Simulation Foundations, Methods and Applications

Series editor

Louis G. Birta, University of Ottawa, Canada

Advisory Board

Roy E. Crosbie, California State University, Chico, USA
Tony Jakeman, Australian National University, Australia
Axel Lehmann, Universität der Bundeswehr München, Germany
Stewart Robinson, Loughborough University, UK
Andreas Tolk, Old Dominion University, USA
Bernard P. Zeigler, University of Arizona, USA

More information about this series at http://www.springer.com/series/10128

Okan Topçu · Halit Oğuztüzün

Guide to Distributed Simulation with HLA

Springer

Okan Topçu
Middle East Technical University,
 Northern Cyprus Campus (METU NCC)
Kalkanlı, Güzelyurt, Mersin 10
Turkey

Halit Oğuztüzün
Middle East Technical University
Ankara
Turkey

Additional material to this book can be downloaded from http://extras.springer.com.

ISSN 2195-2817　　　　　　　ISSN 2195-2825　(electronic)
Simulation Foundations, Methods and Applications
ISBN 978-3-319-61266-9　　　ISBN 978-3-319-61267-6　(eBook)
DOI 10.1007/978-3-319-61267-6

Library of Congress Control Number: 2017943250

© Springer International Publishing AG 2017
This work is subject to copyright. All rights are reserved by the Publisher, whether the whole or part of the material is concerned, specifically the rights of translation, reprinting, reuse of illustrations, recitation, broadcasting, reproduction on microfilms or in any other physical way, and transmission or information storage and retrieval, electronic adaptation, computer software, or by similar or dissimilar methodology now known or hereafter developed.
The use of general descriptive names, registered names, trademarks, service marks, etc. in this publication does not imply, even in the absence of a specific statement, that such names are exempt from the relevant protective laws and regulations and therefore free for general use.
The publisher, the authors and the editors are safe to assume that the advice and information in this book are believed to be true and accurate at the date of publication. Neither the publisher nor the authors or the editors give a warranty, express or implied, with respect to the material contained herein or for any errors or omissions that may have been made. The publisher remains neutral with regard to jurisdictional claims in published maps and institutional affiliations.

Printed on acid-free paper

This Springer imprint is published by Springer Nature
The registered company is Springer International Publishing AG
The registered company address is: Gewerbestrasse 11, 6330 Cham, Switzerland

*To Tuğçe—the love of my life
and
To Oğuz—the meaning of my life*
Okan Topçu

*To Serpil, Çerağ and Ozan
My circle of love*
Halit Oğuztüzün

Foreword

I have always enjoyed driving boats, but this was a very special day. For the first time in my life, I was driving a huge ship, the 203 meter long, 2500 passenger cruise ship Silja Symphony. I was about to enter the Helsinki harbor when I noticed a small vessel crossing my ship's path. I turned sharply starboard, but nothing happened. I kept turning, and after five seconds the ship reacted and steered sharply toward a quay, completely out of control. In just a few seconds, the ship would crash, causing a major disaster.

Fortunately, all of this took place in a simulator in a ship's pilot school. My heart pounded while I drove the ship, immersed in the virtual environment. A few minutes later, I calmed down over a cup of coffee while the instructor walked through my decisions and mistakes.

Simulations let us experience dangerous situations, and let us learn how to handle them without risking our lives. Training in simulators saves time and money, instead of using real ships or aircraft. Simulators let us try many what-if scenarios, analyze the results, and take better decisions. Simulations take us places where we otherwise cannot go.

Simulation programs were initially developed as monolithic applications by an individual or a group. As simulation technology advanced, several simulation applications could be interconnected. Expertise from several groups can be combined, making it possible to build even more powerful, scalable, and interactive simulations. More complex scenarios can be simulated, scenarios that are more like the real world. Physical equipment, human decision making, sensors, environment, communications, and more can be integrated into one holistic approach, solving important problems in today's complex world.

For more than twenty years, I have been involved in developing distributed simulation systems as well as supporting the evolution of standards for simulation interconnectivity. I have visited a large number of countries, giving advice to distributed simulation projects in places such as Japan, Brazil, Canada, Taiwan, China, USA, and most European countries. Everywhere I've been, I've seen a big demand for know-how about distributed simulation.

It is an honor for me to introduce Drs. Topçu and Oğuztüzün's book, which provides an introduction to simulation as well as valuable insights into the design of distributed simulation systems. This book starts with a history and overview of the

High-Level Architecture (HLA), the leading modern standard for distributed simulation. HLA provides services for information exchange and synchronization between simulations that together form a federation.

To successfully apply HLA to a specific domain, be it pilot training, space mission planning, transportation, or manufacturing, a Federation Object Model, or FOM, is needed. The FOM describes the information that the simulations exchange. The second part of this book covers this interesting area. Today, there are many FOM standardization efforts ongoing around the world, for example, the Space Reference FOM, air traffic management FOMs, the Real-time Platform Reference FOM, road traffic simulation FOMs, and the NATO Education and Training FOM. This part of the book gives a foundation for anyone who wants to understand these FOMs and the architecture of such distributed simulation systems.

In part three, Drs. Topçu and Oğuztüzün show how applications, known as federates, use HLA and how they are structured and developed. While the HLA specification describes each service, this book shows how to put everything together. Various tools and frameworks facilitate HLA development. Drs. Topçu and Oğuztüzün introduce one such framework.

After covering some advanced topics in part four, Drs. Topçu and Oğuztüzün conclude this book with a complete case study. This should be a good time for the reader to gain an understanding of how everything fits together.

Drs. Topçu and Oğuztüzün's book will be very valuable to a large number of simulation developers, ranging from students to advanced practitioners. This book also fills a hole, since an up-to-date book on HLA has been missing for several years. I strongly recommend this book and hope that the reader will enjoy it as much as I did!

2017

Björn Möller
Vice President and Co-founder of Pitch Technologies,
Vice Chair of the IEEE 1516 HLA standard
Linköping, Sweden

Preface

Purpose

This is a hands-on guidebook on distributed simulation (DS), specifically on High Level Architecture (HLA), with a view toward software development. It contains a variety of examples to support learning by doing. It offers practical advice on real-world development issues for the novice engineers and programmers who are entering the field of distributed simulation.

Rationale

The book elaborates the implementation of an HLA federation covering all areas from the object model development to federate application development by exemplifying all the federate interface service areas. More importantly, the federate application development is based on the layered architectural style, which provides a clear separation of concerns. The implementation is based on the latest HLA standard, known as HLA Evolved, yet we point to the related topics with HLA 1.3 specification in the interest of backward compatibility. We also present a running example involving a great deal of variation to illustrate several practical issues of federate application development. The implementation is not based on a specific commercial runtime infrastructure (RTI) software, but rather based on generic and extendible tools that can be obtained freely. One is SimGe, a freeware, which is a fully dressed HLA object model development tool and a code generator. Second is RACoN, which is fundamentally an open-source .NET wrapper for HLA RTI application programming interface (API). The book serves as the only comprehensive reference for both tools by giving downloadable sample case studies with the source code. Moreover, this book contains a unique chapter that shows the practitioner how to employ HLA in (multi) agent-based simulation.

The prominent features are as follows:

- It comes with the tools RACoN and SimGe to enable the reader work at a conceptually high level.

- Numerous step-by-step examples and code snippets help the reader to understand the RTI concepts.
- It includes a running example involving a great deal of variation to illustrate several practical issues of federate application development.
- It includes a larger-scale case study involving multi-agents. The scenario is based on the maritime border surveillance with the help of a fleet of unmanned surface vehicles.
- It includes downloadable sample source code.
- It uses Microsoft .NET platform and the C# programming language for all implemented examples and case study.
- It provides a fast start-up on HLA federation development giving an implemented sample for each service area of the HLA federate interface specification.
- It includes a unique chapter to employ the HLA in multi-agent simulations.
- It covers not only federate application development, but also object model construction.
- Many chapters include questions for review and further study.

Book Overview

The book is structured as follows. Chapter 1 is a high-level introduction to the essential concepts of modeling and simulation, while highlighting DS as the focal area of interest. Chapter 2 introduces the fundamental concepts and the principles of HLA. Chapter 3 takes a look into federation development and presents development guidelines. These three chapters together lay the technical background for federation development.

The remaining chapters constitute three major parts of the book: object model development, federate implementation, and advanced topics. Chapters 4 and 5 present an introduction to object model development and then elaborate on the subject through a case study. Using the object model in the case study, Chaps. 6–8 elucidate the details of implementing a federate application. Last, Chap. 10 considers some advanced topics by discussing the connection between agent-based simulation and HLA. Then, Chap. 11 provides a complete case study to put it all together.

The chapters are structured in a layered way so that the initial chapters include more generalized topics such as M&S and HLA concepts. As we proceed, each chapter brings more specialized topics relying on the knowledge of the preceding ones.

Web Material

The software tools and examples used in the book are freely available on the web.

Audience

This book is intended for students of distributed simulation, based particularly on High Level Architecture. It can be used as a textbook or reference book for an upper undergraduate/lower graduate course, probably named as distributed simulation or distributed interactive simulation.

Final

We believe that the most prominent contribution of this book is to provide a starting point and all-in-one resource for HLA-based distributed simulation development without depending on any commercial tools. The book is complementary, in regard to its implementation slant, to model-based engineering approach for distributed simulations.

Edirne, Turkey	Okan Topçu
Ankara, Turkey	Halit Oğuztüzün

Acknowledgements

We would like to acknowledge our associate editor Simon Rees for smooth editorial assistance.

Okan would like to thank his parents Selime and Bekir for their boundless support.

Halit would like to thank all his graduate students, especially those who graduated from the MODSIM master of science program at METU.

For various chapters of this book, we have adapted parts of the following articles/chapters:

Topçu, O., Durak, U., Oğuztüzün, H. & Yılmaz, L., 2016. Distributed Simulation: A Model Driven Engineering Approach. 1st ed. Cham(Zug): Springer International Publishing. Parts adapted and reprinted with permission from Springer appear in Chaps. 1, 2 and 7.

Contents

Part I Introduction

1 Introduction 3
  1.1 Modeling and Simulation 3
    1.1.1 What Is Model? 4
    1.1.2 What Is System? 5
    1.1.3 What Is Simulation? 6
    1.1.4 Model to Simulate and Model to Build 7
    1.1.5 Simulation Engineering 8
    1.1.6 Time and Change 9
  1.2 Distributed Simulation 10
    1.2.1 SIMNET 12
    1.2.2 DIS Protocol 12
    1.2.3 Aggregate Level Simulation Protocol 13
  1.3 High Level Architecture 13
  1.4 Tools 15
    1.4.1 SimGe 16
    1.4.2 RACoN 16
  1.5 Introduction to Case Studies 17
    1.5.1 Strait Traffic Monitoring Simulation 17
    1.5.2 Maritime Border Surveillance Using Unmanned
           Surface Vehicles 19
  1.6 Book Outline 22
    1.6.1 Summary of Chapters 22
    1.6.2 Typeface Conventions 23
  1.7 Summary 24
  1.8 Questions for Review 24
  References 25

2 High Level Architecture 29
  2.1 Prelude 29
    2.1.1 What Is HLA? 30

xv

	2.2	Basic Components	31
		2.2.1 Federate and Federation	32
		2.2.2 Runtime Infrastructure	33
	2.3	HLA Rules	34
		2.3.1 Federation Rules	34
		2.3.2 Federate Rules	35
	2.4	HLA Data Model and Data Communication	36
		2.4.1 HLA Data Communication Pattern	36
		2.4.2 Object Exchange: Publish/Subscribe Pattern	38
		2.4.3 Data: Objects, Interactions, and HLA Classes	39
		2.4.4 Object Model Template	42
		2.4.5 HLA Object Models	44
		2.4.6 Object Model Modularity	45
	2.5	Interface Specification	46
		2.5.1 Federation Management	50
		2.5.2 Declaration Management	54
		2.5.3 Object Management	59
		2.5.4 Ownership Management	60
		2.5.5 Data Distribution Management	62
		2.5.6 Time Management	64
	2.6	Full Life Cycle of a Federation Execution	68
		2.6.1 Initialization	71
		2.6.2 Operation	71
		2.6.3 Termination	71
	2.7	Example Federation Deployment	72
	2.8	Federation and Federate States	72
		2.8.1 Federation Execution States	73
		2.8.2 Federate States	73
	2.9	Summary	74
	2.10	Questions for Review	75
	References		77
3	**Federation Development At-A-Glance**		79
	3.1	Process Model	79
	3.2	Federation Development and Guidelines	81
		3.2.1 Federation Design	81
		3.2.2 Federate Design	87
		3.2.3 Federate Implementation	89
		3.2.4 Target Platform	89
		3.2.5 Integration with Local Simulations/Games	89
	3.3	Implementation Steps	91
	3.4	Summary	92
	3.5	Questions for Review	92
	References		93

Part II Object Model Development

4 Introduction to Object Model Development 97
   4.1   SimGe Overview 97
   4.2   Managing SimGe Projects 98
        4.2.1   The Main User Interface 98
        4.2.2   Creating a Project 100
        4.2.3   Loading a Project 100
        4.2.4   Saving and Closing a Project 102
        4.2.5   Project Start Page 102
        4.2.6   Project Settings 102
        4.2.7   Options 103
   4.3   Federation Architecture Modeling 104
        4.3.1   Creating a FAM 105
        4.3.2   Federation Structure 106
   4.4   Summary 108
   4.5   Questions for Review 108
   References 109

5 Object Model Construction 111
   5.1   Overview 111
   5.2   Creating a Federation Object Model from Scratch 112
   5.3   Loading an Existing SimGe Object Model 112
   5.4   Removing Object Model 113
   5.5   Importing a FED/FDD File 113
   5.6   Exporting the FED/FDD Files 114
   5.7   Object Model Editor 115
        5.7.1   OME Toolbar 115
   5.8   Table Editor 116
        5.8.1   Object Model Identification 118
        5.8.2   Objects 121
        5.8.3   Interactions 122
        5.8.4   Attributes 123
        5.8.5   Parameters 125
        5.8.6   Dimensions 125
        5.8.7   Time Representations 128
        5.8.8   User-Supplied Tags 128
        5.8.9   Synchronization 128
        5.8.10   Case Study: Synchronization 129
        5.8.11   Transportations 129
        5.8.12   Update Rates 131
        5.8.13   Switches 131
        5.8.14   Data Types 133
        5.8.15   Case Study: Data Types 140
        5.8.16   Notes 141

		5.8.17	Interface Specification Services	141
		5.8.18	OMT 1.3 Support	142
	5.9	Textual View		143
		5.9.1	Textual View for FED and FDD Files	143
	5.10	Validating the FDD File		144
	5.11	MOM Integration		145
	5.12	OM Explorer		146
		5.12.1	Functionality for Traverse	147
		5.12.2	Functionality for Modification	149
	5.13	Report Generator		149
	5.14	Summary		150
	5.15	Questions for Review		151
	References			152

Part III Federate Application Development

6	**Code Generation**			157
	6.1	Overview		157
	6.2	User Interface		158
		6.2.1	Code Explorer	159
		6.2.2	Code Viewer	159
	6.3	Architectural Style		159
		6.3.1	Code Generation for Object Model	162
		6.3.2	Code Generation for Federate	163
		6.3.3	Code Generation for Data Type	163
		6.3.4	Code Generation for MOM	164
	6.4	Code Generator Configuration		164
		6.4.1	General Settings	165
		6.4.2	Callback Settings	165
		6.4.3	Runtime Settings	165
	6.5	Summary		167
	References			168

7	**Federate Application Development Based on Layered Architecture**			169
	7.1	Federate Application Architecture		169
		7.1.1	Presentation Layer	170
		7.1.2	Simulation Layer	170
		7.1.3	Communication Layer	171
		7.1.4	Integration of Layers	171
		7.1.5	Encapsulation of Simulation Local Data Structures	172
		7.1.6	The Federation Foundation Library	174

	7.2	Development Environment Configuration	174
		7.2.1 Prerequisites	175
		7.2.2 Operating Environment Configuration	175
		7.2.3 IDE Configuration	177
	7.3	Case Study: Running the STMS Federation	179
		7.3.1 User Interface	179
	7.4	Summary	180
	References		181
8	**Federate Implementation: Basics**		**183**
	8.1	Case Study: Federate Architecture	183
	8.2	The Basics	184
		8.2.1 Namespace	184
		8.2.2 RACoN Methods	184
		8.2.3 Creating the Simulation Manager	185
		8.2.4 Creating the Federate Class	186
	8.3	Implementing the Simulation Object Model	188
		8.3.1 Defining an Object Class and Its Attributes	190
		8.3.2 Defining an Interaction Class and Its Parameters	191
		8.3.3 Connecting SOM and Federate	191
	8.4	Calls and Callbacks	192
		8.4.1 Events	192
		8.4.2 Event Handling	193
		8.4.3 Tracing the RTI	193
	8.5	Federation Management	196
		8.5.1 Federation Execution Creation	196
		8.5.2 Joining the Federation Execution	197
		8.5.3 High-Level Method for Initialization	198
		8.5.4 Finalization of Federation Execution	198
		8.5.5 Connection Lost	199
	8.6	Declaration Management	200
	8.7	Object Management	201
		8.7.1 Implementing Simulation Objects	201
		8.7.2 Registering Objects	203
		8.7.3 Updating the HLA Object Attributes	204
		8.7.4 Discovering Objects	206
		8.7.5 Reflecting the Attribute Values	207
		8.7.6 Request an Update for Attribute Values	208
		8.7.7 Deleting and Removing an Object Instance	209
		8.7.8 Sending an Interaction	210
		8.7.9 Receiving an Interaction	210
	8.8	Main Simulation Loop	212
		8.8.1 Console Applications	213
		8.8.2 Windows Forms Applications	213

		8.8.3	Windows Presentation Foundation (WPF) Applications	213
	8.9	Parameter and Attribute Marshaling/Unmarshaling		214
		8.9.1	Supported Data Types.........................	215
	8.10	Summary		215
	8.11	Questions for Review		216
	References			217

Part IV Advanced Topics

9 Federate Implementation: Advanced 221

	9.1	Time Management		221
		9.1.1	Time-Regulating Federates	221
		9.1.2	Time-Constrained Federates...................	224
		9.1.3	Time Advancement.........................	224
		9.1.4	Queries..................................	227
		9.1.5	Changing Preferred Order Types	229
		9.1.6	Sending and Receiving TSO Messages	229
		9.1.7	Message Retraction.........................	231
	9.2	Federation Synchronization		231
	9.3	Federation Save-and-Restore		235
	9.4	Data Distribution Management........................		238
		9.4.1	Case Study 1: STMS	238
		9.4.2	Creating Regions	241
		9.4.3	Subscribing an Object Class with Regions.........	242
		9.4.4	Registering an Object Instance with Regions	243
		9.4.5	Associating Regions for Updates	243
		9.4.6	Case Study 2: Extended Chat Application	244
		9.4.7	Subscribing Interactions with Regions.............	246
		9.4.8	Sending and Receiving Interactions Using Regions..............................	246
	9.5	Ownership Management		247
		9.5.1	Ownership Management Services	247
		9.5.2	Pull Strategy	248
		9.5.3	Push Strategy.............................	249
		9.5.4	Case Study: Transferring Tracks Among Traffic Stations............................	251
		9.5.5	Querying the Ownership	252
		9.5.6	Problems in OwM of HLA 1.3.................	253
	9.6	Handling Multiple Federation Executions		253
	9.7	One Federate Application, Multiple Federates		255
	9.8	Summary		257
	9.9	Questions for Review		258
	References			259

10	**Integration of Agents into HLA**		261
	10.1	Agent-Based Simulation	261
		10.1.1 A Cognitive Agent Architecture	262
	10.2	Integration of Agents into HLA-Based Simulations	264
		10.2.1 Architectural Approaches	264
		10.2.2 A Concrete Architecture	266
		10.2.3 Using HLA as Agent Communication Medium	267
	10.3	Summary	270
	References		271
11	**A Complete Case Study**		273
	11.1	Prelude	273
		11.1.1 Simulation Environment	274
	11.2	Naval Simulation	275
		11.2.1 Virtual Environment	275
	11.3	Agent-Based Simulation	277
		11.3.1 Goal Reasoning	278
		11.3.2 Agent Manager	279
		11.3.3 USV Agent	280
	11.4	Object Model	282
	11.5	Federation Structure	286
	11.6	Deployment and Execution	287
	11.7	Federate Application with Intensive Graphics	287
	11.8	Main Simulation Loop	290
	11.9	Graphics API Integration	291
	11.10	Summary	292
	11.11	Questions for Review	292
	References		292

Appendix A: SimGe Installation and Remarks 295

References 301

Index 303

Abbreviations

ACL	Agent Communication Language
AgentFdApp	Agent Manager Federate Application
ALSP	Aggregate Level Simulation Protocol
AMG	Architecture Management Group
AOR	Area of Responsibility
API	Application Programming Interface
ARPA	Advanced Research Projects Agency
C2	Command and Control
CGB	Coast Guard Boat
CGF	Computer Generated Force
CodeGen	Code Generator (of SimGe)
CogAgentLib	Coherence-based Agent Framework
COTS	Commercial off-the-shelf
CRUD	Create, read, update, and delete operations
D/A	Divest/Acquire
DDM	Data Distribution Management, Detailed Design Model
DeCoAgent	Deliberative Coherence Driven Agent
DIF	Data Interchange Format
DIS	Distributed Interactive Simulation
DLC	Dynamic Link Compatibility
DLL	Dynamic Link Library
DM	Declaration Management
DMAO	Distributed Simulation Engineering and Execution Process Multi-Architecture Overlay
DMSO	U.S. Defense Modeling and Simulation Office
DoD	U.S. Department of Defense
DOI	Digital Object Identifier
DSEEP	Distributed Simulation Engineering and Execution Process
DUB	Dimension Upper Bound
EnviFd	Environment Federate
EnviFdApp	Environment Controller Federate Application
FAM	Federation Architecture Model
FAME	Federation Architecture Modeling Environment

FAMM	Federation Architecture Metamodel
FAP	Federation Architecture Project
FDD	FOM Document Data
FED	Federation Execution Details
FEDEP	Federation Development and Execution Process
FedMonFd	Federation Monitor Federate
FedMonFdApp	Federation Monitor Federate Application
FFL	Federation Foundation Library
FIPA	Foundation for Intelligent Physical Agents
FM	Federation Management
FOM	Federation Object Model
fps	Frame per Second
GALT	Greatest Available Logical Time
GPS	Global Positioning System
GUI	Graphical User Interface
HLA	High Level Architecture
IDE	Integrated Development Environment
IEEE	Institute of Electrical and Electronics Engineers
IF	Interface Specification
IP	Internet Protocol
ISBN	International Standard Book Number
KQML	Knowledge Query and Manipulation Language
LITS	Least Incoming Timestamp
M&S	Modeling and Simulation
MariSim	Maritime Simulation
MCV	Model-View-Controller
MDE	Model-Driven Engineering
MIM	MOM and Initialization Module
MOM	Management Object Model
MRU	Most Recently Used
MS	Microsoft
MSF	Maritime Surveillance Federation
NavySim	Naval Simulation
NSTMSS	Naval Surface Tactical Maneuvering Simulation System (pronounced "Nistmiss")
OM	Object Model, Object Management
OME	Object Model Editor (of SimGe)
OMG	Object Modeling Group
OMT	Object Model Template
OOP	Object Oriented Programming
OOW	Officer of the Watch
OwM	Ownership Management
P/S	Publish/Subscribe
PDU	Protocol Data Unit
POC	Point of Contact

RACoN	RTI Abstraction Component for .Net
RB	Refugee Boat
RID	RTI Initialization Data
RO	Receive Order
RPR-FOM	Real-time Platform Reference FOM
RTI	Runtime Infrastructure
ShipFd	Ship Federate
ShipFdApp	Ship Federate Application
SimGe	SIMulation Generator
SISO	Simulation Interoperability Standards Organization
SL	Semantics Language
SOM	Simulation Object Model
SS	Support Services
StationFd	Station Federate
StationFdApp	Station Federate Application
STMS	Strait Traffic Monitoring Simulation
T/A	Transferable/Acceptable
TC	Time-Constrained
TC&TR	Both TC and TR
TM	Time Management
TMS	Traffic Monitoring Station
TR	Time-Regulating
TSO	Time Stamp Order
TSS	Tracking Sub-System
U/R	Updateable/Reflectable
UI	User Interface
UML	Unified Modeling Language
URL	Uniform Resource Locator
US DoD	United States Department of Defense
USV	Unmanned Surface Vehicle
VS	Visual Studio
WiX	Windows Installer XML
WPF	Windows Presentation Foundation
XML	Extensible Markup Language

Part I
Introduction

Introduction

1

In his popular Sci-Fi book series "Foundation," Isaac Asimov described modeling and simulation as the simplification of a phenomenon to such a degree that only the characteristics that are essential to understand it (Asimov 1988). Further than science fiction, Modeling and Simulation (M&S) became a solid interdisciplinary scientific and engineering endeavor including many subfields such as discrete event simulation, continuous simulation, distributed simulation, and parallel simulation. In this chapter, we introduce some fundamental concepts of M&S keeping distributed simulation (DS), specifically High Level Architecture (HLA) in focus. We aim to familiarize the user with the terminology and concepts used frequently in this book. First, we introduce the basic concepts from the theory of M&S and then present a historical perspective on DS and related standards. And the case studies used for illustration throughout the book are introduced. The chapter concludes with a detailed outline of the book chapters incorporating a chart for chapter dependency. This introduction chapter is a slight adaptation of the first chapter of Topçu et al. (2016).

1.1 Modeling and Simulation

Modeling and simulation revolves around certain concepts, such as reality, model, simulation, computer, and results and relations among these elements. Figure 1.1 depicts the basic elements, relations, and processes of the modeling and simulation enterprise, for example, the model of reality, which we want to simulate, and the model of the simulation software, which we want to run on a computer. Let us clarify these essential concepts that keep occurring in our discussions throughout this book.

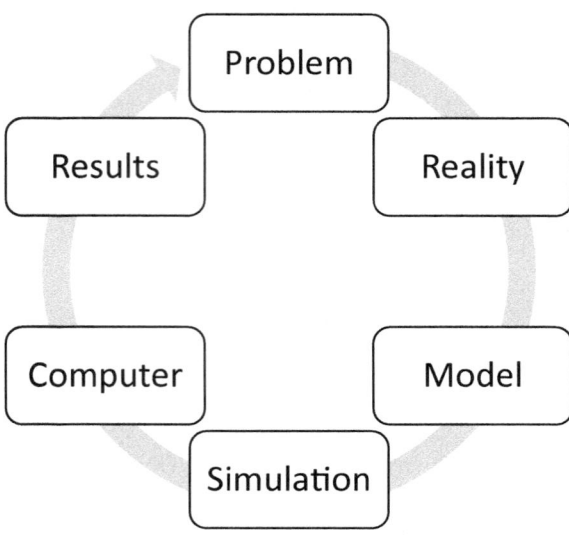

Fig. 1.1 The basic elements, relations, and processes of the modeling and simulation endeavor

1.1.1 What Is Model?

A *model* is construed as a representation of reality and modeling as the activity of creating a model. Admittedly, this formulation is rather terse. We need to be a bit more explicit about what our notion of "reality" is, what kinds of "representation" are admissible, what sort of processes can be followed to come up with representations that will be useful for a certain purpose, and how we can put them into use. By the term *reality*, we mean the world that exists independently of our minds, or the imagined or hypothetical world that exists only in our minds, or any mixture of the two. Consider, for example, the hydrodynamics model of an existing ship and that of a ship being designed. They would be indistinguishable as representations. Further, suppose we are planning modifications to an existing ship, say, by upgrading its engine, then the future ship is a mixture of the existing one (so that we can keep its geometric model) and the envisioned one (so that we have a new propulsion model reflecting the new engine capabilities). Therefore, the notion of reality that is subject to modeling does not necessarily have a material counterpart. It is often undesirable to experiment with reality directly and in many cases, too dangerous or plainly impossible. Suppose we would like to study the wave actions that might cause our ship to capsize. This is when the use of models becomes indispensable. We can experiment with models safely in our offices.

At any moment, we are concerned with only a confined part or a certain aspect of reality, because we have a particular purpose. We have a particular problem to solve, a decision to be made, or, more basically, we need a better understanding of the state of affairs. Thus, we have to limit the scope of our modeling effort accordingly. Perhaps, for example, the navigation system of the ship is not of immediate concern; then, it is out of our modeling scope. For the same reason, we

1.1 Modeling and Simulation

need to put a limit on the level of detail we can have in our models. For example, the wear and tear of the ship's engine may be ignorable if we are only interested in the maximum torque it can produce. After all, we cannot duplicate reality. This means, in modeling, we seek some deliberately simplified view of reality.

Abstraction refers to the fact that a model explicitly represents those aspects of reality that are of interest to us while omitting other aspects that are not of concern. Suppose we are interested in studying the maneuverability of a ship. Then, parameters related to its mass, geometry, propulsion, and rudder will be taken into consideration, while the material used in its construction will be safely ignored.

What is subjected to modeling, the part of reality which is known as the *simuland*, can involve entities, systems, events, and processes. The term *entity* is used in quite a generic sense, meaning any recognizable and identifiable thing, tangible or intangible, in the domain of application, such as a wheel of a car or percept of a sensor. An entity can have identity, attributes, states, functional behavior, and relationships with other entities, just like an object in the sense of object-oriented programming.

The intended uses of a model constitute its purpose. There are several kinds of practical uses for models: First, perhaps the most common, use is communication among stakeholders. It is easier to share our ideas and intuitions about reality if we are referring to the same model. Second, the model can be subjected to rigorous analysis, using computational methods, for example. This way we can predict a system's performance. Third is the generation of the behavior of a system from the system's model. The behavior of a system is some ordering (possibly, partial) of the system's actions over time. An action consists of taking some inputs or producing some outputs, or both. The inputs come from the system's environment, and the outputs create some effect on it.

1.1.2 What Is System?

A system is an organized collection of components that interact with each other according to a pattern in order to achieve some purpose or functionality. A component is any entity that can exhibit an input–output behavior through a well-defined interface. A *system's purpose* is realized through its interactions with its environment. The environment *of a system* is the part of reality where the system is situated in so that the system receives inputs from and provides outputs to the environment. Consider, for example, a ship as a system, within an environment consisting of the captain and the crew and passengers on board as well as the stretch of water it moves on, and other ships nearby in the maritime traffic.

In the context of discrete event systems (Cassandras and Lafortune 2010), an event refers to an indivisible action, whereas a *process* refers to a sequence of events. For modeling purposes, an event is usually thought of as being instantaneous while a process as consuming time. Hence, we may want to assign a time instant to an event and a time interval to a process. For example, for a ship, changing the course can be regarded as an event, and following a route can be a process.

1.1.3 What Is Simulation?

The term *simulation* has many meanings. Tuncer Ören has surveyed about a hundred definitions of it (Ören 2011). The view we adopt for this book is simulation as a mechanism to move a model over time. We define simulation as a method of generating behavior from a model, given input data, and information on the environment. Evidently, a computer-based or software-intensive system is the most common way of realizing a simulation. The term *simulation application* is used to emphasize the view of simulation as application software. In this regard, Fig. 1.1 depicts the basic notions and relationships that we have discussed thus far.

The *simulation user*, who could be an analyst, researcher, decision maker, trainer, or trainee, has an interest in a real-world issue, say, the maneuverability of a certain class of ship. He (or she) builds a mathematical model of the ship that accounts for the significant factors that can affect the maneuverability of the ship. He implements this model in a programming language, say, Java. The simulation in Java runs on a computer getting inputs in accordance with a scenario. The user examines the results produced by the simulation run, or multiple runs, and hopefully gains an understanding of the maneuverability of the ship under the conditions dictated by the scenario—without actually handling the ship.

The generation of behavior requires that the model is provided with input data over time. This is where the notion of *scenario* comes in. A scenario specifies the initial data and the data to be fed to the model in a timely manner, or at least a prescription of how that data will be generated. A scenario also contains a description of the environment. It is the job of the computer, specifically, the simulation engine, to enact the scenario.

A particular instance of applying a simulation (as a method) with a given scenario is known as a *simulation run* (or *simulation execution*). A simulation run, therefore, consists of events that take place over the time axis. In everyday usage, the terms simulation and simulation run (or execution) are often used interchangeably. In this book, however, we take care to keep the distinction clear.

The description of the above steps reveals several issues that need to be addressed in a simulation study: What are the input, output, and control variables and system parameters to be studied and what is the objective of our study: comparison and optimization? What is the required level of accuracy (*fidelity*)? Did we include all factors that matter to achieve the objectives (*level of detail*)? Did we implement the mathematical model faithfully as a program (*verification*)? Is the scenario adequate given the objectives (*input data analysis*)? How far can we rely on the outputs produced by the simulation runs (*results validation*)? Trying to discuss these issues adequately in this book would divert us from our main objective, which is to show how to implement an HLA-compliant distributed simulation. Fortunately, several excellent books are available for the readers who want to build a strong foundation on M&S, such as Law (2007), Sokolowski and Banks (2010), and Banks et al. (2010).

In some cases, it is easy to distinguish the model and the simulation. For example, the model could be in a mathematical form, say, as a linear system of ordinary differential equations, and the simulation could take the form of software that implements a solver for this system of equations. Given the power and prevalence of software, the distinction between a model and simulation is not always made clear. In many cases, the model is directly expressed in an *executable form*, say, in a general-purpose programming language such as Java, simulation-oriented programming language such as SIMSCRIPT III (Rice et al. 2005), a mathematical programming language, such as MATLAB (Chapman 2015), or a language with development and execution environment specifically designed for simulation such as SIMAN/ARENA (Kelton et al 2014). In such cases, the model does not have a separate representation, but embodiment as the source code. Then, people may refer to that code as a *simulation model*. When it is not important or not practical to separate the model and the simulation, you may even hear people using the terms model and simulation interchangeably. In this book, however, we will be clear about the separation between these two concepts.

1.1.4 Model to Simulate and Model to Build

In M&S, we model systems to simulate them. In software and systems engineering, we model systems to build them. The modeling activity is common to most scientific and engineering endeavors though each subject area has its own conventions and traditions in regard to modeling techniques and tools Beyond the subject area, the difference in purposes can lead to a big difference in modeling approaches. The model of the ship hull to be constructed by engineers and the model of the ship to be analyzed for its certain structural properties, say, its radar cross section, or behavioral properties, say, its stability, would look drastically different. This is no surprise as we know that any model is a purposeful abstraction of reality.

When we start building models to simulate systems, we face the issue of fidelity. *Fidelity* can be defined as the degree of accuracy of a model (Cross 1999) compared with the actual system. In other words, it is a measure of how accurately the model represents the reality. The *level of detail* is one aspect of fidelity. Which control surfaces are represented in an aircraft aerodynamics model is a level of detail issue, for example. *Resolution* is another aspect. The number of cells represented in the finite grid of certain dimensions is a matter of resolution. In any case, the fidelity required of a model depends on the intended uses of the model. In a formation flight training scenario, for example, we would probably need a higher fidelity level for our own aircraft compared to our wingmen's aircraft.

We may want to measure the fidelity of a model by comparing the results from the simulation runs with the data obtained by observing the real world, provided, of course, that such data, called the *referent*, are available. This activity can be a part of a validation process—results validation, to be more specific. One must be aware of the numerical precision and instability problems that might be introduced as the model is implemented as simulation software.

Fidelity requirements of simulations are often in conflict with an important constraint, namely the cost of both development and operation. Deciding what the right level of fidelity is in any simulation project is tricky. The situation is even more complicated when we need to reuse legacy simulation components with varying degrees of fidelity.

When we start building models to build operational systems, the accuracy and precision requirements are usually unequivocally derivable from system requirements. Therefore, the level of detail or resolution that the system must support for its correct operation can be determined similar to other derived requirements.

By and large, the fidelity issue is what separates simulation software from operational software; the issue is much less clear in simulation. Overlapping with the fidelity issue, the range of possibilities for the notion of time also sets simulations apart from other kinds of software. Operational systems, such as control systems, normally operate in real time, while for simulations real time is just one of the possibilities. The smallest time step for the simulation clock is clearly a matter of resolution.

The simulation conceptual model is the most appropriate place to settle the fidelity and time issues. A *simulation conceptual model* involves the domain entities, along with their attributes and actions, and the relationships between the entities in a level of detail in accordance with the targeted level of fidelity. These must carry over to the model of the simulation software to be developed. So, a simulation conceptual model answers how the domain concepts and relationships can be represented on a computer and gives the associated algorithms at a level of detail so that a capable engineer can implement them in the form of simulation software. Taking an object-oriented view, for example, the tangible and intangible entities in the field may map to classes and the whole-part relationships between entities to aggregations between classes, and so on. We can find a way of transforming the simulation conceptual model to a design model for the simulation system either informally as in this book or formally using model-driven engineering (MDE) techniques as promoted in Topçu et al. (2016). For the logical data model part of design, the mapping can be easier to see as we can leverage our object-oriented analysis and design (OOA&D) experience. For the behavioral part of design, however, the transition is less straightforward, and we may need help from conceptual scenarios.

1.1.5 Simulation Engineering

Simulation engineering is the engineering of simulation systems. It is essentially a subdiscipline of systems engineering that focuses on simulation systems. As simulation engineers, we are interested in building simulation systems, which are the systems whose functionality is to unfold a model over time. Therefore, we would be interested in modeling the simulation systems themselves. This is the case when the part of reality that we target for modeling is the simulation itself as a software application, or a computer-based system, in general.

Modeling of digital systems has long been an area of active research and industrial practice. Modeling of computer and network systems for the purpose of performance evaluation, for example, has a long history (Kleinrock 1976). Modeling digital systems as finite-state machines for the purpose of model checking for safety and liveness properties turned out to be important to achieve reliability (Clarke et al. 1999). Modeling of object-oriented software for analysis and design purposes goes back to the earlier work by object-oriented methodologists that culminated in the development of UML (OMG 2015). Requirements of the modeling of computer-based or software-intensive systems that involve not only software but also hardware, people, and process elements led to the development of SysML (OMG 2012).

Many simulation systems today such as training simulators for operators of all sorts of platforms and equipment, embedded simulators, war games, fall into the category of software-intensive systems. Engineering of such systems requires more of a systems engineering effort, rather than a purely software engineering effort. Development of simulation systems can obviously benefit from the modeling technology available for software-intensive systems. Rewards would be even bigger when systems modeling is linked with simulation conceptual modeling.

1.1.6 Time and Change

The reality we are interested in modeling inevitably has a *time* dimension. For many phenomena in the physical world that we experience directly, time seems to be flowing continuously. Consider, for example, the motion of a ball on a billiards table. The movement of the ball from the instant it is hit by the cue until it stops or falls into one of the holes would seem like a continuous motion. In fact, classical physics-based models of the ball's motion would assume the time as an independent variable ranging over the domain of nonzero real numbers. The smooth motion of the ball would undergo an abrupt change as it hits another ball or bounces off the edge of the table. An observer can record the instants of such events along the time axis. We can define the state of the ball at a time instant t as a vector comprising the ball's position on the table, and its translational and rotational velocity. The state of the ball goes through continuous changes as time flows and instantaneous changes as it experiences events.

When we model such a system, we need to account for both continuous developments in state and abrupt changes. Such abrupt, instantaneous changes in state are brought about by *discrete events*. Thus, we have the notion of time that keeps increasing continuously (with unit speed) and the system state that is continuously changing with time and instantaneously changing in response to discrete events.

In some cases, one may be able to simplify the situation by ignoring one or the other aspect of time and state change and arrive at a continuous time model or discrete event model. *Continuous time models* frequently arise in scientific and engineering domains, and *differential equations* are the modeling technique of choice. *Discrete event models* frequently arise in the modeling of service and manufacturing systems and social systems; various sorts of *state-based formalisms*, e.g., Petri nets (Reisig 1991), are used. Going back to the billiards example, if we are interested in foreseeing when and where two balls will collide, we need to maintain the notion of state continuously changing with time but also subject to discrete events that can happen any moment in time. Formal groundwork has been laid for such models, called *hybrid automata*. We refer the reader to Alur et al. (1993) for the fundamentals of hybrid systems modeling.

Models with continuous time and continuously changing state variables can be quite satisfactory from the modeler's perspective, but from the simulation engineer's perspective, there is a problem: A continuous variable is impossible to realize as is on a digital computer due to the limited precision of floating point number representations. Fortunately, an extensive body of knowledge on numerical methods exists that allow the simulation engineers to solve approximately the models expressed as various kinds of differential equations up to desired accuracy, limited by the precision of floating point number representation on the computer, by making the size of time steps sufficiently small.

What if we let the time variable take on integer values only? This can make sense, for example, when we are modeling a synchronous digital circuit, which is driven by a hardware clock. This amounts to deciding to ignore what happens between two successive time instants, say t and $t + 1$. Then, the state variables can only be updated at those instants of time, at the clock ticks. Such system models are known as *discrete-time models*. The mathematical tool of choice to express such models is *difference equations* (Luenberger 1979).

Once we switch to a discrete notion time, it would seem easier to accommodate discrete events. After all, the ticking of the clock is just another kind of discrete event. The catch is, although ordinary discrete events can occur any time in principle, they can only be processed when the clock ticks.

Once we have the notion of time progressing in regular intervals, we may wonder whether the intervals can be allowed to be irregular. Indeed, this is possible, in so-called event-driven simulations, quite popular for discrete event system simulation, for example, in queueing system simulations. Instead of letting the time variable (the simulation clock) advance on its own accord, we allow it advance only when an event happens. We leave the thorough treatment of time advancement mechanisms to Fujimoto (2000).

1.2 Distributed Simulation

Often, the subject reality (simuland) inherently involves multiple interacting entities. Imagine a fleet of drones flying in formation. We can of course have one monolithic simulation model including all the drones and their interactions with each other and with the physical environment. An alternative might be to have individual models of each drone and the environment, and let these models interact with each other via a well-defined and agreed-upon interface. The second approach might be preferable for several reasons. First, the load of simulation can be shared

1.2 Distributed Simulation

by multiple processors. These processors can be distributed over a network or can be housed on a single host computer. Roughly speaking, the latter leads to *parallel simulation*, while the former leads to *distributed simulation*.

What distinguishes parallel simulation from distributed simulation in the M&S jargon is the former's emphasis on speed, which can be measured by the number of events processed per second. The speedup is the ratio of the speed of sequential simulation to the parallel or distributed simulation. The primary concern for parallel simulation implementers is to speed up simulation execution to the extent possible with the available high-performance computing technology. ==Physical distribution usually works against performance as the processors need to communicate by exchanging messages over the network and the network is usually the bottleneck (rather than the processors).== However, in situations where the message traffic is not overwhelming, which could be the case when we have loosely coupled models to run together, or replicated runs of the same model, the load-sharing argument can win.

Mind you that being distributed is largely a point of view. Two flight simulators, located in faraway facilities, flown by pilot trainees in a coordinated flight exercise, no doubt constitute a distributed simulation. When we consider an individual flight simulator, we can see a single unitary aircraft simulator or a distributed structure inside specialized models of the mission computer, sensors, controls, aerodynamical models, image generators for a variety of displays, and so on, exchanging data and commands over a bus or local network. Hierarchical composition of systems is a well-known idea, and at which level in the hierarchy we start to have a distributed view of the system is up to the simulation engineer.

The second, perhaps more fundamental, reason to go distributed is that the nature of our models is distributed. The simuland is readily decomposable by its nature; all we need to do is let the simulation system architecture follow the structure of the simuland. This is quite apparent in a gaming situation, such as a war game, where the players interact with models and other players in their own workstations, connected through a network. In general, human-in-the-loop simulations for the purpose of team training tend to be distributed.

In some cases, some simulation components require special hardware located in certain hosts on a network. Visualization needs (e.g., availability of high-end graphics processors), location of certain databases and related services (say, message format conversion), and location of required storage (e.g., large disks for logging) all lead to a distributed configuration for the simulation system.

An additional advantage of working with composite models rather than big monolithic models is *reusability*. In many cases, some dependable models are already existing and we would like to reuse them in a new setting. To be sure, composition of models can take place in a centralized setting as well. Generally, distribution promotes the loosely coupled approach that facilitates model development by modules and composition of those modules.

Distributed simulation promotes heterogeneity and dispersion, linking simulation components of various types (e.g., discrete vs. continuous) at multiple locations to create a virtual environment (battlefields, multi-player games, multi-agent systems, virtual factories, supply chains, etc.) with a common notion of space and time. Networked virtual environments are early examples of distributed simulation systems (Singhal and Zyda 1999).

In general, engineers can leverage the known benefits of distributed systems, such as fault tolerance and load balancing, for simulation. However, they must face the known challenges, too, such as interoperating heterogeneous system components, and difficulty of determining global states.

In this book, we focus on the development of distributed simulations, which are composite simulations that consist of multiple individual simulations distributed over a network of hosts.

1.2.1 SIMNET

The early efforts of US Defense Community on developing distributed simulation technology culminated in the SIMNET (Simulation Networking) project. SIMNET's vision was to create a new generation of networked simulators. Starting from late 1970s till the late 1980s, for about a decade, the technological foundations of distributed simulation, from communication protocols to dead-reckoning algorithms, were developed (Cosby 1995).

First conceptual demonstration of distributed interactive simulation was conducted in 1984 (see Fig. 1.2). The out-of-the-window graphics were integrated to the distributed simulation in 1985, and in 1986, SIMNET demonstrated a platoon-level scenario. When SIMNET project ended, it was noted that there were 250 simulators installed at eleven sites, seven of which in the USA and the rest in Europe (Miller and Thrope 1995).

1.2.2 DIS Protocol

The simulation communication protocol, developed in SIMNET to connect simulators, became an industry standard in 1993 as IEEE 1278 distributed interactive simulation (DIS) standard protocols (IEEE 1993). DIS is a message passing

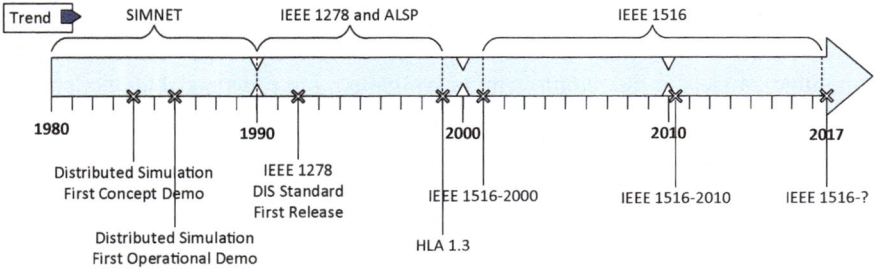

Fig. 1.2 Timeline of distributed simulation

protocol standard that defines the messages and the procedures for communication among the simulators. It specifies standard message packets called *protocol data units* (PDUs). PDUs are transmitted over the network. Among a number of PDUs specified by the standard, most commonly used ones are Entity State, Fire, Detonation, and Simulation Management PDUs.

DIS (IEEE Std 1278.1–2012, 2012) protocol is an application protocol originally approved in 1992 by IEEE DIS which is composed of PDUs, used for sending and receiving data across a network. A set of PDUs, used for different purposes, are predefined in the standard. If a new PDU type is required due to changing requirements, then the new PDUs should be defined and added to these standards.

1.2.3 Aggregate Level Simulation Protocol

In SIMNET, the focus was on individual weapon simulators for operator/pilot training, rather than the aggregate-level combat simulations for commander training. The aggregate-level simulations had their challenges of being distributed and run in an unprecedented scale. Therefore, the US Advanced Research Project Agency (ARPA) sponsored another effort, *Aggregate Level Simulation Protocol* (ALSP), to target distributed simulation of aggregate-level simulations in 1990. Some of the important unique challenges of ALSP include time management, data management, and architecture independence. ALSP brought forth several concepts that then became the foundations of High Level Architecture, such as objects, attributes, interactions, confederation, confederation model, and an infrastructure software (Weatherly et al. 1996; Wilson and Weatherly 1994).

1.3 High Level Architecture

Using experience gained from the DIS and ALSP efforts, US Department of Defense (DoD) presented a Modeling and Simulation Master Plan (DoD 1995) to create a common technological framework for modeling and simulation. The first objective was to develop a high-level simulation architecture to facilitate interoperability among simulations as well as operational systems, which is later called as *High Level Architecture* (HLA). Architecture Management Group (AMG), which was composed of major defense modeling and simulation bodies, drafted an initial technical architecture in 1996 In 1998, HLA became a DoD standard, and the reference RTI implementation for HLA version 1.3 was released (Dahmann et al. 1998). Then, in 2000, HLA became an IEEE standard and named as Modeling and Simulation (M&S) High Level Architecture IEEE 1516-2000 series (IEEE Std 1516-2000, 2000; IEEE Std 1516.1-2000, 2000; IEEE Std 1516.2-2000, 2000).

After the IEEE release, HLA gained wider visibility and acceptance all over the world. It has been employed not only by military projects, but also by civilian applications albeit on a much smaller scale (Boer et al. 2009). Alternative implementations, both proprietary and open-source, of the RTI are available for the user communities with a wide range of requirements. Simulation Interoperability Standards Organization (SISO) became one of the major platforms that hosts working groups and conducts conferences to discuss and evolve the related standards and recommendations. New-generation HLA is called *HLA Evolved*. After years of discussions and constant feedback from the implementers, and in an effort to accommodate the emerging service-oriented computing paradigm, HLA Evolved was published in 2010 as IEEE 1516-2010 series.

The latest HLA standard incorporates three specifications, namely the HLA Framework and Rules Specification (IEEE Std 1516-2010, 2010), the HLA Federate Interface Specification (IEEE Std 1516.1-2010, 2010), and the HLA Object Model Template (IEEE Std 1516.2-2010, 2010). Moreover, two standards that serve as process model complete the major specifications. The IEEE standard embodies five related standards shown in Table 1.1.

HLA Framework and Rules specifies the elements of systems design and introduces rules for a properly operating distributed simulation system. The second volume, *HLA Object Model Template*, presents the mechanism to specify the data model—the information produced and consumed by the members of the distributed simulation. The last volume *HLA Federate Interface Specification* introduces the functional interface that enables distributed simulation execution. Thus, this standard specifies the capabilities of the software infrastructure of HLA (i.e., *runtime infrastructure*—RTI). A federate application is a simulation member application (a piece of software) in terms of HLA. A federate is an executable component capable of participating in a federation, where a federation is the distributed simulation environment. Chapter 2 presents a detailed introduction of HLA.

Moreover, there exist some standards supporting HLA from other organizations. Table 1.2 summarizes those standards.

Later standardization efforts focus on the generalization of some HLA principles to distributed simulation systems life cycle. Table 1.3 presents those standards. One is the Recommended Practice for Distributed Simulation Engineering and Execution Process (DSEEP). In this standard, a *member application* is defined as "An

Table 1.1 IEEE 1516 standards

Standard	Explanation
IEEE 1516-2010	IEEE standard for modeling and simulation (M&S) HLA framework and rules, August 18, 2010
IEEE 1516.1-2010	IEEE standard for M&S HLA federate interface specification, August 18, 2010
IEEE 1516.2-2010	IEEE standard for M&S HLA object model template (OMT) specification, August 18, 2010
IEEE 1516.3-2003	IEEE recommended practice for HLA federation development and execution process, April 23, 2003 (IEEE Std 1516.3-2003, 2003)
IEEE 1516.4-2007	IEEE Recommended Practice for Verification, Validation, and Accreditation of a Federation: An Overlay to the HLA FEDEP, December 20, 2007 (IEEE-1516.4-2007, 2007)

Table 1.2 Other HLA standards

Standard	Explanation
SISO-STD-004-2004	SISO standard for dynamic link compatible (DLC) HLA API standard for the HLA interface specification (version 1.3). Reaffirmed in December 08, 2014
SISO-STD-004.1-2004	SISO standard for dynamic link compatible HLA API standard for the HLA interface specification (IEEE 1516.1 version). Reaffirmed in December 08, 2014

Table 1.3 DS standards

Standard	Explanation
IEEE Std 1730-2010	IEEE recommended practice for distributed simulation engineering and execution process (DSEEP), approved September 30, 2010. Revision of IEEE Std 1516.3-2003
IEEE Std 1730.1-2013	IEEE recommended practice for distributed simulation engineering and execution process multi-architecture overlay (DMAO), approved August 23, 2013

application that is serving some defined role within a simulation environment. This can include live, virtual, or constructive simulation assets, or can be supporting utility programs such as data loggers or visualization tools" (IEEE Std 1730-2010, 2010), whereas a *simulation environment* is defined "A named set of member applications along with a common simulation data exchange model (SDEM) and set of agreements that are used as a whole to achieve some specific objective" (IEEE Std 1730-2010, 2010).

1.4 Tools

Throughout the book, we will use a toolset to illustrate the practical implementation and development issues arising from the case studies. Therefore, here we briefly introduce the tools before summarizing the chapters. For a detailed account and use of those tools, please refer their related documentation. The toolset consists of a model development tool, which is freeware application, called *SimGe*, and an open-source library, called *RACoN*. The toolset is specifically developed to support laboratory activities in a graduate-level distributed simulation course. Therefore, the intended use of the toolset is for education, where the students can develop HLA-based simulation projects during a one-semester course.

1.4.1 SimGe

SimGe (Simulation Generator) is a simulation design and development environment for HLA-based distributed simulations. SimGe includes an object model editor and a code generator. The editor allows the user to manage the object model and enables the creation and modification of the HLA Object Model Template and object models and the import and export of the HLA related files (i.e., Federation Execution Details (FED),[1] Federation Object Model (FOM) Document Data (FDD)[2]), which contains configuration data for the federation execution. The code generator automatically generates code for the target platform, that is, RACoN in our case.

Currently, SimGe can generate all the RACoN compatible classes of a simulation object model using the federation execution configuration files (i.e., FDD/FED). A preview of the tool and sample projects can be obtained from SimGe Web site as a freeware (SimGe 2015).

1.4.2 RACoN

Many HLA simulations are developed on top of an abstraction layer over RTI as abstraction layer (wrapper) over RTI is a popular approach in many HLA-based development projects (PNP-Software 2007; Savaşan 2008; Chen et al. 2008), since this approach offers more maintainable, robust, easy to use, and portable methods. Thus, to explain the simulation implementation details, we will first use an RTI abstraction component for .NET (RACoN), targeted for Microsoft .NET environments, which provides the .NET wrapper classes for the RTI and RTI-specific data structures. There are also available COTS tools that provide abstraction layers for HLA such as MAK VR-Link (VT MAK 2017).

RACoN deals with the HLA runtime infrastructure-level communication to access the federation-wide data (the objects and interactions exchanged in a federation). RTI is a middleware software that manages the federation execution and management, and object exchanges throughout a federation execution.

The RACoN provides the .NET wrapper classes for the RTI and RTI-specific data structures. RACoN encapsulates the entire RTI low-level class interface to simplify the repetitive, error-prone, and low-level implementation details of the HLA federate interface. For instance, data contracts are used to enforce the federate interface specification in service usage to diminish the runtime errors caused by using wrong RTI services. With the help of RACoN, any .NET language can be selected to implement an HLA federate. The major rationale for the development of RACoN is to prepare an HLA version-free platform with the aim of code generation. RACoN is an open-source distributed library and can be obtained from RACoN (2016).

---

[1]FED file is used by RTIs that conform to the HLA 1.3 specification. See Chap. 2.
[2]FDD file is used by RTIs that conform to the HLA 1516 specification. See Chap. 2.

1.5 Introduction to Case Studies

There are two major case studies in this book. In this section, we will present a short introduction to both. The first one, Strait Traffic Monitoring Simulation, is a basic distributed simulation that consists of two applications. It will serve for introducing the HLA concepts as a running example scattered throughout the book. The second one is a larger case study, presented in a devoted chapter to show all the simulation development activities in one place. Furthermore, it will serve as an example involving multi-agents.

1.5.1 Strait Traffic Monitoring Simulation

Strait Traffic Monitoring Simulation (STMS) is used to explain the basics of the HLA-based simulation development. Its scenario first appeared in Topçu et al. (2008). Here, we first introduce the scenario of case study and give the rationale for it. The complete of the source code of the case study is available with RACoN library.

1.5.1.1 Definition

A *traffic monitoring station* tracks the ships passing through the strait. Any ship entering the strait announces her name and then periodically reports her position to the station and to the other ships in the strait using the radio channels. *Channel-1* is used for ship-to-ship, and *channel-2* is used for ship-to-shore communication. The traffic monitoring station tracks ships, and ships track each other through these communication channels. All radio messages are time-stamped to preserve the transmission order. The conceptual view of the application is presented in Fig. 1.3.

1.5.1.2 Rationale
While selecting this case study, the following highlights were in mind:

- Evidently, the essence of this simple simulation environment is an example of a set of objects tracking each other. It is a common scenario/interaction pattern for most distributed simulations.
- We believe that this example has a simple conceptual model, which will make it easily understandable and capture your attention immediately. Thus, it will push you focus on the modeling part than on the example itself.
- Moreover, the sample simulation naturally includes some advanced HLA services such as time management, ownership management, and data distribution management services in addition to the base services (e.g., federation management services) See Chap. 2 for the HLA services.
- The sample simulation environment involves two distinct member applications, and it has a potential to support multiple simulation environments.

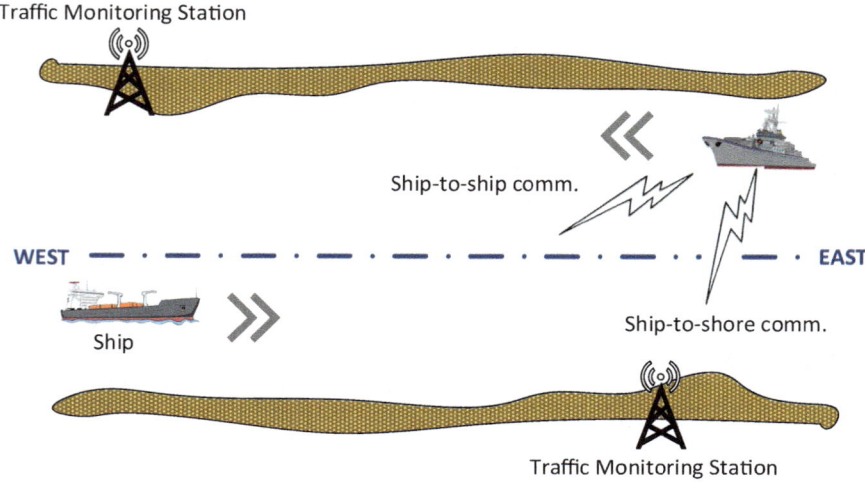

Fig. 1.3 A conceptual view for STMS application. Here, the strait is divided into two sea lanes for regulating the ship traffic. The entities (i.e., the ships and stations) may communicate with each other

- It provides some simple user interactions based on textual interface during execution (e.g., sending a radio message on request), which makes it as an interactive simulation. Thus, it presents how to model a simulation that involves the user interactions.

1.5.1.3 Road Map for Case Study

Case study is dispersed throughout the book chapters and used as a running example. Figure 1.4 presents a road map to the dispersion of case study to the book chapters.

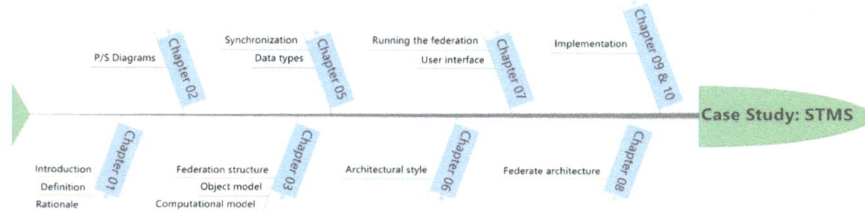

Fig. 1.4 Road map for the running example: STMS

1.5.2 Maritime Border Surveillance Using Unmanned Surface Vehicles

Maritime Border Surveillance Federation (MariSim) is a complete large case study including multi-agents.

1.5.2.1 Scenario

Maritime surveillance, especially on unpopulated or scarcely populated areas, is an important factor of border security. Continuous surveillance is necessary to increase the situational awareness in complex maritime environments, specifically to control and stop illegal immigration followed through by sea.

To perform continuous maritime surveillance, a fleet of unmanned surface vehicles (USVs) is formed to detect and identify refugee boats on sea border and to support current border control systems and manned (coast guard) boats.

A USV patrols and monitors its assigned area of responsibility (AOR). It is capable of detecting and identifying the refugee boats. When it identifies a refugee boat, it sends a message to command center and it escorts the refugee boat until a manned boat arrives and then continues with its regular surveillance activities. USV is fully autonomous and modeled as an intelligent agent and implemented as a federate, which is capable of making its own decisions (i.e., selecting which goal/task to persuade).

A refugee boat (RB) is a boat full of refugees. It is a computer-generated federate.

A coast guard boat (CGB) is a manned surface vehicle; when it receives a contact message from the USV, it navigates to the area and seizes the refugee boat. CGB is modeled as a three-dimensional (3D) graphics federate application operated by a human.

A conceptual screen is depicted in Fig. 1.5.

While selecting this case study, the following highlights were in mind:

- This case study involves a human-in-the-loop federate application, CgBoatFdApp (i.e., coast guard boat), which is a nearly real-time simulation.
- CgBoatFdApp is also a 3D graphics application, which allows us to discuss how to integrate a federate application with an intensive graphics application.
- The case study incorporates intelligent software agents, which are autonomous and have the ability to choose which goal or task to follow themselves. This point is raised to discuss the synergy between an agent-based simulation and a distributed simulation.
- The agents are modeled as computer-generated forces.
- The case study is non-trivial, resembling real-life projects.
- The federate application has the capacity to enhance the simulation execution with variations such as trying different time management schemes.

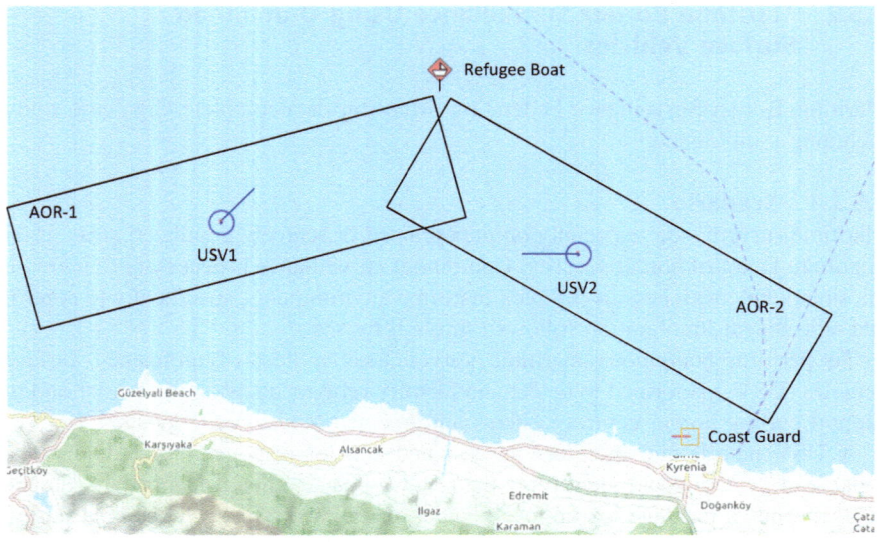

Fig. 1.5 Maritime surveillance conceptual view

- It has parts both for civilian use and military use. It includes components for autonomous systems for civilian use.
- The case study involves a scenario. So, scenario management activities, such as scenario start/stop, can be introduced.

1.5.2.2 Federation Architecture

As the environment manager, a part of an existing maritime simulation, called Naval Surface Tactical Maneuvering Simulation Systems (NSTMSS) (MariSim 2017; NSTMSS 2016; Topçu and Oğuztüzün 2005), is used to model the environment and to control the environment parameters. NSTMSS is an HLA-based distributed simulation that is composed of three-dimensional (3D) ship handling simulators, a tactical level simulation of operational area, a virtual environment manager (Environment Controller Federate Application—EnviFdApp), and simulation management processes (i.e., scenario management and simulation monitoring tools).

This case study uses the EnviFdApp both to model the environment and to control the environmental (i.e., sea) effects (e.g., sea state and waves) and the atmospheric (i.e., weather) effects (e.g., fog, wind, and time of day) in the virtual environment. The USVs and RBs are part of the simulation scenario. Scenario management is provided by the agent manager to specify the USV and RB models (e.g., the number of RBs, their paths, and speeds). In other words, the agent manager is responsible to instantiate the USVs and RBs according to the scenario. See Topçu and Oğuztüzün (2010) for scenario management practices. Both

1.5 Introduction to Case Studies

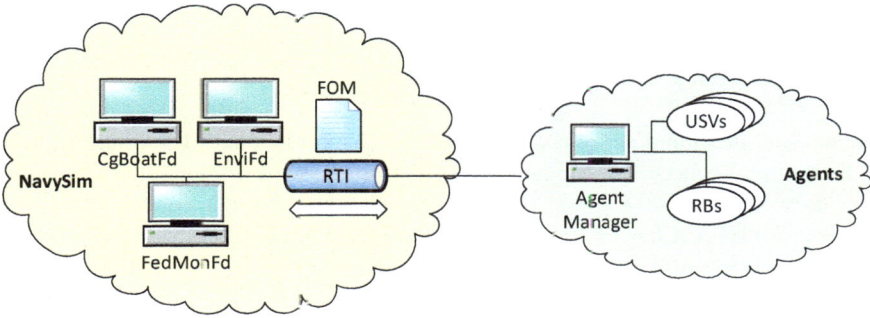

Fig. 1.6 MariSim architecture

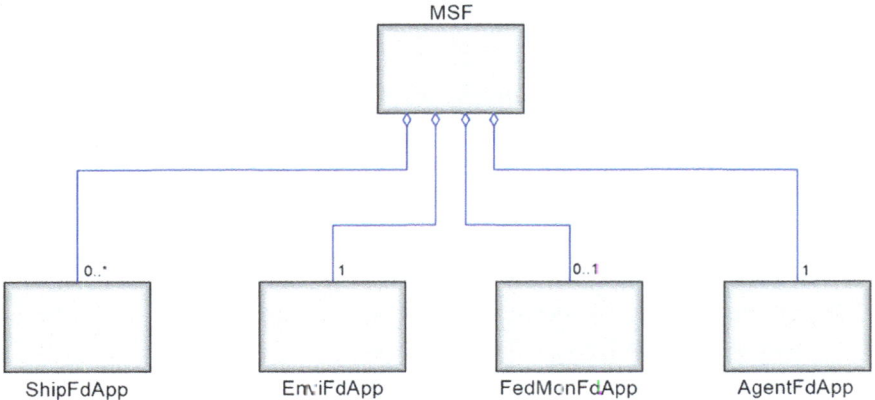

Fig. 1.7 MariSim federation structure

applications enable us to create a dynamic and an adversarial environment. EnviFdApp enables us to run the simulation under different environmental parameters (e.g., clear vs. foggy weather).

The Federation Monitor Federate Application (FedMonFdApp) is used to monitor the interactions among federates.

The simulation architecture is depicted in Fig. 1.6. Agent manager and NSTMSS federates communicate over HLA runtime infrastructure (RTI) by exchanging objects specified by a federation object model (FOM). Hence, the agent manager can be seen as an HLA wrapper for the agents.

The federation structure of MariSim Federation (MSF) is depicted in Fig. 1.7. There must be one agent manager application (AgentFdApp) to create and manage the USV federates and RB federates. The ship federate application represents the CGB federates. The FedMonFdApp is not essential for simulation execution, but required in case RTI-related data logging is needed. Therefore, it can be viewed as a stealth federate.

1.6 Book Outline

1.6.1 Summary of Chapters

The book is structured as follows. The present chapter is a high-level introduction to the essential concepts of Modeling and Simulation, while highlighting DS as the focal area of interest. Chapter 2 introduces the fundamental concepts and the principles of HLA. Chapter 3 takes a look into federation development and presents the development guidelines. These three chapters together lay the technical background for federation development.

The remaining chapters constitute three major parts of the book: object model development, federate implementation, and advanced topics. Chapters 4 and 5 present an introduction to object model development and then elaborate on the subject by using a case study. Using this object model, Chapters from 6 to 8 explain the details of implementing a federate application. Last, Chap. 10 considers some advanced topics by discussing the connection between agent-based simulation and HLA. Then, Chap. 11 provides a detailed case study to put it all together.

The chapters are structured in such a layered way (see Fig. 1.8), where the chapters in top layer include more generalized topics such as M&S and HLA concepts, and as we proceed to bottom layers, more specialized topics are covered such as implementing time management services.

The contents of each chapter and the appendix are broken down as follows:

- This chapter provides an overview of the M&S concepts, distributed simulation, the tools used in this book, and the case studies.
- Chapter 2 presents a detailed introduction to the HLA.
- Chapter 3 presents federation development at-a-glance.
- Chapter 4 gives an introduction to object model development and explains the simulation development process.
- Chapter 5 presents the details and hands-on practices of the object model construction with SimGe object model editor.
- Chapter 6 presents the code generation with the SimGe code generator.
- Chapter 7 presents an introduction to the federate application development.
- Chapter 8 elaborates on the fundamentals of federate implementation.
- Chapter 9 delves into some advanced topics in federate implementation such as ownership management.
- Chapter 10 brings forward the synergy between agent-based simulation and distributed simulation.
- Chapter 11 presents a complete case study to demonstrate the integration of agent-based simulation with HLA.
- Appendix A specifies the hardware and software requirements and the installation steps of SimGe.

1.6 Book Outline

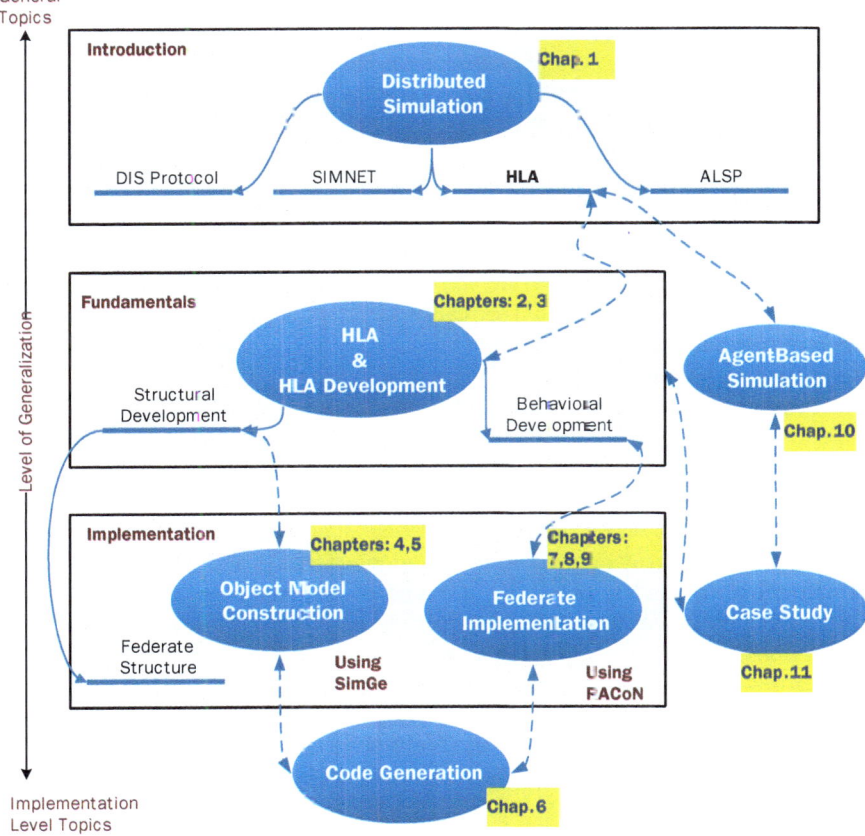

Fig. 1.8 Road map to book outline

Please note that many chapters include a *Questions for Review* section to provoke the reader into further thinking about the topics.

1.6.2 Typeface Conventions

This book uses the following typeface conventions:

- All code examples/snippets are printed in a Consolas Font.
- At the introduction or definition of a major term, the term is shown in *italics*.
- All references to classes, attributes, and other elements of a model are shown in Courier New font.
- *Italics* is used for emphasized words or phrases in running.

1.7 Summary

In this chapter, we presented an introduction to the concepts and principles of modeling and simulation. In this regard, we tried to clarify all the essential concepts such as model, system, and simulation that keep occurring in our discussions throughout this book. A model is construed as a representation of reality and modeling as the activity of creating a model. A system is an organized collection of components that interact with each other according to a pattern in order to achieve some purpose or functionality. Behavior of a system involves its outputs in response to its inputs. We define the simulation as a method of generating system behavior from the system model. The reality we are interested in modeling also has a time dimension. According to time and state change, we arrive at a continuous time model or discrete event model.

In case the subject reality (simuland) inherently involves multiple interacting entities, then we need alternatives instead of one monolithic simulation model for the purpose of balancing the load of simulation can be shared by multiple processors. These processors can be distributed over a network or can be housed on a single host computer, where we characterize the latter parallel simulation while the former as the distributed simulation. We also looked into (briefly) the history of DS from SIMNET to HLA as presenting the related standards.

Moreover, in this chapter, we presented the book structure and introduced the toolset, SimGe and RACoN, used throughout the book. SimGe is mainly a tool for constructing a simulation object model, whereas RACoN is an abstraction layer to the RTI, which is the main orchestrator software of HLA.

Lastly, we introduced two main case studies used in this book. The first one, Strait Traffic Monitoring Simulation, is a basic distributed simulation, where it serves as introducing the HLA concepts and employed as a running example scattered throughout the book. The second one is a large case study, where it shows all the simulation development efforts in one place and serves as an example involving agent-based simulation.

1.8 Questions for Review

1. What is the difference between a real-time simulation and a real-time application?
2. Describe Zeigler's Modeling and Simulation Theory (Zeigler 1976) by giving major elements and relations among them.
3. What is the difference between distributed simulation and parallel simulation?
4. Can a simulation application be classified as both distributed simulation and parallel simulation?
5. Referring to Fig. 1.1, you see the fundamental concepts and relations among them. So, each concept is cycled with another. Considering this cycle, is any

shortcut possible between concepts? For example, think about a direct relation between "simulation" and "results" concept skipping the "computer" concept.
6. The DIS Vision issued by Institute for Simulation and Training (IST) in May 1994 stated the following:

> The primary mission of DIS is to define an infrastructure for linking simulations of various types at multiple locations to create realistic, complex, virtual "worlds" for the simulation of highly interactive activities. This infrastructure brings together systems built for separate purposes, technologies from different eras, products from various vendors, and platforms from various services and permits them to interoperate. DIS exercises are intended to support a mixture of virtual entities (human-in-the-loop simulators), live entities (operational platforms and test and evaluation systems), and constructive entities (wargames and other automated simulations).
>
> The DIS infrastructure provides interface standards, communications architectures, management structures, fidelity indices, technical forums, and other elements necessary to transform heterogeneous simulations into unified seamless synthetic environments. These synthetic environments support design and prototyping, education and training, test and evaluation, emergency preparedness and contingency response, and readiness and warfighting.

Investigate to what extent HLA helped realize the DIS Vision. You may use Internet resources to search for success stories.

References

Alur, R., Courcoubetis, C., Henzinger, T. A. & Ho, P. H. (1993). Hybrid automata: An algorithmic approach to the specification of hybrid systems. In: *Hybrid systems, lecture notes in computer science* (Vol. 736, pp. 209–229). Berlin: Springer.

Asimov, A. (1988). *Prelude to foundation*. New York: Collins. (New Ed 1994).

Banks, J., Carson, J. S., II, Nelson, B. L., & Nicol, D. M. (2010). *Discrete-event system simulation* (5th ed.). Upper Saddle River, CA: Pearson Education.

Boer, C., de Bruin, A., & Verbraeck, A. (2009). A survey on distributed simulation in industry. *Journal of Simulation, 3*, 3–16.

Cassandras, C. G., & Lafortune, S. (2010). *Introduction to discrete event systems* (2nd ed.). Boston, MA: Springer.

Chapman, S. J. (2015). *MATLAB programming for engineers* (5th ed.). Boston, MA: Cengage Learning.

Chen, D., Turner, S., Cai, W., & Xiong, M. (2008). Decoupled federate architecture for high level architecture-based distributed simulation. *Journal of Parallel and Distributed Computing, 68*(11), 1487–1503.

Clarke, E., Grumberg, O., & Peled, D. (1999). *Model checking*. Cambridge, MA: MIT Press.

Cosby, L. (1995). *SIMNET: An insiders' perspective*. Retrieved from http://oai.dtic.mil/oai/oai?verb=getRecord&metadataPrefix=html&identifier=ADA294786

Cross, D. C. (1999). Report from the fidelity implementation study group. In *Spring Simulation Interoperability Workshop*.

Dahmann, J., Kuhl, F., & Weatherly, R. (1998). Standards for simulation: As simple as possible but not simpler the high level architecture for simulation. *Simulation, 71*(6), 378–387.

DoD. (1995). *Modeling and simulation (M&S) master plan*. Alexandria: DoD.
Fujimoto, R. M. (2000). *Parallel and distributed simulation systems*. New York, NY: Wiley.
IEEE Std 1278.1-2012. (2012). *IEEE standard for distributed interactive simulation–application protocols*. IEEE.
IEEE Std 1516.1-2000. (2000). *Standard for modeling and simulation (M&S) High level architecture (HLA)—Federate interface specification*. IEEE.
IEEE Std 1516.1-2010. (2010). *Standard for modeling and simulation (M&S) high level architecture (HLA)—Federate interface specification*. IEEE.
IEEE Std 1516.2-2000. (2000). *Standard for modeling and simulation (M&S) high level architecture (HLA)—object model template (OMT) specification*. IEEE.
IEEE Std 1516.2-2010. (2010). *Standard for modeling and simulation (M&S) high level architecture (HLA)—Object model template specification*. IEEE.
IEEE Std 1516.3-2003. (2003). *Standard for IEEE recommended practice for high level architecture (HLA) federation development and execution process (FEDEP)*. IEEE.
IEEE Std 1516-2000. (2000). *Standard for modeling and simulation (M&S) high level architecture (HLA)—Framework and rules*. IEEE.
IEEE Std 1516-2010. (2010). *Standard for modeling and simulation (M&S) high level architecture (HLA)—Framework and rules*. New York: IEEE.
IEEE Std 1730-2010. (2010). *IEEE recommended practice for distributed simulation engineering and execution process (DSEEP)*. New York: NY: IEEE.
IEEE-1516.4-2007. (2007). *IEEE recommended practice for verification, validation, and accrediation of a federation: An overlay to the high level architecture federation development and execution process*. IEEE.
IEEE. (1993). *Protocols for distributed interactive simulation applications—entity information and interaction*.
Kelton, W. D., Sadowski, R., & Zupick, N. (2014). *Simulation with arena* (6th ed.). New York: McGraw-Hill Education.
Kleinrock, L. (1976). *Queueing systems: Computer applications* (Vol. 2). New York, NY: Wiley.
Law, A. M. (2007). *Simulation modeling & analysis* (4th ed.). Singapore: McGraw-Hill.
Luenberger, D. G. (1979). *Introduction to dynamic systems: Theory, models, and applications*. New York, NY: Wiley.
MariSim. (2017). *Maritime simulation (MariSim)*. Retrieved January 8, 2017 from https://sites.google.com/site/okantopcu/marisim
Miller, D., & Thrope, J. A. (1995). *SIMNET: The advent of simulator networking*, pp. 1114–1123
NSTMSS. (2016). *Naval surface tactical maneuvering simulation system (NSTMSS) web site*. Retrieved January 8, 2017 http://www.ceng.metu.edu.tr/~otopcu/nstmss/
OMG. (2012). *OMG systems modeling language (SysML) version 1.3*. OMG.
OMG. (2015). *OMG unified modeling language (OMG UML) version 2.5*. Object Management Group.
Ören, T. I. (2011). The many facets of simulation through a collection of about 100 definitions. *SCS M&S Magazine*, 82–92.
PNP-Software. (2007). *EODiSP*. Retrieved October 29, 2014 http://www.pnp-software.com/eodisp/index.html
RACoN. (2016). *RACoN project website*. Retrieved May 19, 2017 https://sites.google.com/site/okantopcu/racon
Reisig, W. (1991). Petri nets and algebraic specifications. *Theoretical Computer Science, 80*(1), 1–34.
Rice, S., et al. (2005). The SIMSCRIPT III programming language for modular object-oriented simulation. In M. E. Kuhl, N. M. Steiger, F. B. Armstrong, & J. A. Joines (Eds.), *Proceedings of the 2005 Winter Simulation Conference* (pp. 621–630), Orlando, FL.
Savaşan, H. (2008). *The RToolkit: An open source object oriented distributed simulation framework*. SISO: Orlando.

References

SimGe. (2015). *SimGe web site*. Retrieved April 07, 2017 https://sites.google.com/site/okantopcu/simge

Singhal, S., & Zyda, M. (1999). *Networked virtual environments: Design and implementation*. Reading, MA: Addison-Wesley.

Sokolowski, J. A., & Banks, C. A. (2010). *Modeling and simulation fundamentals*. Hoboken, NJ: Wiley.

Topçu, O., Adak, M., & Oğuztüzün, H. (2008). A metamodel for federation architectures. *Transactions on Modeling and Computer Simulation (TOMACS), 18*(3), 10:1–10:29.

Topçu, O., Durak, U., Oğuztüzün, H., & Yılmaz, L. (2016). *Distributed simulation: A model driven engineering approach* (1st ed.). Cham: Springer International Publishing.

Topçu, O., & Oğuztüzün, H. (2005). Developing an HLA based naval maneuvering simulation. *Naval Engineers Journal, 117*(1), 23–40.

Topçu, O., & Oğuztüzün, H. (2010). Scenario management practices in HLA-based distributed simulation. *Journal of Naval Science and Engineering, 6*(2), 1–33.

VT MAK. (2017). *VR-Link*. Retrieved April 23, 2017 https://www.mak.com/products/link/vr-link

Weatherly, R., et al. (1996). *Advanced distributed simulation through the aggregate level simulation protocol* (pp. 407–415).

Wilson, A. L., & Weatherly, R. M. (1994). *The aggregate level simulation protocol: An evolving system* (pp. 781–787). IEEE.

Zeigler, P. B. (1976). *Theory of modeling and simulation*. New York: Wiley-Interscience Publication.

High Level Architecture

In this chapter, we want to provide you a detailed introduction to High Level Architecture (HLA) to lay the technical background for the rest of the chapters. HLA is both a de facto and de jure standard for distributed simulation. HLA is a simulation systems architecture framework for distributed simulation. Interoperability, along with reusability, is a major design aim of HLA. And it is commonly used in many application domains, specifically in the military realm. In this chapter, various aspects of the standard will be reviewed to furnish user with a comprehensive introduction. This chapter extends the third chapter of (Topçu et al. 2016).

2.1 Prelude

As we provided the historical perspective of distributed simulation in Chap. 1, HLA is the latest de facto and de jure standard for distributed simulations. The efforts began to realize a common technical framework for M&S through (initially) the defense domain, to enable the interoperability of various simulation systems by urging the stakeholders (e.g., the vendors, users, etc.) to a common architecture, which is called as High Level Architecture (DoD 1995). Today, it is commonly used in many application domains, in both military and civilian realm.

The evolution of HLA begins with the U.S. DoD HLA 1.3 specification, then to an IEEE standard in 2000 and then evolving once more in 2010 to its current version, which is called *HLA Evolved*, published in 2010 as IEEE 1516.2010 series (IEEE Std 1516-2010 2010; IEEE Std 1516.1-2010 2010; IEEE Std 1516.2-2010 2010). Unfortunately, the three versions of HLA specifications are not fully compatible with each other both in terms of software and framework, which increases the confusion of users as a result. In this regard, this book is generally based on the HLA Evolved version. Whenever we want to clarify the difference, we explicitly spell the version. For consistency throughout the book, we will refer to the HLA versions as presented in Table 2.1 to eliminate confusion.

Table 2.1 HLA versions

HLA specification	Referrant
The U.S. DoD HLA 1.3 specification	HLA 1.3
IEEE 1516-2000 standard	HLA 1516-2000
IEEE 1516-2010 standard	HLA 1516-2010 or HLA evolved

Today, the studies for the improvement of HLA actively continue spearheaded by Simulation Interoperability Standards Organization (SISO).

The major enhancements to IEEE 1516.2010 series were summarized as modular federation object models (FOMs) and simulation object models (SOMs), Web services communication, improved support for fault tolerance, smart update rate reduction, and dynamic link compatibility (DLC) (Möller et al. 2008).

2.1.1 What Is HLA?

Its standard defines HLA as a simulation systems architecture framework with the aim to facilitate the reuse and the interoperability of simulations (IEEE Std 1516-2010 2010). Cost-effectiveness, quality, and timeliness concerns necessitate reuse of assets not only in simulation domain, but also in all software-intensive domains. Systematic reuse, however, can only be achieved by assets that are designed for reuse. Component-based modularity with loose coupling of components at the heart of HLA is a key enabler for both interoperability and reusability. The interoperability can be defined as the capability of simulations to exchange information in a useful and meaningful way (Yilmaz 2007). The realization of interoperability requires a means of communication between the components.

As pointed out earlier, the motivation of HLA is to provide a common architecture for distributed simulation (Kuhl et al. 1999). Thus, the simulations, whatever their type might be (live, constructive, or virtual), interoperate on a single infrastructure to achieve the simulation objectives (e.g., to train a pilot in an engagement, or to produce data to input to a decision-making process). In a distributed environment, the infrastructure can be based on a direct communication (point-to-point) or an indirect communication (using a mediator) among components. In this regard, HLA adopts the latter approach, especially, to promote the reuse of components by decreasing the coupling of each component with others using a mediator, where *coupling* specifies the degree of the functional interdependency (in terms of communication) between components. This mediator is called *runtime infrastructure* (RTI), and its task is to provide services for the management of distributed simulation, components, and the data communication.

The HLA standard defines an architecture framework as "major functional elements, interfaces, and design rules, pertaining as feasible to all simulation applications and providing a common framework within which specific systems architecture can be defined" (IEEE Std 1516-2010 2010). While functional elements specify the feature set that will be provided, interfaces define the way that user will consume them. Design rules introduce the practices to be employed to use these functions over the described interfaces to build up a system. This trio, namely, functional elements, interfaces, and rules, constitutes a common framework for developing simulations.

To wrap up, in a broad sense, the standard defines an architectural framework whose aim is to enable component-based, loosely coupled simulation development. The basic assumptions and motivations underneath this effort are summarized as follows (Dahmann et al. 1997).

- Diverse user requirements of today's simulation systems cannot be fulfilled by a single or monolithic structure. Thus, HLA supports decomposing large simulation problems into smaller parts.
- Today's simulations sweep a wide range of domains so that no single group of developers possesses all required knowledge to develop the whole simulation. Thus, HLA supports composing smaller parts into a big simulation system.
- Simulations can be used for more than one application some of which cannot be foreseen during development. Thus, HLA supports reusable simulations that can be composed into various simulation systems that have different requirements.
- Simulations have long life spans so that the technology that uses them is subject to changes. Thus, HLA provides an interface between the simulations and their users that insulates their use from the changing technology such as network protocols, operating systems, and programming languages.

As an historical fact, HLA was originated from the requirements of the defense modeling and simulation community. Early requirements for distributed simulations for collective training, and later, for aggregate simulations for analyzing battlefield situations led to a worldwide accepted simulation standard, HLA. Today, the user community of the standard spreads beyond defense applications. Since the standard was first published, there have been numerous distributed simulation applications in homeland security, space, aeronautics, disaster recovery, air traffic management, transportation systems, and medical domains that take advantage of it.

2.2 Basic Components

HLA is not software, but an architectural framework. It is a set of specifications, which is comprised of three parts:

- *HLA Framework and Rules* specifies the principles of systems design and introduces "a set of rules that must be followed to achieve proper interaction of simulations (federates) in a federation. These describe the responsibilities of simulations and of RTI in HLA federations" (IEEE Std 1516-2010 2010).

- *Interface Specification (IF)*: "The HLA Interface Specification defines the interface between the simulation and the software that will provide the network and simulation management services. RTI is the software that provides these services" (IEEE Std 1516.1-2010 2010). This standard specifies the capabilities of the software infrastructure of HLA, namely *RTI*.
- *Object Model Template (OMT)* presents the mechanism to specify the data model—the information produced and consumed by the elements of the distributed simulation. More formally "the OMT describes a common method for declaring the information that will be produced and communicated by each simulation participating in the distributed exercise" (IEEE Std 1516.2-2010 2010).

Before presenting each major standard in detail, let us begin with introducing some basic terminologies such as federate and federations and runtime infrastructure in this section.

2.2.1 Federate and Federation

A *federate application* is a (simulation) member application that conforms to the HLA standard and implements the interfaces specified in the HLA Federate Interface Specification to participate in a distributed simulation execution (IEEE Std 1516-2010 2010). When we refer to a simulation member as a piece of software, we call it a federate application, and, as an executable component capable of participating in a federation, we call it a *federate*. In order to interact with other federates (through the RTI) in the distributed simulation execution, a federate must join the simulation execution; then it is called as a *joined federate*.[1] A federate application may join the same execution multiple times or may join into multiple executions, creating a new joined federate each time.

It is worth noting that the standard is interested only in the interface of the federate, not how a federate application is structured. The motivation is that a legacy simulation application can be wrapped as a federate, thus, can participate in a federation. Simulations of systems or phenomena, simulation loggers, monitoring applications, gateways, and live entities all can be federate applications. Federate technically can be defined as a single connection to the RTI. So, we can identify it as a unit of reuse (IEEE Std 1516.2-2010 2010) and a member of a federation as depicted in Fig. 2.1. It can be a single process or can contain several processes running on more than one computer. It can be a data consumer, producer, or both. Best practices advocate designing a reusable set of simulation features as a federate. It can represent one platform such as a ship in an aggregate-level simulation or a frigate hydrodynamics model that can be a federate in a full mission training simulator.

---

[1]Throughout the book, application is used as a short form for "federate application", and federate is used as a short form for "joined federate", unless otherwise indicated.

2.2 Basic Components

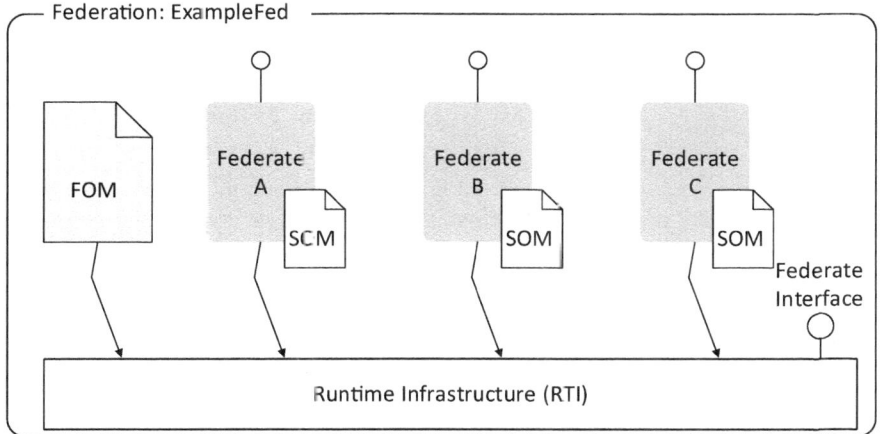

Fig. 2.1 Federation and federates

Federation is a simulation environment with a name, which is composed of the set of federates that share a common specification of data communication that are captured in *federation object model* (FOM) (i.e., *simulation data exchange model* in DS jargon) and interact via the RTI. As presented in Fig. 2.1, federates, whose data communication requirements are documented in their *simulation object models* (SOMs), are composed and interoperate over the runtime infrastructure throughout the federation execution. The information exchange requirements that include class relationships, data representations, parameters, and other relevant data of a federate are documented in the FOM. FOM is composed from the participating federate capabilities (documented as SOM).

Federation execution is a runtime instantiation of a federation; that is an actual simulation execution.

To exemplify the concepts introduced so far, consider a maritime simulation, which is composed of multiple ships, data loggers, and simulation control applications, where all share the same virtual environment and the notion of time. Here, the whole simulation is a federation with a common object model (i.e., FOM) shared by each participant. Each one of the participating members, e.g., a ship, a data logger, or a simulation controller, which is capable to participate in this federation, is a federate with its own object model (i.e., SOM). Assuming this federation is intended for analyzing the traffic management of a strait, then each simulation run is called as a federation execution.

2.2.2 Runtime Infrastructure

Most software architectures rely on infrastructures to enable their promises. HLA also comes with an infrastructure to enable interfederate communication. RTI is the

HLA's underlying software infrastructure, a *middleware*. Federates interact with RTI through the standard services and interfaces to participate in the distributed simulation and exchange data. RTI supports the HLA Rules with the services it provides over the interfaces specified in the Interface Specification (IEEE Std 1516.1-2010 2010).

The first public available RTI, called RTI 1.3, implements the HLA 1.3 specification and was released in 1998 (Kuhl et al. 1999). Since then, there have been more than 20 RTIs produced as open-source, freeware, or commercial software. Some of the major commercial ones are pRTI™ from Pitch Technologies (Pitch 2013), MÄK RTI (2013) from VT MÄK. And some popular open-source RTIs are Portico (2013), OpenRTI (2011), CERTI (2002), EODiSP HLA (PNP-Software 2007), and Open HLA (2016).

2.3 HLA Rules

The principles that a distributed simulation system must adhere to be considered HLA compliant are specified in the standard (IEEE Std 1516-2010, 2010). They are categorized under two headings, namely federation rules and federate rules.

2.3.1 Federation Rules

- Federation shall have an HLA FOM, documented in accordance with the HLA OMT.

  The formalization of information exchange is one of the key points of HLA; it thus enables domain-independent interoperability. FOM is a major part of any federation agreement. So, any federation shall have a FOM, in which all the data (object and interaction) exchange that can happen during a federation execution is specified.

- In a federation, all simulation-associated object instance representation shall be in the federates, not in the RTI.

  HLA aims to separate federate-specific (domain-specific) functionality from the support for general purpose (simulation) capabilities. So, it is the federates' responsibility to keep the copies of the object instance attribute values they are interested in. RTI does not provide a storage medium for shared data; rather, it provides a medium of transmission.

- During a federation execution, all exchange of FOM data among joined federates shall occur via the RTI.

  To permit coherency in data exchange among the participants, federates shall utilize the RTI for data exchange as specified in the FOM. Then, the RTI can manage the execution and data exchange of the federation. Allowing a backdoor for communication would create hidden dependencies among federates, thus, hindering their reusability.

- During federation execution, joined federates shall interact with the RTI in accordance with the HLA Interface Specification.

    Two-way interaction between the federate and the RTI shall conform to the federate interface specification. This specification is the base documentation for both the RTI implementers and the federate application developers. A federate uses this standard interface to employ the RTI services.

- During a federation execution, an instance attribute shall be owned by at most one joined federate at any given time.

    To promote data integrity, only one federate can own instance of an object attribute at a time. Initially, the creator of an object is the owner of all its attributes. The ownership of an attribute confers the owner the right to update it. Transfer of ownership from one federate to another during execution is mediated by the RTI. Notice that ownership is at the attribute level; the attributes of the same object instance can be shared between different owners, thus allowing implementation of distributed objects.

2.3.2 Federate Rules

- Federates shall have an HLA SOM, documented in accordance with the HLA OMT.

    Interoperability and reuse are only possible with an explicit specification of the capabilities and needs of the federates. This is the advertisement part. The object classes, class attributes, and interaction classes with their parameters shall be specified for every federate in its SOM. SOM is mainly used for documentation.

- Federates shall be able to update and/or reflect any instance attributes and send and/or receive interactions, as specified in their SOMs.

    Federates can interact with others over updating or reflecting object instance attributes and sending or receiving interactions as specified in their SCMs. Thus, the reuse is enabled. This and the next two rules simply say "No false advertisement!"

- Federates shall be able to transfer and/or accept ownership of instance attributes dynamically during a federation execution, as specified in their SOMs.

    As specified in the SOM, federates shall support transferring or accepting the ownership of object instance attributes during execution. This provides flexibility for federation designers in terms of the allocation of responsibility.

- Federates shall be able to vary the conditions (e.g., thresholds) under which they provide updates of instance attributes, as specified in their SOMs.

    To take part in various federations, or cope with different phases of the same federation execution, a federate must be able to vary its object attribute update rates or interaction send rates, within the limits set forth in its SOM.

- Federates shall be able to manage local time in a way that will allow them to coordinate data exchange with other members of a federation.

  Being a simulation on its own, a federate shall be able to manage its own time. Moreover, it must cooperate with the federation so that the RTI can maintain a notion of federation time. HLA supports federates with different time advancement mechanisms, such as time-driven or event-driven, via time management services. HLA also supports different time management strategies, such as conservative and optimistic, within a federation.

2.4 HLA Data Model and Data Communication

In the heart of distributed simulation is the simulation data exchange model which governs the data communication between simulation members. It is essential to understand how data are represented and shared during a federation execution.

In this respect, we introduce the HLA data communication pattern, the design time, and runtime data structures, and we present the HLA object exchange. Here, we answer what an HLA class is and then explain the related concepts, particularly, HLA OMT and the HLA object models. Chapters 4 and 5 demonstrate how to develop an HLA object model using SimGe tool.

2.4.1 HLA Data Communication Pattern

In a communication pattern, it is important to specify the policy of how data are exchanged among components. There are two important aspects of this specification. First, it is important to know what to exchange and how. For the latter question, in general, the participating member applications in a simulation environment can communicate directly in point-to-point manner (Fig. 2.2a) or they can employ a mediator (i.e., broker), part of a middleware, for communicating indirectly (Fig. 2.2b).

For the former question, what to exchange, there are two common approaches for data communication: *message exchange* (Fig. 2.3a) and *object exchange* (Fig. 2.3b).

In case of HLA, HLA specifies data communication via object exchange using a middleware (Fig. 2.4).

Now, we can describe how HLA exchanges objects among federates. The RTI plays the role of a mediator and routes the objects to the related federates. In the point-to-point communication, adopted by Distributed Interactive Simulation (DIS) protocol, the sender must know the receiver. In particular, the sender must know the network Internet Protocol (IP) address of the receiver. But, the middleware architecture model, which HLA adopts, uses a middleware to route the data among federates. Consequently, there is no need, in principle, for a federate to know about other federates. The RTI performs data routing using a *Publish/Subscribe Pattern*. In the following subsections, we will give the details of this pattern.

2.4 HLA Data Model and Data Communication

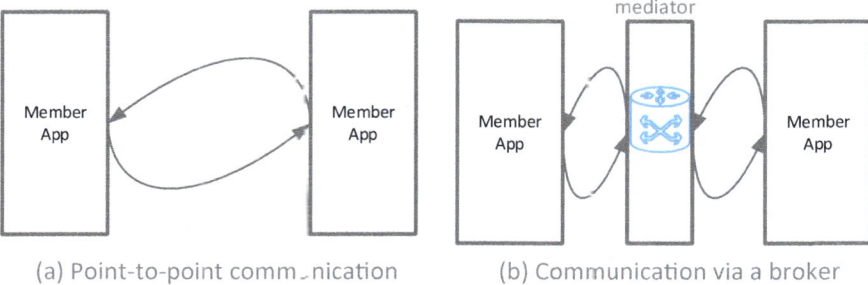

Fig. 2.2 How to exchange? **a** point-to-point **b** using a mediator. We can think of brokerage as a service provided by the middleware (in general terms)

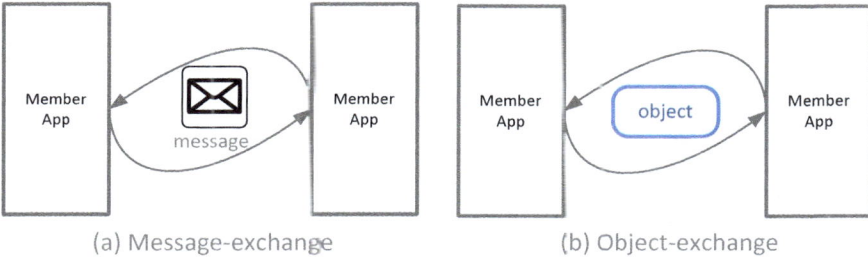

Fig. 2.3 What to exchange? **a** message **b** object

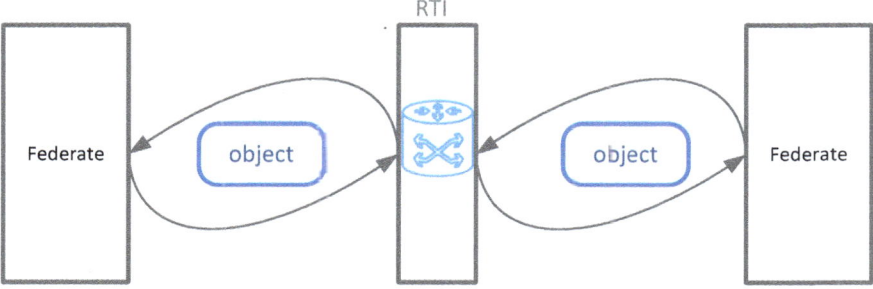

Fig. 2.4 HLA data communication pattern

The answer for what to exchange is that HLA communication model is based on object-exchange technology. In other words, HLA-compliant federates communicate with each other by exchanging objects. Therefore, the technology differs from classical DIS protocols, where data communication is based on message exchange technology, whereas data are exchanged through well-defined messages using predefined protocol data units (PDUs). The structure of the exchanged data is embedded in DIS protocol. This causes the DIS protocol to be inflexible. For instance, to exchange an entity state, DIS protocol specifies an entity state PDU. Therefore, the simulation engineer can only use those predefined PDUs. You cannot create or define new data structures as all are specified with the standard. In contrast, HLA separates the data and its architecture. In this regard, HLA defines the structure of the data that will be exchanged by the help of a template of what to exchange at design time. This is done by employing the HLA Object Model Template. The simulation engineer can model new data structures, in terms of *HLA classes*, using the HLA OMT specification. The collection of those specified data structures is called an *HLA object model*. In the following subsections, we will expand both OMT and the object models.

2.4.2 Object Exchange: Publish/Subscribe Pattern

In this pattern, the sender and receiver components (i.e., federates) do not know each other. They just declare (to the RTI) what they need and what they can provide to the federation execution. In a federation execution, it is essential to express the relationship between a federate and particular federation objects. Therefore, a crucial federation design activity is to define the *Publish and Subscribe (P/S)* interests of federates with the objects of conceptual model at hand.

The Publish/Subscribe pattern forms the basis of the model of communication used by HLA between federates in terms of objects and interactions. *Publishing* means declaring willingness (and ability) to provide data, which is composed of object classes and their attributes, and interaction classes that the federate is able to update or send. *Subscribing* means declaring interest and the needs in receiving certain data. RTI dynamically routes the data from publishers (producers) to subscribers (consumers).

As shown Fig. 2.5, at runtime, federates can declare to the RTI, which plays the role of an object router, a set of data templates they can provide (i.e., publish), and a set of data templates they are ready to receive (i.e., subscribe) according to the *Federation Execution Details (FED)* for HLA 1.3 federations or *FOM Document Data (FDD)* for HLA 1516 federations, which both are derived from the FOM documented using the OMT specification. Following data declaration, federate can create an object (i.e., register) or can send an interaction, which it published. Afterward, the RTI finds the federates who subscribed to the class of the objects or interactions and then routes the object/interaction to the subscribers. So that, a subscriber federate can receive the interaction or discover the object. Updating the values of the object attributes works the same way. The publisher federate updates the value of an object attribute (i.e., update), and then the update is reflected to the subscriber federates (i.e., reflect).

Now, let us look at closely what an object, class, and an object model mean in HLA.

2.4 HLA Data Model and Data Communication

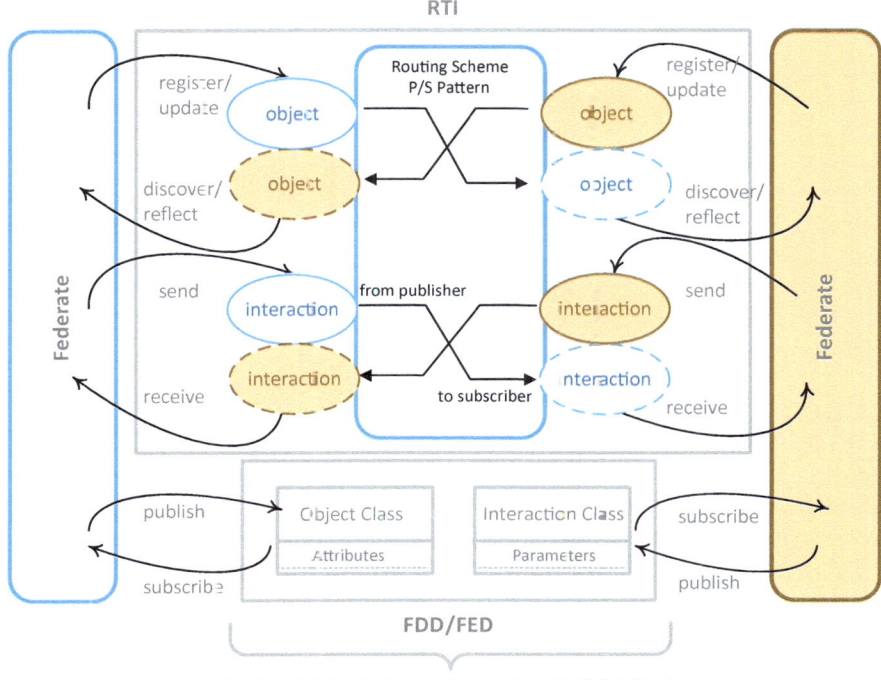

Fig. 2.5 Object exchange based on P/S pattern

2.4.3 Data: Objects, Interactions, and HLA Classes

2.4.3.1 Object Instances and Interactions

The *objects*, also known as *object instance* or *HLA object* are the primary means of communication in a federation. They can be regarded as the abstractions of simulated entities. A simulated entity may have a lifetime that is as long as the simulation execution time span. And for sure, more than one federate can share an interest over that simulated entity. While one controls the entity, some others may only observe it. Good examples of HLA objects can be platforms or sensors in combat simulations or airplanes in air traffic simulations. Only joined federates can create or delete an object in a federation execution. The lifetime of an object is the duration between its creation and deletion. Only the federate that publishes the object class can create an object that is an instance of that class. Deletion of an object can be done only by the federate, which owns the privilege to delete. This is explained later in the ownership management section.

Object modelers identify the objects to facilitate an organizational scheme. There are *attributes* associated with an object. The values of the attributes determine the object state. The owner federate provides the attribute values by updating them, and others (that are subscribed to those attributes) receive the values by reflecting those attributes. The position and velocity of a platform object can be examples of attributes.

Interactions, on the other hand, represent an occurrence or an event (analogous to events in the sense of discrete event simulation). So conceptually, they are not durable entities of interest but instantaneous events or occurrences of interest, such as sending of a message or landing of an aircraft. An interaction possesses a collection of data that is related to the occurrence or the event. The members of this data collection are called *parameters*. The parameters of an interaction are analogous to the attributes of an object. The difference is that the parameters of an interaction form a single indivisible group, while the attributes of an object can be grouped in different ways.

2.4.3.2 HLA Classes

Both objects and interactions are unique instantiations of HLA classes (see Fig. 2.6) because each object has a unique handle given by the RTI. *Handles* are the unique identifiers managed by the RTI. In classical sense, a class is "a description of a group of items with similar properties, common behavior, common relationships, and common semantics" (IEEE Std 1516.2-2010 2010). There are two types of HLA classes: *object class* and *interaction class*. An object class is "a template for a set of characteristics that is common to a group of object instances" (IEEE Std 1516.2-2010 2010), where an interaction class is "a template for a set of characteristics that is common to a group of interactions" (IEEE Std 1516.2-2010 2010).

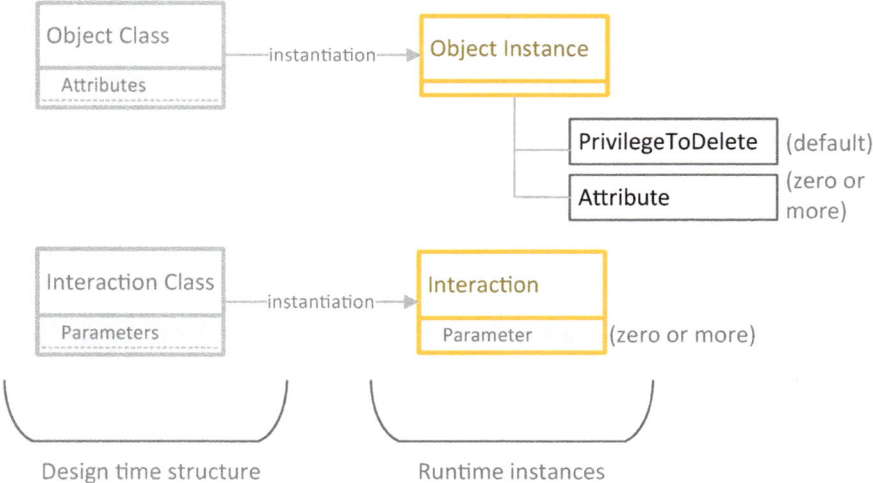

Fig. 2.6 HLA data structure. Each object has a default attribute called as `PrivilegeToDelete`. See Sect. 2.5.4 for the purpose of this attribute

2.4 HLA Data Model and Data Communication

An object class and an interaction class can be thought of as design time structures. They must be documented conforming to the OMT specification before federation execution as a part of the federation object model.

2.4.3.3 Comparison with Object-Oriented Paradigm

Many (computer/software) engineers take a course on object-oriented programming (OOP) in their undergraduate education, so they are tempted to compare and sometimes confuse it with the HLA object/class terminology. In the OOP literature, an object is defined as a software encapsulation of data (state) and behavior (methods) with an identity. In HLA, objects are defined by characteristics (i.e., attribute or parameter) that are exchanged between federates (the visible portion of state) during execution. Behavior is generated by the federates rather than directly by objects. HLA objects do not have methods.

The HLA standard also mentions this topic. It points out that while class objects are encapsulations for data and the operations, HLA objects are defined by the data that are exchanged between federates during federation execution (IEEE Std 1516-2010 2010). Of course, nothing prevents a federate application from implementing, say, a ship object internally in an object-oriented fashion, perhaps as a Java object, and exposing it to the federation as an HLA object instance via encapsulation. Encapsulation of an (OOP) object into an HLA object is explained in Chap. 7.

Moreover, attributes are treated as first-class structures in HLA, where attribute ownership is subject to change at runtime. A federate other than the one that created an object can update an attribute of the object. Thus, it is possible for an object to be distributed among multiple federates.

2.4.3.4 Class Hierarchy

For a complete object model, it is not sufficient to specify the object and interaction classes separately; there is a need to specify the relationships among them as well. HLA only allows class hierarchy using "is-a" relationship between classes, known as *single inheritance*. In OMT, there is a predefined root class for object classes, called HLAobjectRoot, and for interaction classes, called HLAinteractionRoot. A class that generalizes a set of properties that may be extended by more specialized classes is called *superclass* (base class in the OOP terminology), and a class extended from it is called a *subclass* (derived class). A subclass inherits all the properties of its superclass. For instance, Ship object class is a superclass for CargoShip, RoRo, and Tanker classes as depicted in Fig. 2.7. Here, Tanker class inherits the Name and Location attributes, and in addition, it declares a new attribute, OilCapacity.

As we go top-down (from root to leaves), the generalization decreases and specialization increases. Consequently, as the subclasses provide more concrete domain objects, the superclasses provide the classification of classes and reusability.

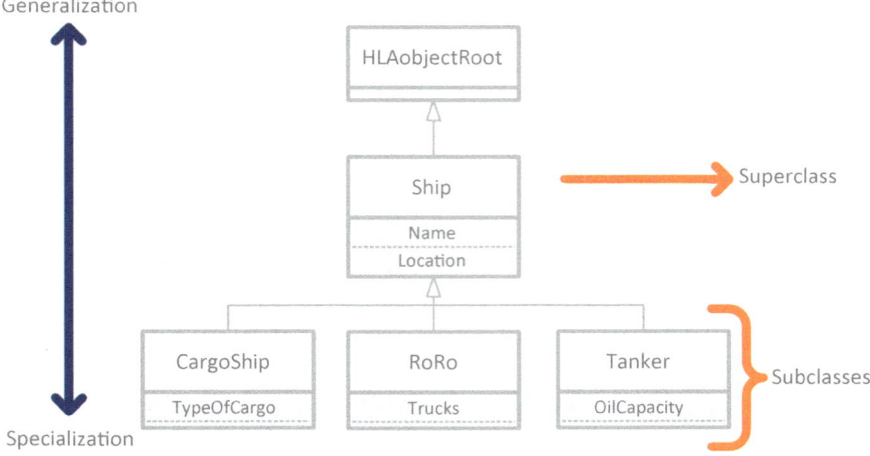

Fig. 2.7 Class hierarchy

2.4.4 Object Model Template

Object Model Template (OMT) is a metamodel (thought of as a template) both for specifying the data exchange and for providing a mechanism for the general coordination as a federation agreement (SISO FEAT 2017) among federates (in the form of FOM). It describes the structure of object models, as well as other relevant information such as synchronization points, via specifying the syntax and the format. Furthermore, the motivation behind developing a template for object models is presented in the standard is to provide an established mechanism for defining capabilities of the participants of the federation over their data exchange specifications (in the form of SOM) and to enable the development of common tool sets for object model development (IEEE Std 1516.2-2010 2010).

OMT is basically represented in tabular format and serialized in OMT data interchange format (DIF). As *federation agreements* involve more than data exchanged, it consists of a number of components in the form of tables, which can be listed as Object Model Identification Table, Object Class Structure Table, Interaction Class Structure Table, Attribute Table, Parameter Table, Dimension Table, Time Representation Table, User Supplied Tag Table, Synchronization Table, Transportation Type Table, Update Rate Table, Switches Table, Datatypes Table, Notes Table, Interface Specification Services Usage Table, and FOM/SOM lexicon. These tables are created for all federations and individual federates. While some require specifications from the designer, certain tables may be left empty depending on the situation.

While the reader is gently advised to go through the standard for the details of all the tables, we would like to introduce some of the important ones. First to mention is the *Object Model Identification Table*. The purpose of this table is to annotate the

2.4 HLA Data Model and Data Communication

object model with the information about how the federate or the federation has been developed. The information provided in this table includes version, modification date, purpose of the object model, its limitations, point of contact, and references. An example Object Model Identification Table, for our running example STMS, is given in Table 2.2.

In the *Object Class Structure Table*, the hierarchical relationship of the classes is specified. This table also indicates if a federate can publish, subscribe, or publish and subscribe these classes. A sample object class hierarchy is depicted in Table 2.3. In this example table, we can easily see the object class hierarchy. The

Table 2.2 Object Model Identification Table example for strait traffic monitoring simulation (STMS) federation

Category	Information
Name	StmsFom
Type	FOM
Version	2.0
Modification data	17/11/2016 12:00 AM
Security classification	Unclassified
Release restriction	NA
Purpose	A sample federation object model for this book
Application domain	HLA general
Description	This object model is provided as a sample project in SimGe object modeling tool
Use limitations	NA
Use history	Topçu et al. (2008, 2016)
Keyword	
Taxonomy	Simulation, maritime traffic management
Keyword	HLA, strait traffic management
POC	
POC Type	Sponsor
POC Name	Okan Topçu
POC organization	Okan Topçu
POC telephone	+1 (111) 111-1111 (fictitious)
POC e-mail	otot.support@outlook.com
References	
Type	Stand-alone
Identification	NA
Other	Created by SimGe at 11/14/2016 19:06:49
Glyph	**STMS**

Table 2.3 Object Class Structure Table example for STMS federation

HLAobjectRoot (N)	Ship (N)	CargoShip (PS)	
		RoRo (PS)	ConRo (PS)
			RoLo (PS)
		Tanker (N)	GeneralPurposeTanker (PS)
			MediumRangeTanker (PS)
			LongRangeTanker (PS)
			VeryLargeCrudeTanker (PS)

Table 2.4 Parameter Table example for STMS federation

Interaction	Parameter	Data type	Available dimension	Transportation	Order
Radio message	Call sign	String	VHF	Hlabesteffort	Timestamp
	Message	String			

Ship object class, which acts as a superclass for the derived classes: CargoShip, RoRo, and Tanker. Moreover, we see that Ship is marked with N, indicating it is neither publishable or subscribable (which can be thought of an abstract class) while CargoShip is both publishable and subscribable (PS).

The *Interaction Class Structure Table*, likewise, consists of class–subclass relations of interaction classes as well as their publish/subscribe capabilities. The *Attribute Table* is used to specify the characteristics of object classes that are subject to change in the course of federation execution. They are updated by the RTI and made available to the related members of the federation. This table includes data type, update type such as periodical or conditional, if it is conditional, the update condition, ownership policy, publish/subscribe status, its dimensions, its transport method, and its order of delivery. The *Parameter Table* specifies the parameters that characterize the interaction classes (see Table 2.4 for an example). One must note that while the attributes can be published and subscribed on an individual basis, interaction parameters cannot be. So, although the Parameter Table looks like the Attribute Table, one should keep this difference in mind. Thus, a Parameter Table only possesses data type at the parameter level, while having dimensions, transportation, and order at the interaction class level.

All the OMT components are given in detail in Chap. 5.

2.4.5 HLA Object Models

The HLA standard specifies three types of object models. These are simulation object model (SOM), federation object model (FOM), and Management Object Model (MOM).

2.4 HLA Data Model and Data Communication

2.4.5.1 Federation Object Model

The participants of distributed simulation require a common understanding about the communication among themselves. FOM provides a standard way of defining a major part of federation agreements (SISO FEAT 2017). FOM mainly describes the format and the structure of data and events that can be exchanged among federates in a federation execution in form of objects and interactions with their attributes and parameters, respectively. Using FOM, designers can specify the data exchange in their federation in a standard format. There is one FOM per federation. So FOM can be regarded as an *information contract* that enables the interoperability among federates. FOM takes the form of a file at runtime, called FDD/FED file, which is supplied to the RTI in the federation execution. A new FOM can be developed from scratch for each federation as well as an existing reference FOM can be reused. The HLA Evolved standard also supports the modular federation object models (FOMs). The details of the FOM modularity are discussed in the following sections.

The reference FOMs are developed for increasing the interoperability by the simulation communities to agree on a common data model. For instance, real-time platform-level reference FOM (RPR-FOM) is developed to provide a preready reference FOM for real-time platform-level simulations targeting in general the pre-HLA simulations that use the DIS protocol (SISO 2015).

2.4.5.2 Simulation Object Model

With SOM, federates specify their capabilities and data interfaces. Thus, SOM serves as the specification for describing the capabilities of federates to promote reusability. You can determine the suitability of a federate for participation in a federation by examining its SOM. The HLA OMT format is also applicable to define SOMs.

2.4.5.3 Management Object Model

The HLA MOM is used to define the constructs for controlling and monitoring of a federation execution. Federates require insight about the federation execution as well as controlling the execution of individual federates, federation execution, or the RTI. MOM utilizes the Object Model Template format and syntax to define the information to be monitored and the control parameters. Its inclusion is compulsory for all FOMs. This inclusion can be accomplished by consolidating MOM data by HLA Standard *Management and Initialization Module* (MIM). MIM can be defined as a subset of FOM that contains the tables that describe the MOM. All FOMs have a default MIM that is specified by the standard, which can be overridden by a user-supplied MIM.

2.4.6 Object Model Modularity

The HLA Evolved standard brings support for object model modularity, so that SOM and FOM can be composed of one or more modules and one MIM. The previous HLA versions used a monolithic object model. In the HLA Evolved, the modules are introduced as the partial object models that lay out a modular component to create more flexible and scalable object models (Möller et al. 2008). The major aim is to separate the local (custom) object models from the standardized object models (a.k.a. reference FOMs) such as RPR-FOM. Thus, as a design pattern, one may extend the standardized object model by introducing a partial and custom object model module, which is established upon a base stand-alone module and then inherit all object classes from these base classes. This capability makes the modules smaller and also promotes the reusability of object models for maintainable federations.

There are two types of FOM modules: *stand-alone module* and *dependent module*. A stand-alone module can be used without other FOM modules, so that it serves as a base object model that can be extended by other modules. A dependent module contains some references defined in another FOM module. A reference can point to a superclass (either an object class or an interaction class), a data type, a transportation type, a dimension, or a note defined in another module (Möller et al. 2007). Because of this dependency, the dependent modules cannot be used as a stand-alone FOM.

The stand-alone modules may contain references only to a MOM module. Therefore, a MOM module is always required for FOM modules but optional for SOM modules. One or more stand-alone modules together with a MOM module can be used to build a FOM unless the definitions of concepts do not conflict in the modules. Dependent modules can be built upon one or more stand-alone modules or other dependent modules. But a dependent module cannot be used without a stand-alone module.

The OMT Object Model Identification Table includes a type and identification pair in its references section. So, one may specify the type of FOM/SOM as stand-alone or dependent. If the type is `dependency`, then the identification field must include all the dependent FOM/SOM module names.

As the RTI uses a subset of data from FOM in the form of an FDD file, the file designators (i.e., the full name of the FDD file) are provided to the RTI in time of creating the federation execution and joining the federation execution. See Chaps. 8 and 11 for implementation details and for how to use multiple FOM modules.

2.5 Interface Specification

The HLA federate interface specification (IEEE Std 1516.1-2010 2010) defines the standard services and interfaces between the RTI and the federate applications to support interfederate communication. In other words, this specification provides a basis for functionally interfacing between a federate application and the RTI component. The functional interface is defined in terms of *RTI services*, which are arranged as seven groups:

2.5 Interface Specification

- *Federation management* (FM) provides the services to create, control, and terminate a federation execution.
- *Declaration management* (DM) provides the services for federates to declare their intentions on publishing or subscribing object classes and sending and receiving interactions.
- *Object management* (OM) provides the services to register, modify, and delete object instances, and to send and receive interactions.
- *Ownership management* (OwM) provides the services to transfer ownership of attributes of object instances among the federates.
- *Time management* (TM) provides the services and the mechanisms to enable delivering messages in a timely manner.
- *Data distribution management* (DDM) provides the services to refine data requirements at the instance attribute level in terms of values, thus enables reducing unnecessary data traffic.
- *Support services* (SS) includes the utilities for federates such as name-to-handle, handle-to-name transformations, and getting update rate values.

The interface specification provides a description of the functionality of each service and the arguments (both the supplied and returned) and *preconditions* necessary for use of the service. *Post-conditions* specify any changes in the state of the federation execution resulting from the call. *Exceptions* give all exceptions that can be thrown by the service routine. The parts of interface specification are the following:

- Interface name and brief description of service;
- Supplied arguments;
- Returned arguments;
- Preconditions;
- Post-conditions;
- Exceptions;
- Related services.

Let us give an interface specification example for the *confirm synchronization point* service, which is an RTI-initiated service provided under the FM service group. This service is used to indicate the result of a federation synchronization point registration (see following section for a detailed explanation of federation synchronization). Its supplied arguments are a synchronization point label, registration-success indicator, and an optional failure reason. It has no defined returned arguments. The interface specification also defines its preconditions such that the federate needs to be joined to the federation execution and the joined federate has invoked *register federation synchronization point* service for the specified label argument. As a post-condition, it is specified what will be done in case of a positive registration-success indicator. And the standard specifies one exception for this service, which is *federate internal error*.

An RTI service defines an interface in a programming language independent way, where an *RTI method* is an implementation of that service using a particular programming language such as C++, Java, and C#. An RTI service can be mapped to more than one methods because of the different argument sets due to the optional arguments in the service specification or because of indicating a success or failure behavior of a service. For example, the "Confirm Synchronization Point" service, discussed above, can be mapped to two methods showing the result as a success or a failure. Below C++ method declarations are given:

```
// 4.12
virtual void synchronizationPointRegistrationSucceeded(
       std::wstring const & label)
       throw (rti1516e::FederateInternalError);

virtual void synchronizationPointRegistrationFailed(
       std::wstring const & label,
       rti1516e::SynchronizationPointFailureReason reason)
       throw (rti1516e::FederateInternalError);
```

In connection with the points mentioned, the RTI methods provided for a programming language constitute an *Application Programming Interface* (API) for interfederate communication. Consequently, each federate must interact with RTI by making method *calls*. The methods, which are provided to user federate applications, constitute the *federate interface*. The methods are grouped into (i) *federate-initiated* methods and (ii) *RTI-initiated* methods, to stress the direction of the communication. The RTI-initiated methods are also called as *callback* methods (see Fig. 2.8) *callback methods*. The Requests for calls should be included in *try-catch* blocks to catch the exceptions thrown so that appropriate action may be taken for error processing.

Typically, we make method calls when we want to instruct the RTI to do something. For example, the federate, `WhiteFdApp`, in Fig. 2.9, calls the method *Request Federation Save* to make the RTI to initiate a federate save. In response, the RTI initiates a federate save by informing each federate with a callback method "Initiate Federate Save." Figure 2.9 depicts the federate interface and two-way communication represented as a Unified Modeling Language (UML) sequence diagram[2] (Fowler 2003). Here, all the interfederate communication is done by using this federate interface (i.e., using the methods and callbacks). In some specific RTI distributions (e.g., DMSO RTI 1.3 NG v6), a central process (e.g., RtiExec) is required to run RTI software. *RtiExec* (RTI Executive) is a global process, where each federate communicates with `RtiExec` to initialize its RTI components, whereas each `FedExec` manages a federation execution.

---

[2]Throughout the book, we will specify the interactions among federates and the RTI as a UML Sequence Diagram. In the diagram representations, we generally tend to use the UML diagrams as a sketch, informal and incomplete, not to loose the focus and simplicity with a strict formalism. So, the user without a deep UML background can folllow the diagrams easily. The reader may refer to Fowler (2003), Larman (2004) for UML introduction.

2.5 Interface Specification

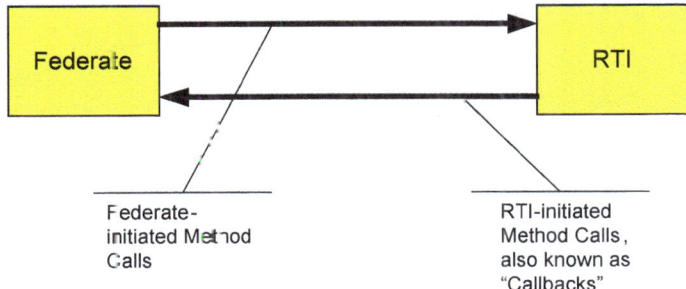

Fig. 2.8 RTI/federate-initiated methods

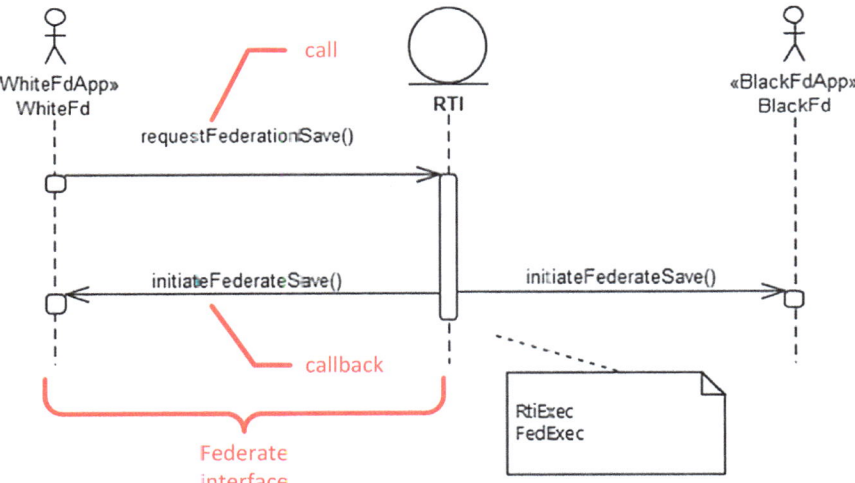

Fig. 2.9 The federate interface

The federate-initiated methods are called via a module, generally known as *RTI Ambassador*, and the callbacks are received by *Federate Ambassador* (see Fig. 2.10). The Federate Ambassador handles two types of incoming messages: *time-stamp-order (TSO) messages* to receive messages delivered in order of timestamp and *receive order (RO) messages* to receive messages delivered in order received. So, the federate must iterate through the queues to process the waiting callbacks. This operation is known as *ticking* or *evoking*.

Fig. 2.10 Ambassadors

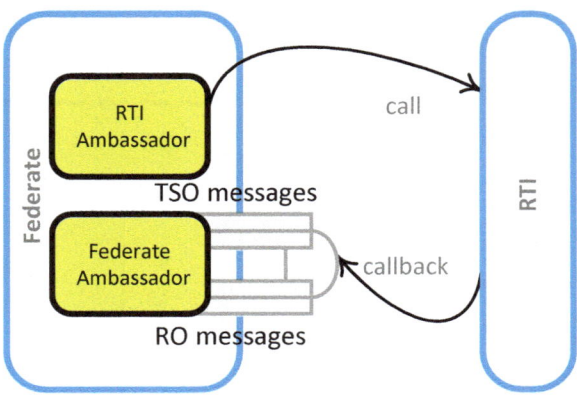

2.5.1 Federation Management

Federation management involves the services to initialize, finalize, monitor, and dynamically control (e.g., saving and restoring) a federation execution.

2.5.1.1 Initialization and Finalization

Initialization services are used to connect to the RTI, to create a federation execution, and to join a federation execution. Before any interaction takes place between the un-joined federate and the RTI, a federate application must establish a connection. After a connection is established, federate can interact with the RTI to create a federation execution or to join a federation execution. During connect method, we specify the callback model that the federate prefers. Although the federate interface specification defines two types of callback model, which are *immediate callback model* or *evoked callback model*, a native RTI implementation may implement only one mode or both. In immediate callback model, the RTI shall invoke callbacks immediately. In the evoked mode, the federate must explicitly call a method (i.e., evoke callback or evoke multiple callbacks) to cause the callbacks to be executed. In HLA 1.3 specification, there is no specification for connect service. In this case, a federate can directly interact with the RTI after instantiating an RTI Ambassador and a Federate Ambassador. In this case, to invoke callbacks, the tick service is used.

Finalization services include resigning from the federation execution, destroying the federation execution, and lastly terminating the connection between the federate and the RTI.

2.5.1.2 Federation Execution Monitoring Services

Monitoring services are generally employed by applications to monitor the federation executions. So, a federate may request a list of federation executions that are currently running. The RTI replies this call with a list of federation execution

2.5 Interface Specification

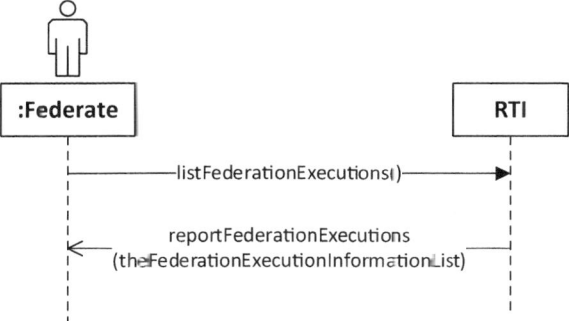

Fig. 2.11 UML sequence diagram for monitoring federation executions. Notice the use of synchronous (method calls by federate) and asynchronous (callbacks from the RTI) messages. Synchronous ones have *solid arrowheads*. The *open arrowheads* are for asynchronous messages

information. Each entry in the list encapsulates a pair of the federation execution name and the logical time implementation name. See Fig. 2.11 for interactions between the federate and the RTI.

2.5.1.3 Synchronization Services

Synchronization mechanism is provided to synchronize activities throughout the federation executions. A *synchronization point* is used to specify a synchronization activity. The synchronization points are declared in the OMT *Synchronization Table*.

Federation synchronization begins with a federate requesting a synchronization point registration (see Fig. 2.12 msg. 1). The RTI informs the requested federate whether registration is successful (msg. 2) or not (msg. 3). The reason for a failed synchronization point registration can be in case where a synchronization point label is not unique. For instance, assume that a federate has registered a synchronization point and as the synchronization process continues, another federate tries to register the same synchronization (i.e., with the same label) and so gets a failure. After a successful synchronization point registration, the RTI announces the synchronization point to the related federates (or all federates) according to the parameter selection on registration (msg. 4). When a synchronization point is announced by the RTI, each federate receiving this callback (msg. 5) replies with a *Synchronization Point Achieved* message after it successfully fulfills the synchronization point requirement. When all the related federates report achievement (either with success or failure), the RTI informs the related federates that the synchronization is completed and reports the failed federates (msg. 6).

See Chap. 5 on how to declare synchronization points in the HLA OMT and Chap. 9 how to implement the federation synchronization.

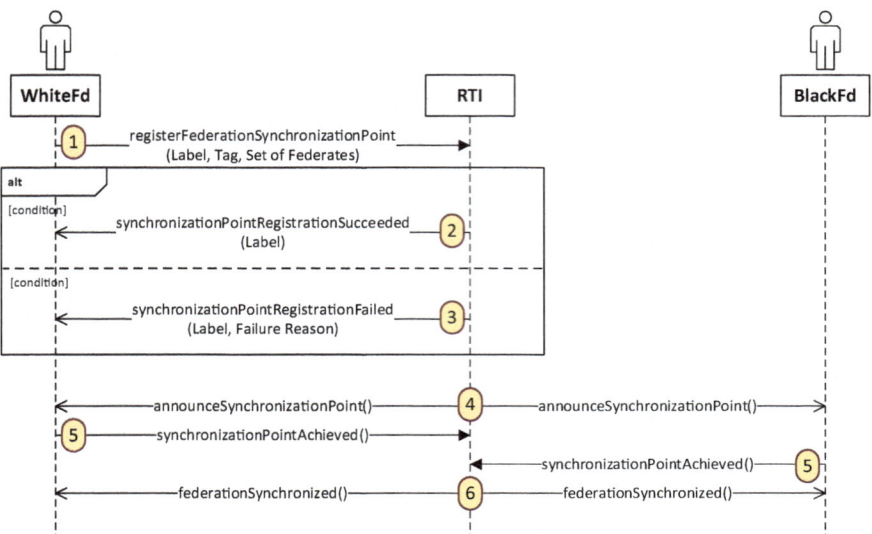

Fig. 2.12 UML sequence diagram for federation synchronization

2.5.1.4 Save/Restore Services

Another important federation management service area is to save a federation execution and then to restore it later to its state when the save is performed.

The interactions between federates and the RTI are depicted in Fig. 2.13. The federation execution save is initiated with a *Request Federation Save* message (Fig. 2.13 msg. 1). Here, the requesting federate provides a federation save label, which will be used in restore operation. The federate may also supply a timestamp to indicate the logical time for federation save. The timestamp can only be provided by a time-regulating federate (see time management section below for time-related concepts). When a timestamp is not present, then the RTI orders all joined federates to save state as soon as possible with a initiate federate save service (msg.2). Now, all joined federates are informed about a save operation. When a federate begins a save operation, it informs the RTI with a federate save begun call (msg.3). So, the federates may begin to save their application-specific data (whatever they want to keep to restore its state again) in a data store (a file or a database). When the federate completes its save operation, it informs the RTI by issuing a *Federate Save Complete* message (msg.4). Finally, the RTI informs the joined federates either the federation save operation is successfully completed or not by sending a federation saved message (msg.5). In case of a successful federation save indication, then the federates may shut down safely. Note that only one federation save can be in progress (IEEE Std 1516.1-2010 2010).

To support the federation save operation, there are some additional services provided by RTI interface (see Fig. 2.14). A federate may abort federation save

2.5 Interface Specification

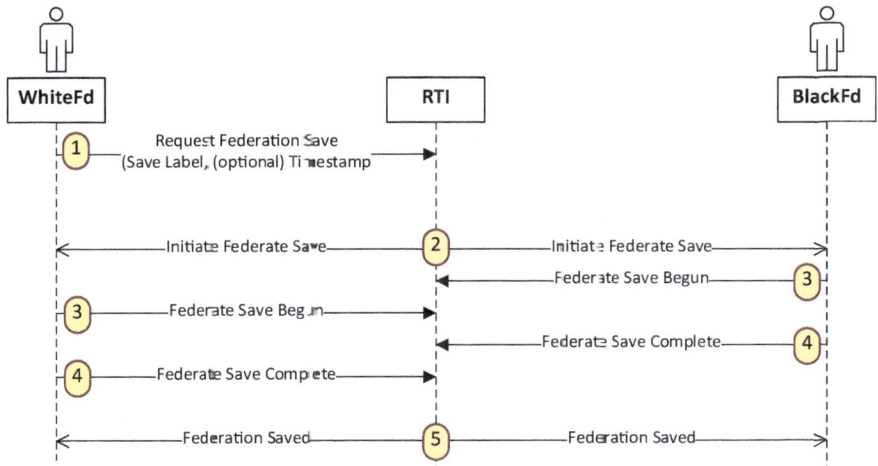

Fig. 2.13 UML sequence diagram for federation save

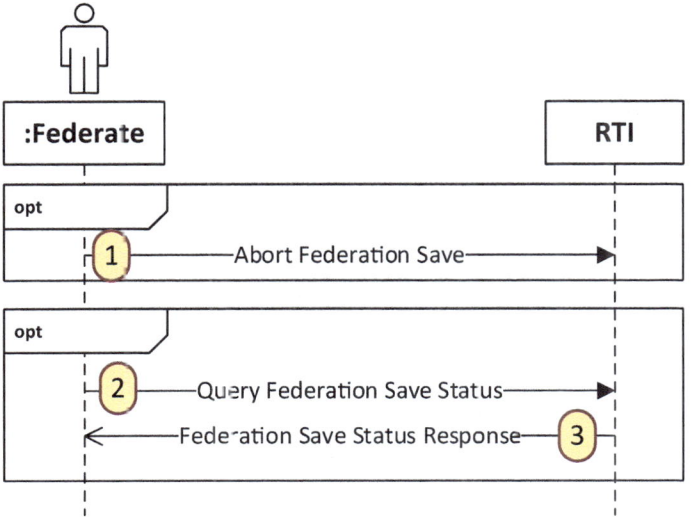

Fig. 2.14 UML sequence diagram presenting the additional services for federation save

(msg.1) or may query the federation save status (msg.2). When a query is requested, the RTI answers with a federation save status callback (msg.3). Note that these additional services are unavailable in HLA 1.3 specification.

The federation restore operation is similar to the federation save operation. The process begins with a *Request Federation Restore* service call (see Fig. 2.15, msg.1). This call must be supplied with a federation save label argument. A valid request is confirmed by the RTI using a confirm federation restoration request sent

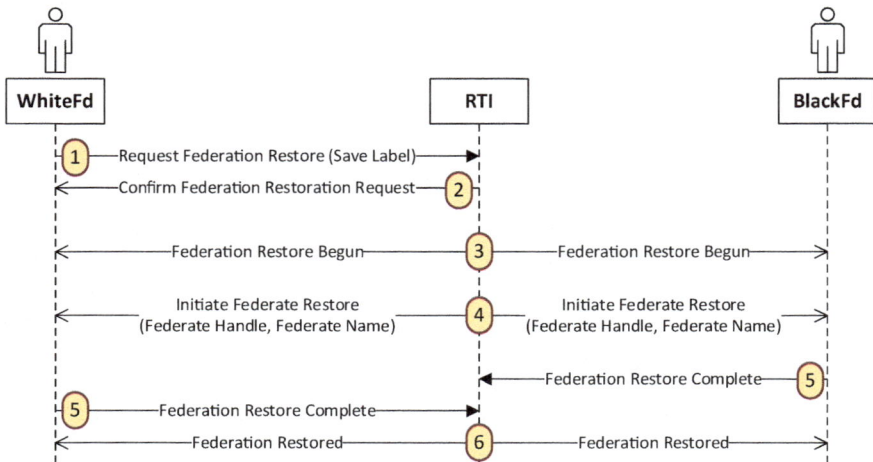

Fig. 2.15 UML sequence diagram for federation restore

to the requesting federate (msg.2). Then, the RTI informs all the federates that a federation restoration is about to happen by issuing a *Federation Restore Begun* callback (msg.3). Thus, the federates stop providing new information (e.g., updating attribute values) to the federation and wait for an initiate order. The RTI instructs the joined federate to initiate a federate restore (msg.4). The federate must return to its previous state indicated by the federation save label. Here, the federate loads its saved application data kept in the federation save and as a result of this service invocation, the federate's handle and name change according to the provided arguments by the RTI from the values taken by the join federation execution service. After federate completes its restoration, it informs the RTI by calling the *Federate Restore Complete* service (msg.5) and waits for the invocation of the federation restored service (msg.6).

Similar to the save operation, additional services exist for aborting and querying a federation restore.

2.5.2 Declaration Management

As pointed in the previous (HLA Data Model) section, HLA uses publish and subscribe mechanism to exchange objects at runtime. In this regard, the *declaration management* services provide all the required means for a federate to declare their capability and interests in a federation execution.

2.5 Interface Specification

2.5.2.1 Functional Description

Before a federate involves in any data exchange during a federation execution, it must declare its capability (i.e., data it will produce) and its interests (i.e., data it will consume) to the RTI.

To declare capability, the federate uses the *Publish Object Class Attributes* and *Publish Interaction Class* services. Alternatively, a federate can change its declarations by using *Unpublish Object Class Attributes* or *Unpublish Interaction Class* services. To declare interest, the federate uses the corresponding *Subscribe/Unsubscribe* services such as *Subscribe Interaction Class* service.

Furthermore, there are additional services to help the federate fine tune when to start registration or begin sending interactions. Those services are listed below, and how to use them is shown in Chap. 8.

- Start/Stop Registration For Object Class: When a federate is interested with the data you can provide, the RTI informs you using this service. In other words, if a federate A subscribes to an object class, which is published by federate B then B is notified by the RTI that it can begin registration of the object instances related to that class. In the same manner, if there is no federate left subscribed to the object class, then the RTI informs the publishing federate to stop registrations. A federate loses its interest when it unsubscribes or leaves the federation execution.
- Turn Interactions On/Off: This works the same, but for interactions. When a subscriber is found, then the RTI informs the publishing federate to begin sending interactions.

The use of publish and subscribe services must conform to the FOM. For instance, an object class must be specified as publishable in the FOM. So, a federate can publish this object class.

2.5.2.2 Publish/Subscribe Diagrams

Publish and Subscribe Diagrams are introduced in (Topçu et al. 2003) as design artifacts to focus on the object/interaction interests among the federates. The P/S diagrams present the system in a snapshot view. Initially, all the federate interests are being hard coded at system start-up. During a run, however, a federate can change and re-declare its interests.

The general P/S diagram is a graph of Publish and Subscribe association stereotype elements connected by their various static relationships. It depicts all of the capabilities of member federates in terms of the objects and interactions that they produce or they are interested in.

The rectangular shapes in the diagrams represent the HLA objects, which are exchanged through federation. The oval shapes represent the (joined) federates. The directed arc from a federate to an object means that the federate has the capability to publish the object, and on the other hand a directed arc from an object to a federate means that the federate is subscribed to the object or is interested in the published object and its attributes or possibly subsets thereof.

HLA 1.3 standard allows *routing space* definitions to define the object-exchange regions by utilizing the RTI data distribution management capabilities. In that case, all the exchanges of objects take place in *Default Space* predefined by the RTI.

The diagrams can be expanded to reflect the system in detail by focusing on the different views: The Class-based P/S diagrams and the Federate-based P/S diagrams.

Class-Based P/S Diagrams

The *Class-based P/S diagrams* emphasize the P/S issues between a particular object and a federate. Class-based P/S diagrams show all the common HLA objects and interactions, and their parameters and attributes one by one while depicting the interests of federates over these objects and interactions.

This type of diagram is suitable for federate designers. For example, assume that a federate designer wishes to add a new federate into a federation. The first thing to do is to design the P/S interests with the existing federation objects and interactions.

Notation: As in the stereotype notation, the "P" stands for "publishes," "S" stands for "subscribes," and "PS" stands for "both publishes and subscribes." It is possible for a federate to publish or to subscribe a subset of the available attributes for a given class. The sign "*" means "all attributes." For interaction classes, it is not possible to specify a subset. Interactions are produced and consumed as a single piece.

Federate-Based P/S Diagrams

The *Federate-based P/S diagrams* depict the capability and interest of a particular federate. It can be used when reviewing existing federates for reuse. From these diagrams, the user can easily check which classes that the federate is capable of creating or needing.

2.5.2.3 Case Study: P/S Diagrams

Here, we provide the publish and subscribe interests of STMS federation. First, we will present the class-based P/S diagrams and then we will give the federate-based diagrams.

Ship object-class P/S diagram: Fig. 2.16 depicts the ship object class and its attributes. The focus of the diagram is a specific object class. The Ship object encapsulates the major properties of a ship that entered the strait. As shown Fig. 2.16, only the ShipFd can create and update a ship object and its attributes. StationFd is informed when a ship object is created or when its attributes are updated to reflect the changes in their traffic display. The StationFd only subscribes a subset of the attributes of the ship object. Those are the ship name (Callsign) and its location.

Station object-class P/S diagram: Fig. 2.17 depicts the Station object class and its attributes. Station object encapsulates the major properties of a traffic station located along the strait. The diagram shows that only the station federate is responsible to create and update a station object. The ShipFd is informed about traffic stations around them.

2.5 Interface Specification

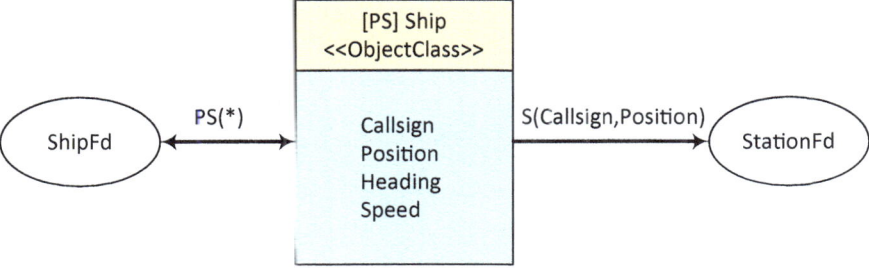

Fig. 2.16 Ship object class P/S diagram

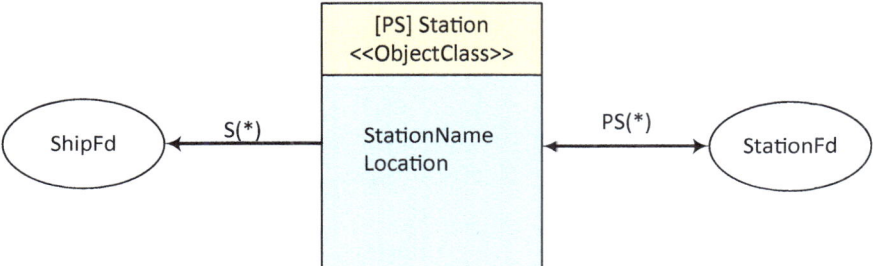

Fig. 2.17 Station object class P/S diagram

Fig. 2.18 Track object class P/S diagram

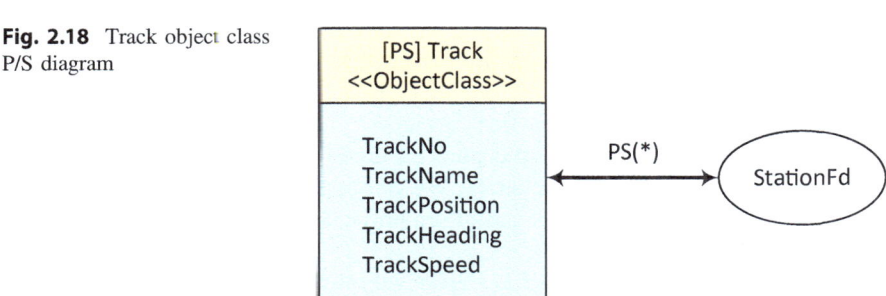

Track object-class P/S diagram: Fig. 2.18 depicts the Track object class and its attributes. Track object is the encapsulation of a ship which is found in the area of responsibility of a station, and it is used to exchange the track information between traffic stations. Each track is managed only by one station when a ship is within its area of responsibility. When ship passes to another area, which is managed by a different station, then track ownership is also exchanged between stations. Only the StationFd can create and update a track object and its attributes.

Radio message interaction-class P/S diagram: Fig. 2.19 depicts the RadioMessage interaction class and its parameters. Radio message interaction is the encapsulation of a radio transmission between ships and stations. It consists of

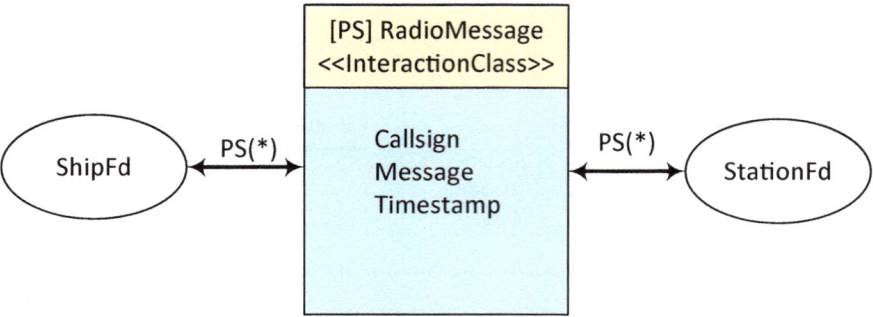

Fig. 2.19 Radio message interaction class P/S diagram

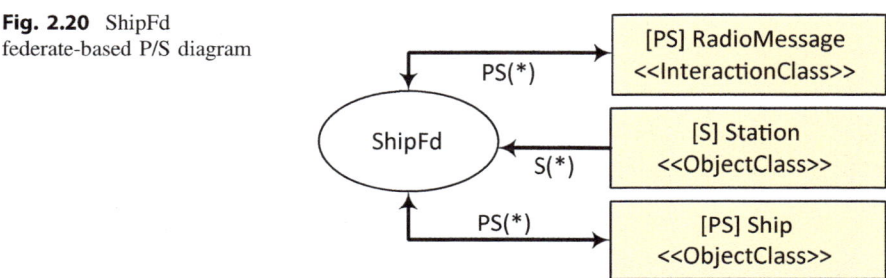

Fig. 2.20 ShipFd federate-based P/S diagram

three parameters: Callsign, Message, and Timestamp for the transmission. Remember that an interaction typically corresponds to an event in the sense of discrete event systems. The primary difference between objects and interactions is persistence: Objects persist, interactions do not.

ShipFd P/S diagram: Fig. 2.20 depicts all the P/S status of the ShipFd. Now, the focus of the diagram is the federate. We can easily deduce that the ShipFd is capable of generating ship objects and of sending radio message interactions while it requires a station object.

StationFd P/S diagram: Fig. 2.21 depicts all the P/S status of the StationFd. It is capable of generating station and track objects and of sending radio message interactions while it requires a ship object to generate tracks.

2.5.2.4 Smart Update Reduction

Support for *smart update reduction*Update reduction is a new feature in the HLA Evolved. An *update rate* is defined as the rate that attribute values are provided either (i) by the RTI to a subscribing federate or (ii) by the owning federate to the RTI (IEEE 1516.1-2010 2010). The update rates are defined by giving a name and a maximum rate in the FOM of a federation according to the OMT and it is a part of the FDD file used by the RTI at runtime.

The update rate can be specified as a supplied argument (as *update rate designator*) when subscribing to object class attributes. In this case, the RTI provides

2.5 Interface Specification

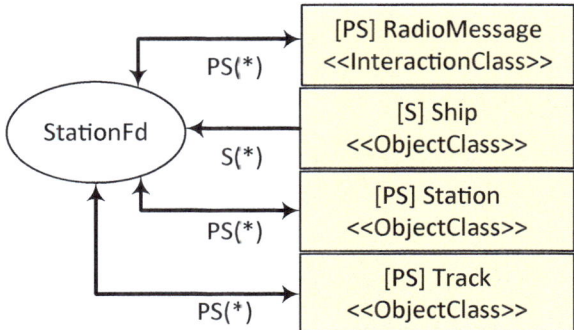

Fig. 2.21 StationFd federate-based P/S diagram

the value updates to the subscribing federate at a maximum update rate specified by the designator. In case an update rate designator is not supplied in the subscription step, then no update reduction takes place.

The update rate is also notified to the owning federate (i.e., the responsible federate, which will update the attribute values) by the RTI with *Turn Updates On for Object Instance* service (see the following section) as a returned argument (i.e., update rate designator). Thus, the owning federate can regulate its update rate with respect to the maximum rate provided by the designator conforming to the federation agreement for update scheme.

Using the RTI support services, a federate can ask the RTI about the actual update value of a specified update rate designator using *Get Update Rate Value* service or the update rate value of a specific attribute using *Get Update Rate Value for Attribute* service.

2.5.3 Object Management

In Sect. 2.4, we explained the object instances and object exchange. Now, let us see which services are used. The object exchange is done by using the *object management* (OM) services A publishing federate must be capable of:

- Registering (i.e., creating) an object instance;
- Updating the values of the instance attributes;
- Sending an interaction;
- Deleting an object instance.

A subscribing federate must be capable of:

- Discovering an object instance;
- Reflecting the values of the instance attributes;
- Receiving an interaction;
- Removing an object instance (the RTI informs when an object is deleted by the owner).

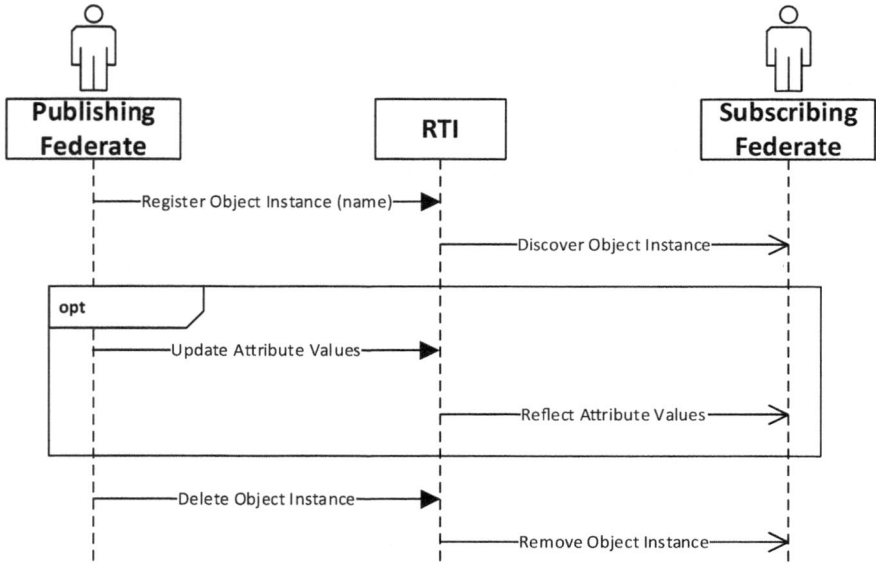

Fig. 2.22 Object management services for an object instance

The services for interaction exchange are simply *Send Interaction* and *Receive Interaction* services. The major object management services used in object-exchange interaction is depicted in Fig. 2.22. When registering an object instance, the federate may supply an *object instance name*. In this case, before invoking the registration service, the name must be reserved by the registering federate using *Reserve Object Instance Name* service.

As a design principle, for the sake of bandwidth utilization, a federation object or interaction is only sent through network when interested federates join the federation execution, instead of periodically sending a heartbeat-like message. For example, when EnviFd joins the federation, it only creates an environment object if there exists an interested federate (i.e., a federate that has subscribed to the environment object class) or not. If it exists, it registers the environment object. Again, the RTI informs the registering federate to turn updates on (or off) for the object instance. So, the federate can begin to update its attribute values, resulting in diminished network load. See Chap. 8 for the details and the implementation of *Start/Stop Registration for Object Instance* and *Attribute Relevance Advisory Switch* services.

2.5.4 Ownership Management

The responsibility of deleting an object instance and updating its attribute values is initially given to the creator federate. By using the *ownership management*

2.5 Interface Specification

(OwM) services, it is possible to share the responsibility for updating and deleting object instances. To enable this, each attribute of an object instance has an owner. The owning federate has the privilege to update the attribute. Thus, the ownership of attributes of an object instance can be shared by more than one federate. To delete an object, a special attribute, named as `privilegeToDelete` for HLA 1.3 and `HLAprivilegeToDeleteObject` for HLA Evolved, exists for all object instances by default. The federate that owns this attribute for an object instance has the right to delete the object. If the federate owns the privilege-to-delete attribute of an object instance, then it has the delete responsibility for that object. The OwM services enable federates to transfer the ownership of an attribute including the ownership of the privilege-to-delete attribute.

The transferability of the ownership of an attribute is specified in the FOM during design time. Each attribute has a property to indicate if the ownership of an attribute of an object instance can be transferred to other federates or not. Transfer is possible by *divesting* or *acquiring* the ownership. See Chap. 5 on how to specify attribute ownership transferability in a FOM.

We can roughly talk about two strategies to deal with the ownership transfer: the pull and push strategies. In general case, the federates try to negotiate to hand over the ownership in both strategies. The conceptual views (without an RTI) for both strategies are depicted in Fig. 2.23.

In the *pull strategy*, a federate tries to acquire the ownership of some of the attributes of a specific object instance. The specified attributes can be either unowned (*orphaned*) or owned by some federate. In case of unowned attributes, the RTI simply informs the acquiring federate whether the ownership is transferred or not. This method is known as *orphaned-attribute pull*. In case the attributes are owned by a federate, then the willing federate and the owned federate must agree on transfer. The willing federate (acquiring federate) explicitly asks the RTI to acquire the ownership of the attributes of a specific object instance. The owned federate either accepts the transfer of the ownership or does not. This method is known as the *intrusive pull*.

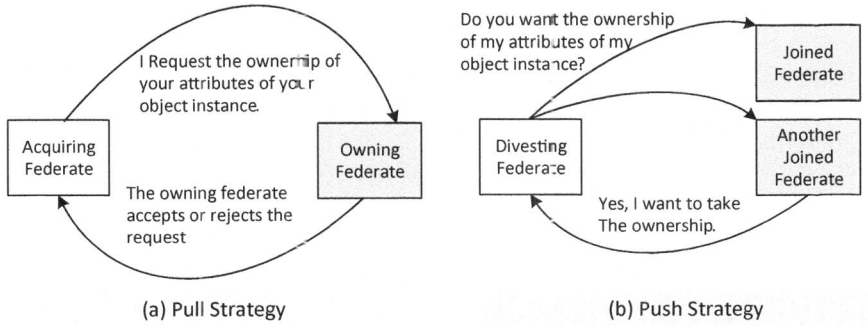

(a) Pull Strategy   (b) Push Strategy

Fig. 2.23 Conceptual views for pull and push strategies

In the *push strategy*, a federate does not want the ownership of some attributes of a specific object instance that it owns. In this strategy, there are two methods to push the ownership. In the first method, the federate may unconditionally give up the ownership of some attributes to immediately relieve its responsibility of updating and/or deleting an object instance. This is called as *unconditional push*. The specified attributes become *unowned*. And the RTI seeks for a willing federate to own those attributes until attributes are owned. The second method is called *negotiated push*. In this case, there is a federate, which is willing to divest the ownership of all or some of its attributes of an object instance. The ownership transfer is completed as the result of negotiation when a willing federate is found. The willing federate follows a pull strategy to take the ownership. See Chap. 9 on how to implement these strategies.

2.5.5 Data Distribution Management

Data distribution management (DDM) services are employed to filter data distribution to reduce the volume of both the transmission and the reception of federation-wide data. Federates may create data filters to refine data transmission and reception in the form of distribution regions.

DDM services are related with other RTI services. Therefore, we can group DDM services into three categories. The first category includes core DDM services, used to manage the regions based on the dimensions defined in the FOM. The other categories involve the services related with the declaration management and object management services to transmit and receive data with regions. The regions are associated with an object class attribute or with an interaction class for subscription.

The core DDM services are the following:

- Create region;
- Commit region modifications, and
- Delete region.

The DDM services related with the declaration management services are as follows:

- Subscribe object class attributes with regions;
- Unsubscribe object class attributes with regions;
- Subscribe interaction class with regions;
- Unsubscribe interaction class with regions.

The DDM services related with the object management services are listed below. The regions are associated with an object instance attribute or with an interaction (in send operation).

2.5 Interface Specification

- Register object instance with regions;
- Request attribute value update with regions;
- Send interaction with regions;
- Associate regions for updates, and
- Unassociate regions for updates.

The implementation of services is explained in Chap. 9 with some case studies. Here, we will provide a theoretical background for DDM services by giving definitions of important concepts, on which DDM services are based.

- A *dimension* is the fundamental DDM concept, which is defined as "a named interval of non-negative integers" (IEEE Std 1516.1-2010 2010). The interval begins with zero to a dimension upper bound specified in the FOM (i.e., FDD). A federation object model may specify one or more dimensions so that each attribute or interaction can be associated with a set of available dimensions. See Chap. 5 on how to specify a dimension and how to associate an attribute or an interaction class with a set of dimensions in a FOM.
- A *range* is "a continuous half-open interval on a dimension" (IEEE Std 1516.1-2010 2010). The range has end points denoted by a lower bound and an upper bound. Since the interval is half-open, the lower bound is closed (where it is denoted by a square bracket and the value is included) and the upper bound is open (where it is denoted by a parenthesis and the value is excluded). According to the HLA Evolved specification, the upper bound must be greater than the lower bound and the minimum possible difference between them can be one.
- A *region* can be a one-dimensional region or multi-dimensional region based on the region specification.
- A *region specification* "is a set of ranges. The dimensions contained in a region specification shall be the dimensions of the ranges that are included in the region specification. A region specification shall contain at most one range for any given dimension." (IEEE Std 1516.1-2010 2010). Each range is a region specification is normalized as zero to dimension's upper bound. In specification, the upper bounds are not included.
- Note that dimensions are design entities while regions are runtime entities (i.e., they are created at runtime).
- A *region template* is "an incomplete region specification where one or more dimensions have not been assigned ranges." (IEEE Std 1516.1-2010 2010).
- When a region specification is associated with the related element (i.e., object class attribute or interaction class for subscription, object instance attribute for update, and interaction for sending), then it is defined as a *region realization* (IEEE Std 1516.1-2010 2010).

The RTI provides a *default region* including a range beginning from zero to the dimension's upper bound for each dimension specified in the FDD.

For a hypothetical example, let us assume that a FOM declares two dimensions called as X and Y. These dimensions define a two-dimensional coordinate system

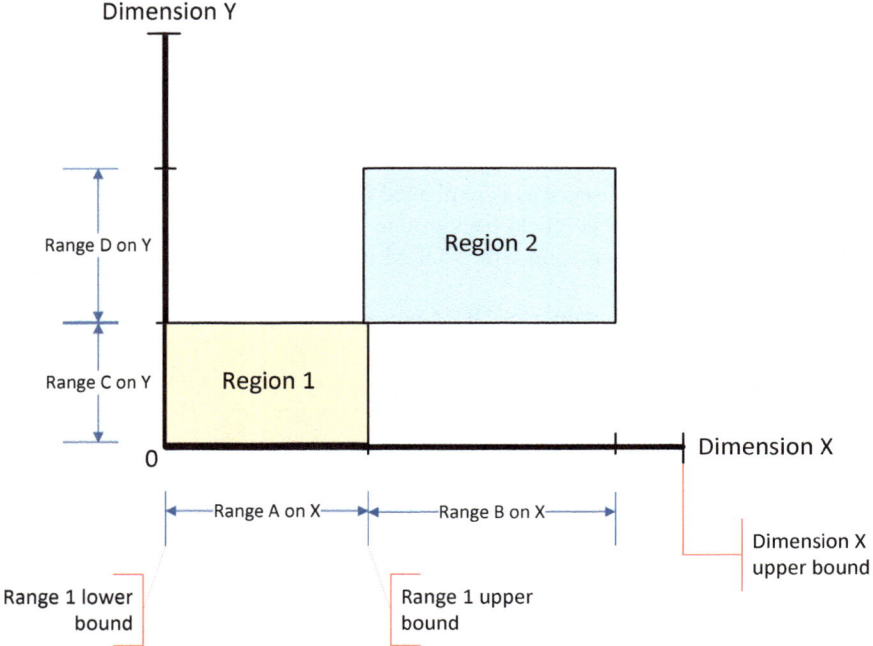

Fig. 2.24 Two-dimensional coordinate system and sample regions

(see Fig. 2.24), for which federates may express an intention to send or receive data by associating its attributes and interactions with the dimensions. To realize the intention, the regions must be created for subscription and update purposes. In Fig. 2.24, two regions are illustrated. Both regions are defined using the ranges specified on the dimensions. As shown in the figure, the ranges are specified by a lower and upper bounds on a specific dimension. For instance, Region 1 is specified by the Range A on X and Range C on Y.

2.5.6 Time Management

The main concern of services and mechanisms provided by *time management* (TM) is to coordinate the advance of (logical) time of each federate and to deliver messages in a consistent order during the federation execution. For this purpose, there are total 23 time management services, four of which are RTI-initiated callbacks (IEEE Std 1516.1-2010 2010).

2.5.6.1 Basics

Before giving the details of time management services, it would be useful reviewing some terms related to time issues in HLA and the RTI. As we introduced time and

2.5 Interface Specification

change in a general sense in Chap. 1, time in HLA is regarded as a point in the *HLA time axis*, whereas the time will advance in intervals through these points. So, a federate can reference these points on the time axis to associate itself or some of its messages (IEEE Std 1516.1-2010 2010). *Messages* are events or some activities such as sending an interaction. Association of a federate with the HLA time axis in terms of discrete time creates a federate *logical time*. Associating the activities means that the federate assigns a *timestamp* (a designation of logical time) to the message with related to the HLA time axis. A major purpose of TM services is to enable sending and receiving TSO messages ordered with a timestamp.

Each federate is assigned a logical time in joining a federation execution, and then the joined federates may advance along the time axis during the federation execution. To advance time in the federation and to advance federates along the HLA time axis, we need *time advancement strategies*, also referred as *time management mechanisms*. Since the specific strategy used for time management is driven by the purpose of the simulation, it is important to control the advancement of federates along the time axis in light of differing internal time management mechanism implemented by the federate applications. So, another major purpose of the time management services is to control the advancements of federates. In general, a federate may advance its time using the following strategies (Fujimoto 1998):

- Time step advancement. Federate advances its time in fixed (time) steps.
- Event-based advancement. Federate advances its time to the timestamp of the next TSO message (event).
- Optimistic advancement. Federate is free to advance its time, but in case it receives a message with a timestamp less than its current logical time, then it roll backs its time.

The first two strategies are known as the *conservative time management* and the third strategy is known as the *optimistic time management* (Fujimoto 2000). The logical time advancement of a federate may be constrained by another federate. In general, there are four main federate types in relation to time as depicted in Table 2.5.

By default, all federates start out as "Neither." During federation execution, federates can change their states dynamically. See Chap. 9 on how to implement the federate types related to time management.

All regulating federates (meaning both TR and TC&TR federates) are responsible to regulate advancement of (TC) federates along the time axis. To guarantee that a regulating federate would not send any TSO message during a time period, TR federates have a *lookahead* value. The lookahead value represents a duration of time (i.e., a time interval), whereas this value also can be modified during the execution. Only TR federates have the capability to send a TSO message with a timestamp. "Semantic differences exist between the way time is represented for the purpose of depicting timestamps versus calculating lookahead. When depicting timestamps, time can be considered to be an absolute value on the HLA time axis,

Table 2.5 Federate types per time management

Types	Explanation
Time-constrained (TC)	A constrained federate can receive TSO messages, but cannot send. Besides, their time advance is constrained by regulating federates
Time-regulating (TR)	A regulating federate can send a TSO message. It can still receive a TSO message but as an RO message. In addition, they can progress any time without any constraint. So, they regulate the federation time flow
Both TC and TR (TC and TR)	Federates that are both constrained and regulating have the union of the constrained and regulating federates' characteristics. In other words, they can send and receive TSO messages (receive with time information), can regulate federation time flow, and are constrained by other regulating federates
Neither TC and TR	Federates that are neither constrained nor regulating do not participate in federation time management. So, they have complete freedom in managing their own time advance. They cannot send TSO messages, but they can receive TSO messages without time information

and thus, time comparisons can be done to determine if one timestamp is greater than another. Lookahead, in contrast, represents a duration of time, which can be added to timestamps but is generally not used for comparison purposes." (IEEE Std 1516.2-2010 2010).

TC federates can receive TSO messages, and they are volunteered to be regulated by a TR federate for its time advancement. The RTI guarantees that no additional TSO message with a timestamp less than the TC federate's current logical time will be delivered to the TC federate. To insure this, a bound is associated with the federate by the RTI, so the federate cannot advance beyond its bound. This bound is called as the *Greatest Available Logical Time* (GALT), which specifies the greatest logical time to which the RTI insures it can grant an advance without having to wait for other joined federates to advance. So, a constrained federate cannot advance beyond its GALT. In general, GALT is important for the TC federates to advance their logical time, but actually all federates have a GALT value, because they may want to switch into constrained and to set a new logical time. GALT is calculated by the RTI with regard to some parameters such as the logical time, lookahead, and requests made by TR federates to advance time. If there is no TR federate, then GALT is undefined, whereas a federate may advance its logical time to any point in the time axis.

Moreover, each federate has a *Least Incoming Time Stamp* (LITS), which specifies the smallest timestamp a federate will receive in the future.

For further details, the reader is gently advised to go through (IEEE Std 1516.1-2010 2010; IEEE Std 1516.2-2010 2010) for HLA 1516-2010 and (DMSO 2002; Fujimoto 1998) for HLA 1.3 standard.

2.5.6.2 HLA Services Related with Time

The messages that can be associated with time are summarized below. The messages correspond the activities in terms of RTI services.

2.5 Interface Specification

- OM services
  - Update attribute value;
  - Reflect attribute values;
  - Send interaction;
  - Receive interaction;
  - Delete object instance;
  - Remove object instance.

- DDM services
  - Send interaction with regions

The message order type (i.e., either TSO message or RO message) for delivery must match the *preferred order type* of data specified in the FOM for each object class attribute and interaction parameter (see Chap. 5 on how to specify the message order type). A federate may change the preferred order type of an interaction or an attribute at runtime by using the *Change Interaction Order Type* and *Change Attribute Order Type* services, respectively.

The exact order type of a sent message and a received message is somewhat complex, and it is dependent on some conditions such as the preferred order type of data declared, whether a timestamp is supplied or not, and whether the federate is regulating or constrained. The details are presented in (IEEE Std 1516.1-2010 2010). To summarize:

- The order type of a sent message is TSO if and only if preferred order type is TSO, the sending federate is regulating, and a timestamp is supplied with the message.
- The order type of a received message is TSO if and only if order type of sent message is TSO, and the receiving federate is time-constrained.

2.5.6.3 Advancing Time

Each federate is assigned a logical time upon joining a federation execution and then the joined federates may only advance along the time axis during the execution with *Time Advance Grant* after invoking the TM services such as *Time Advance Request* or *Next Message Request* (the full list is displayed in Fig. 2.25) according to their time advancement strategies. See Chap. 9 on how to achieve advancing time.

2.5.6.4 HLA 1.3

In HLA 1.3 specification, the TM jargon differs. See Table 2.6 for a map. The keywords change in service naming. For example, *Query "Logical" Time* service corresponds to *Query "Federate" Time* service in HLA 1.3 or *Next "Message" Request Available* service corresponds to *Next "Event" Request Available* service in HLA 1.3. For further details of time management in HLA 1.3, see (DMSO 2002).

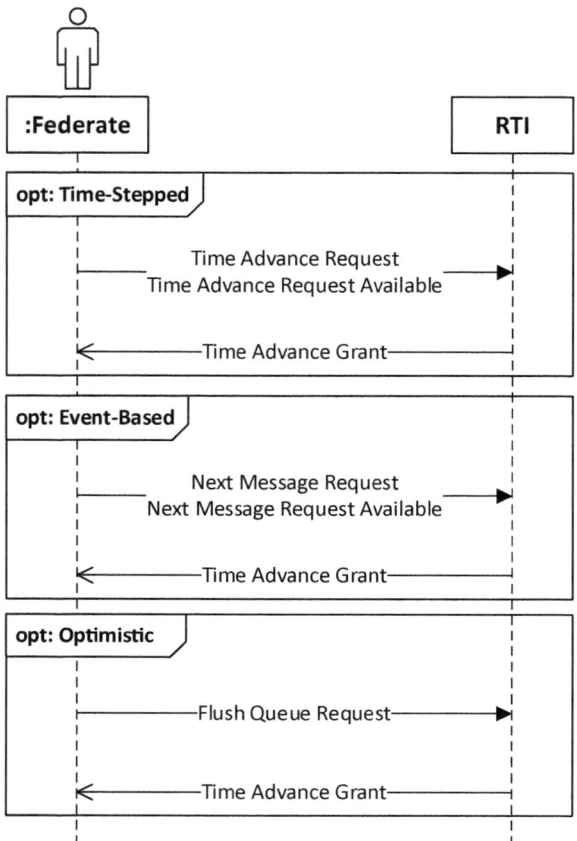

Fig. 2.25 UML sequence diagram for advancing time

Table 2.6 HLA1.3 and IEEE 1516-2010 TM Jargon

IEEE 1516-2010 keywords	HLA 1.3 keywords
Logical time	Federate time
Message	Event
GALT	LBTS (lower bound timestamp)
LITS	Min. next event time

2.6 Full Life Cycle of a Federation Execution

For introduction, here we describe the full life cycle of a federation from the perspective of a federate. So, we will know what kinds of services a federate and a federation needs. A typical federation execution life cycle starts with the connection to the RTI as depicted in Fig. 2.26, and then:

2.6 Full Life Cycle of a Federation Execution

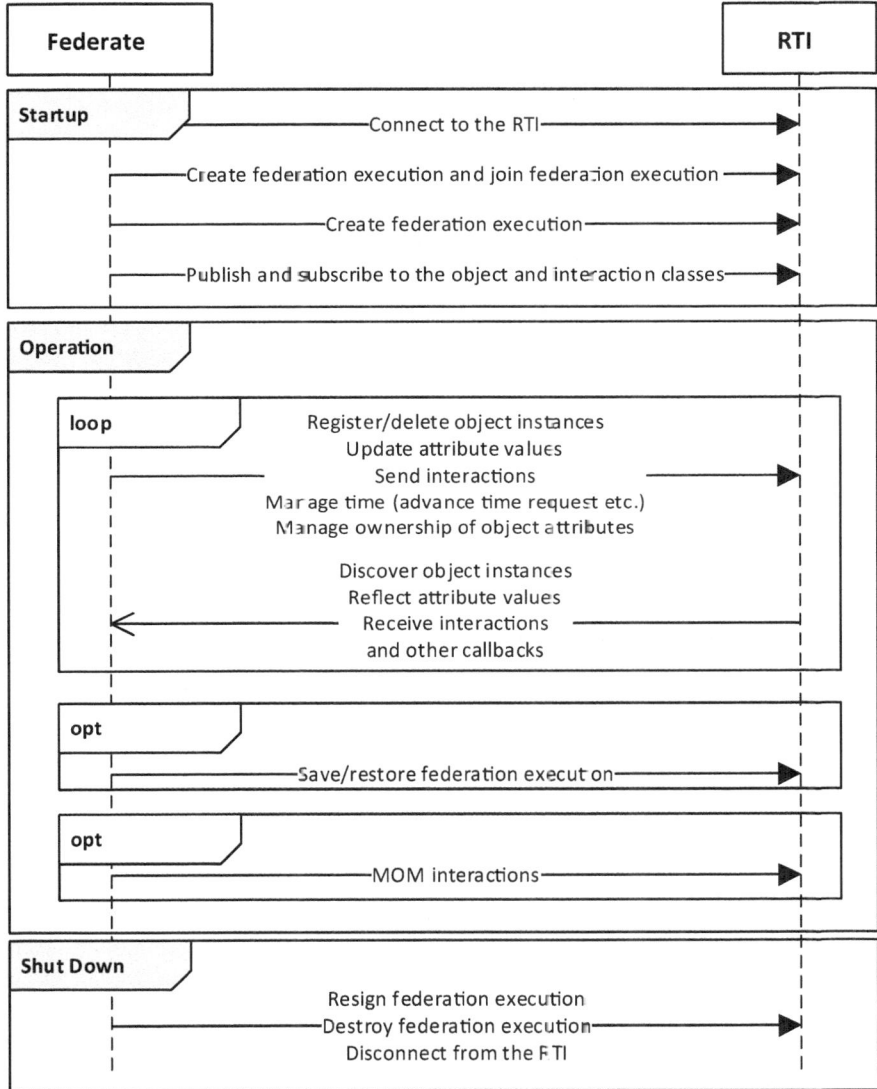

Fig. 2.26 Typical federation execution from the perspective of a federate

- Federate application connects to the RTI to use federate services and interact with the RTI.
- Federate first tries to create the federation execution if not created till then and then joins the federation execution. After joining the federation execution, a joined federate instance in the RTI is created that represents the federate in the federation execution.

- Federate should inform the RTI about its capabilities and interests by publishing and subscribing the object classes and interaction classes. Thus, it establishes its initial data requirements.
- Federate registers (creates) objects that it will provide to other federates.
- Federate may register new objects or update the values of the instance attributes that it registered; may discover new objects, that are created by other federates; may receive updates for the subscribed attributes; and may send and receive interactions.
- Federate deletes objects, which it holds the privilege to delete (generally the objects that created by the federate itself) before leaving.
- Federate manages its time according using RTI time management services (e.g., Time Advance Request), if it specifies a time management policy (e.g., time-regulating federate).
- Federate manages ownership of attributes, if necessary.
- Federate resigns and tries to destroy the federation execution and succeeds if it happens to be the last federate.
- Federate disconnects from RTI.

The order is important. For example, you cannot register an object instance before publishing the related object class. Or, you cannot join the federation execution before connecting to the RTI.

This typical federation execution life cycle affects the design of federates. With no surprise, basic program flow of federates is divided into three phases: system initialization (start-up), main application loop (operation), and system termination (shut down) (Fig. 2.27).

System initialization and termination phases include the RTI *initialization* and *termination* phases, which involve some federation-wide principles. Generally, there are two federation management models: *centralized* and *non-centralized* models. In the centralized model, a specific federate is responsible for the initialization and termination of the federation execution. In non-centralized models, each federate has the equal responsibility for initialization and termination. Initialization and termination phases also include the initialization and termination activities for the scenario play-out, respectively.

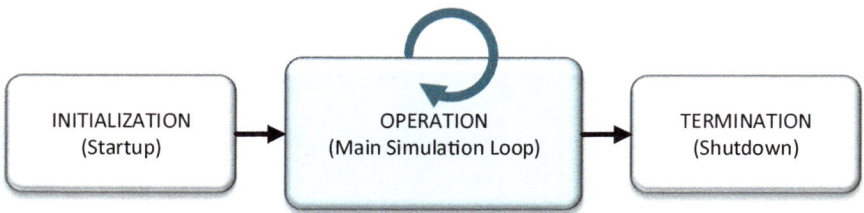

Fig. 2.27 Basic program flow of a typical federate

2.6 Full Life Cycle of a Federation Execution 71

2.6.1 Initialization

HLA does not mandate the creation of a federation execution to the privilege of a particular federate. This policy provides flexibility and non-centralization. One may design that the first job of any one of the federate applications is to try to create a federation execution. The first federate succeeds to create the federation execution if the specified federation execution does not exist, while subsequent federates receive an exception, which indicates that the federation execution does already exist and then they directly join the federation.

In some RTI releases, if joining the federation execution is attempted immediately after the creation of the federation execution, the federation execution may not yet be initialized to communicate with the federate (e.g., the Fedexec process is not forked and initialized in case of HLA 1.3). Beforehand, we cannot assume which federate is the first, so the join logic will loop until the join is successful or until some predetermined number of join attempts are exhausted.

The creation of a federation execution requires a *federation name*. It designates a unique federation execution, and the participating federates use it to join into the specified federation execution. All member federates should agree on the unique federation execution name. Therefore, the federation execution name either should be distributed by hand to all participants at start-up or the federation execution name should be hard coded in federates.

2.6.2 Operation

The operation phase generally includes the *main simulation loop* and an alternative behavior path. The main simulation loop specifies the behavior of the federate for the normal federate execution, which includes the object management, time management, and the ownership management services, while the alternative behavior path is used for abnormal situations such as when save and restore is requested in the federation execution or when MOM interactions are required. The main simulation loop is elaborated in Chap. 8, and, furthermore, it is extended for a graphics-intensive federate application in Chap. 11.

2.6.3 Termination

The shutdown/termination of federation execution is accomplished by the federate that resigns from the federation execution last. In a non-centralized simulation, the same rule applies here; all federates, while resigning, attempt to terminate the federation execution. The last one succeeds while others receive an exception because the federation still has members and resign from the federation without terminating it.

The termination phase consists of three stages (Fig. 2.28): RTI termination, local model termination, and graphics termination. At *RTI termination* stage, the created

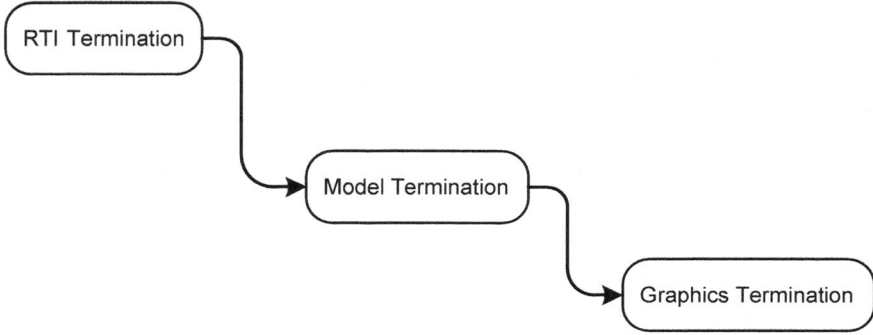

Fig. 2.28 Termination of a federation (Topçu et al. 2016)

objects are deleted and other federates are informed, and then the federate resigns and tries to destroy the federation. At *model termination* stage, the local objects that represent the simulation entities are deleted to free up the application memory, and finally at *graphics termination* stage, the graphics subsystem is shut down.

2.7 Example Federation Deployment

UML deployment diagrams are used to plan and design the execution environment in software-intensive systems by depicting the hardware components and software components. In this context, the specialized and extended form of deployment diagrams can be employed to capture the execution details of federation requirements such as *node* (i.e., hardware component) information (e.g., physical location, IP address, port number, operating system, etc.), *network information* (e.g., network type, bandwidth, etc.), and which federates (i.e., software component) hosted by which nodes (Topçu et al. 2003; Topçu and Oğuztüzün 2005).

An example UML deployment diagram for an HLA federation execution is presented in Fig. 2.29. Here, we can see that there are five hosts, where four of them are distributed in a TCP/IP network and one (Node 4) is a Web client connecting from Internet. The diagram shows us which federate is executed on which host and gives some information about the host (e.g., the host's operating system).

2.8 Federation and Federate States

During a federation run, federates and the federation execution can be found in specific states from the viewpoint of the RTI. Those states are useful to define the context of federates and the federation execution during simulation run.

2.8 Federation and Federate States

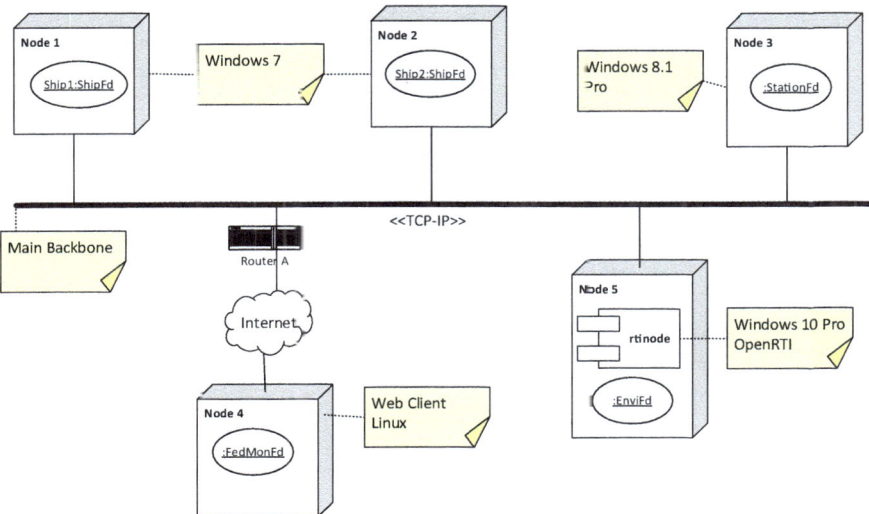

Fig. 2.29 Typical federation execution deployment. The federate applications can be deployed to execute on heterogeneous environments such as Linux/Windows or various versions of Windows

2.8.1 Federation Execution States

Federation execution states are depicted in Fig. 2.30. Initially, the federation execution is in Federation Execution Does Not Exist state when no federation execution exists (either it is not created yet or is destroyed). The directed links show the events that trigger the transition from one event to another event. After the federation execution is created and running, the federation execution state transits to Federation Execution Exists state. This state is a *composite state* that encapsulates two substates: No Joined Federates and Supporting Joined Federates. The substates are not essential from the viewpoint of federate developer. Therefore, we do not go into the details further. The RTI implementers may refer to (IEEE Std 1516.1-2010 2010) for details.

2.8.2 Federate States

A federate is either connected or not connected according to its connection with RTI. Figure 2.31 depicts the basic state diagram from a federation management perspective. The Connected state is a composite state including the states where a federate is joined the federation execution (Joined state) or not (Not Joined state). The joined federate state also includes some substates such as active federate state, federate save in progress state, and federate restore in progress state from the perspective of the RTI (IEEE Std 1516.1-2010 2010).

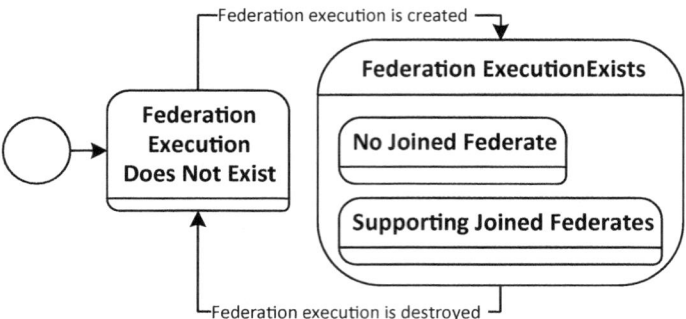

Fig. 2.30 UML state diagram for federation execution

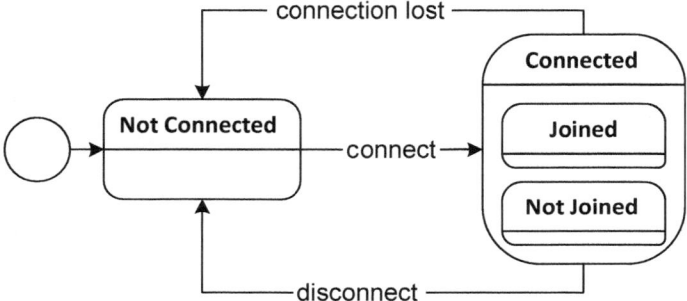

Fig. 2.31 UML state diagram for a federate

Most distributed interactive simulations use scenarios to drive the simulation execution. Using a federation-wide scenario slightly changes the lifetime of federate introducing new states for a scenario-dependent run. See (Topçu and Oğuztüzün 2010; Topçu et al. 2016) for the details of the scenario-related federate states.

2.9 Summary

In this chapter, we presented a thorough introduction to the concepts and principles of HLA mostly from the perspective of a federate application developer. Various aspects of the standard, including its historical roots, concepts, and the rules that govern its operation, have been covered.

HLA provides a prominent software framework for distributed simulations with special emphasis on interoperability and reusability of simulation components (Dahmann et al. 1997). HLA has been evolving constantly since its introduction. Currently, HLA is at its third stage, known as HLA Evolved. The HLA standard consists of three main components: the HLA Rules, Interface Specification, and the Object Model Template. The rules specify some policy that federates and federation executions must conform. The interface specification presents a standard interface for the interaction between a federate and the RTI. The OMT specifies the standard for the HLA object models, namely FOM, SOM, and MIM. HLA uses an object-exchange mechanism employing the RTI as the mediator between publishers and subscribers. The RTI library also provides an API with programming language bindings such as Java and C++ for federation developers exposing all the federate service areas; federation management, declaration management, object management, data distribution management, time management, and ownership management. A typical life cycle of a federation execution from the perspective of a federate involves initialization, operation, and termination phases. In the initialization phase, a federate joins the federation execution and then declares its capability and interests to the RTI. During the operation phase, which involves the main simulation loop, the federate registers its objects, updates the attribute values, and sends interactions as it can discover new objects, receive interactions, and reflect the attribute value updates. The federate may also transfer the ownership of some of attributes of its objects to another federates. Of course, time is an important aspect of simulation. Therefore, a federate can interact with the RTI to manage its time policy. In the termination phase, the federate resigns from the federation execution.

As it became a widely accepted standard in the area of distributed modeling and simulation over the last decade, and we see that many new distributed simulation applications in both the civilian and, to a larger extent military realm are being built to be HLA compliant. In this regard, this chapter lays the technical background to develop HLA-compliant distributed simulations.

2.10 Questions for Review

1. Is it a requirement that all the federates use the time management services?
2. Explain the FOM Modularity in HLA Evolved. Show the extension and union techniques in sample FOM modules.
3. What is WSDL? Explain the relation of it with HLA.
4. What is DLC API?
5. Explain the "Connect and List Services" property in HLA Evolved.
6. Discuss the differences of HLA federation management services specified in HLA 1.3 and HLA Evolved standards.
7. Discuss the differences of HLA time management services specified in HLA 1.3 and HLA Evolved standards.

Table 2.7 Time data for federation execution

Federate	Time management scheme	Federation time $t_{current}$	Lookahead $t_{lookahead}$	Time step
Fd-1	R	17	10	5
Fd-2	RC	N/A (late joining)	–	–
Fd-3	RC	16	4	4
Fd-4	C	18	–	4
Fd-5	RC	16	5	5
Fd-6	N	0	–	6

8. Discuss the differences of HLA data distribution management services specified in HLA 1.3 and HLA Evolved standards.
9. Discuss the pros and cons of a wrapper API around RTI. In this respect, discuss RACoN API.
10. Explain the class-based filtering and value-based filtering in HLA by giving examples.
11. What are the major components of HLA? Explain each shortly.
12. Table 2.7 presents the time information of federates in a federation execution. In this regard, draw a time diagram for each federate and then:

    a. Show LBTS value for each federate and state whether the federate will proceed or not.
    b. Assume that the federate Fd-2 joins the federation execution at time $t = 20$. Calculate the LBTS value for Fd-2.

13. Answer the below questions regarding to the two-dimensional space depicted in Fig. 2.24.

    a. Draw the region specified by the range A on the dimension X and the range D on the dimension Y.
    b. Draw the region specified by the range B on the dimension X and the range C on the dimension D.
    c. If we want to cover all the distribution space (in other words, if we want to create a single region equal to the default region), what should we do?

14. Why is it desirable to have larger lookahead values? Consider time-driven and event-driven federates separately.
15. It is often remarked that HLA compliance, by itself, does not guarantee interoperability of simulations. What else is required on the part of developers?

References

CERTI. (2002). *CERTI*. http://savannah.nongnu.org/projects/certi. Accessed April 08, 2017.

Dahmann, J. S., Fujimoto, R. M., & Weatherly, R. M. (1997). *The department of defense high level architecture* (pp. 142–149). Atlanta, GA: IEEE.

DMSO. (2002). *High level architecture run-time infrastructure RTI 1.3-next generation programmer's guide version 6*, s.l. Department of Defense Defense Modeling and Simulation Office.

DoD. (1995). *Modeling and simulation (M&S) master plan*. Alexandria: DoD.

Fowler, M. (2003). *UML distilled: a brief guide to the standard object modeling language* (3rd ed.). Boston: Addison-Wesley

Fujimoto, R. M. (1998). Time management in the high level architecture. *Simulation, 71*(6), 388–400.

Fujimoto, R. M. (2000). *Parallel and distributed simulation systems* (1st ed.). New York, NY: Wiley.

IEEE 1516.1-2010. (2010). *Standard for modeling and simulation (M&S) high level architecture (HLA)—Federate interface specification*. New Jersey, NJ: IEEE.

IEEE Std 1516-2010. (2010). *IEEE standard for modeling and simulation (M&S) high level architecture (HLA)–Framework and rule*. New York: IEEE.

IEEE Std 1516.1-2010. (2010) *Standard for modeling and simulation (M&S) high level architecture (HLA)—Federate interface specification*. New Jersey, NJ: IEEE.

IEEE Std 1516.2-2010. (2010) *Standard for modeling and simulation (M&S) high level architecture (HLA)—Object model template specification*. New Jersey, NJ: IEEE.

Kuhl, F., Weatherly, R., & Dahmann, J. (1999). *Creating computer simulations: An introduction to the high level architecture*. Upple Saddle River, NJ: Prentice Hall PTR.

Larman, C. (2004). *Applying UML and patterns: An introduction to object-oriented analysis and design and iterative development* (3rd ed.). Upple Saddle River, NJ: Prentice Hall.

Mäk, V. (2013). *HLA RTI—Run time infrastructure: MÄK RTI*. Retrieved from http://www.mak.com/products/link-simulation-interoperability/hla-rti-run-time-infrastructure.html

Möller, B., Löfstrand, B., & Karlsson, M. (2007). *An overview of the HLA evolved modular FOMs*. Orlando: SISO.

Möller, B., et al. (2008). *HLA evolved—A summary of major technical improvements*. SISO: Orlando, FL.

Open HLA. (2016). *Open HLA*. Retrieved from https://sourceforge.net/projects/ohla/. Accessed April 08, 2017.

OpenRTI. (2011). *OpenRTI project website*. Retrieved from https://sourceforge.net/projects/openrti/files/. Accessed October 11, 2016.

Pitch. (2013). *Pitch pRTI™—Connect your systems*. Retrieved from http://www.pitch.se/products/prti

PNP-Software. (2007). https://www.pnp-software.com/eodisp/home.html. Retrieved from https://www.pnp-software.com/eodisp/home.html. Accessed April 08, 2017.

Portico. (2013). *The portico project*. http://www.porticoproject.org/. Accessed August 30, 2015.

SISO FEAT. (2017). *FEAT user's guide reference for the federation engineering agreements template*. Orlando, FL: Simulation Interoperability Standards Organization.

SISO, & Siso, F. E. A. T. (2015). *Standard for real-time platform reference federation object model v2.0*. Orlando, FL: Simulation Interoperability Standards Organization (SISO).

Topçu, O., Adak, M. & Oğuztüzün, H. (2008). A metamodel for federation architectures. *Transactions on Modeling and Computer Simulation (TOMACS), 18*(3), 10.

Topçu, O., Durak, U., Oğuztüzün, H., & Yılmaz, L. (2016). *Distributed simulation: A model driven engineering approach* (1st ed.). Cham (Zug): Springer International Publishing.

Topçu, O., & Oğuztüzün, H. (2005). Developing an HLA based naval maneuvering simulation. *Naval Engineers Journal, Winter, 117*(1), 23–40.

Topçu, O., & Oğuztüzün, H. (2010). Scenario management practices in HLA-based distributed simulation. *Journal of Naval Science and Engineering, 6*(2), 1–33.

Topçu, O., Oğuztüzün, H., & Hazen, M. (2003). *Towards a UML profile for HLA federation design. Part II* (pp. 874–879). Montreal, Canada: SCS.

Yilmaz, L. (2007). *Using meta-level ontology relations to measure conceptual alignment and interoperability of simulation models* (pp. 1090–1099). Washington, DC: IEEE.

Federation Development At-A-Glance

3

In this chapter, we will elaborate for beginners how to start developing an HLA simulation from scratch. In this respect, this chapter presents some development guidelines and hints. Please keep in mind that we do not try to either present a full simulation development process or supersede the existing process models such as FEDEP (IEEE Std 1516.3-2003 2003) or DSEEP (IEEE Std 1730-2010 2010). We advise you to refer (Topçu et al. 2016) for a full-blown federation development process model based on model-driven engineering (MDE) principles (Schmidt 2006).

3.1 Process Model

A process model specifies the life cycle and activities throughout the development and execution of a distributed simulation. It specifies where to begin and how to proceed and what to produce in each step. It is very useful as a road map for simulation developers.

Distributed simulation engineering and execution process (DSEEP) (IEEE Std 1730-2010 2010) is an important standard specifying a process model for distributed simulation development and execution and is independent of any simulation environment architecture. DSEEP can be viewed as a generalization of High - Level Architecture (HLA) Development and Execution Process (FEDEP) (IEEE Std 1516.3-2003 2003) with the purpose of supporting distributed simulation approaches in a generic way independently of a specific architecture. DSEEP can also be useful in supporting processes involving multiple simulation architectures. In the context of a project, however, developers need a more specific process model adapted to a particular DS architecture such as HLA In this case, overlays of DSEEP come to play. For HLA, the annex-A of standard (IEEE Std 1730-2010 2010) presents an HLA process overlay to the DSEEP. Here, we do not cover either the DSEEP, overlays of DSEEP, or FEDEP. To see a discussion and a gentle introduction to them, refer to (Topçu et al. 2016).

Besides standards, which basically promote an activity-driven paradigm, from the perspective of MDE, an MDE-based process model is quite practical with emphasis on models and transformations among them to enable tool support and automation (Topçu et al. 2016). In this book, our intention is not to go into details of MDE and related process model, but to use a simple process for model-based development. Figure 3.1 presents this simple process for HLA-based simulation

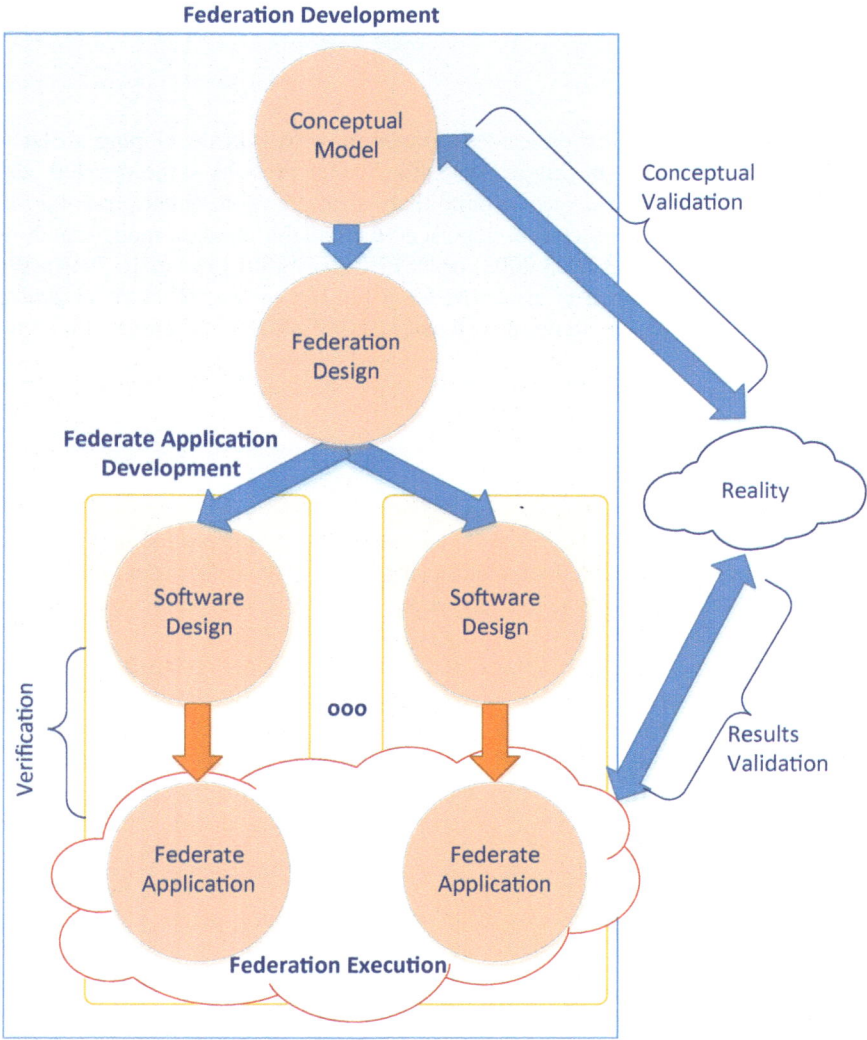

Fig. 3.1 Simple simulation development process

development where each bubble represents a model. In the federation development, we tend to talk about models in general: a (simulation) conceptual model, a federation design (i.e., high-level design of a simulation system), a software design (i.e., detailed design focusing on software), and the executable model (i.e., application). A (simulation) *conceptual model* is a (problem) domain model, in which simulation concerns are addressed. It is the highest level abstraction of reality representing the concepts and the relations among them in the problem domain. Regarding the *reality* (or the referent system), a conceptual model is validated to evaluate the realism of the model according to the objectives of the simulation (Am I building the right system?). This validation is known as the *conceptual validation*. Subject-matter experts or domain experts play a significant role on the development and the validation of this model. The reality is also employed to validate the output results of the federation execution, known as *results validation*. The conceptual model is the major resource to design the federation (*federation design*), and then, both are used to design the federate applications (*software design*). Then, you can implement the application using a programming language such as C# (*federate application*). In software engineering, we also need to make sure that the implementation is correct with respect to the design, which is known as (software) *verification* (Am I building the system right?).

The development of a conceptual model is the first step of the federation development. A conceptual model can be either formal or informal. That said, because the focus of this book is on federation implementation, we will use an informal form of conceptual model. So, the introduction of each case study, in Chap. 1, serves as an informal conceptual model for our purpose.

The following section will explain each activity and present development guidelines.

3.2 Federation Development and Guidelines

3.2.1 Federation Design

Designing a federation is an activity to specify a *federation architecture* that captures the static and the dynamic aspects of a federation.

The major parts of a federation architecture that reflects the static view of the federation incorporate:

- A federation structure and
- Object model, which is a set of federation object model (FOM) per federation.

The dynamic aspect of a federation architecture includes:

- Specifying the behaviors of participating federates (so that they can fulfill their responsibilities within the federation).

The representation of a federate architecture can be formal or informal. Although a formal federation architecture model is very useful especially for code generation (Topçu et al. 2008), in this book, we will use an informal federation architecture representation to keep the presentation conceptually simple and not to shift the focus of the book.

3.2.1.1 Federation Structure

A federation structure depicts the participating federate applications in a federation execution. An example is shown in Fig. 3.2. This diagram is colloquially known as a *lollipop diagram*. Diagrammatic representations can be more informative such as in Fig. 3.5, where it also shows the multiplicity information of (joined) federates.

The important activity in this stage is to specify the federate applications and the (joined) federates. We have a federate application (software), and it is replicated to realize multiple federates. In general, it is a one-to-one relation, where a federate application represents one federate in the federation execution. For instance, a federate application can manage (e.g., joining federation execution) a ship federate and its objects in the execution. The multiple copies of a (ship) federate application are executed where each copy is a federate that simulates the same kind of ship (see Fig. 3.3).

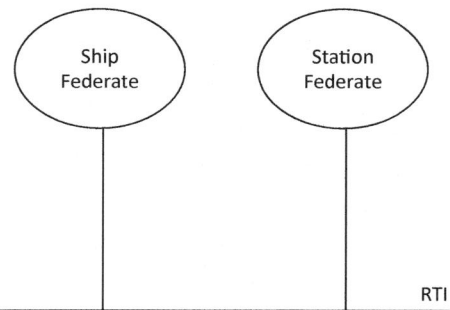

Fig. 3.2 STMS federation structure depicted as a lollipop diagram

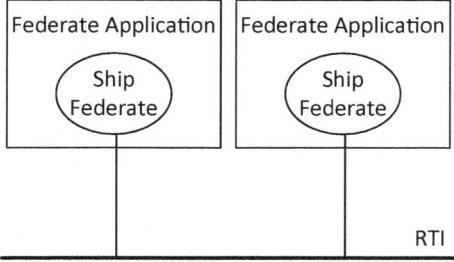

Fig. 3.3 One-to-one relation between a federate application and a federate. Here, the federate application is run as much as the ship federates required in a federation execution

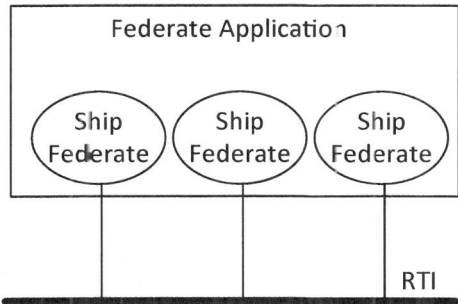

Fig. 3.4 One-to-many relation between a federate application and multiple federates. Here, there is only one application that manages multiple federates

But for some cases, a federate application will replicate multiple federates (one-to-many) (see Fig. 3.4). For instance, computer-generated entities such as all enemy ships (as a federate each) with their related objects can be managed by only one application. Although there is one application, there will be multiple ships (federates not objects) joined in the federation execution.

Do not confuse with where, as a design issue, this could be a single federate creating and updating multiple (ship) objects. See Chap. 9 for an example implementation.

This approach is a useful design for incorporating the agents (of an agent-based simulation) as federates (of an HLA federation) as agents are generally managed by a single application (i.e., agent manager). See Chap. 11 for an example implementation of agents as federates.

In large-scale simulations, a federate can participate in multiple federation executions at the same time. This is useful, for example, to bridge different federation executions. See Chap. 9 for how to implement such a case.

3.2.1.2 Case Study: Federation Structure

We will begin to open up this running example by specifying its federation architecture informally. For the complete formal federation architecture model, which comprises the federation and the behavioral models for each participating federate along with other supporting material, the reader is referred to (Topçu et al. 2016).

When we analyze the (informal) conceptual model (introduced in Chap. 1) of our running example, STMS, two conceptual entities (actors) stand out: the traffic monitoring station and the ship(s). They are represented with two types of applications; a station application and a ship application, respectively. There is an ongoing interaction among the stations and the ships.

The *ship application* (ShipFdApp) is an interactive application allowing the user to pick up a unique ship name, a direction (eastward or westward), and a constant speed by means of a textual interface. Joining a federation execution corresponds to entering the strait (either from east or west according to its initial position), and resigning from the federation corresponds to leaving the strait.

The *station application* (StationFdApp) is a monitoring federate, where each has an *area of responsibility* (AOR) for monitoring task. During execution, each station keeps track of the ships in its AOR; a track consists of the ship name, position, direction, and speed. And then, it merely displays the tracks. Tracks are also exchanged between stations as ships move from one AOR to another.

We need to think about how many joined federates may participate in a specific federation execution and which federate applications will support those federates. A joined federate can be seen as a role that a federate application plays in a federation execution.

Now, let us think about a specific federation execution, call it as D-Strait, assuming the strait is Dardanelles and there are two traffic stations, where one is located in the east and the other in the west, dividing the strait into two AORs. This imposes the requirement that during federation execution, there must be exactly two station federates participated in. On the other hand, the ships enter and exit the strait. Here, we can model a distribution function using the past statistics of the traffic of ships regarding the D-Strait. So, a federation execution may have zero or more ship federates during the execution, while the station federate is limited to two in this specific scenario.

Remember that a federation structure shows the participating federate applications in a federation execution, and the multiplicity of joined federates is allowed. The federation structure, depicted in Fig. 3.5, reflects our D-Strait federation execution. Chap. 4 will show how to build this federation structure using a modeling tool, namely SimGe.

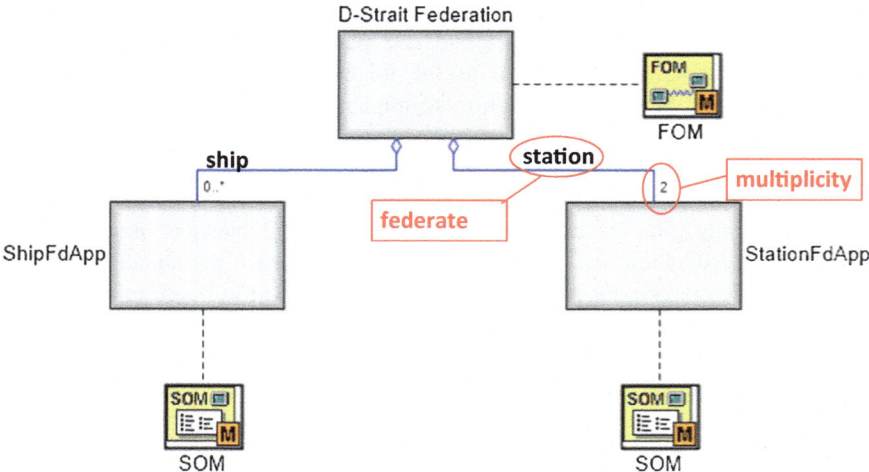

Fig. 3.5 Federation structure for D-Strait. Here, ShipFdApp represents a ship federate as StationFdApp represents two station federates. In the diagram, they are shown as a role along with the multiplicity

Also, notice that each federation has a related FOM and each federate has a related SOM. The object model development process is explained in the following section.

3.2.1.3 Object Model Development

The next important step is to develop the object models, which are a FOM, the shared data among federates, and SOMs, one per federate, specifying the capability of the federate in terms of producing/consuming data.

The development activity essentially involves a conceptual domain analysis, where we want to find out the important concepts and their relations with each other. A common and simple method is to conduct a *verb–noun analysis*, where the analyzer tries to identify the important nouns and verbs in a given problem statement. Here, in general, the nouns and the verbs identified correspond to the concepts and the relationships (and actions as well), respectively, in the problem domain.

As the SOMs are mainly used for documentation to promote reusability, our main concern will be the development of a FOM. When we begin federation development from scratch, SOMs will constitute the related parts of the FOM. But if a federate is to be reused in different federations, then its SOM will reflect its capability not for one specific federation, but for all federations it can be used.

Representation

For the documentation purpose, a FOM or a SOM may be represented using tables based on OMT tabular format. But for exchanging and reusing, the representation of a FOM/SOM must be in DIF format. As (a part of) FOM is used in runtime by the RTI, its representation must be in FDD/FED format.

Therefore, the best practice for representing an HLA object model is to use an object model development tool, found under various names such as FOM editor and object model editor. In this book, Simulation Generator (SimGe) will be used to construct an object model. Using a tool has many advantages, the prominent one being the automated generation of the FED/FDD file, which is required at runtime by the RTI. Moreover, if there is an existing FED/FDD file, you may reuse it (by import) to construct your object model.

3.2.1.4 Case Study: Object Model

In our running example, the object model involves three object classes, namely Ship, Station, and Track, and one interaction class, namely RadioMessage. The object class and interaction class hierarchies of the object model are presented in Fig. 3.6.

Ships and stations can detect ships in the environment, say, using a radar. So, ship object class represents the ships in the virtual environment. Station object class specifies a station in the virtual environment. Track object class is the representation of a ship created for traffic monitoring stations and is used to exchange tracks between stations. The object classes and the related attributes are presented in Table 3.1.

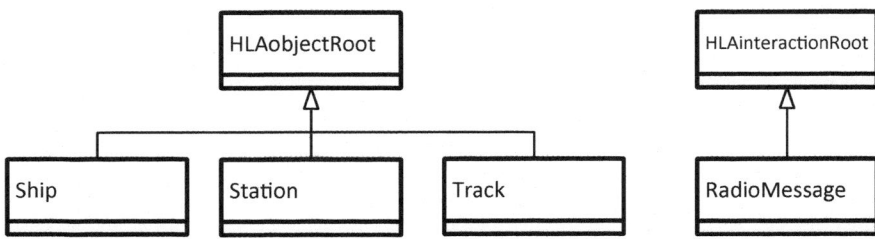

Fig. 3.6 A part of the STMS FOM

Table 3.1 Object classes and their attributes

Object class	Attributes	Explanation
Ship	Call sign	Radio name of the ship
	Position	X and Y coordinates
	Heading	Either east or west
	Speed	Enumeration value of {very slow, slow, fast, very fast}
Station	Station name	Name of the traffic monitoring station
	Location	Either east or west
Track	Track number	Track number is the same with the call sign of the ship for simplicity
	Track position	X and Y coordinates
	Track heading	Either east or west
	Track speed	Enumeration value of {very slow, slow, fast, very fast}

Table 3.2 Interaction classes

Interaction class	Parameters	Explanation
Radio message	Call sign	The name of the entity that sent the message
	Message	The content of the message (e.g., free text saying "I entered strait")
	Timestamp	Date and time the message sent

The radio message interaction class is used to represent a free-text radio message sent and received by ships and stations. The interaction class and its parameters are presented in Table 3.2.

The construction of an object model using SimGe will be shown in Chap. 5 in detail.

3.2.2 Federate Design

3.2.2.1 Federate Architecture

A federate architecture defines the architectural style of an application. Many software architectures may be used in order to develop a federate, but we suggest and use a layered architecture throughout the book A layered architecture specific to HLA is introduced in detail at (Topçu and Oğuztüzün 2013; Topçu et al. 2016). See Chap. 7 for further details and some examples.

3.2.2.2 Behavioral Specification

The Observable Behavior
The behavioral specification of a federation encompasses all the observable interactions among participating federates from the viewpoint of the RTI in a federation execution. The interactions are federate-specific, so they will be a part of federate application design, also called as *detailed (application) design*. A federate application design incorporates an architecture style (i.e., *federate architecture*), intra-object communication of its internal software objects, and interfederate communication with other applications.

From the perspective of federation development, the important part of the interfederate communication involves the interaction of the federate application with the RTI in terms of management services based on HLA federate interface specification (the other parts are such as user interface interaction). Therefore, our focus of this book is on the federate implementation (i.e., implementing the RTI interface) based on a given federate architecture.

The observable behavior of our running example will be presented in chapters through Chaps. 7–9. In these chapters, the representation of behavior of a federate application will be in a programming language. But when required, we will specify a behavior informally either using descriptions in natural language or using a UML (OMG 2015) diagram (e.g., sequence diagrams) for complex behaviors. For a formal specification of the behavioral aspect of a federation, readers may refer to (Topçu et al. 2016).

3.2.2.3 Federate Internal Behavior

As we outlined in the first two chapters, the applications do simulate an abstract model and share the state of the objects in the model with other members in a distributed simulation execution. In fact, an object (in HLA sense) captures a part of the state of a federate (or the simulated system). In this regard, the simulated entities include a computational model. For instance, if we simulate a ship, we need a computational model for its movement regarding to the hydrodynamic forces. From the perspective of HLA, the local simulation of models is encapsulated within the federate applications, which make them application-specific and internal to the application. Therefore, as the focus of our book is on the observable part of the federate applications, we leave the topic of federate internal behavior to other simulation books. But, here we will introduce the simulation computational model of our running example for a better understanding and for the sake of completeness of the case study.

3.2.2.4 Case Study: Simulation Computational Model

As the station federate only tracks the ships in the strait, here we will explain the computational model for ships. The ships in our simulation environment are basic simulation entities when they enter a strait (i.e., join to the federation execution); they simply follow a predefined straight path throughout the strait. So, our simple computational model involves the real-time movement of the ship only in one dimension.

Before presenting the dynamics, we will explain the coordinate system we applied in the simulation of the movement of the ship. As ships move in a straight axis, we use a two-dimensional coordinate system as depicted in Fig. 3.7. The area represents a strait of 4 km in width and 20 km in length. There are two regions, which are called the areas of responsibility, allocated to the stations. The initial location for each ship is determined by the user at runtime either as east or as west (see Chap. 7 for the user interface). So, the position of a ship is fixed as an X–Y coordinate. The initial position coordinates are $(-10, -1)$ and $(10, 1)$ for east and west locations, respectively. Also, the heading of the ship is determined as the opposite direction according to its initial location. For instance, if its initial location is west, then its heading is east.

When the simulation execution starts, the ship is moving in the direction of its heading in real time. The distance change (Δx) is simply calculated with the help of parameters: time increment (Δt) and ship's constant speed (V) using the formula:

$$\Delta x = V \times \Delta t \tag{3.1}$$

The speed is also taken from the user as an enumeration (very slow, slow, fast, very fast) and converted to a constant value. Consequently, a very slow ship takes 10 min to pass the strait, while a very fast ship takes 1 min. As you see, our ships are too fast according to the real ones.

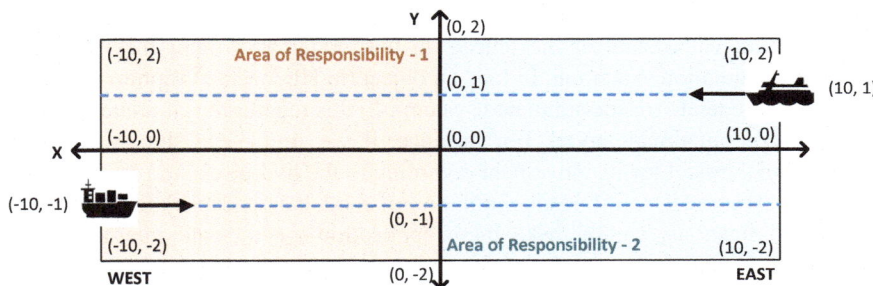

Fig. 3.7 Two-dimensional coordinate system for ship dynamics

3.2 Federation Development and Guidelines   89

Please note that in real-life applications, the vehicle dynamics involves the nature forces affecting the ship posture in a 3D environment. In a rigid body coordinate system, the oscillations of a vessel by its hydrodynamics include rotational changes: yawing, rolling, and pitching motions as well as heaving (up–down), surging (forward–backward), and swaying (left–right), known as six degrees of freedom (6-DOF). An interested reader is referred to (NSTMSS 2016) for a more elaborate hydrodynamics model.

Furthermore, for a more elaborate coordinate system for real-life applications, see our second case study presented in Chap. 11. There, we use a *geodetic coordinate system*, where the position of a ship is represented with latitude and longitude values. It is the most commonly used coordinate system in navigation, and therefore, it is applicable to the real-life cases.

3.2.3 Federate Implementation

After the design phase, federate implementation may start. At this stage, some code generators may help to generate the skeleton code of the entire federation according to the FOM and the federation structure. In our book, we will use SimGe to automatically generate code. This really boosts the development effort as many RTI code is repetitive in nature. See Chap. 6 for details.

3.2.4 Target Platform

The Application Programming Interface (API) of the RTI supports many programming languages, specifically C++ and Java. But if you plan to develop the federate in a Microsoft.NET Environment, using Visual Studio, which is an *integrated development environment*, then you must find a compatible RTI that supports .NET. Using RTI abstractions is also another popular approach. RTI abstractions generally extend the support to more programming languages missing in the original RTI. Using abstractions has many advantages. They mostly simplify the complexity inherent in the RTI API. In this book, the RTI abstraction component for .NET (RACoN) will be used to implement the federates. RACoN provides .NET interface for OpenRTI, Portico, and DMSO RTI NG. Remember that when using an abstraction component, you must install the native RTI library that the component supports. For using RACoN, either OpenRTI (OpenRTI 2011), DMSO RTI NG (DMSO 2002), or Portico RTI (Portico 2016) must be installed first.

3.2.5 Integration with Local Simulations/Games

Actually, the visualization of many simulations is implemented using *graphics libraries* (e.g., OpenGL) or *game engines* (e.g., Unity) for user interaction. For instance, if you develop a game or want to modify an existing game as a federate for some simulation environment, then you must integrate it with the RTI instead of implementing a federate application from scratch. Here, the layered architecture helps a lot as far as it provides the separation of concerns.

Each game object that must be shared within federation must be encapsulated as an HLA object or interaction. Therefore, when developing FOM, it is important to specify which of the existing game/simulation local data must be shared in the federation execution. The RTI abstraction components may help to encapsulate the local data. This is another advantage of the abstraction libraries. In this regard, RACoN facilitates full encapsulation of local data. So, when you develop a simulation/game in C# language and want to use the RTI interface services in your simulation/game, then RACoN provides the necessary constructs.

Figure 3.8 depicts the integration of a game (or a non-HLA simulation application) and the RTI. The objects related to the game/local simulation application (e.g., o1 and o2) are required to be encapsulated as HLA objects (e.g., ho1 and ho2) before sending them through the RTI.

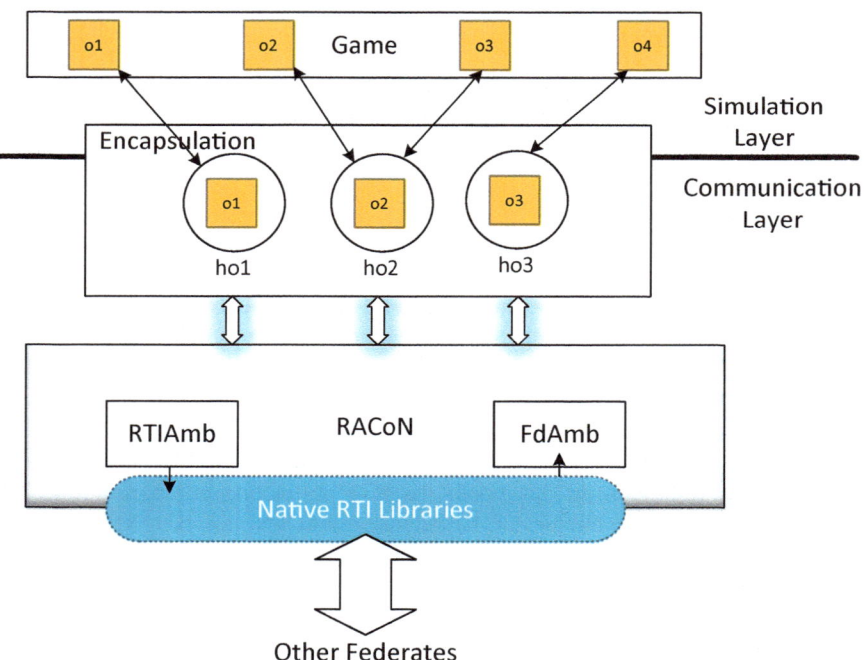

Fig. 3.8 Integration layers of a game with the RTI

3.3 Implementation Steps

From this point forward, we will begin the implementation of federate applications. Here is an overview at-a-glance for implementation order and some quick steps to be ready for the implementation.

- Install OpenRTI (2011), (Portico 2016), or if you intend to use only HLA 1.3 specification, DMSO RTI (2002).
- Download the RACoN library (2016).
- Download the Visual Studio project of Strait Traffic Monitoring Simulation (STMS) sample (RACoN 2016).
- Compile and run the STMS federation.
- If the federate applications run as expected, that is if you send and receive messages, then your machine is ready for an execution environment.
- Download and install SimGe (2015) and use SimGe (refer to Chaps. 4–6 for how to use SimGe):
  - Model federation structure,
  - Develop FOM considering the conceptual model of your application or the game/local simulation objects that you want to share,
  - Export the FED file for HLA 1.3 or the FDD file for HLA IEEE versions, and
  - Generate code.
- Prepare your development environment as described in Chap. 7.
- In MS Visual Studio, create a project for your application or in case of an existing game/simulation, open it, and then create another layer (as a separate project or as a folder in the current project) and import the generated code files.
- Encapsulate the game objects you want to share by employing the RACoN.
- Use the RACoN methods for HLA services (e.g., to update an object) as described in Chaps. 8 and 9.
- In case of interoperating an agent-based simulation and the RTI, refer to Chaps. 10 and 11.
- Deploy your application as introduced in Chap. 2.

3.4 Summary

This chapter has presented a global look at federation development without going into the implementation details. Here, the development guidelines and the steps to follow are presented to give a road map to the reader.

Federation development involves simulation conceptual model development, federation design, federate application design, and then implementation. A conceptual model is the representation of the reality (problem domain). It incorporates assumptions, approaches, and simplifications over the reality. In fact, actually what we simulate is the conceptual model. The most common representation of a conceptual model is informal representation, where we describe the problem, our objectives, and the requirements. Federation design is how we map conceptual entities and the relationships among them to a federation architecture. In general, we describe a federation architecture by depicting its static and dynamic aspects. We specify what the federates are and what data will be shared among federates as well as the time management policy and other management issues such as synchronization among federates. Then, we need to design our federate applications, their internal structures, where this basically involves software design techniques. After design phase, the implementation of the application begins. Implementation requires a thorough understanding of the RTI API at hand. Finally, the application must be deployed for execution.

3.5 Questions for Review

1. What is a Lollipop Model?
2. Discuss and exemplify the static and the dynamic aspects of a federation. And then explain how we can design a federation based on these aspects.
3. In our case study presented in Sect. 3.2, why do we model a ship as a federate and as an HLA object? What are the differences?
4. Which of domain concepts are modeled as an object and as an interaction?
5. What do we mean by "interfederate communication"?
6. DSEEP/FEDEP methodology does not address the federate development issues specifically. Can you think of reasons why?
7. HLA can be regarded as a "component integration architecture." What do you think is meant by this statement?

References

DMSO. (2002). *High level architecture run-time infrastructure RTI 1.3-Next generation programmer's guide version 6*. s.l.: Department of Defense Modeling and Simulation Office.

IEEE Std 1516.3-2003. (2003). *Standard for IEEE recommended practice for high level architecture (HLA) federation development and execution process (FEDEP)*. s.l.: IEEE.

IEEE Std 1730-2010. (2010). *IEEE recommended practice for distributed simulation engineering and execution process (DSEEP)*. New York, NY: IEEE.

NSTMSS. (2016). Naval surface tactical maneuvering simulation system (NSTMSS) Web site. Retrieved from http://www.ceng.metu.edu.tr/~otopcu/nstmss/. Accessed November 26, 2016.

OMG. (2015). *OMG unified modeling language (OMG UML) version 2.5*. s.l.: Object Management Group.

OpenRTI. (2011). *OpenRTI project website*. Retrieved from https://sourceforge.net/projects/openrti/files/. Accessed October 11, 2016.

Portico. (2016). *The poRTIco project*. Retrieved from http://timpokorny.github.io/public/index.html. Accessed October 11, 2016.

RACoN. (2016). *RACoN project website*. Retrieved from https://sites.google.com/site/okantopcu/racon. Accessed August 30, 2016.

Schmidt, D. (2006). Model-driven engineering. *IEEE Computer, 39*(2), 25–32.

SimGe. (2015). *SimGe web site*. Retrieved from http://www.ceng.metu.edu.tr/~otopcu/simge/. Accessed 2015.

Topçu, O., Adak, M., & Oğuztüzün, H. (2008). A meta model for federation architectures. *Transactions on Modeling and Computer Simulation (TOMACS), 18*(3), 10.

Topçu, O., Durak, U., Oğuztüzün, H., & Yılmaz, L. (2015). *Distributed simulation: A model driven engineering approach* (1st ed.). Cham(Zug): Springer International Publishing.

Topçu, O., & Oğuztüzün, H. (2013). Layered simulation architecture: A practical approach. *Simulation Modelling Practice and Theory, 32*, 1–14.

Part II
Object Model Development

Introduction to Object Model Development

In this chapter, we present how to begin object model construction and we introduce the SimGe tool for the HLA-based distributed simulations. First, we will give an overview of SimGe. And then, we will show how to manage federation development, federation architecture modeling, and object model construction in form of SimGe projects.

4.1 SimGe Overview

SimGe is a design and development environment for High Level Architecture (HLA)-based distributed simulations (IEEE Std 1516-2010 2010; IEEE Std 1516.1-2010 2010; IEEE Std 1516.2-2010 2010). SimGe consists of an object model editor, a federation architecture modeling environment, a report generator, and a code generator. The *object model editor* allows the user to manage the object model and enables the creation and modification of HLA object models and the import and export of the HLA-related files (i.e., Federation Execution Details

(FED),[1] Federation Object Model (FOM) Document Data (FDD)[2]), which contains configuration data for the federation execution. The object model editor is described in Chap. 5 in detail. The code generator automatically generates code for the target platform, which is an HLA runtime infrastructure (RTI) abstraction layer, namely the RTI abstraction component for .NET (RACoN 2016). The architecture of the generated code by SimGe conforms to the layered simulation architecture as described in (Topçu and Oğuztüzün 2013). The *code generator* is described in Chap. 6 in detail. The *report generator* fully generates the OMT tables as per the HLA 1516-2010 specification (IEEE Std 1516.2-2010 2010) for documenting purposes. The details of the report generator are given in Chap. 5. The *federation architecture modeling environment* is used to develop federation architectures, specifically the federation structure. The details of federation architecture modeling are presented in Sect. 4.3.

The major highlights of SimGe:

- State-of-the-art user interface—easy to use,
- Table-style object model editor,
- Support for multiple FOMs,
- Project-based environment,
- Sample projects—provided for a fast start,
- Validation services,
- Compatible with RACoN, and
- Freeware—downloadable from SimGe (2015).

For the installation manual for SimGe, see Appendix A.

4.2 Managing SimGe Projects

SimGe organizes simulation development efforts using a project-based approach. A *simulation project* is the main container and organizer for the federation architecture and code generation. A simulation project is composed of the structural and the behavioral parts of a federation architecture. A project file saves all the development data and the project's settings. Therefore, whenever running SimGe, the user must either create a new project or open an existing one.

4.2.1 The Main User Interface

The project user interface has two main sections divided by a vertical slider. On the right side is the project explorer, and on the left side is the project workspace (see Fig. 4.1).

---

[1]Used by the RTIs that conform to the HLA 1.3 specification.
[2]Used by the RTIs that conform to the HLA 1516 specification.

4.2 Managing SimGe Projects

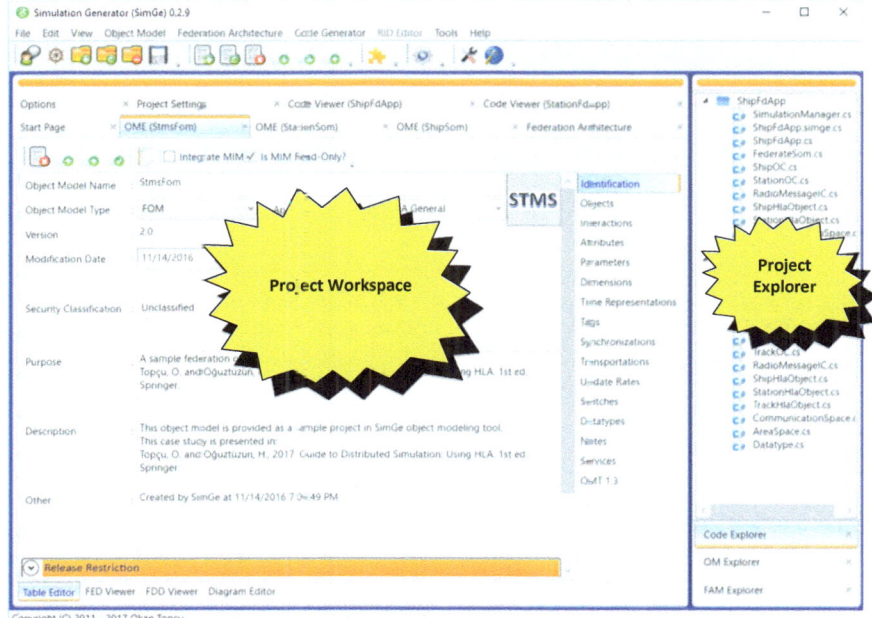

Fig. 4.1 SimGe user interface

The *project workspace* area includes the various workspaces used in the construction of the simulation in a tab view environment. The workspaces currently supported are as follows: (i) new project wizard, (ii) start page, (iii) project settings, (iv) options, (v) object model editor, and (vi) code viewer. The new project wizard is used to create a simulation project from scratch (see the following section). The start page presents the metadata about the project and the object model such as project name and the object model name, respectively (see Sect. 4.2.6). The project settings workspace is used to set the project settings such as the namespace for code generator (see Sect. 4.2.7). The options workspace is where you customize the properties of the SimGe application such as the maximum number of most recently used projects showed in the file menu (see Sect. 4.2.8). The object model editor includes the necessary tools to create and work with HLA 1.3 and HLA 1516-2010 object models and is described in Chap. 5 in detail. The code viewer depicts the generated code files for each federate application and is explained in Chap. 6.

The *project explorer* area includes various explorers. An explorer is a tree view of the simulation project areas such as the object model management. There are mainly three explorers: code explorer, object model (OM) explorer, and federation architecture model (FAM) explorer.

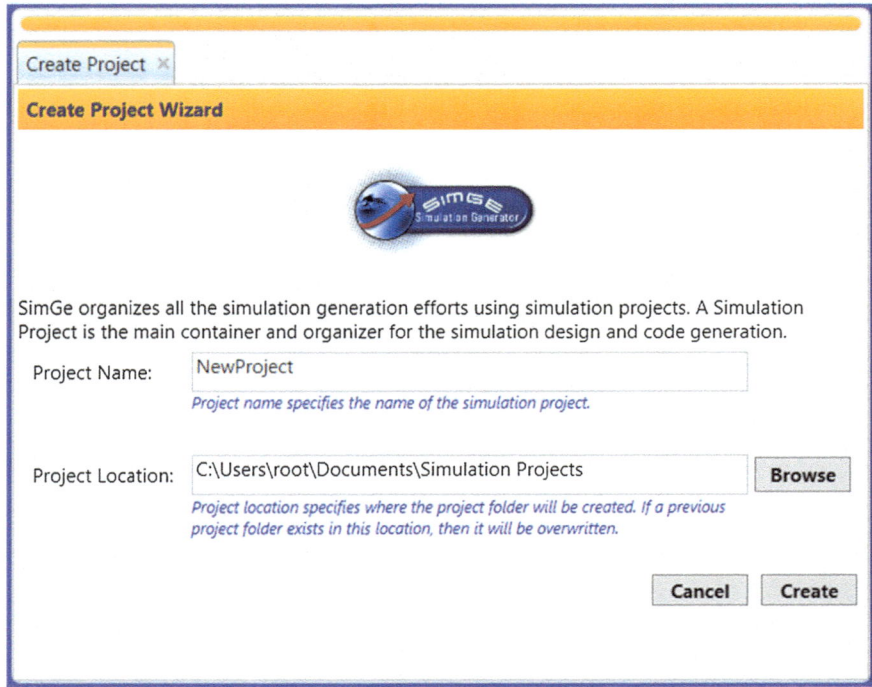

Fig. 4.2 Create project wizard. You can create a new project by specifying its name and its location

4.2.2 Creating a Project

After running the SimGe application, the user can select to create a new project either by using the File menu or by pressing the new project icon at the toolbar menu. The create project wizard is depicted in Fig. 4.2. Here, the user enters a name and selects the root folder, where the project-related folders will be created afterward.

4.2.2.1 Project Folders
Project and its related files are located under the project home folder. The default *project home folder* has the name of the project and is located under the simulation projects folder found in the user's "my documents" folder. The project home folder includes, by default, the folders specified in Table 4.1.

4.2.3 Loading a Project

4.2.3.1 Loading an Existing Project
To load an existing project, press the open project button. An open dialog will appear to select an existing project file. The project files are XML files with ".fap"

4.2 Managing SimGe Projects

Table 4.1 Default folders for a SimGe project

Folder	Explanation
Project home folder	It takes the name of the project and is located under the *simulation projects* folder found in the user's "my documents" folder
FOM	The *FOM Folder* is the home folder where the project object model is kept. It contains the Object Model Template (OMT) documentation and the FOM structure
FAM	The *FAM Folder* is the home folder, where the project federation architecture is kept
SourceCode	The *Source Code Folder* is the container for the generated code source files

extension. After selecting the project file, SimGe will load all the project files. FAP stands for Federation Architecture Project.

4.2.3.2 Loading a Sample Project

SimGe provides two default sample projects, called *Chat Federation* and *Strait Traffic Monitoring Simulation* (STMS). STMS is introduced in Chap. 1 and used as a running example throughout the book.

Chat Federation is an HLA-based distributed interactive application that provides basic chatting functionalities such as selecting a nickname, entering a chat room. A *chat room* is a virtual space where the chat messages are exchanged. By using the *chat client*, a federate application, one can exchange messages with his or her friends in a chat room. Before entering a chat room, you have to pick a unique nickname. The chat client provides a graphical user interface for user interaction and deals with RTI communication. The conceptual view of the application is presented in Fig. 4.3.

4.2.3.3 Loading a Recently Used Project

SimGe keeps the most recently used projects (called *Most Recently Used* (MRU) list) and displays them in File menu. The MRU list currently is kept in an XML file (i.e., RecentProjects.xml) in the operating system common application

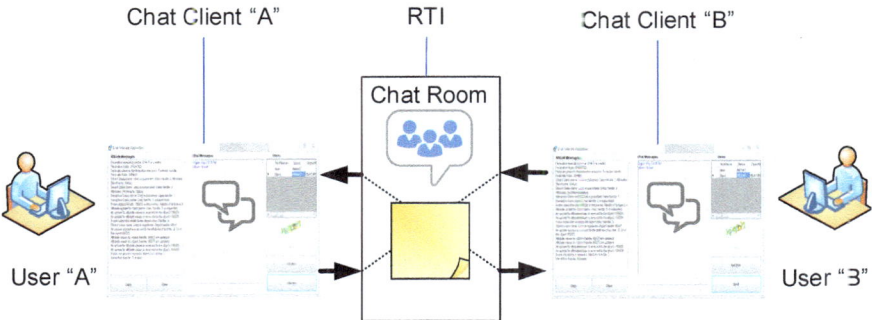

Fig. 4.3 Chat Federation conceptual view

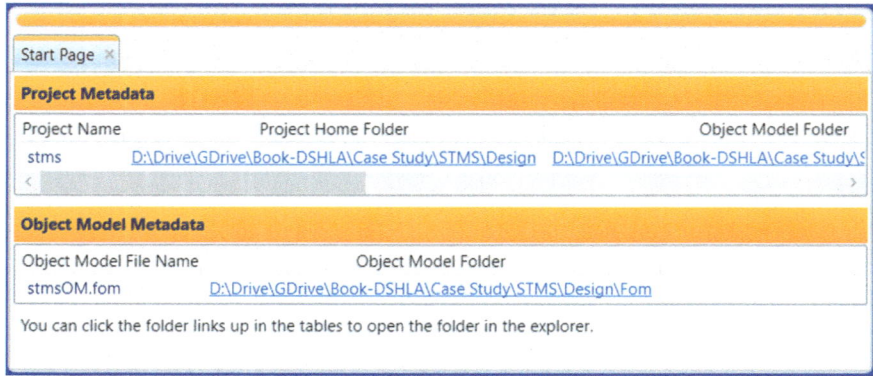

Fig. 4.4 The screen shot of STMS depicting the project start page

data folder (i.e., generally C:\ProgramData\SimGe). The user may adjust the max number of files to be kept using `options` menu.

4.2.4 Saving and Closing a Project

Use the `Save` or `Close` buttons found in the `File` menu. SimGe will save the project file in the project home folder. When the Close button is pressed and there are some open project files that need to be saved, then SimGe will save them before exiting the application. The save process, particularly in the first save, can take a while due to the serialization of the object model.

You can also save a project under a different name using `Save As` command in the `File` menu. Select the folder and a new project name for the project. Note that SimGe saves only the project file and the object model as one can always regenerate the code and the reports.

4.2.5 Project Start Page

After creating a new project, the project user interface is loaded and the *Project Start Page* is displayed (Fig. 4.4). The project start page displays the metadata of the project and the object model. It shows the user the default folders that are set for the project. All folder paths are clickable links; hence, the container folder is opened when clicked on the related link.

4.2.6 Project Settings

Project settings are the project-specific preferences such as the project home folder and they are saved with the project. The project settings tab allows you to configure

4.2 Managing SimGe Projects

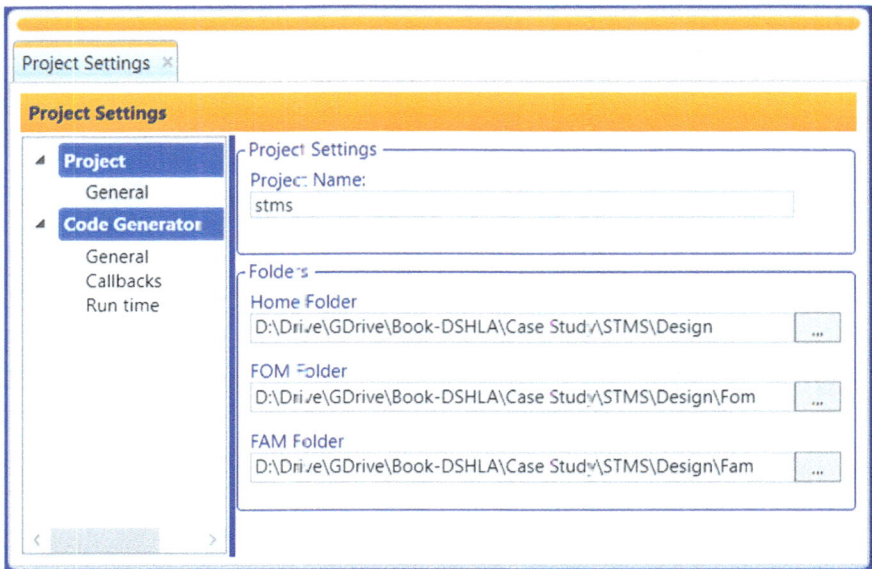

Fig. 4.5 The screen shot for depicting the project settings—specific to STMS

Table 4.2 Preferences for project settings

Parameter	Explanation
Project name	The user can change the project name here: (i) The project name is the default namespace for the code generation (ii) The project name is the file name of the project when saved
Home folder	This is the project home folder. When you change this, all default folders automatically set accordingly
FOM folder	This is the home folder where SimGe object model is saved
FAM folder	This is the home folder where federation architecture model is saved

the project and the code generator settings. See Chap. 6 for details about code generation configuration preferences.

The project part of settings contains (i) the project settings and (ii) folders as depicted in Fig. 4.5.

Table 4.2 summarizes and explains the project settings.

4.2.7 Options

Options are the preferences for the SimGe program such as "Show Status Bar." They are used to configure the SimGe actions and view. All the configuration

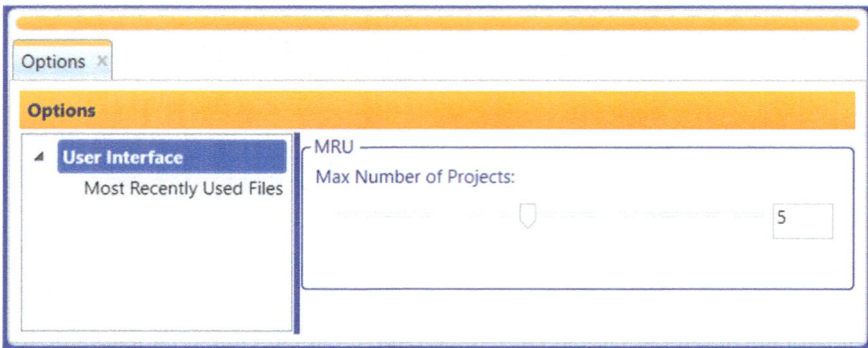

Fig. 4.6 User interface for SimGe options

Table 4.3 MRU options

Parameter	Explanation
Max. number of projects	SimGe keeps track of the recently used projects. The user can adjust the max number of files to be kept. Default value is 5.

options adjusted by the user persist. Options are automatically loaded when the program is started and the changes are automatically stored when the program is closed. The options are kept in an XML file (i.e., options.xml) located in the SimGe installation folder.

A screen shot depicting the MRU options is presented in Fig. 4.6. In this screen, you can specify the maximum number of projects remembered by SimGe using the slider.

Table 4.3 summarizes and explains the MRU options.

4.3 Federation Architecture Modeling

One of the major activities for federation development is to specify the federation design, specifically, the federation architecture. The federation architecture is composed of a federation structure and a federation object model as explained in Chap. 3.

federation architecture modeling environment (FAME) is the design environment for constructing a federation architecture model (FAM), or, in short, Federation Architecture. For the detailed definition of FAM, please refer to (Topçu et al. 2008). For a fully graphical environment that supports modeling formal federation architectures including their behavioral model, see (FAMM 2011).

SimGe supports only modeling a federation structure, where the user can specify the properties of the federation execution and the participating federates.

4.3 Federation Architecture Modeling

4.3.1 Creating a FAM

The user can create a new FAM using the `Federation Architecture` menu as shown in Fig. 4.7. If the project has a federation architecture, then the command for creating the FAM is disabled.

SimGe will adjust a modeling environment, which consists of a new workspace (Federation Architecture) and a new explorer (FAM explorer) to model and to design a federation architecture as shown in Fig. 4.8. The properties shown in Fig. 4.8 are explained in the following sections.

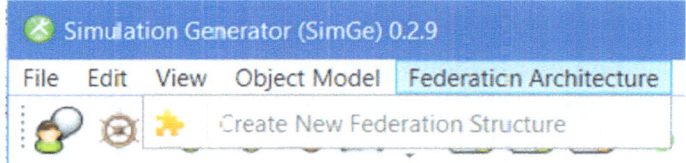

Fig. 4.7 FAM creation. Use the Federation Architecture menu to create a new federation structure. If the project has one, then the command is disabled

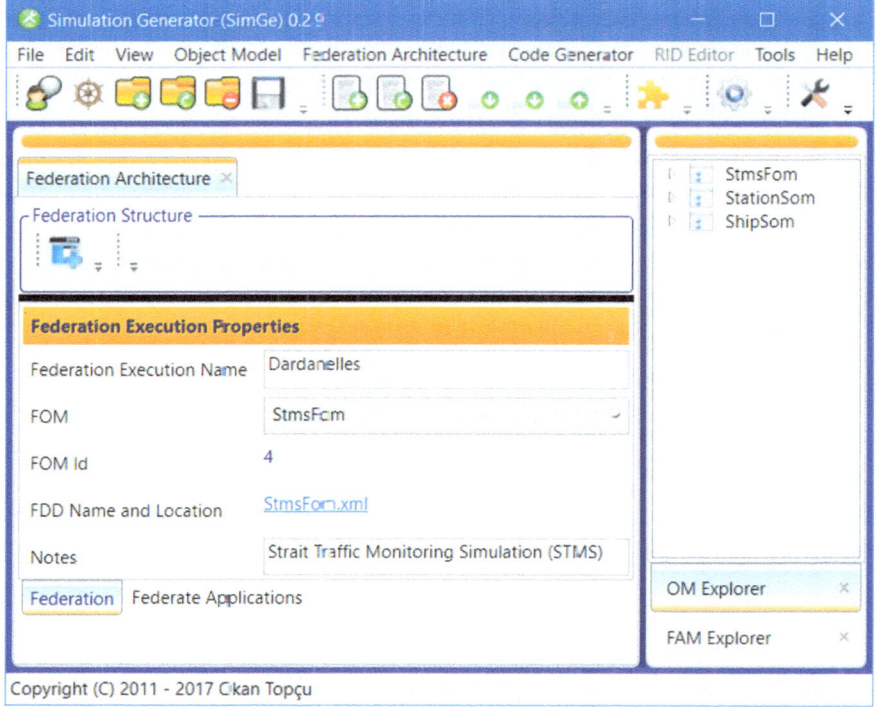

Fig. 4.8 FAME user interface for federation execution properties

4.3.2 Federation Structure

The federation structure is the place where the static structure of the federation is designed. The federation structure contains information about federation execution, such as the location of the FOM Document Data file, the link for the related FOM, and the structure of the federation, where the participating federate applications and their corresponding simulation object models are linked. The details are presented in the following sections.

4.3.2.1 Federation Execution Properties
The federation execution properties include properties such as the name of the federation execution. Table 4.4 summarizes the federation execution properties.

4.3.2.2 Federate Applications
The user can add and remove federate applications to the federation structure. The user interface and the properties of the ShipFdApp of our case study STMS is depicted in Fig. 4.9. FAME toolbar consists a button (the only button) to add a new federate application. Each added application will appear in its own tab. In order to remove a federate application, press the Close button in its tab.

Table 4.5 summarizes the Federate Application Properties.

4.3.2.3 Setting Project FOM
In the OM Explorer, first select the FOM and then right click. In the context menu (as shown in Fig. 4.10), click "Set as Project FOM." Now, you can start working on the object model editor with the selected FOM.

Table 4.4 Federation execution properties

Property	Explanation
Federation execution name	Federation execution name is the name of the federation registered to RTI when the federation is created
FOM	FOM property links the federation execution with the object model. When code is generated, the FDD and FED files will be automatically generated using this FOM
FOM Id	This is internally generated by SimGe. It is read-only. The user cannot set it. It is unique for each object model found in the project
FDD name and location	When code is generated, a FED and a FDD file is generated and placed in the source code folder. When the user clicks the link, a folder explorer will be opened
Notes	Comments about the federation execution

4.3 Federation Architecture Modeling

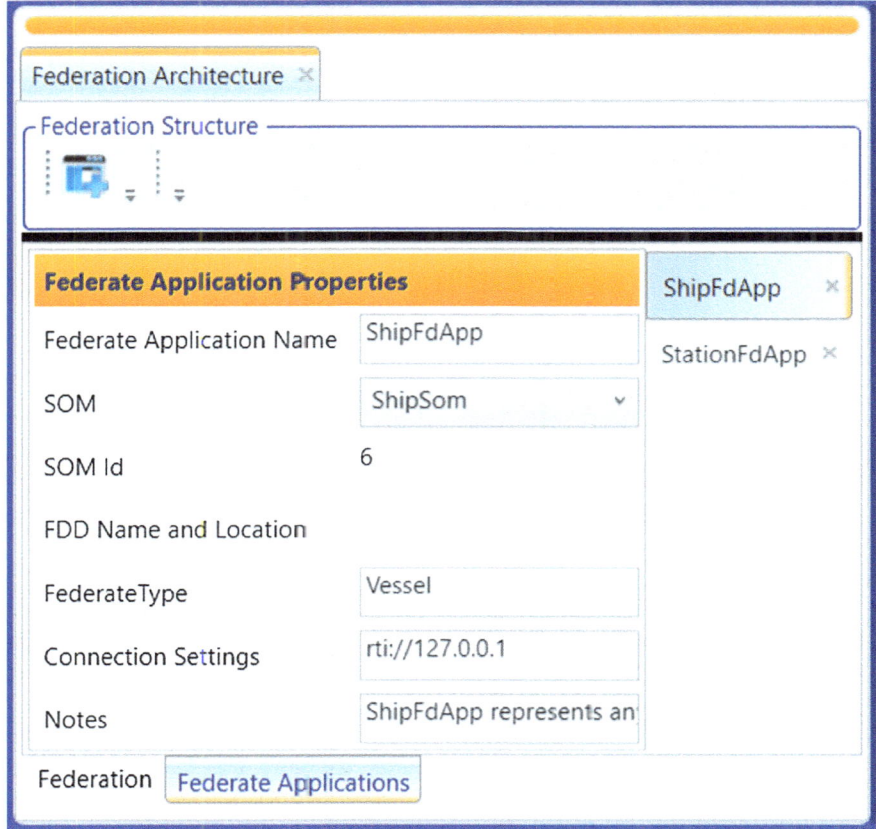

Fig. 4.9 Federate application properties. SOM Id is unique in the project and it is internally generated by SimGe

Table 4.5 Federate application properties

Property	Explanation
Federate application name	Federate application name. In this book, we name the federate applications by adding "FdApp" suffix to a name. For example, for the ship federate application in STMS, we name the application as ShipFdApp
SOM	SOM property links the federate with the object model. When code is generated, the FED/FDD file is automatically generated using this specified SOM
SOM Id	This property is internally used by the SimGe. It is unique for each object model in the project. It is also a read-only property
FDD name and location	This depicts the FED/FDD file generated and its location. The location is a hyperlink where you can click the link to open the containing folder
Notes	Comments about the federate application

Fig. 4.10 Setting Project FOM using the context menu in the OM Explorer

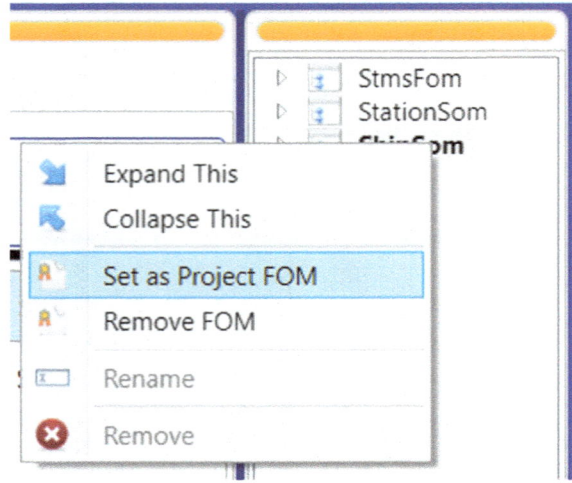

4.4 Summary

Development begins with forming a federation architecture and proceeds with developing an Object Model for federation execution. It is suggested to use an object model development tool that may go by names such as FOM Editor and Object Model Editor. In this chapter, the SimGe modeling environment has been introduced, and in Appendix A, its installation is shown step-by-step. We also explained how to prepare the environment to manage SimGe project files. Now, we are ready to develop an object model. Chapter 5 will explain how to construct an object model in detail.

SimGe is freeware and obtainable from SimGe (2015). Note that here we only covered the major functionalities. For the most functionalities, please refer to its Web site.

4.5 Questions for Review

1. Discuss why we relate a federation execution with a FOM and a federation application with an SOM in the federation structure.
2. SimGe uses a project-based environment for modeling federation architectures. In this regard, what are the advantages of a project-based environment for modeling a federation architecture?
3. Load the sample Chat Federation project and make some changes (e.g., change the project name or add a new object class). As you notice, you can make

changes, but you cannot save/keep the changes you made. Using this sample project, can you figure out how you can create your own customized Chat project?

References

FAMM. (2011). *FAMM website*. [Online] Available at: https://sites.google.com/site/okantopcu/famm. Accessed November 08 2016.

IEEE Std 1516-2010. (2010). *Standard for modeling and simulation (M&S) high level architecture (HLA)—Framework and rules*. New York: IEEE.

IEEE Std 1516.1-2010. (2010). *Standard for modeling and simulation (M&S) high level architecture (HLA)—Federate interface specification*. s.l.: IEEE.

IEEE Std 1516.2-2010. (2010). *Standard for modeling and simulation (M&S) high level architecture (HLA)—Object model template specification*. s.l.: IEEE.

RACoN. (2016). *RACoN project website*. [Online] Available at https://sites.google.com/site/okantopcu/racon. Accessed August 30, 2016.

SimGe. (2015). *SimGe website*. [Online] Available at: https://sites.google.com/site/okantopcu/simge. Accessed April 14, 2017.

Topçu, O., Adak, M., & Oğuztüzün, H. (2008). A metamodel for federation architectures. *Transactions on Modeling and Computer Simulation (TOMACS), 18*(3), 10:1–10:29.

Topçu, O., & Oğuztüzün, H. (2013). Layered simulation architecture: A practical approach. *Simulation Modelling Practice and Theory, 32*, 1–14.

Object Model Construction 5

In this chapter, we will show how to construct an object model, which is a major development step of federation development process. HLA object models are introduced in Chap. 2. Here, we will give the details of object model components by presenting examples for each component. We also show how to create and use them by using the SimGe object model editor. Therefore, the focus will be on the object model editor component of SimGe, rather than the federation architecture specification and code generation components.

5.1 Overview

SimGe *Object Model Editor* (OME) is a fully dressed HLA object model editor that enables you to work with HLA 1.3 and HLA 1516-2010 object models (OMs). The prominent features of OME can be summarized as follows. We will elaborate each feature in the following sections.

- OME supports both HLA OMT 1.3 specification (DoD 1998) and HLA OMT 1516.2010 specification (IEEE Std 1516.2-2010 2010);
- OME allows creation and import of a SimGe project object model;
- OME allows import and export of an HLA 1.3 FED file;
- OME allows import, export, and validation of an HLA 1516.2010 (a.k.a. HLA Evolved) FDD file;
- OME allows modification of the object model using a table-style user interface;
- OME supports interface specification services usage;
- OME validates the user input according to the HLA 1516-2.2010 OMT specification;
- OME supports working with multiple object models at the same time by enabling an OME for each.

SimGe provides three options to begin the construction of an object model (i.e., FOM and SOM) for the simulation project. The user can opt to construct an object model (OM) by the following:

- Option-1: developing it from scratch (i.e., by creating an empty object model);
- Option-2: loading a previously saved SimGe object model; or
- Option-3: importing an existing FED file or FDD file [e.g., a generic FOM, i.e., RPR-FOM file (SISO 2015)].

The following sections explain how to begin the construction of an object model using these options.

5.2 Creating a Federation Object Model from Scratch

After creating a new project, you can start constructing the object models (i.e., FOM and SOM) for your federation and the federate applications. As said before, you can either create an empty object model (option-1), load a previous SimGe object model (option-2), or import a FED or FDD file (option-3) as depicted in Fig. 5.1 using the `Object Model` file menu. When the user selects the "Create New FOM/SOM," an empty object model is created and initialized using HLA Standard Management and Initialization Module (MIM) file (IEEE 1516-2010 Downloads 2010).

The user can create multiple object models. A separate OME will be dedicated to each federation object model for editing so that the user can work on the SOMs of interrelated federates without creating any inconsistency.

5.3 Loading an Existing SimGe Object Model

Remember that SimGe provides a project-based environment for federation development. To promote the modular structuring of a project, its parts, such as the federation architecture and the object model, are separately kept. Thus, the object

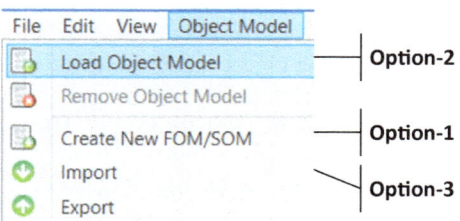

Fig. 5.1 Beginning to construct an object model. Here, you have three options. You can either create a new object model, load an existing one, or you can import a FED or FDD file

model is saved as a separate file to increase its reusability. Consequently, you can reuse an object model in any SimGe project.

SimGe object model is an internal representation specific to SimGe. It does not conform to HLA 1516-2010 OMT or data interchange format (DIF) schemas. The object model of a SimGe simulation project is kept in an XML file in the project FOM folder, named "Fom" in the project home folder. (See Chap. 4 for default folders for a SimGe project, and see Appendix A for file extensions for SimGe-related files.) The name of the file is the name of the project with the suffix "OM." You always work with an object model in OME, which is a workspace of SimGe user interface. OME allows you to modify the object model content in an OMT table view/style.

If you want to use a previously saved object model file, you can import the existing file by using the "Load Object Model" menu item. The imported OM file is copied to the project FOM folder.

5.4 Removing Object Model

You can remove the object model from the project and then create, load, or import another one. When you remove the object model, all opened OMEs and their related federation object models will be discarded. Although the saved object model will remain, it will not be a part of the project anymore. Of course, you can reload it to relate with your project.

5.5 Importing a FED/FDD File

After creating a new project, the user can import an existing FED/FDD file by selecting the Import FED/FDD menu item from the Object Model menu or by pressing Import FED/FDD button in toolbar. The user can select the FED/FDD file by browsing folders on the open file dialog (Fig. 5.2). Please note that SimGe does not copy the FED/FDD file to the project folder.

For a successful import, the FED file format must conform to the HLA FED file specification (DoD 1998) and the FDD file must conform to the HLA1516-2010 FDD schema (IEEE1516.1-2010 FDD Schema 2010). The FDD importer validates the source FDD file using the HLA1516-2010 FDD schema and reports the validation results. See Sect. 5.8.10 for more on validation.

After importing a FED/FDD file, the user can edit the OM and then the code generator is ready to generate SOM code for the federate application.

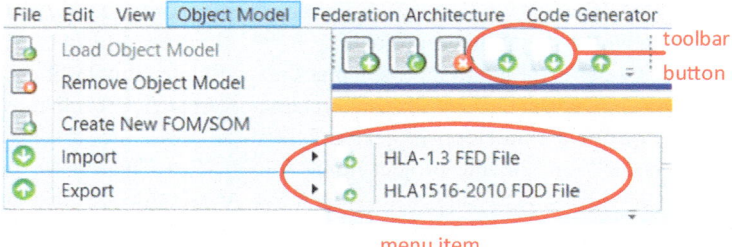

Fig. 5.2 Importing a FED or FDD file. You can use either the menu item or the toolbar buttons

5.6 Exporting the FED/FDD Files

SimGe supports exporting a FED or an FDD file as well as importing it. This is done by using the `Export` menu item in the `Object Model` menu. As SimGe supports multiple object models, the export utility asks for the source object model and the target format as depicted in Fig. 5.3.

Each object model can also be exported by using its related OME toolbar. See the next section for more on this point.

FDD Exporter validates the generated FDD file and reports the result to the user as shown in Fig. 5.4.

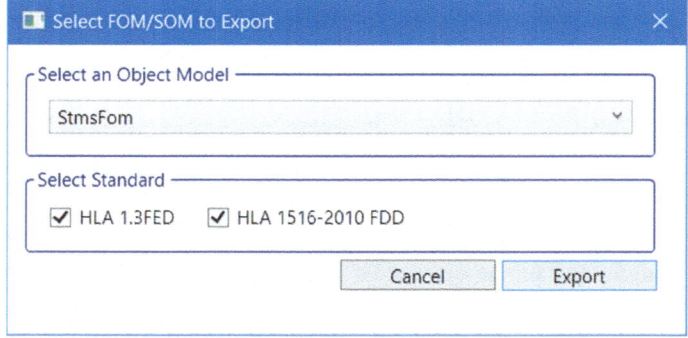

Fig. 5.3 Configuration screen when exporting the object model to a FED or FDD

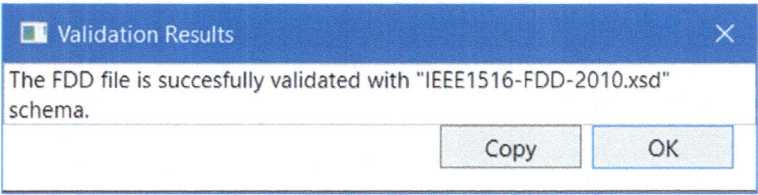

Fig. 5.4 Dialog showing the validation results

5.7 Object Model Editor

The object model content is displayed in three forms: (i) as a tabular form in a table editor that supports OMT, (ii) as a text view (FED viewer and FDD viewer), and (iii) as a diagram using a diagram editor (some tools support diagrams for representing object models but this feature is not implemented in the current version of SimGe).

OME supports working with multiple object models at the same time. This feature provides some important benefits:

- First, you need a FOM and a SOM per federate application. Consider the STMS application, in its FOM, the Ship object class is defined as both *Publishable* and *Subscribable*. In the SOM of the ShipFdApp, the Ship object class is defined as only *Publishable*, whereas the Ship object class is defined as only *Subscribable* in the SOM of the StationFdApp. Moreover, the code is generated according to the definitions with respect to the related SOM for each federate application. So, the ship federate can publish and the station federate can subscribe to it.
- Second, you can work with multiple versions of an object model. This feature allows you flexibility in the federation development. So, you can switch to back and forth between SOM and FOM versions by relating them with the federation or with the federate, respectively.
- Third, remember that HLA Evolved supports multiple FOM modules. So, you can work with multiple modules in your project in one place.

You can add many object models to the project. Each object model can be worked in its own OME. The OM workspace, as introduced in Chap. 4, is added to the project user interface as a new tab (see Fig. 5.5).

5.7.1 OME Toolbar

Each OME has its own toolbar (see Fig. 5.6). The major toolbar commands are the following: remove current federation object model, export to FED/FDD, validate

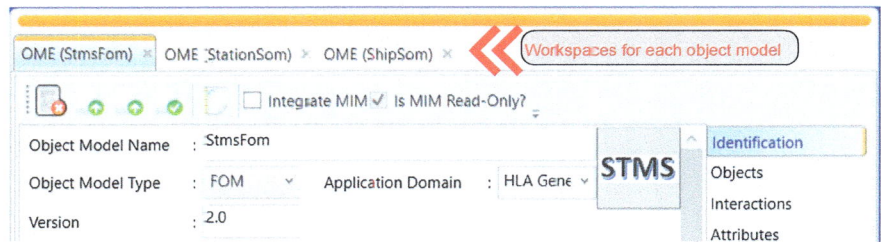

Fig. 5.5 Multiple OMEs for each object model in the project

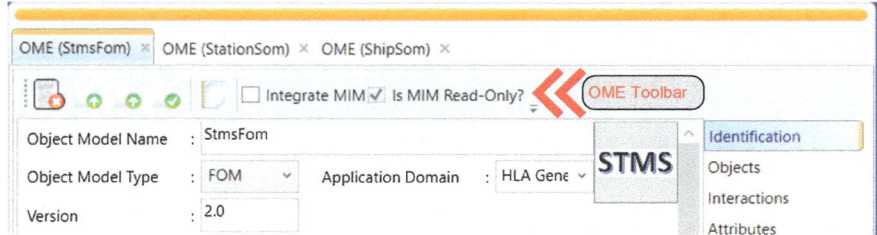

Fig. 5.6 OME toolbar that enables actions such as export and import

FDD, generate OMT report, integrate MIM, and set MIM as read-only. All these commands are specific to the object model opened in that OME.

The first button on the OME toolbar is used to remove only the related federation object model from the project. Please note that this is an irreversible action as each model in OME is kept within the SimGe object model. When you remove it from the project, it no longer is in the SimGe object model. As a precaution, you can always export the federation object model as an FDD before removing.

Another way to remove the current object model is to use the commands on the OM Explorer, see Sect. 5.12.

5.8 Table Editor

The Table editor presents a working area to edit the OMT tables. It allows the user to perform basic table operations, namely, create, read, update, and delete, known by the acronym CRUD. The Table editor is composed of all the OMT tables found in the HLA 1516.2010 OMT specification tables (IEEE Std 1516.2-2010 2010). Moreover, it also supports the HLA OMT 1.3 specification tables (DoD 1998) for routing spaces.

Some rows in the OMT tables are read-only rows, and they are indicated with a lock symbol in the header of the row and the row is grayed (see Fig. 5.7). The read-only rows are the compulsory built-in OMT elements (e.g., `ObjectRoot`, `RTIprivate`) or the MOM elements (e.g., `Manager`, `Federation`, `Federate`). The white rows are eligible for CRUD operations.

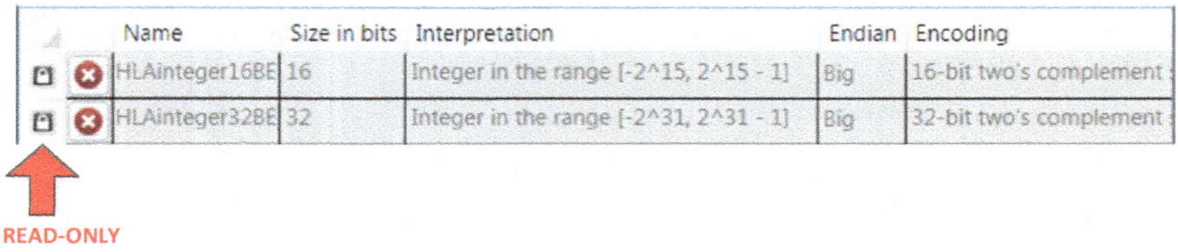

Fig. 5.7 Read-only OMT elements

5.8 Table Editor 117

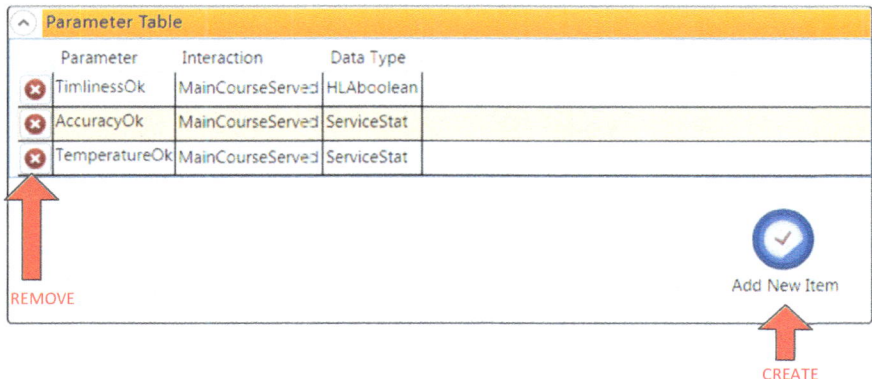

Fig. 5.8 Adding/removing an OMT element

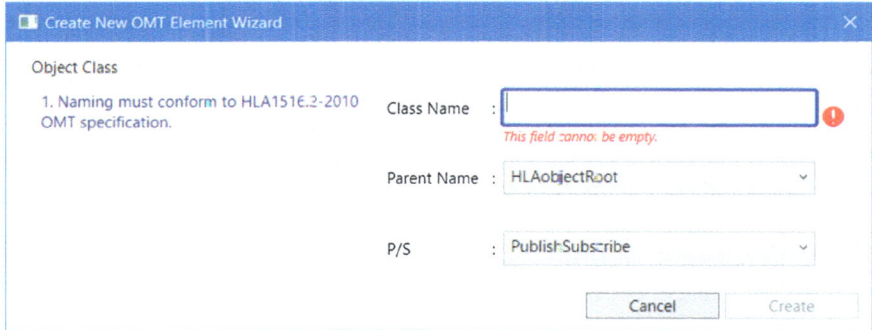

Fig. 5.9 Object class data input screen. The user interface warns you when a compulsory field is missing

The user can create a new OMT Element by clicking the "add new item" button at the end of each table (see Fig. 5.8). To delete an OMT element, simply select the row and then click the remove icon (found in each row) or press the delete key on keyboard.

A data input wizard for each element is popped up as shown in Fig. 5.9. All data input is validated according to (IEEE Std 1516.2-2010 2010). In case of a validation error, you are informed about the error with a possible cause (e.g., "this field cannot be empty").

This wizard is only used for the creation of an OMT element. To modify an existing one, double click the cell where modification is required.

Mostly, the columns in an OMT table provide all the possible values that you can select. For example, when setting the Parent of an object class, only the object classes defined so far in the OMT are shown to you (Fig. 5.10).

Fig. 5.10 Value selection. In most cases, SimGe will provide the possible values for an element

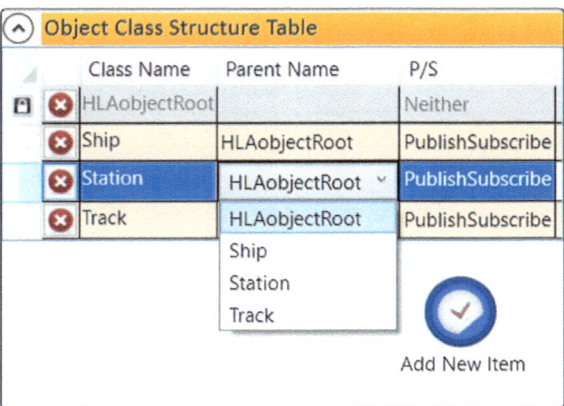

Whenever you save the project, the object model (without MOM elements) is also saved.

For a formal semantics of all tables and columns, refer to (IEEE Std 1516.2-2010 2010; DoD 1998). The following sections cover the major elements and how we define them in SimGe.

5.8.1 Object Model Identification

The OM identification interface consists of an area for object model metadata and explorers for points of contact (POCs), use history, keywords, and references of the object model. Figure 5.11 presents a screen shot of the GUI for a well-known example, the Restaurant example, found in the specification (IEEE Std 1516.2-2010 2010; IEEE 1516.2-2010 Restaurant FOM Module 2010).

5.8.1.1 POC
The POCs explorer displays all the POCs in a table view. When you click a user row, additional details about the user showing the phone numbers and e-mails are displayed (see Fig. 5.12). You can add, delete, or modify. The predefined POC types are provided as you can define new ones.

5.8.1.2 Keywords
The keywords table displays the taxonomy and keyword value (see Fig. 5.13). You can add, delete, or modify new/existing keywords.

5.8.1.3 References
The References table keeps links to external resources. A reference is composed of a reference type and an identification (Fig. 5.14). In general, a type identifies the type of the resource such as a Web resource or a text document, while the identification field holds the location of the resource with the help of an identifier

5.8 Table Editor

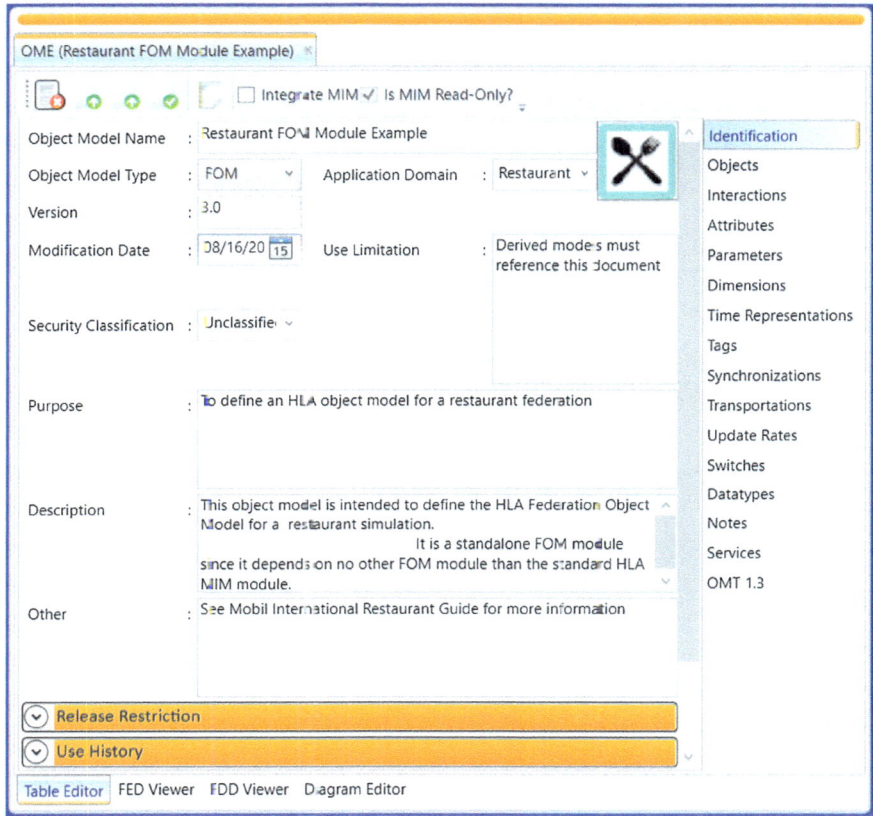

Fig. 5.11 Table editor—identification information for restaurant federation. Here, you can see all the metadata of the object model, along with its icon

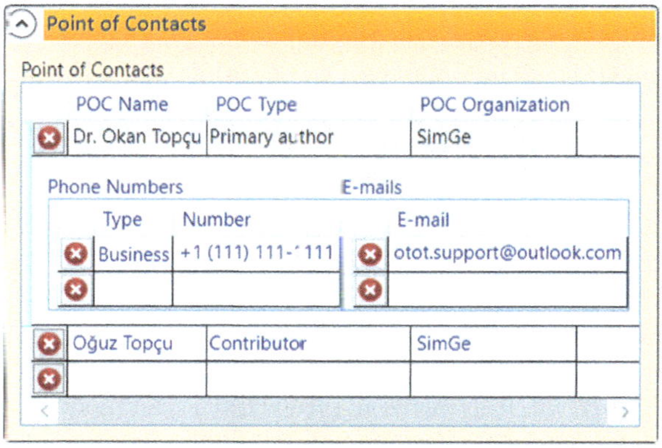

Fig. 5.12 POC details for STMS federation. When you click on a POC, then the details form is expanded for information such as phone numbers

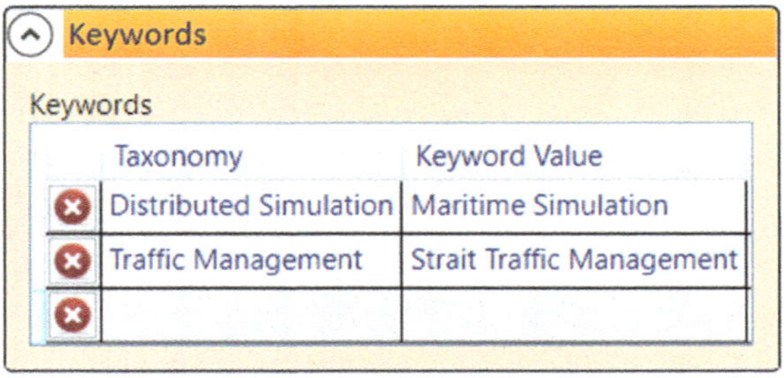

Fig. 5.13 Keywords for STMS federation

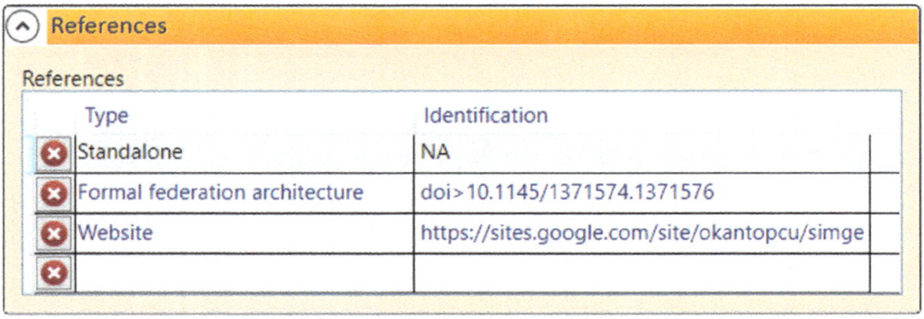

Fig. 5.14 References for STMS

(pointer), for instance, in the form of a DOI for an academic article, a URL for a Web document, or an ISBN for a book. In specific cases, where the object model is intended as a FOM/SOM module, then the type can be either *standalone*, *composed from*, or *dependency*. If the type is stand-alone, then the identification field must have a null value, which is represented with "NA." In case of dependency, the identification field must specify the name of all the dependent modules. In case of type is "composed from," then the identification field provides the names of all the models that are composed to build this model.

5.8.1.4 Use History
The Use History table displays the history of the object model (see Fig. 5.15). This table is very useful in keeping track of the past applications where this object model is employed.

5.8.1.5 Glyph
SimGe fully supports glyph import and export from an FDD file. At the top-right, the user can set a new glyph for the object model by clicking the image area. The glyph attributes, namely, height, width, and type, are automatically set.

5.8 Table Editor

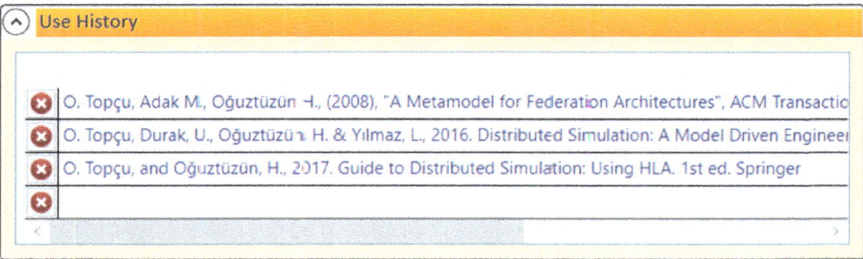

Fig. 5.15 Use history for STMS

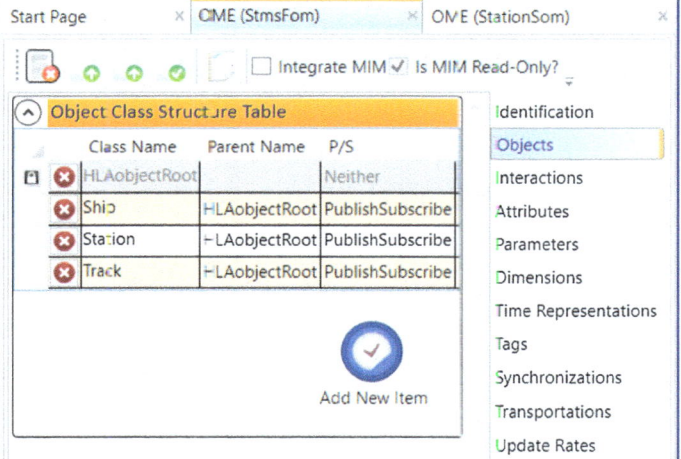

Fig. 5.16 Object classes, part of the FOM of STMS

5.8.2 Objects

The objects tab is used to edit the HLA object classes. A screen shot showing the object classes of STMS is presented in Fig. 5.16.

You can create a new object class by clicking add-new-item button at the end of each table. The Parent field is used to build object class hierarchy. Therefore, the parent of the newly created class must always be set (if it is a top class, then its parent is set as the HLAobjectRoot). The class hierarchical relationships (class-subclass relation) among the HLA classes in SimGe are defined differently from the OMT specification counterpart. In SimGe, the hierarchical relationships are defined simply by specifying the parent of each class, whereas in the OMT specifications, the hierarchical relationships are defined by column order (see Chap. 2). The P/S field shows the publish and subscribe status. It is set to Neither by default, and you can change it according to your needs. For the data input screen, see Fig. 5.9.

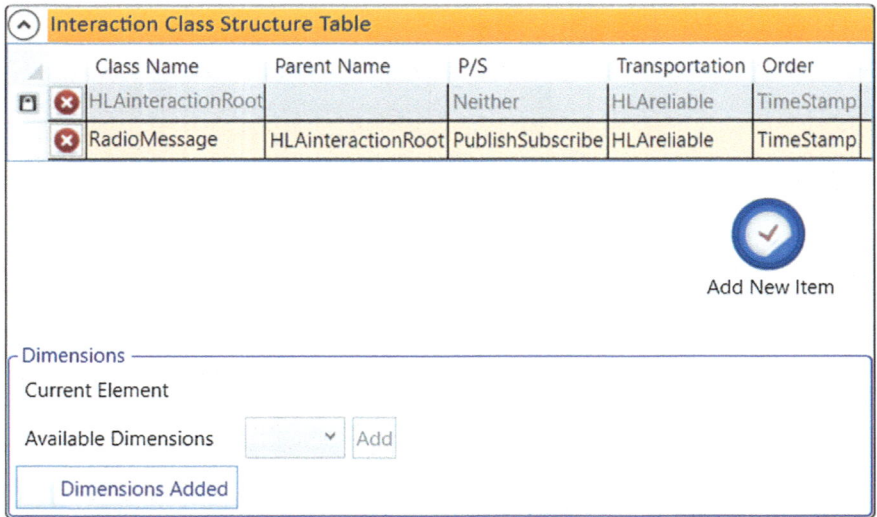

Fig. 5.17 Interaction classes of the STMS FOM

5.8.3 Interactions

The *Interaction Class Structure Table* is used to create/edit/delete the HLA interaction classes. A screen shot for STMS interaction classes is shown in Fig. 5.17. The interaction class structure table includes a default interaction class, HLAinteractionRoot, which acts as the root for the class hierarchy. The hierarchy between the interaction classes is set up using the Parent field as in the Object Class Table.

The Interaction Class Structure Table provided here is slightly different than its OMT counterpart. In HLA OMT, the interaction class structure template only allows to specify the P/S capabilities for interaction classes. But, in SimGe, we allow to specify transportation, ordering, and dimensions properties in the Interaction Class Structure Table instead of the Parameters Table, since these properties apply to all the parameters of an interaction class. In other words, the set of interactions parameters is treated as an indivisible unit. The dimensions, transportation, and the order (of delivery) specified for an interaction is valid for all its parameters. Therefore, in SimGe, these properties are defined in the Interaction Class Structure Table, differently from the OMT specification.

The order of delivery for interaction and its parameters can be either selected as *receive* or *timestamp* to indicate a receive order (RO) or a timestamp order (TSO) message, respectively (see Chap. 2 for the order of delivery). The transportation field specifies the transportation method for the interaction. The values for the transportation field comes from the *Transportation Table* (see Sect. 5.8.11).

Each attribute and interaction class has a set of dimensions (specified in the *Dimensions Table*—see Sect. 5.8.6). In the table view, the dimensions are provided

5.8 Table Editor

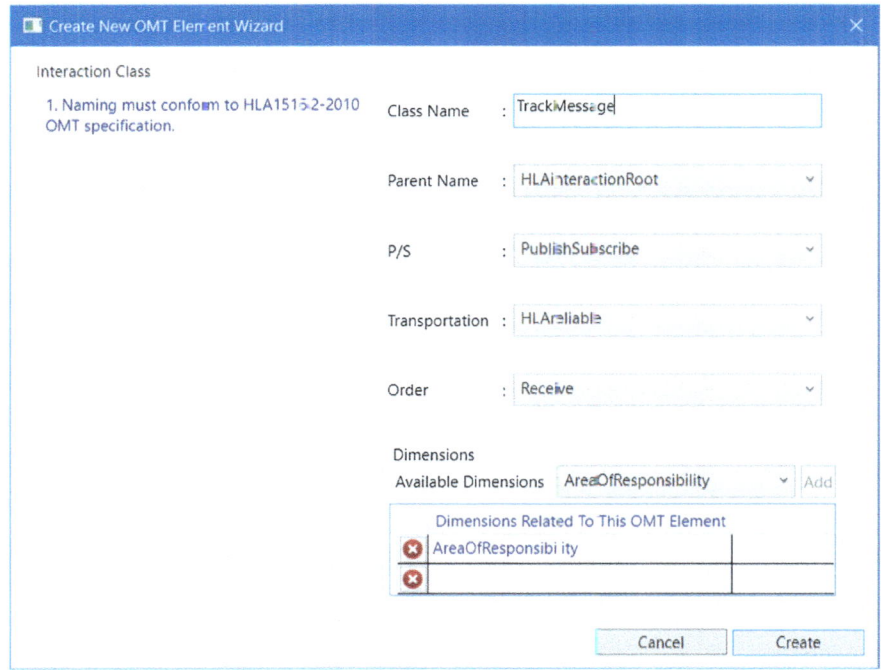

Fig. 5.18 Interaction class data input user interface

in a detail table when the related row of attribute or interaction is selected as shown in Fig. 5.17. The user can add dimensions to the selected attribute/class from the available dimensions presented in a drop-down menu. If you want to remove a dimension, then just select the dimension you want to delete in the table and then press delete key. The dimensions of the attributes and the interactions can also be added to the dimension set, while creating the attribute/interaction class element using the data input screen as shown in Fig. 5.18.

5.8.4 Attributes

The attributes tab is used to edit HLA object attributes. A screen shot depicting the attributes of the STMS FOM is presented in Fig. 5.19 Notice that HLAprivilegeToDeleteObject is default for the HLAobjectRoot (therefore, it is grayed) (see Chap. 2 on how to delete objects). Another important thing to do is to associate an attribute with an object class. For instance, the attribute CallSign is an attribute of the Ship object class. Dimensions for the selected attribute are provided in the detail table where the user can add or remove a dimension (see Sect. 5.8.6 to how to specify a dimension).

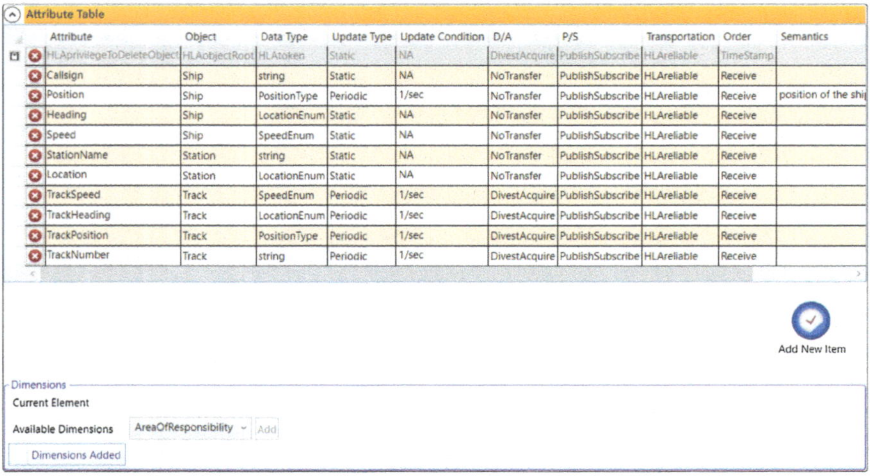

Attribute	Object	Data Type	Update Type	Update Condition	D/A	P/S	Transportation	Order	Semantics
HLAprivilegeToDeleteObject	HLAobjectRoot	HLAtoken	Static	NA	DivestAcquire	PublishSubscribe	HLAreliable	TimeStamp	
Callsign	Ship	string	Static	NA	NoTransfer	PublishSubscribe	HLAreliable	Receive	
Position	Ship	PositionType	Periodic	1/sec	NoTransfer	PublishSubscribe	HLAreliable	Receive	position of the shi
Heading	Ship	LocationEnum	Static	NA	NoTransfer	PublishSubscribe	HLAreliable	Receive	
Speed	Ship	SpeedEnum	Static	NA	NoTransfer	PublishSubscribe	HLAreliable	Receive	
StationName	Station	string	Static	NA	NoTransfer	PublishSubscribe	HLAreliable	Receive	
Location	Station	LocationEnum	Static	NA	NoTransfer	PublishSubscribe	HLAreliable	Receive	
TrackSpeed	Track	SpeedEnum	Periodic	1/sec	DivestAcquire	PublishSubscribe	HLAreliable	Receive	
TrackHeading	Track	LocationEnum	Periodic	1/sec	DivestAcquire	PublishSubscribe	HLAreliable	Receive	
TrackPosition	Track	PositionType	Periodic	1/sec	DivestAcquire	PublishSubscribe	HLAreliable	Receive	
TrackNumber	Track	string	Periodic	1/sec	DivestAcquire	PublishSubscribe	HLAreliable	Receive	

Fig. 5.19 Interface showing the attributes table related to the STMS FOM

Data input screen is shown in Fig. 5.20. Update type can be *static* (update is provided upon registration and when requested), *periodic* (update at regular time intervals), or *conditional* (update when a condition is met). If the federate does not provide a value, then the update type will be "*NA*." In the update condition column, for periodic types, we need to identify the rate for the number of updates per time unit (e.g., 1/s), and for condition types, we need to identify the condition, if the update type is static or NA, then NA shall be entered. Each attribute may have a data type specified in the Data Types Table (see Sect. 5.8.14). Regarding the ownership field, see the following section.

5.8.4.1 Ownership Management

Each attribute must have a designation of its ownership transferability. The D/A column indicates this property, where D/A stands for *Divest/Acquire*. The ownership of an attribute can be specified as one of the elements of {D, A, N, DA}. *Divest* (D) is used to specify that some federate that publishes the object class attribute can divest the ownership of an instance of this attribute. *Acquire* (A) specifies some federate, capable of publishing the related object class, can acquire the ownership. DA shows that some federate is capable of both divesting and acquiring the ownership. Finally, N means *no transfer*, meaning that the ownership of the instance of the attribute is not transferable. Chapter 9 shows how to implement divesting and acquiring ownership.

5.8 Table Editor

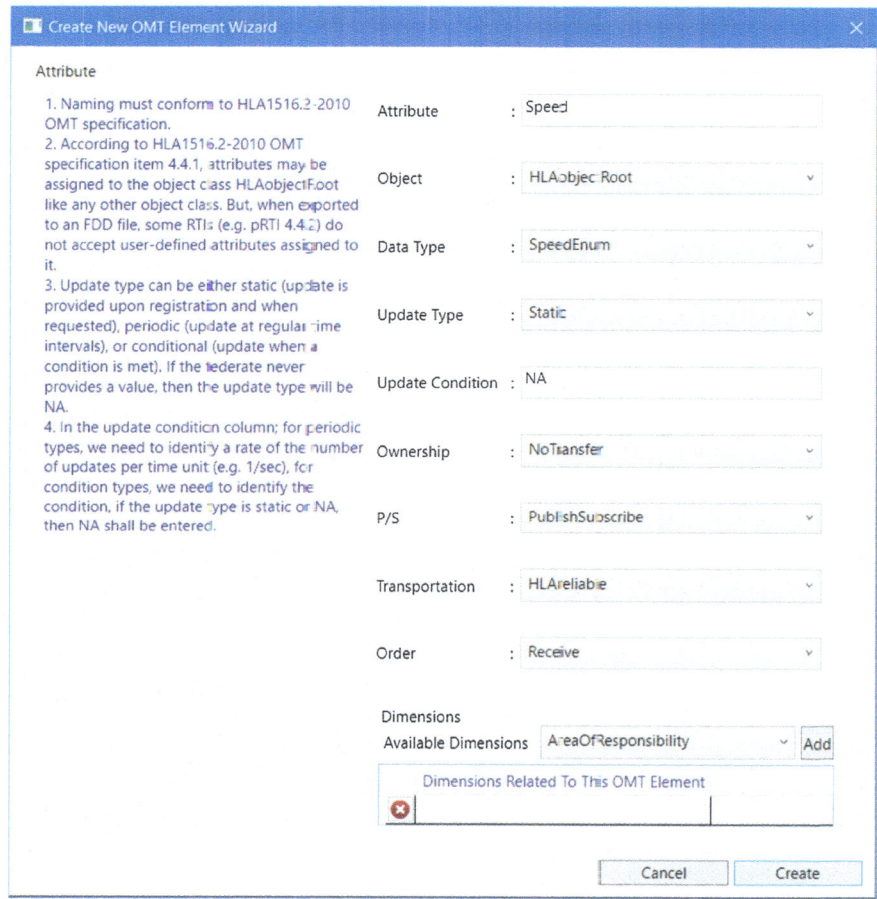

Fig. 5.20 Data input screen for attributes

5.8.5 Parameters

The parameters tab is used to edit HLA interaction parameters. Each parameter belongs to an interaction. A screen shot is presented in Fig. 5.21. The data type of a parameter must be specified in the data type table. For example, the data type of Message parameter of RadioMessage interaction is specified in the *Array Datatype Table*. Data input screen is shown in Fig. 5.22.

5.8.6 Dimensions

A common agreement among federates is required for a successful implementation of data distribution policy in the federation execution. In this regard, dimensions are

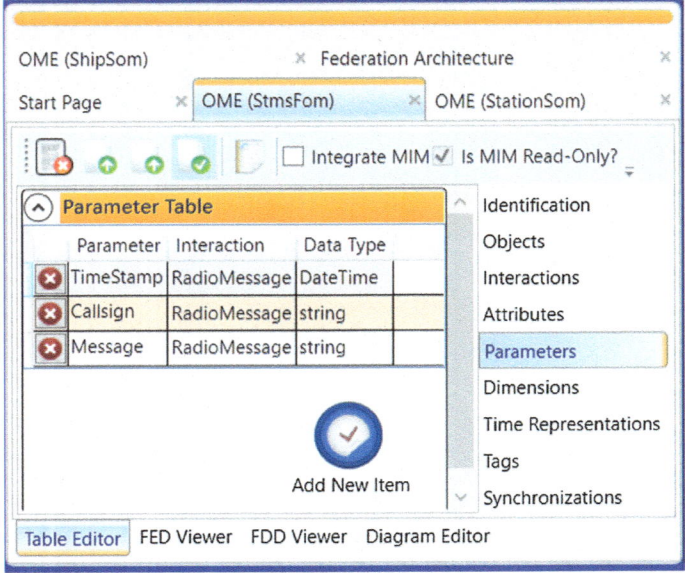

Fig. 5.21 Parameters related to the STMS FOM

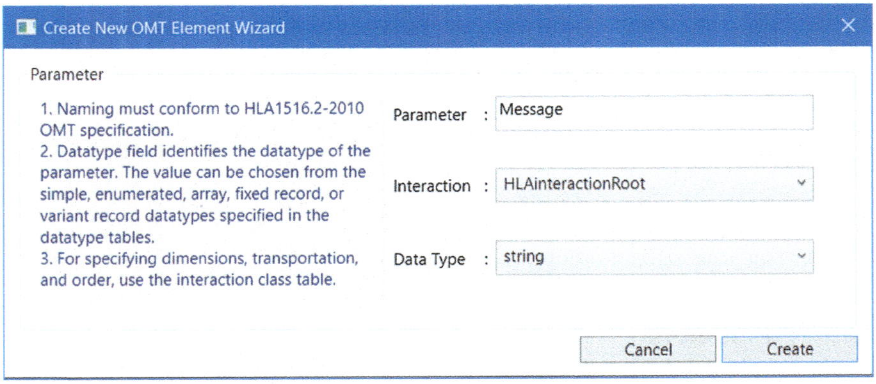

Fig. 5.22 Parameter data input screen

the essential DDM concepts of this agreement. The dimensions of a FOM are specified in the Dimensions Table of the OMT. In SimGe, the *dimensions* tab is used to create and edit dimensions as depicted in Fig. 5.23.

Each dimension has an interval beginning from zero (this is fixed) to an upper bound (specified by you). Data input screen is shown in Fig. 5.24. A unique name must be given to each dimension. A dimension data type can be either a simple data type or an enumerated data type (see Sect. 5.8.14 for data types).

5.8 Table Editor

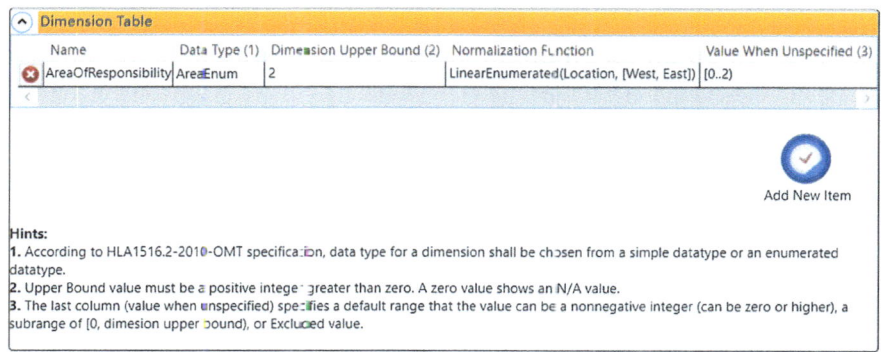

Fig. 5.23 Dimensions defined in STMS FOM

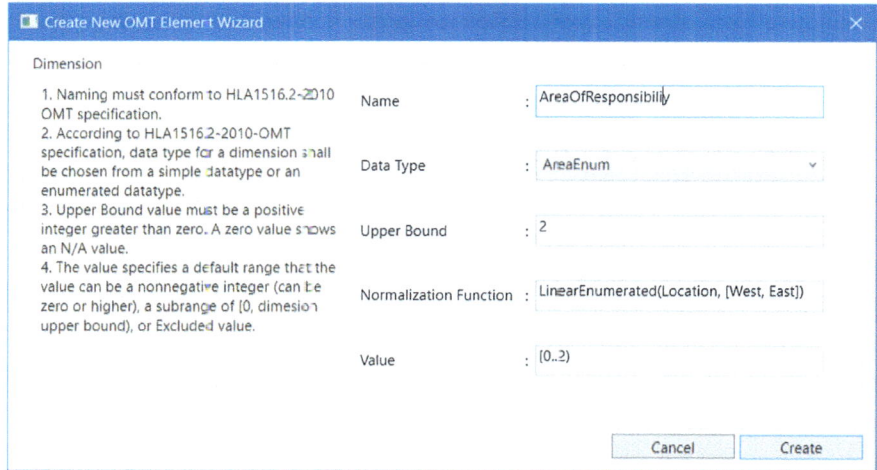

Fig. 5.24 Data input screen for dimensions

Normalization function defines how to normalize (map) the federate's view of the region's bounding coordinates (e.g., a domain value) to subranges of the dimension interval specified (remember that a dimension lower bound is always fixed to 0). Some common normalization functions are listed in Annex B of IEEE Std 1516.2-2010 (2010). See Chap. 9 for how we use the dimensions to create distribution regions and how a normalization function maps a value.

After specifying the dimensions, the attributes and the interactions can be associated with a set of dimensions defined here.

Time Representation Table		
Category	Data Type	Semantics
timeStamp	HLAinteger64Time	Default time representation in secs
lookahead	HLAinteger64Time	Default time interval in secs (non-negative)

Fig. 5.25 Time representations

5.8.7 Time Representations

As the representation of the HLA logical times (points in the HLA time axis) and timestamps (attached to time-related messages) requires the same data types, we need an agreement on how logical times are represented in the federation among the federates. The Time Representations Table provides these representations. By default, two types of time representation categories (i.e., timestamp and lookahead) are defined (Fig. 5.25). The user cannot add new ones or delete the existing ones. Yet, the (abstract) data type and semantics cells of two time representations are available for modification. Remember that while timestamp is a HLA time (i.e., a point in time axis), lookahead is a time interval. The data type for a lookahead must normally provide nonnegative numbers. Zero lookahead is allowed for handling algebraic calculations in models (where time does not progress), but the loops in calculations require special treatment. See Chap. 2 for the details of time concepts and Chap. 9 for how to implement time management policies.

5.8.8 User-Supplied Tags

The user-supplied tags are employed to add additional coordination and control for specific HLA services such as indicating a reason for deleting/removing an object. The User-Supplied Tags Table provides all the default tag categories (see Fig. 5.26). The user cannot add new ones or delete the existing ones. Furthermore, only the data type and semantics cells of the present ones are available for modification. An empty value for data type and semantics column corresponds to NA value meaning no tag is specified for the service category.

5.8.9 Synchronization

Synchronization mechanism is provided to synchronize the federation-wide activities at designated points during the federation execution. A *synchronization point* is used to specify a synchronized activity. The synchronization points are declared in the OMT Synchronization Table. In SimGe, the synchronizations tab is used to edit synchronizations. You can add, modify, or delete a synchronization point.

5.8 Table Editor

Fig. 5.26 User-supplied tags for STMS

User-supplied Tag Table		
Category	Data Type	Semantics
updateReflectTag		
sendReceiveTag		
deleteRemoveTag	string	Reason for deletion
divestitureRequestTag		
divestitureCompletionTag		
acquisitionRequestTag		
requestUpdateTag		

The *Synchronization Table* is only used to document the synchronization agreements for federation. Each synchronization point is specified with a label. The tag data type column indicates the data type for a user-supplied tag. If a user-supplied tag is not provided, then the value of tag data type will be "NA." Then, the value of the capability column must be "NA" for all FOMs. For SOMs, the user may select any provided enumeration value such as "Achieve." Data input screen is shown in Fig. 5.27.

See the next section for an example of declaring synchronization points.

5.8.10 Case Study: Synchronization

In our case study, STMS, the synchronization points are used to synchronize the speed of all ships in the federation. A station federate may announce a speed limitation for the ships in the strait in case of an emergency event. This scenario is implemented using the synchronization points. Figure 5.28 depicts a Synchronization Table for SOM of the StationFd, whereas the StationFd has the capability to register these synchronization points to control the speed of all the ships in the strait.

On the other hand, when a synchronization point is announced, the ship federates must achieve this request by adjusting their speeds as shown in Fig. 5.29. The ship federates do not have synchronization point registration capability.

In Chap. 9, we show how we implement these defined synchronization points in the federation execution.

5.8.11 Transportations

Transportation is a kind of "quality of service" specification for the transportation of interactions and attribute values. Two transportations are available by default, namely, *HLAreliable* and *HLAbestEffort*. As implied by their names, `Reliable` indicates a reliable communication in the sense of TCP (Transmission Control

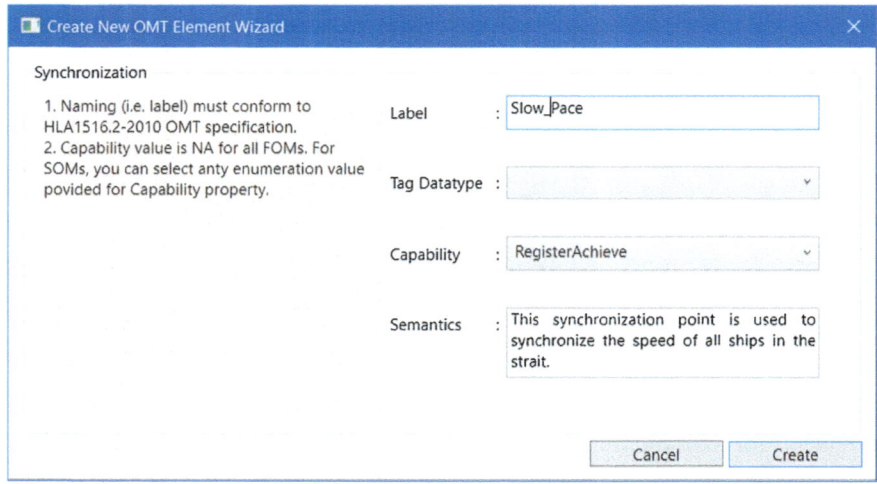

Fig. 5.27 Data input screen for defining a synchronization point

Synchronization Table			
Label	Tag Datatype	Capability	Semantics
❌ SlowPace	string	Register	This is used to limit the speed of ships in case of emergency
❌ FastPace	string	Register	This is used to limit the speed of ships in case of emergency

Fig. 5.28 Synchronization points for StationFdApp. Notice that a station federate has only register capability

Synchronization Table			
Label	Tag Datatype	Capability	Semantics
❌ SlowPast	string	Achieve	This is used to limit the speed of ships in case of emergency
❌ FastPace	string	Achieve	This is used to limit the speed of ships in case of emergency

Fig. 5.29 Synchronization points for ShipFdApp. Notice that a ship federate has only achieved capability for the synchronization points

Protocol) reliable delivery with an acknowledgement mechanism, and `BestEffort` implies an unreliable communication in the sense of UDP (User Datagram Protocol) best effort delivery of packets (Fig. 5.30). You cannot delete or modify those, but you can add new transportations as provided by the RTI. Data input screen is shown in Fig. 5.31.

5.8 Table Editor

	Name	Reliability	Semantics
	HLAreliable	Reliable	Provide reliable delivery of data in the sense that TCP/IP delivers its data reliably
	HLAbestEffort	BestEffort	Make an effort to deliver data in the sense that UDP provides best-effort delivery
	LowLatency	Reliable	Choose the delivery mechanism that results in the lowest latency from service

Fig. 5.30 Transportations Table. Each transportation can be either reliable or best effort. In case of reliable transportation, data are guaranteed to be delivered. In case of best effort, the delivery is not guaranteed

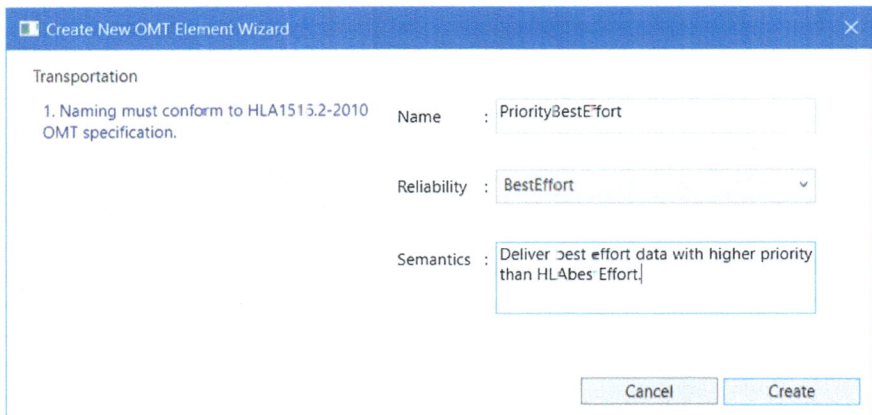

Fig. 5.31 Transportation data input screen. Writing the semantics is a good practice for developing well-documented federation models, and it helps to increase its understandability

5.8.12 Update Rates

The support for *smart update reduction* is a new feature in the HLA Evolved (see Chap. 2). An *update rate* is defined as the rate that attribute values are provided either by the RTI to a subscribing federate or by the owning federate to the RTI (IEEE 1516.1-2010 2010). The *Update Rate Table* is used to manage the update rates. Data input screen is shown in Fig. 5.32. Each update rate has a unique name and a value for the maximum update rate. The maximum update rate is a decimal number greater than zero in hertz (Hz). See Chap. 9 to how smart update reduction works.

5.8.13 Switches

A *switch* is a setting for the RTI to perform some actions for federates such as advising the object class relevance or what to do on resign. The *Switches Table*,

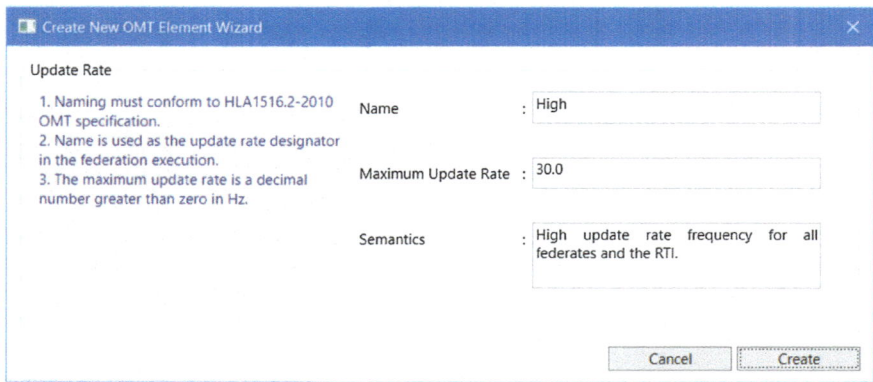

Fig. 5.32 Data input screen for update rates. Update rates are associated with the object class subscription in the federation implementation

Fig. 5.33 Switches Table

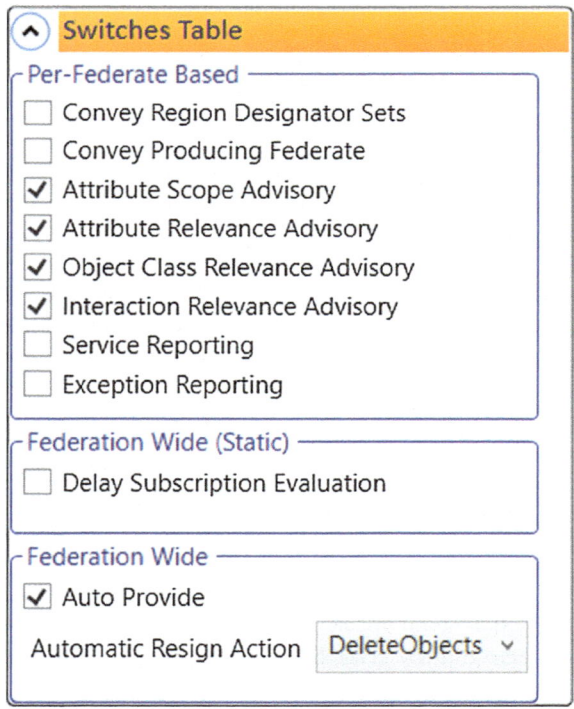

Fig. 5.33, provides all the initial settings for default switches categorized as either federation or federate basis. You can set a switch by clicking the checkbox. You can select the desired value for *Automatic Resign Action* switch using a drop-down menu.

5.8.14 Data Types

SimGe OME supports all data type tables and data representations available in HLA. These are detailed in the succeeding subsections.

5.8.14.1 Basic Data Representations

SimGe OME loads all the predefined data representations and does not let the user change them. The user can create or remove new ones.

Each predefined data representation in the *Basic Data Representations Table* (see Fig. 5.34) is appended with a suffix either BE or LE referring to the *endianness* of data. BE stands for big-endian, LE little-endian. Endian column indicates endianness, which shows which byte of a "memory word" holding a number is stored/loaded first in/from memory from the perspective of computer architecture (a.k.a. CPU-endianness) and the order of byte transmission from the perspective of network communication (a.k.a. network-endianness). For big-endian, the most significant byte is first. Contrarily, the least significant byte is first for little-endian. Although it is a hardware (i.e., CPU architecture)-dependent issue (e.g., Motorola series are big-endian, Intel x85-64 series are little-endian), by a majority, Windows operating system and .NET supports little-endian.

Data input screen is shown in Fig. 5.35.

Name	Size in bits	Interpretation	Endian	Encoding
HLAinteger16BE	16	Integer in the range [-2^15, 2^15 - 1]	Big	16-bit two's complement signed
HLAinteger32BE	32	Integer in the range [-2^31, 2^31 - 1]	Big	32-bit two's complement signed
HLAinteger64BE	64	Integer in the range [-2^63, 2^63 - 1]	Big	64-bit two's complement signed
HLAfloat32BE	32	Single-precision floating point number	Big	32-bit IEEE normalized single-p
HLAfloat64BE	64	Double-precision floating point number	Big	64-bit IEEE normalized double-
HLAoctetPairBE	16	16-bit value	Big	Assumed to be portable among
HLAinteger16LE	16	Integer in the range [-2^15, 2^15 - 1]	Little	16-bit two's complement signed
HLAinteger32LE	32	Integer in the range [-2^31, 2^31 - 1]	Little	32-bit two's complement signed
HLAinteger64LE	64	Integer in the range [-2^63, 2^63 - 1]	Little	64-bit two's complement signed
HLAfloat32LE	32	Single-precision floating point number	Little	32-bit IEEE normalized single-p
HLAfloat64LE	64	Double-precision floating point number	Little	64-bit IEEE normalized double-
HLAoctetPairLE	16	16-bit value	Little	Assumed to be portable among
HLAoctet	8	8-bit value	Big	Assumed to be portable among
UnsignedShort	16	Integer in the range [0, 2^16 - 1]	Little	16-bit unsigned integer

Fig. 5.34 Basic data representations. There are many predefined data representations (shown in the *gray rows*). On the other hand, you can always define new data representations according to your federation needs

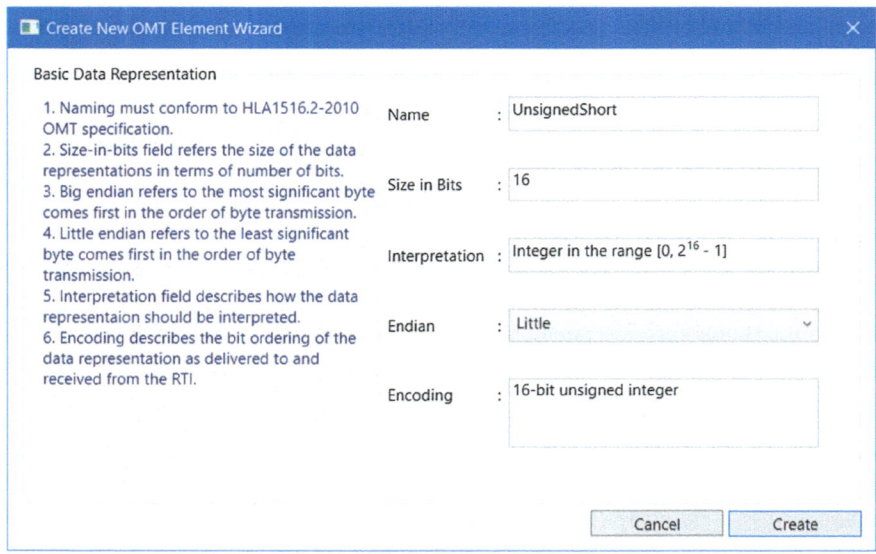

Fig. 5.35 Data input screen for customized data representations. Notice that the *left* segment of the user interface gives explanation about the data fields in the form

	Name	Representation	Units	Resolution	Accuracy	Semantics
	HLAASCIIchar	HLAoctet	NA	NA	NA	Standard ASCII character (see ANSI Std x3.4
	HLAunicodeChar	HLAoctetPairBE	NA	NA	NA	Unicode UTF-16 character (see The Unicode
	HLAbyte	HLAoctet	NA	NA	NA	Uninterpreted 8-bit byte
	HLAinteger64Time	HLAinteger64BE	NA	1	NA	Standardized 64 bit integer time
	HLAfloat64Time	HLAfloat64BE	NA	4.9E-308	NA	Standardized 64 bit float time
	uint	HLAinteger32LE	NA	NA	NA	.NET 32 bit unsigned integer. Range: 0 to 42

Fig. 5.36 Simple data types

5.8.14.2 Simple Data Types

A *simple data type* represents scalar data (a single value) such as an integer or float. The representations (Fig. 5.36) can be selected from the Basic Data Representations Table. SimGe OME automatically provides the available representations in a drop-down list. Whenever the user changes a data representation in the Data Representations Table, the change is automatically applied here.

Data input screen is shown in Fig. 5.37. Units show the units of measure (e.g., cm, kg, or kbps), if applicable for the data type. Here, NA value means no units exist for the data type. Resolution field identifies the precision of measure, "the smallest

5.8 Table Editor

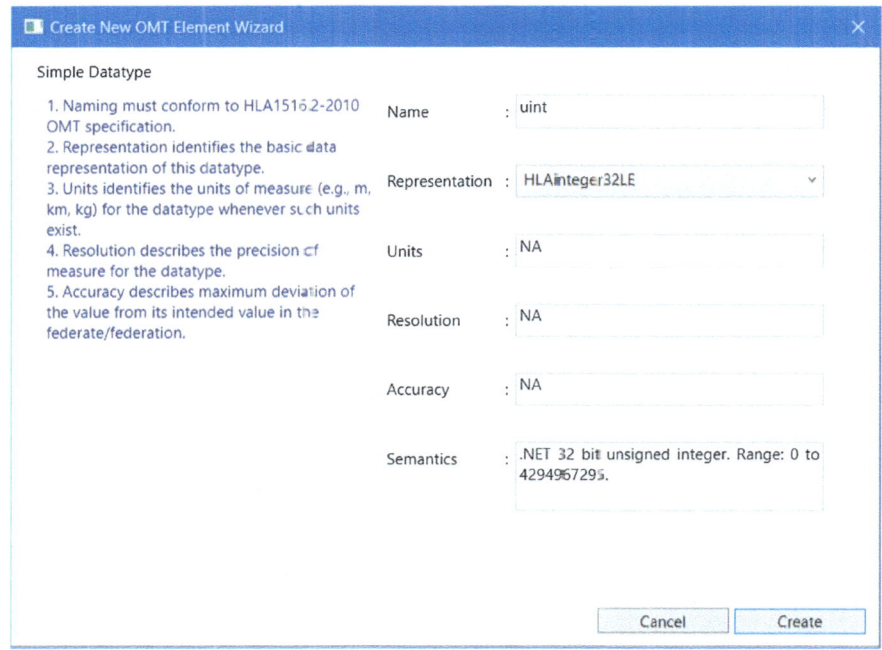

Fig. 5.37 Data input screen for simple data types

resolvable increment between different values that can be effectively discriminated" (IEEE Std 1516.2-2010 2010). The accuracy indicates the maximum deviation from its intended value in the federate/federation.

5.8.14.3 Enumerated Data Types
Enumeration is a set of named values, where each name is called an *enumerator*. In SimGe, the data input screen for creating an enumerated data type is shown in Fig. 5.38.

When the user clicks a row in the *Enumerated Datatype Table*, then enumerators associated with that data type is shown as a nested table[1] (see Fig. 5.39). The user can create new enumerators by entering the last row in the table. Each enumerator has a name and a value. The value must be consistent with the data representation specified in the enumerated data type.

SimGe generates the related codes for the enumerated data types as explained in Chap. 6.

5.8.14.4 Array Data Types
Array data type is a data type to define an indexed collection of homogenous elements (i.e., all elements have the same data type), simply referred to as *arrays*.

---
[1]In general, this type of usage is called as *Master-Slave Table* view.

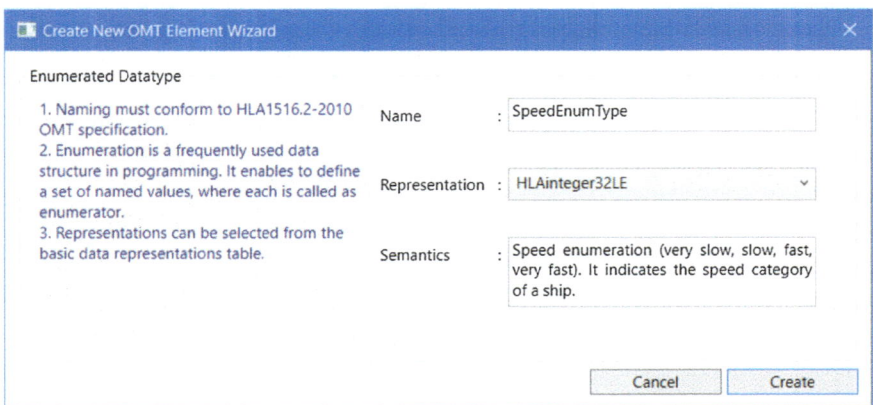

Fig. 5.38 Data input screen for enumerated data type. Enumerators can be added using the Enumerated Table

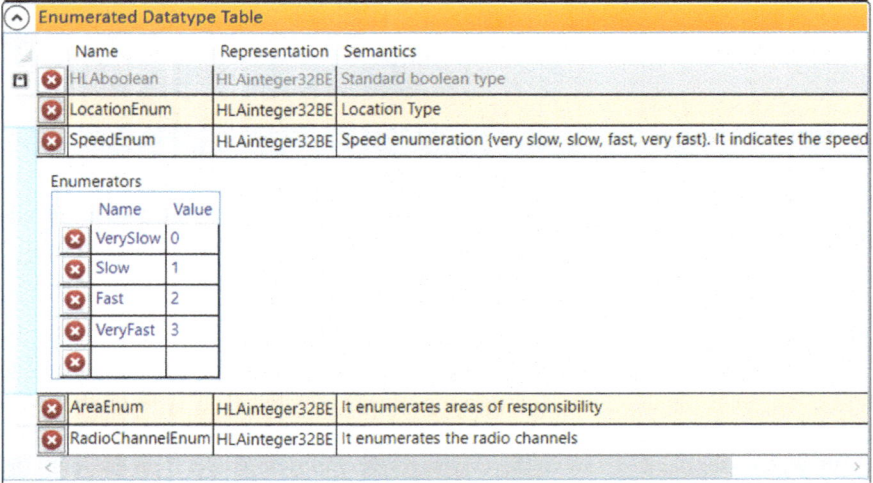

Fig. 5.39 Enumerated data type table

Element type in the Array Datatype Table refers the data type of each element in the array and is linked to the other types defined (Fig. 5.40). Cardinality specifies the number of elements in the array. Multidimensional arrays can be specified by comma-separated values, each indicating one dimension. If the number of elements in an array varies, then the "Dynamic" keyword must be used in the cardinality column. Data input screen for creating an array data type is shown in Fig. 5.41.

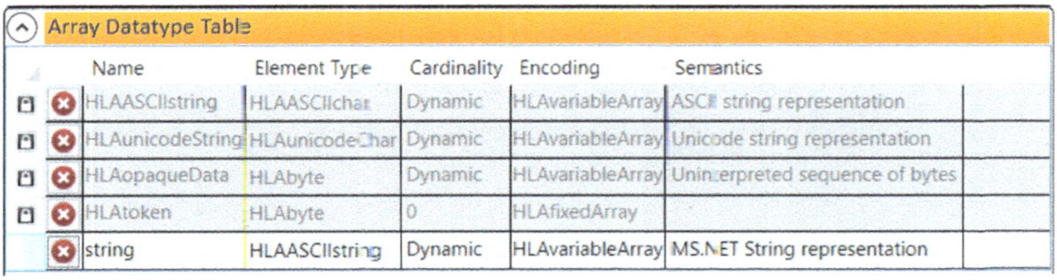

5.8 Table Editor 137

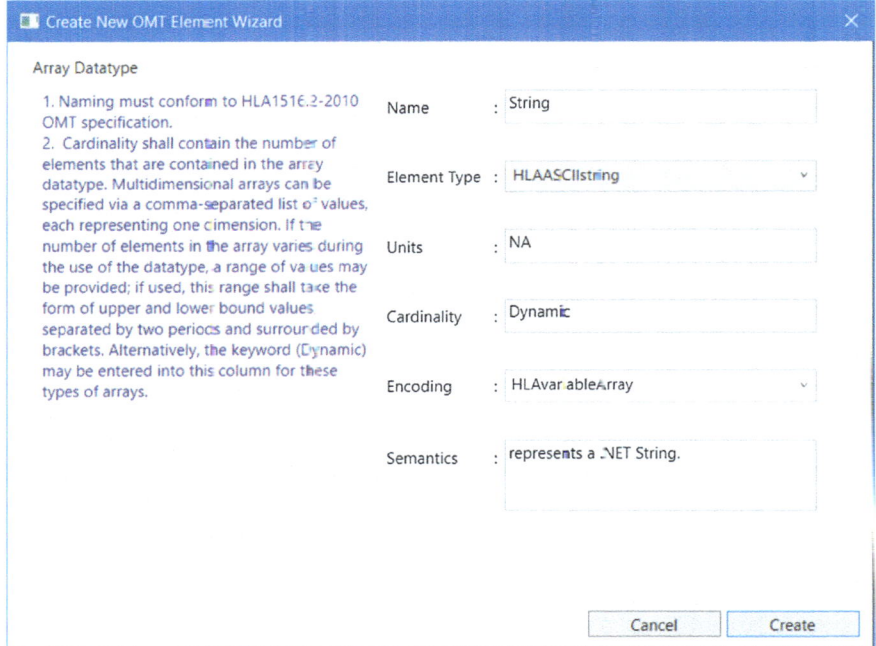

Fig. 5.40 Array data types. The *gray rows* in the table indicate the predefined arrays

Fig. 5.41 Array data type data input screen. Notice that when encoding is selected as HLAvariableArray, then the cardinality field holds dynamic as value

5.8.14.5 Fixed Record Data Types

A *record data type* is used to form an aggregation of previously defined data types. For example, in our case study, the ships maintain a position as (x, y) based on a two-dimensional coordinate system. Therefore, the position data can be specified as an aggregated type such as a record, where it is composed of two floating-point type fields representing the X and Y coordinates. Here, the X and Y are called the *record fields*. The data types of the record fields do not have to be the same; therefore, the record type is said to be heterogenous. Because the types of the record fields are specified in the definition of the record, it is called the fixed record data type. The

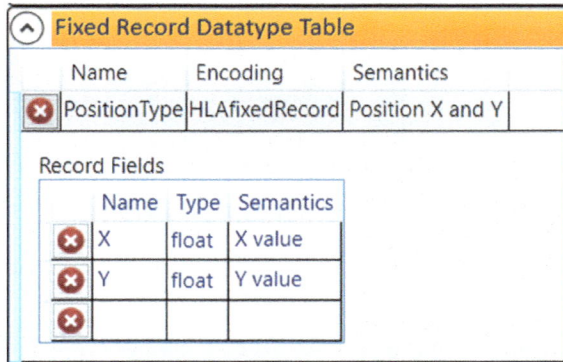

Fig. 5.42 Fixed record data types. The record fields are shown when you select an entry such as PositionType in the data type table

fixed record data type entry for the position is given in Fig. 5.42. When you select a fixed record data type in the table, then a detailed table is shown in order to manage the record fields. You can add/delete a record field or modify the data type of the record field.

Data input screen for creating a fixed record data type is shown in Fig. 5.43. The encoding column shows the predefined encodings for the fixed record data type. You can add new encodings by editing this field.

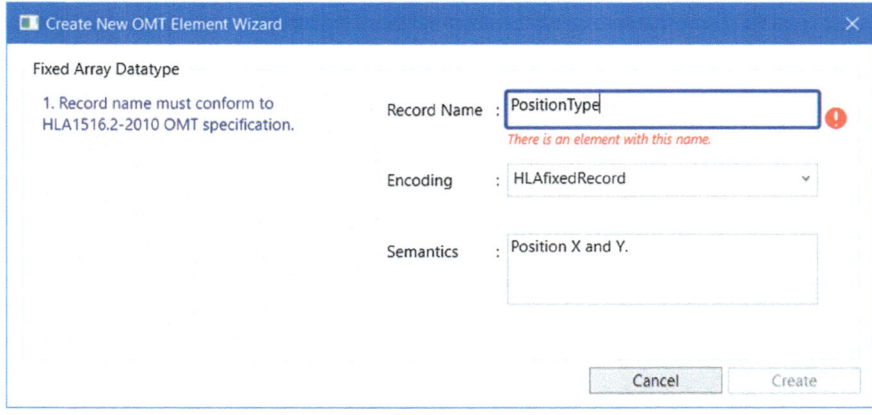

Fig. 5.43 Data input screen for fixed record data type. You are not allowed to create a new record when the table includes a record with the same name

Many high-level programming languages support fixed record data types. For instance, in C#, you can use **struct** to represent a fixed record data type as follows:

```
#region Fixed Record Datatypes
// Position X and Y
public struct PositionType
{
  public float X; // X value
  public float Y; // Y value
}
#endregion
```

SimGe generates all the code for the fixed record data types as explained in Chap. 6.

5.8.14.6 Variant Record Data Types

The idea of a *variant record* is to enable type variations in variables. The variations are chosen using a discriminant of the type. For example, assume that we are modeling a checkout transaction in a store. The payment type in a transaction can be either cash, check, and credit. In case of cash payment, a discount is applied. In case of check payment, we need to keep check number. And in case of a payment with credit card, we need the card number and expiration date. Here, the payment type is the discriminant, and according to its value the alternatives (the variations or the different set of fields) are chosen (Fig. 5.44).

Data input screen for creating a variant array data type is shown in Fig. 5.45. The data type of the discriminant of a variant record can only be an enumerated data type defined in the enumerated data type table. The discriminant enumerators (i.e., the alternatives) are specified after a variant record type is created.

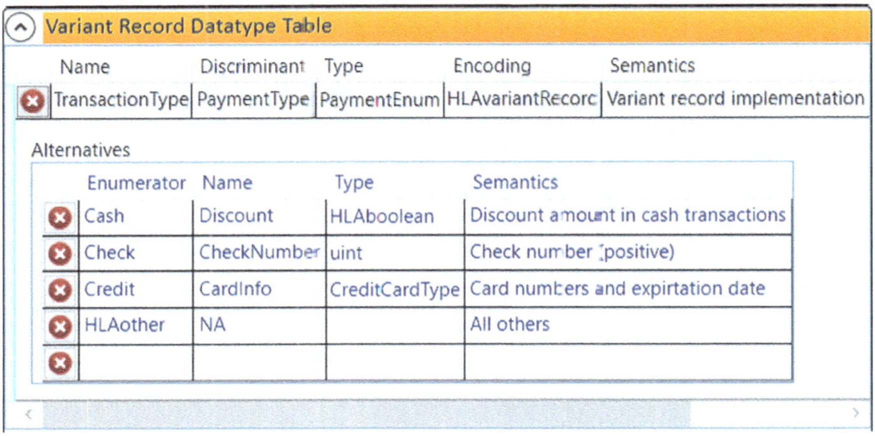

Fig. 5.44 Variant record data types

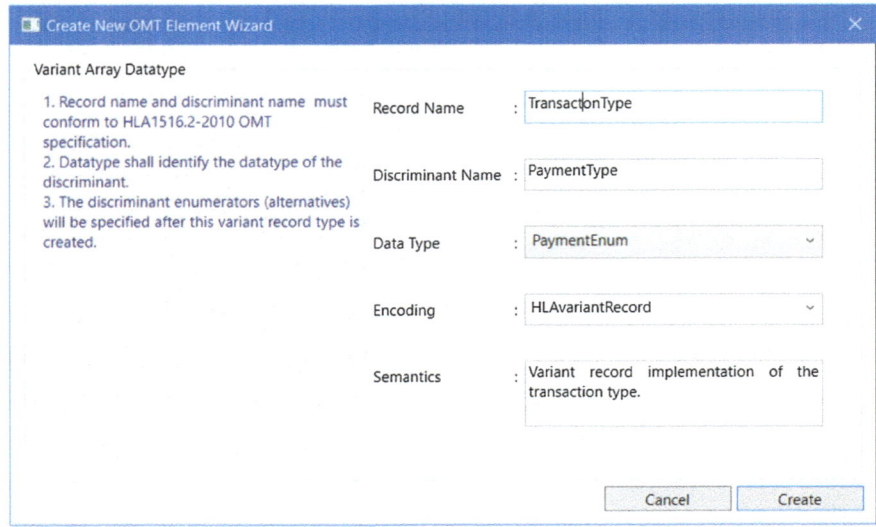

Fig. 5.45 Data input screen for variant record data type

Table 5.1 Data types used in STMS federation

Data type	Explanation
LocationEnum	Enumerated data type: Enumerations {West, East}
SpeedEnum	Enumerated data type: Enumerations {very slow, slow, fast, very fast}
AreaEnum	Enumerated data type: Enumerations {aor1, aor2}. There are two areas of responsibility named as aor1 and aor2
RadioChannelEnum	Enumerated data type: Enumerations {Channel1, Channel2}
PositionType	Fixed record data type: It has two collections of data type: X and Y as float
.NET built-in types	Simple data type: int, float, DateTime Array data type: string

5.8.15 Case Study: Data Types

The federate applications in STMS federation are MS.NET C# applications, and Table 5.1 defines some data types for the attributes and parameters used in the object model.

5.8 Table Editor

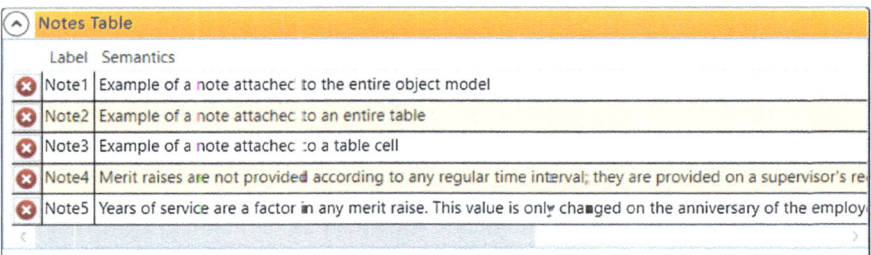

Fig. 5.46 Notes user interface depicting the notes from the Restaurant FOM (IEEE 1516.2-2010 Restaurant FOM Module 2010). Label is the referent for every note pointers

Here are some notes regarding the data types of the case study and .NET:

- Integral .NET C# data types such as int or floating-point types such as float are specified in the Simple Datatype Table.
- The value type, enum, is declared in the Enumerated Datatype Table.
- For structs such as PositionType, the Fixed Record Datatype Table is used.
- String is declared in the Array Datatype Table.

5.8.16 Notes

The *Notes Table* holds the notes that are referenced by any of the OMT components. A *note* provides additional information about individual table entries. Each table entry in the OMT components has a pointer for a note in the notes table. You can add new notes or modify the existing ones. An example is shown in Fig. 5.46.

5.8.17 Interface Specification Services

Interface Specification Services Usage Table is used to track which services are employed for the federation or federate. The table is depicted in Fig. 5.47. The service name, clause of the service, and the callback-or-not information cannot be edited by the user, where all are defined in the specification (IEEE Std 1516.2-2010 2010). All are loaded by default. The only editable column is the usage column. The user can select which services are used by clicking the checkbox of the related service at usage column.

Some services must always be selected as used according to the object model type (i.e., FOM and SOM). If the object model type is FOM, then the services *create/destroy federation execution* and *join/resign federation execution* must be used. In case of SOM, only the *join/resign federation execution* services must be used. According to the user selection, SimGe marks the service row as read-only.

Interface Specification Services Usage Table			
IEEE Std 1516.1-2010 Clause	Service	Usage	Callback
4.2	connect	☐	☐
4.3	disconnect	☐	☐
4.4	connectionLost	☐	✓
4.5	createFederationExecution	✓	☐
4.6	destroyFederationExecution	✓	☐
4.7	listFederationExecutions	☐	☐
4.8	reportFederationExecutions	☐	✓
4.9	joinFederationExecution	✓	☐
4.10	resignFederationExecution	✓	☐
4.11	registerFederationSynchronizationPoint	☐	☐
4.12	confirmSynchronizationPointRegistration	☐	✓
4.13	announceSynchronizationPoint	☐	✓
4.14	synchronizationPointAchieved	☐	☐
4.15	federationSynchronized	☐	✓
4.16	requestFederationSave	☐	☐
4.17	initiateFederateSave	☐	✓
4.18	federateSaveBegun	☐	☐
4.19	federateSaveComplete	☐	☐
4.20	federationSaved	☐	✓
4.21	abortFederationSave	☐	☐
4.22	queryFederationSaveStatus	☐	☐
4.23	federationSaveStatusResponse	☐	✓
4.24	requestFederationRestore	☐	☐
4.25	confirmFederationRestorationRequest	☐	✓

Fig. 5.47 Interface specification services

SimGe also shows the callback column, although it is not specified in (IEEE Std 1516.2-2010 2010).

5.8.18 OMT 1.3 Support

SimGe supports HLA 1.3 OMT files. SimGe Table Editor contains a tab for HLA OMT 1.3 as shown in Fig. 5.48. The OMT 1.3 specification incorporates *routing spaces* which they are supplanted in HLA 1516 specification. You can make necessary routing space operations in this tab. For this purpose, the *Routing Space Table* is added. You can create new routing spaces here. Each *routing space* contains a collection of dimensions. So, the user interface allows adding dimensions to the related routing space. To do this, you first select the routing space row in table then select a dimension from the available dimensions combo box and press Add button. To remove a dimension from the routing space list, click the red icon button at the head of each dimension row.

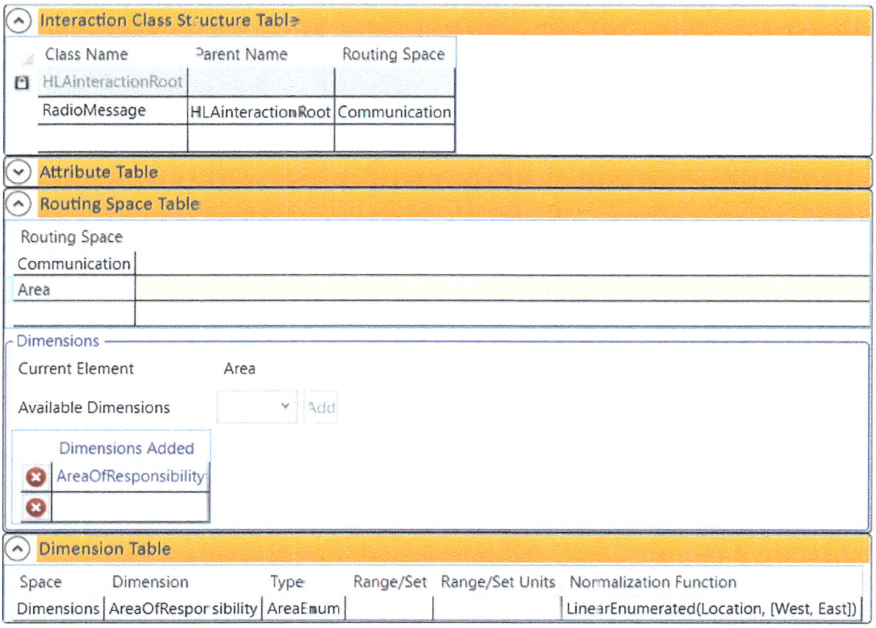

Fig. 5.48 Tab for OMT 1.3 support

Moreover, additional tables are displayed to set up relations between elements that can be related to the routing space, such as interaction class and Attribute Tables.

In HLA 1.3 OMT Attribute Table, the *Transferable/Acceptable* (T/A) column corresponds to *Divest/Acquire* (D/A) in SimGe Attribute Table. In the same way, *Updateable/Reflectable* (U/R) column is mapped to P/S. In Interaction Class Structure Table, the Capability column (i.e., Initiate/Respond/Sense) is matched with the Publish/Subscribe found in the OMT 1516 interaction structure table. P/S attribute is considered in code generation. Dimensions are presented in an additional table.

5.9 Textual View

5.9.1 Textual View for FED and FDD Files

The textual views provide a read-only look into the FED or FDD files generated from the object model. The purpose of the textual view is to provide a quick view for the users who are familiar with the FED or FDD representations for verification of the model they are working on without leaving SimGe. Figure 5.49 depicts the textual view of the FED file content of the STMS.

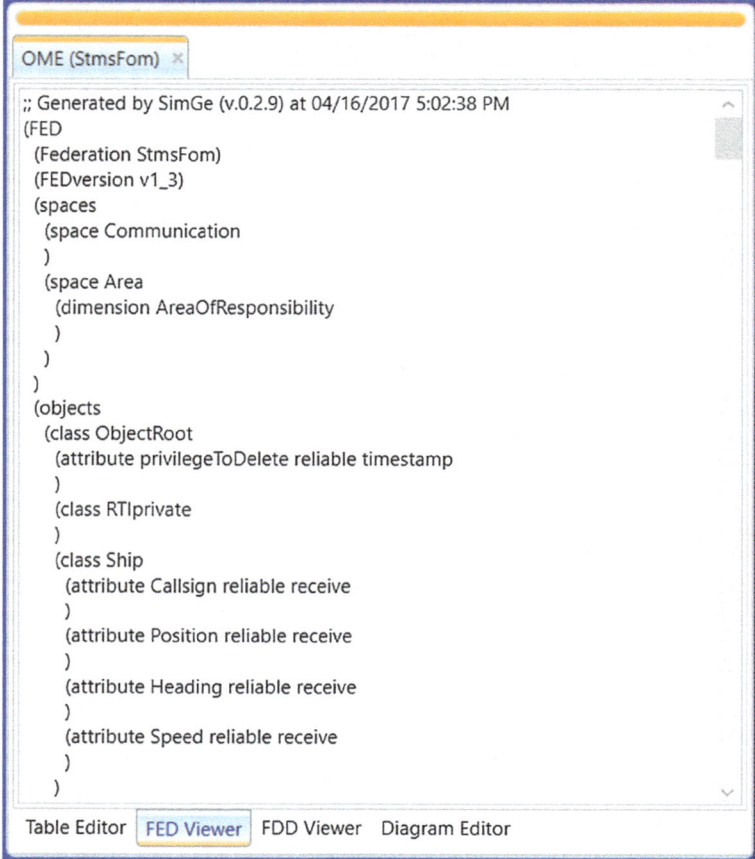

Fig. 5.49 OME FED viewer. The textual view is read-only and shows the content of the FED file generated by SimGe

The FDD viewer depicts the FDD file in an XML-style view as shown in Fig. 5.50. The FDD viewer is implemented as a web browser. When you right click in the area, you see the list of actions to choose from such as "export to Microsoft Excel" or print. When you press `Ctrl+F`, a `Find` dialog appears and you can search for any element you want (Fig. 5.50).

5.10 Validating the FDD File

SimGe OME validates the imported or exported FDD files, when export and import is carried out. Moreover, the user can validate the FDD file generated from object model anytime using the validation menu. The validation results dialog reports the

5.10 Validating the FDD file

Fig. 5.50 OME FDD viewer. Here, you can use Find dialog to search for specific keywords

result. The validation results show the inconsistencies found in the source file. The errors found are reported with the line number in the FDD file. SimGe FDD Viewer does not show the line numbers.

As an example, let us import a well-known sample FOM module, *RestaurantFOMmodule.xml* (IEEE 1516.2-2010 Restaurant FOM Module 2010), provided with the HLA OMT specification as an OMT DIF FOM example. When you import this module, you get two warnings as depicted in Fig. 5.51. The first one indicates that HLAinteractionRoot class has missing mandatory elements, which are transportation and order. The second warning indicates that HLAreliable transportation is not found in the transportations. The warnings arise because the sample is in the DIF format, not in an exact FDD format. Despite warnings, SimGe successfully imports and, if possible, corrects the errors. The user interface for the validation report supports the copy-paste operation. So, you can copy and paste the errors.

5.11 MOM Integration

For all FOMs, the inclusion of the HLA *Management Object Model* (MOM) is required. Moreover, in HLA 1.3, the MOM is a compulsory part of the FED file. Whenever the user imports a FED file, the MOM is imported too. In HLA Evolved, the standard *MOM and Initialization Module* (MIM) (IEEE 1516.1-2010 HLA Standard MIM 2010) includes the MOM and the initialization data.

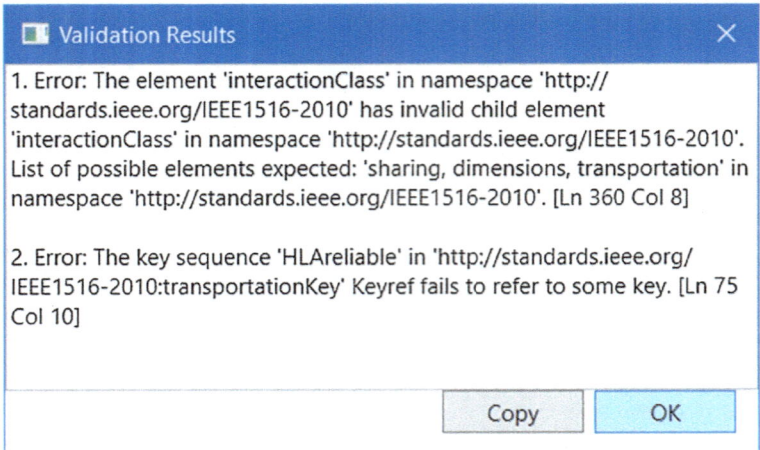

Fig. 5.51 Screen shot showing the validation results after importing the restaurant FOM module

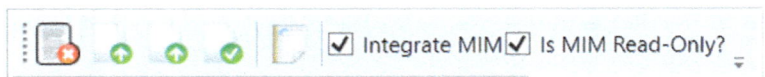

Fig. 5.52 HLA MOM suppression. When you tick the radio button, then the MIM/MOM is integrated to the current view of object model

From the perspective of SOMs, many federate applications do not directly use the MIM. Therefore, SimGe allows suppression of MIM classes. When MIM is suppressed, (i) the table and explorer views do not show the MIM classes, and (ii) the code generator does not generate code for the MIM classes. MIM suppression can be switched from the OME toolbar as shown in Fig. 5.52.

When you want to work with MIM, then you can disable the MIM suppression switch. MIM will show up in the table and explorers view, but it will be read-only (see Fig. 5.53). When you want to modify the properties of the MIM classes (e.g., P/S status of a class), then you can disable the read-only switch from the same menu.

5.12 OM Explorer

The *OM explorer* presents a tree view of the OMT elements. The user can browse the nodes. A star (blue-colored) icon indicates a user-defined element as a red one indicates a built-in element (i.e., a SimGe added element or a MIM/MOM element) (Fig. 5.54).

Class Name	Parent Name	P/S	Transportation	Order
HLAinteractionRoot		Neither	HLAreliable	TimeStamp
RadioMessage	HLAinteractionRoot	PublishSubscribe	HLAreliable	TimeStamp
HLAmanager	HLAinteractionRoot	Neither		Receive
HLAfederate	HLAmanager	Neither		Receive
HLAadjust	HLAfederate	Neither		Receive
HLAsetTiming	HLAadjust	Subscribe		Receive
HLAmodifyAttributeState	HLAadjust	Subscribe		Receive
HLAsetServiceReporting	HLAadjust	Subscribe		Receive
HLAsetExceptionReporting	HLAadjust	Subscribe		Receive
HLAsetSwitches	HLAadjust	Subscribe		Receive
HLArequest	HLAfederate	Neither		Receive
HLArequestPublications	HLArequest	Subscribe		Receive
HLArequestSubscriptions	HLArequest	Subscribe		Receive
HLArequestObjectInstancesThatCanBeDeleted	HLArequest	Subscribe		Receive
HLArequestObjectInstancesUpdated	HLArequest	Subscribe		Receive
HLArequestObjectInstancesReflected	HLArequest	Subscribe		Receive
HLArequestUpdatesSent	HLArequest	Subscribe		Receive
HLArequestInteractionsSent	HLArequest	Subscribe		Receive
HLArequestReflectionsReceived	HLArequest	Subscribe		Receive
HLArequestInteractionsReceived	HLArequest	Subscribe		Receive

Fig. 5.53 Interaction class structure table showing the MIM/MOM elements

Currently, the OM explorer supports the following functions via a context menu (i.e., related to the right mouse click):

- Traversing (expand/collapse all, expand/collapse this);
- Modifying (rename and remove).

A right mouse click is required to use most of those functions. The place where you do a right click is important. For instance, if you select a node and then do a right click, then only the related commands will appear (Fig. 5.55).

The OM explorer also is linked to the table editor. When you select a node, then the table tab (e.g., objects) that contains the related item will appear in the table editor.

5.12.1 Functionality for Traverse

The purpose of traversing is to expand (to show) or collapse (to hide) the nodes of the OMT tree.

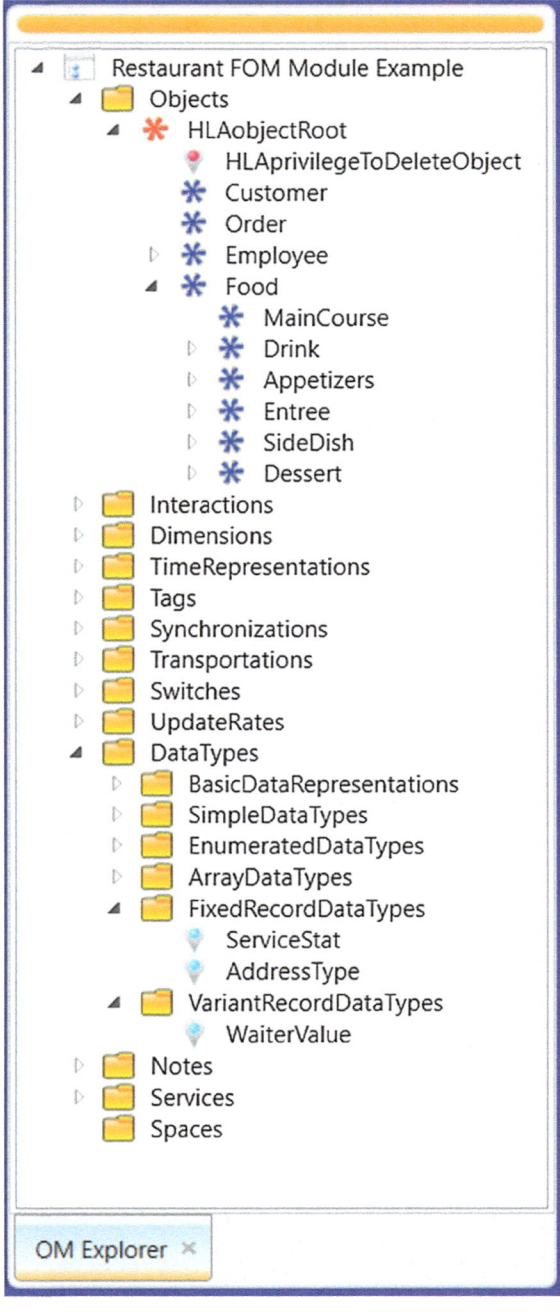

Fig. 5.54 OM explorer depicting the Restaurant FOM elements in a tree-structure view

Fig. 5.55 Context menu of the OM explorer

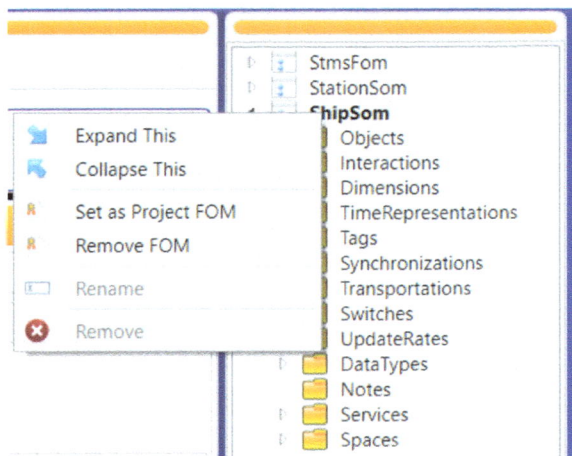

- **Expand all and Collapse all**: This command provides the ability to expand or collapse all nodes at once in the tree.
- **Expand this/Collapse this**: This command expands or collapses all the nodes under the selected node.

5.12.2 Functionality for Modification

The modification includes operations such as renaming or removing an element.

- **Rename**: This command provides renaming of the selected node. To complete renaming, the user must press the enter key.
- **Remove**: This command deletes the selected node and its children (the nodes connected to the selected node) recursively.
- **Remove FOM**: This command removes the current federation object model from the project.

5.13 Report Generator

SimGe Report Generator fully generates HLA OMT 1516-2010 specification (IEEE Std 1516.2-2010 2010) tables for documenting purposes. The report generator can be run using the OME toolbar (see Fig. 5.56), where each report is specific to an object model.

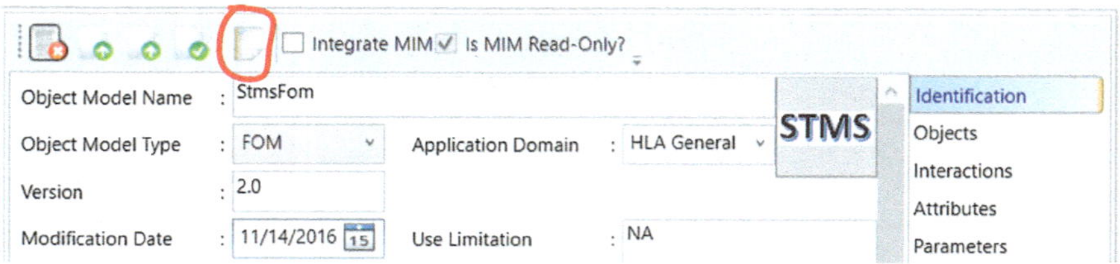

Fig. 5.56 Running the report generator

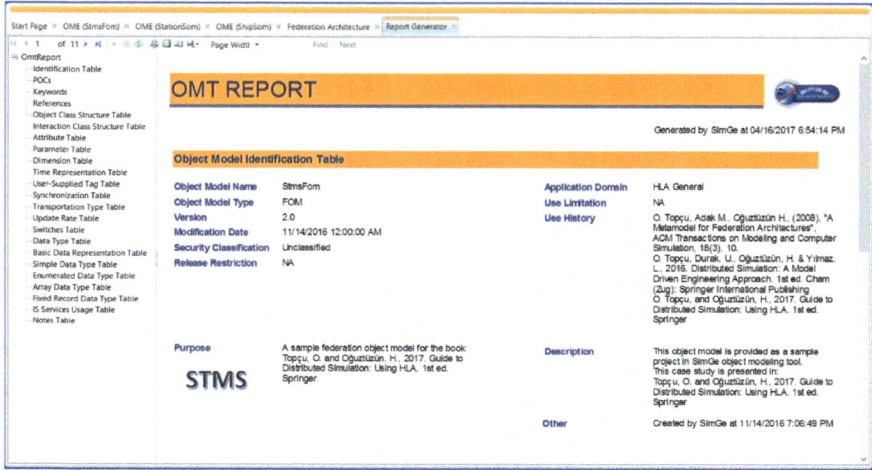

Fig. 5.57 Report generator workspace. In the *left pane*, you see the document map, which refers to the various parts of the report. At the *top* of the workspace, there is a tool menu related to the report for various actions such as exporting the report

When the report generator workspace is displayed (Fig. 5.57), the user can print or export (save) the report to PDF, Microsoft Excel, or Microsoft Word format.

A document map is also created automatically. When you export the report, the document will help you navigate the document (e.g., for a PDF document, the document map will be converted to a list of bookmarks). The sample report for the STMS is provided in the SimGe Web site (SimGe 2015).

5.14 Summary

The one of major steps of federation development is the construction of an object model, where the object model refers both to the data that will be transferred among participating federates and to some settings, which are effective federation-wide. The construction of the simulation object model, both the FOM for the federation

5.15 Questions for Review

1. You are asked to design a data structure for computing the salary of a faculty member with different calculation criteria depending on the faculty rank. The rank can be Assistant Professor, Associate Professor, Full Professor, Visiting Faculty, and Instructor. The salary of the professors is computed according to their title rates, which are 0–2 according to the title orderly. The salary of a visiting faculty is calculated according to his/her experience. There are two levels: novice and expert. Lastly, the salary of an instructor is computed according to his/her weekly class hours.

    (a) What kind of data type is most suitable for this data?
    (b) Define a data type for this data structure in SimGe.
    (c) How can you define this data type in C#?

2. Consider we are modeling a dimension for a course grade. Grading is done ranging from 0 to 100, but in our federation, we will use a scale between 0 and 4. Now, assume that we will use a linear normalization function in the dimension definition as specified in Fig. 5.58.

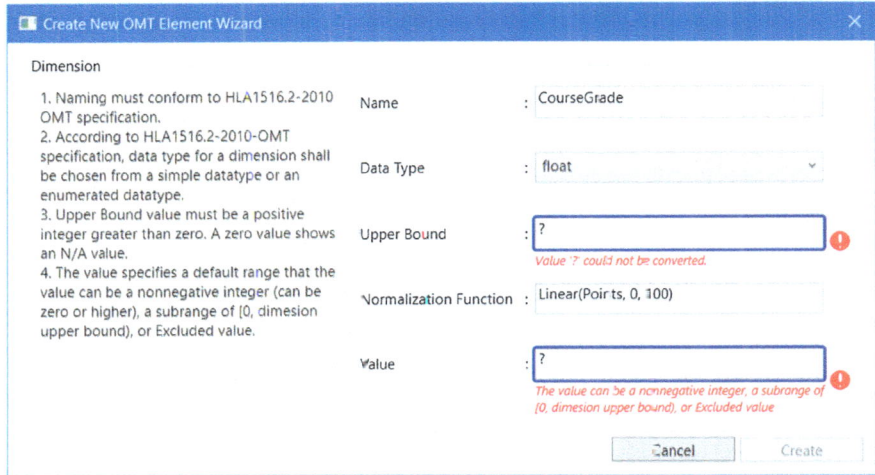

Fig. 5.58 Dimension definition for review question

The function is defined as follows (IEEE Std 1516.2-2010 2010):
Prototype: Linear(domain, dimensionLower, dimensionUpper);
Arguments:

- domain: a non-enumerated value (e.g., integer) known by the federate using the dimension definition;
- dimensionLower: the lower bound on the domain value;
- dimensionUpper: the upper bound on the domain value.

Function:

$$[(\text{domain} - \text{dimensionLower})/(\text{dimensionUpper} - \text{dimensionLower})] \times (\text{DUB} - 1)$$

where DUB is dimension upper bound specified in the definition of dimension.

   (a) What is the dimension upper bound you will define in the dimension (see the first question mark in Fig. 5.58)?
   (b) What is the value you will define (see the second question mark in Fig. 5.58)?
   (c) In case a student gets 75 points, what is the grade in the federation (i.e., the normalized value)?

3. Describe a scenario that includes the use of synchronization and then discuss how you can construct the synchronization points using SimGe.
4. A federate, possibly a member of a naval federation, subscribes to certain attributes, e.g., location, heading, and speed, of a particular class of ships, say, frigates. How can the developer make sure that the federate can still receive the same attribute updates from a new class of ships, say, tankers, in the future?
5. What criteria should be used to choose between reliable delivery and best effort delivery of packets?
6. Imagine a federation where both types of messages, receive order and timestamp order, are used. What could be the contents of such messages?

References

DoD. (1998). *High level architecture federation execution details (FED) file specification (RTI 1.3 Version 3)*. s.l.: DoD.
IEEE 1516-2010 Downloads. (2010). *IEEE-SA supplemental material*. [Online] Available at: http://standards.ieee.org/downloads/1516/. Accessed April 01, 2017.
IEEE 1516.1-2010. (2010). *Standard for modeling and simulation (M&S) high level architecture (HLA)—federate interface specification*. s.l.: IEEE.
IEEE1516.1-2010 FDD Schema. (2010). *IEEE1516-FDD-2010.xsd*. [Online] Available at: http://standards.ieee.org/downloads/1516/1516.1-2010/IEEE1516-FDD-2010.xsd. Accessed April 15, 2017.

References

IEEE 1516.1-2010 HLA Standard MIM. (2010). *HLAstandardMIM.xml*. [Online] Available at: http://standards.ieee.org/downloads/1516/1516.1-2010/HLAstandardMIM.xml. Accessed April 16, 2017.

IEEE Std 1516.2-2010. (2010). *Standard for modeling and simulation (M&S) high level architecture (HLA)—object model template*. New York: IEEE.

IEEE 1516.2-2010 Restaurant FOM Module. (2010). *RestaurantFOMmodule.xml*. [Online] Available at: http://standards.ieee.org/downloads/1516/1516.2-2010/RestaurantFOMmodule.xml. Accessed April 15, 2017.

SimGe. (2015). *SimGe web site*. [Online] Available at: https://sites.google.com/site/okantopcu/simge. Accessed April 14, 2017.

SISO. (2015). *Standard for Real-time Platform Reference Object Model version 2.0*. Orlando, FL: Simulation Interoperability Standards Organization.

Part III
Federate Application Development

Code Generation 6

It is a known observation that coding a federate application is repetitive in nature and involves a large amount of code even for a simple application. In this regard, the code generation is an effective technique that helps rapid prototyping of a federation. Code generation can be seen as a model transformation, which takes a federation architecture as the source model and transforms it to an executable code for a target environment. In this chapter, we show you how code generation for each federate application in a federation architecture can be done using SimGe. The target environment is C# and .NET using RACoN platform as the abstraction layer for the RTI.

6.1 Overview

SimGe can be seen as a rapid federation prototyping tool due to its code generation capability. The target platform of SimGe code generation is the layered federation architecture that uses RACoN as the communication layer, whereas the target environment is C# and Microsoft .NET (Microsoft .NET 2017). The generated code files are intended for a fast start-up to layered federate development. To employ the generated code files, a RACoN project must be created and the generated code files must be added to this project in Visual Studio (Microsoft 2017), an *integrated development environment* (IDE). Then, the simulation developer may continue to implement the federate application by coding manually over the generated code. See Chaps. 7–9 for manual implementation using RACoN.

SimGe code generator (CodeGen) employs the federation architecture model, which includes the federation structure and the object models, as the source. Before generating code, you must construct a simulation object model and a federation structure that includes the federate applications as explained in Chaps. 4 and 5. Code is generated for each federate application separately. So, it is important to specify the simulation object models for each federate.

From the perspective of code generation, we highlight the following features of SimGe:

- Code is separately generated for each federate application found in the federation architecture according to the federate's SOM. The generated code is generally in form of *skeleton code* such as callbacks or in form of full implementation for some functionality such as the implementation of the SOM. A skeleton code is the outline code of a program structure, such as a class or a function, including the declarations of variables. Since we are generating federate code based on its SOM, rather than the FOM, some parts of the generated code might be unused (dead code). As the generated code is generally in form of skeleton code, it usually needs manual intervention specifically for implementing the computation parts of the federate application.
- The structure of the generated code conforms to the *layered architecture* (see Chap. 7 for technical background and Sect. 6.3 for an example).
- The following pieces of code are generated (we will provide the details in the following sections):

    - A class for each HLA class[1] found in the simulation object model,
    - The federate SOM class, which includes and integrates all the separate classes generated for the HLA classes,
    - The skeleton code for the Federate Ambassador callback event handlers for RACoN,
    - The federate class, which deals with the RTI services, and
    - The simulation manager class, which is intended to act as a controller between the federate and the interface.

- Each class is kept in a separate source file.
- Code generation configuration dialog enables the user to select for which management services the callback handler code will be generated.
- A FED and an FDD file is automatically exported to the source code folder according to the federation object model.

6.2 User Interface

To generate code, select `Generate Code` command in the `Code Generator` menu. The C# source code files for each federate application will be created sep-

---

[1]The use of "class" word can be confusing in this chapter. When we use "class" in the text, we need to make sure to distinct that it is used either in the sense of programming language concept or in the sense of HLA terminology. From now on (throughout the rest of the chapters), we reserve the "class" term to refer a class in object-oriented programming, a code template for creating objects, for instance, a federate class for the generated code. Nevertheless, to make the distinction, we use "HLA class," when we are referring to an object class or to an interaction class of an object model.

6.2 User Interface   159

arately and displayed in its own *code viewer*, where a code viewer is a workspace for each federate application to see the content of the related code files (more in the following sections). Each generation also creates a time-stamped folder under the SourceCode folder, which is under the project home folder. Time-stamped format is year + month + day + hour + min + sec (e.g., 20170416111140, which corresponds to the exact time when the code generation is completed). Furthermore, all the generated files are grouped under a folder for each federate application.

6.2.1 Code Explorer

The generated files are reported in the SimGe Code Explorer (see Fig. 6.1). The user can click the hyperlink to open the folder in Windows Explorer.

6.2.2 Code Viewer

The generated code can be seen in the code viewer workspace for each federate application as presented in Fig. 6.2. Please note that this is a read-only view. If editing is required, you must copy or import all the code to the Visual Studio IDE code editor for modification.

The style and naming convention of the generated code conforms to (dofactory 2016).

6.3 Architectural Style

CodeGen generates code that conforms to the *layered simulation architecture* style, which is detailed in Chap. 7. The *presentation layer* heavily depends on the project. Thus, CodeGen targets the *simulation layer* and generates code partially. A sample of the class structure of the generated code for the ShipFdApp is presented in Fig. 6.3. The simulation layer mainly includes a simulation manager, local data structures, and the classes extended from the *communication layer*, in our case from the RACoN. The simulation manager class manages the federate execution (from the viewpoint of the application), and the federate class (CShipFdApp) manages the federate interactions by employing the RACoN API.

At the bottom level, the communication layer (RACoN) interacts with the RTI to communicate with other entities in the federation execution by exchanging objects and interactions. Therefore, the classes for the HLA object model, objects, and the federate class are all extended from the related RACoN classes. For example, the federate class (which acts as both an *RTI Ambassador* and *Federate Ambassador*—see Chap. 2 for the terms) is inherited from the RACoN generic federate class. All

Fig. 6.1 Code explorer screen for STMS

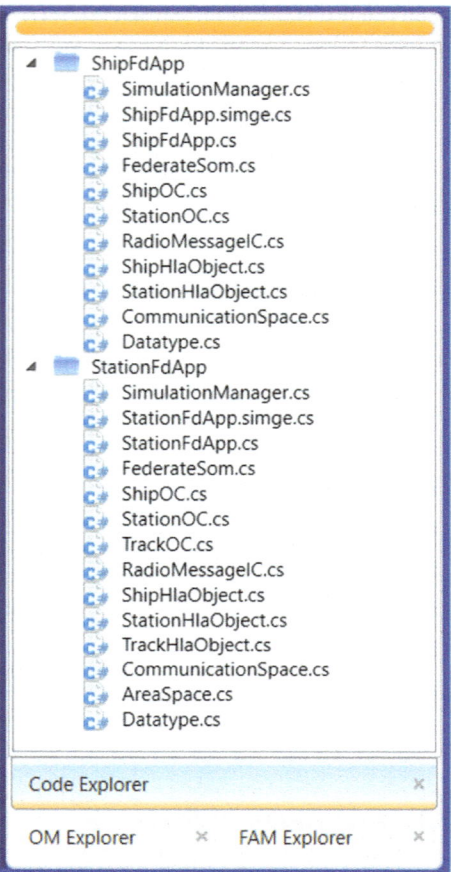

the communication layer-related structures are completely auto-generated, as well as the data types specified in the simulation object model (see Fig. 6.3).

As the simulation layer also deals with the simulation behavior of the application, it also maintains the local data structures to keep track of the entities found in the virtual environment. Local data structures and the simulation local behavior (the computational part) must be manually coded by you.

Each generated class is placed in a separate C# file. Classes are grouped as follows:

- Simulation manager class (i.e., CSimulationManager)
- Federate class (e.g., CShipFdApp)
- HLA object model

6.3 Architectural Style

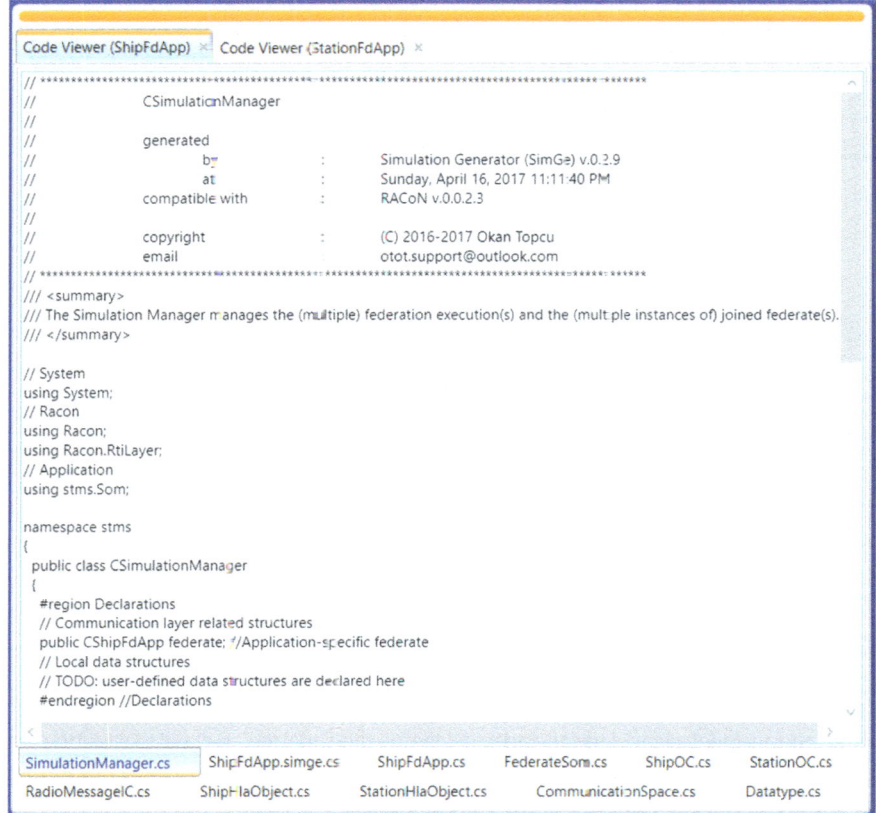

Fig. 6.2 Code viewer and a generated code sample. Notice that there is a separate code viewer for each federate application with multiple tabs (at the *bottom* of the viewer) for each code file

- Federate SOM class (i.e., `FederateSom`)
- Interaction classes for each interaction defined in the SOM, for instance `CRadioMessageIC` class.
- Object classes for each object defined in the SOM, for instance `CShipOC` class.
- Wrapper classes for HLA object instances related to each HLA object class such as `CShipHlaObject`.

- SOM data types

  - Fixed record and enumerated data types for each data type found in the SOM, for instance, `LocationEnum` enumeration and `PositionType` structure.

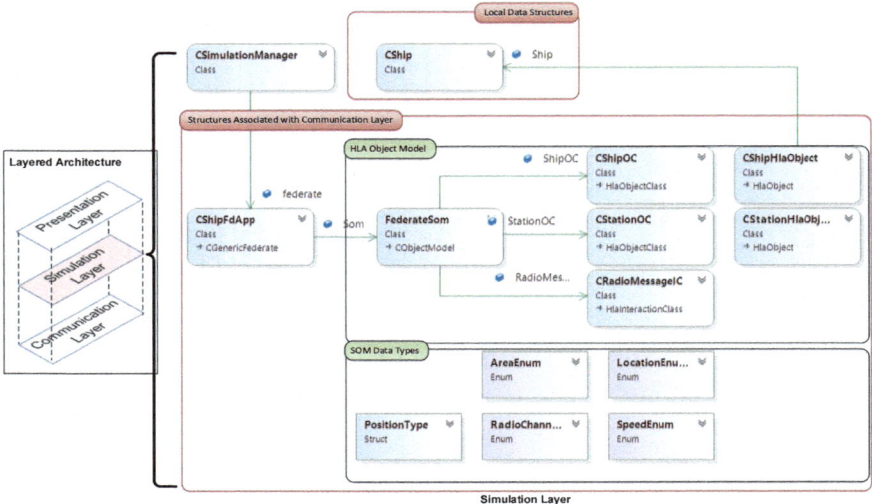

Fig. 6.3 The Partial UML class diagram for ShipFdApp depicting only the simulation layer. The classes associated with the communication layer are all auto-generated by SimGe CodeGen

6.3.1 Code Generation for Object Model

A class is generated for each corresponding HLA class in the SOM. For example, for the Ship object class defined in the SOM of the federate, a class (CShipOC in Fig. 6.3) is generated. Each file for the HLA classes is named by following the rule: "IC" or "OC" is appended to the HLA class name according to the HLA class type, and then, ".cs" extension is added (e.g., CShipOC or CRadioMessageIC). The federate SOM class (i.e., FederateSOM) acts as the main container for each generated class. So the federate class can use a single reference (i.e., Som) to reach all the classes corresponding the FOM.

6.3.1.1 Wrapper Classes for the HLA Object Instances

As the HLA object instances are sustained during the execution, we need to keep track of them in the federation execution. To work with the RTI in conformance, we encapsulate them by wrapping them using local data structures. For instance, CShipHlaObject encapsulates a domain object CShip, so that it can be processed by the RTI (See Chap. 7 for details about object encapsulation). The wrapper classes are generated for each object class found in the object model. They are named by adding the suffix "Object" to the HLA class name.

6.3.2 Code Generation for Federate

6.3.2.1 Federate Class

The federate class code file is named "<Name> FdApp.cs" where <Name> is the federate application name given by you in the SimGe project (e.g., `ShipFdApp.cs`). The federate class includes the skeleton code for the Federate Ambassador callback event handlers (see Chap. 8 for callback event handling). Normally, you will manually edit this class. Therefore, it is generated as a *partial class*, so that it can be dispersed to multiple files. Here, two files are generated for the federate class as depicted in Fig. 6.4. The first one contains the automatically generated code and is named "<Name> FdApp.simge.cs." The second one is for the user to code manually. It is named "<Name> FdApp.cs." The user may edit this file instead of the generated file in order not to lose the changes when it is generated again.

6.3.3 Code Generation for Data Type

CodeGen also supports code generation for the enumerated and the fixed record data types defined in the SOM. For each entry found in the Enumeration Datatype Table of the object model, CodeGen generates enum definitions. An example is depicted in Fig. 6.5. The values are mapped as the enumeration values, and the semantics are mapped as comments.

For each fixed record data type defined in the SOM, a `struct` is generated (see Fig 6.6 for an example). The generated code is kept in `DataTypes.cs` file.

```
ShipFdApp.cs
  public partial class CShipFdApp : Racon.CGenericFederate
  { USER MANUALLY ADDED CODE }
```

```
ShipFdApp.simge.cs
  public partial class CShipFdApp : Racon.CGenericFederate
  { GENERATED CODE }
```

Fig. 6.4 Federate class is generated as a partial class. A partial class allows to split the definition of a class into multiple source files. When the application is compiled, all parts are combined like a class defined in a single source file

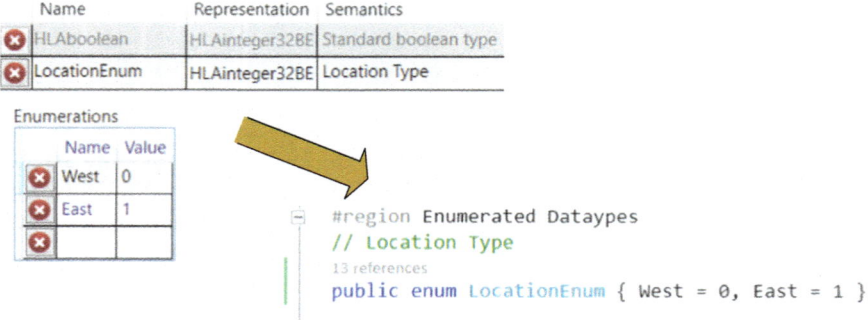

Fig. 6.5 Code generation for each data type defined in the Enumerated Datatype Table of SOM. The presented example, LocationEnum, is from our case study, STMS

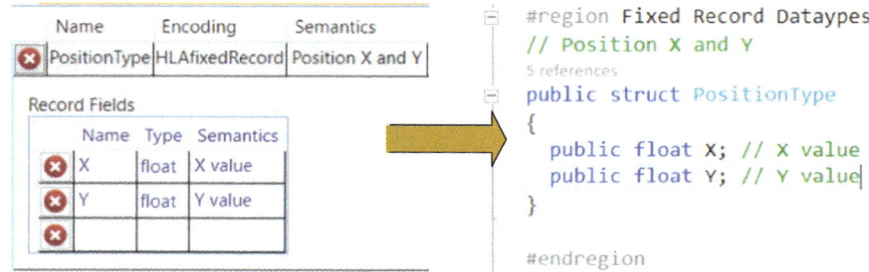

Fig. 6.6 Code generation for the Fixed Record Datatype Table of ShipFdApp

6.3.4 Code Generation for MOM

When MOM suppression is enabled (which is the default behavior), code for the MOM classes will not be generated, otherwise it will.

6.4 Code Generator Configuration

SimGe provides a *Code Generator Configuration Dialog* where the user can select for which management services the callback handler code will be generated. The code generation options are found in Tools/Options menu.

Code generator settings are divided into three groups: (i) general settings, (ii) callback settings, and (iii) runtime settings.

6.4 Code Generator Configuration

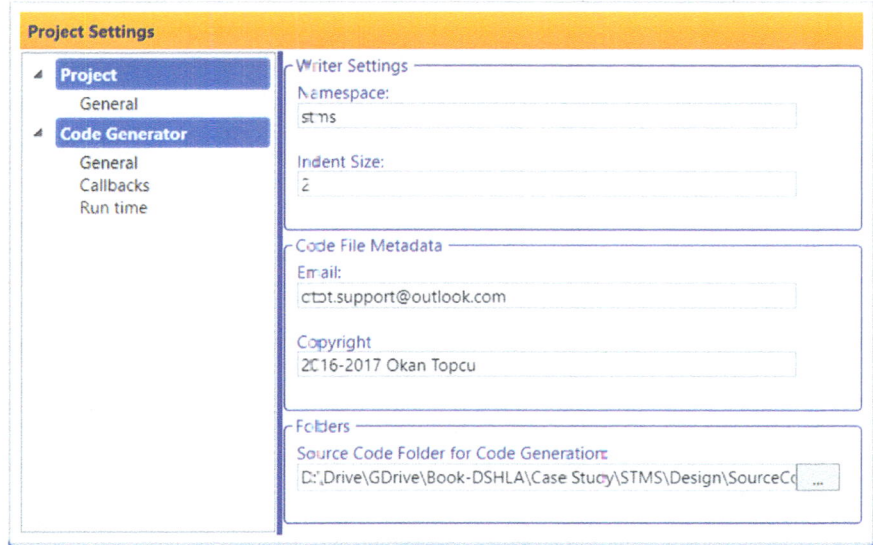

Fig. 6.7 Code generator settings—general

6.4.1 General Settings

General settings contain three groups: (i) the (code) writer settings, (ii) the code file metadata, and (iii) the folders as shown in Fig. 6.7. Settings are kept with the project.

Table 6.1 summarizes the parameters.

6.4.2 Callback Settings

In the callback settings pane, you can select the callbacks, which will be generated by default as shown in Fig. 6.9.

6.4.3 Runtime Settings

Naming scheme slightly differs among the versions of the HLA specifications. The names for the root object class, the root interaction class, and the privilege-to-delete attribute are HLAobjectRoot, HLAinteractionRoot, and HLAprivilegeToDeleteObject for HLA 1516-2010 standard, and ObjectRoot, InteractionRoot, and privilegeToDelete for HLA 1.3 specification, respectively.

Fig. 6.8 Settings that are set in the configuration dialog are reflected in each source file

Table 6.1 Code generator general settings

Parameter	Explanation
Namespace	The namespace of all the classes generated. It is the project name by default. The user may override it here. Note that naming must conform to MS .NET Framework naming rules. See Fig. 6.8
Indent size	It is the indentation (space character) count for the nested codes. Indent size must be equal or greater than zero. See Fig. 6.8
E-mail	The e-mail of the developer. See Fig. 6.8
Copyright	Copyright information. See Fig. 6.8
Code folder	This is the home folder where the code generator will create a time-stamped folder that contains all the code files after code generation is completed

To handle naming variations according to the HLA specifications, these are transformed to appropriate names when generating a workproduct, such as FED, FDD, or code. Before generating code, you can select the target RTI library to determine the appropriate naming. Figure 6.10 depicts the screen shot for this setting. Here, the *RTI library type* is used to select the native RTI supported by SimGe in code generation.

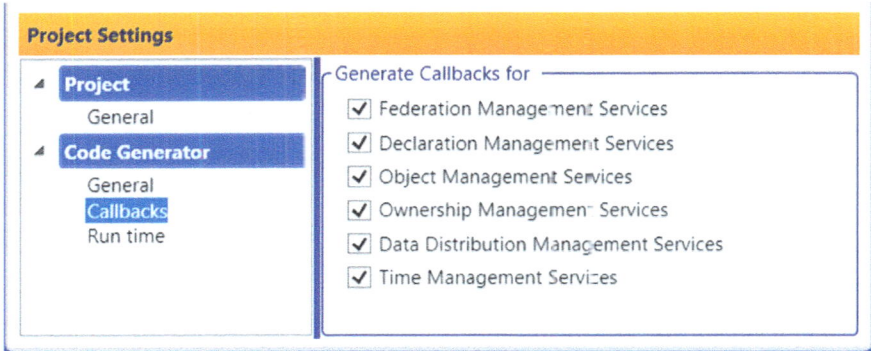

Fig. 6.9 Code generator settings—callbacks

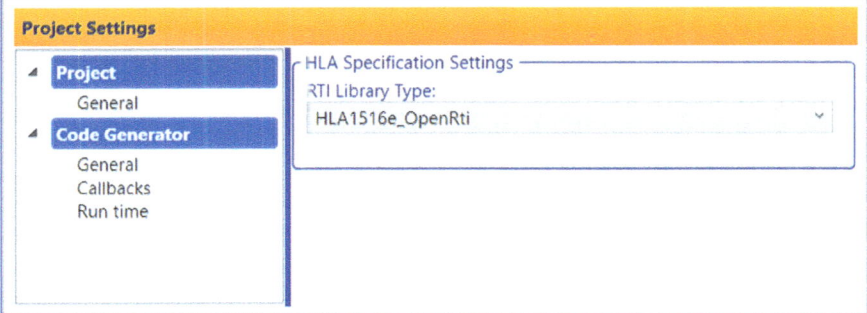

Fig. 6.10 Code generator settings for selecting the target RTI library

6.5 Summary

Code generation enables rapid federation prototyping by using the federation design model. RTI-related code is repetitive in nature; code generation alleviates this burden by generating the skeleton code for all RTI-related services. In this chapter, we showed how code generation can be carried out by using SimGe.

References

dofactory. (2016). *C# coding standards and naming conventions.* [Online] Available at: http://www.dofactory.com/reference/csharp-coding-standards.aspx. Accessed November 12, 2016.

Microsoft. (2017). *Microsoft visual studio.* [Online] Available at: https://www.visualstudio.com/. Accessed April 16, 2017.

Microsoft .NET. (2017). *MS .NET.* [Online] Available at: http://www.microsoft.com/net. Accessed April 16, 2017.

7 Federate Application Development Based on Layered Architecture

In this chapter, we will describe a federate application architecture before giving the implementation details of federate development. The presented architectural style is a layered simulation architecture based on Model Driven Engineering (MDE) techniques. For a general account of Distributed Simulation from a view point of MDE, the reader may consult (Topçu et al. 2016). We also present how to prepare and configure a development environment to begin implementing a federate application using RACoN.

7.1 Federate Application Architecture

Before implementing any federate application, a substantial software engineering effort is required for the analysis and design of that application. Architectural style of an application guides the top view of the simulation modular structure including its components and it shapes how the inner parts of the federate application will cooperate. Although many architectural styles, such as data-centric or event-driven styles, can be used to design a simulation application, with respect to modularity, the layered architectural style (Microsoft 2009) is a promising candidate for the structuring of a federate application.

Layering is an encapsulation of the components by providing separation of concerns regarding three types of tasks:

- The user interaction (graphical output, the user input, and synchronization of data between view and simulation),
- The simulation logic and computation model (representation of the system of interest), and
- The communication, which provides the federation-wide data (objects).

Each concern is addressed by a particular layer in the architecture, respectively, the *presentation layer*, the *simulation layer*, and the *communication layer*. The cross-cutting concerns between the simulation and the presentation layers are addressed by the federation-specific data structures in the form of a shared *federation foundation library* (FFL) (Topçu and Oğuztüzün 2013). Explanations about the layers are given in the following sections.

The separation between the functionality of the layers is clear, and each layer is focused on its own responsibilities (tasks). All the layers are loosely coupled to each other, and they are located on the same physical tier (computer) and operate within the same process. The communication technique between the layers is direct *method calls*, where the upper layers call the public methods of the lower layers and (may) react/handle the *events* in those layers. For instance, a class in the presentation layer can call the methods in the simulation layer. *Event-based notification* is used to inform the upper layer about the changes in lower layers, thus avoiding circular dependencies (Topçu et al. 2016).

7.1.1 Presentation Layer

The presentation layer (also called the *user interface layer*) provides the functions for the pure presentation (view), for input, and for interaction with the user (if involved). It has two major components:

- The *graphical user interface* (GUI), which can be developed using a GUI library [e.g., Windows Presentation Foundation (Microsoft WPF 2017) and Java Swing (Oracle 2017)].
- The *user interface controller* (UI controller) binds the user interface widgets with simulation data, manages and handles the user events and inputs, and iterates over the main simulation loop.

The presentation layer is separately developed for each federate and it depends on its deployment platform. For instance, it can be implemented as a *web client* or a *stand-alone desktop application*.

7.1.2 Simulation Layer

The simulation layer (also called the *processing layer*) includes the computation (the simulation), the local data (the federate-specific objects), and the extended classes from the communication layer. Its main purpose is to generate the federate internal behavior and the observable behavior, viz. the interactions with the RTI by the help of the communication layer. To give an example for the federate internal behavior, consider a ship simulation. The simulation layer includes federate application-specific components, where all the hydrodynamic calculations (e.g., the forces affecting the ship hull) are performed. Therefore, it contains all the model-related data (e.g., inputs and parameters). We call these data structures *local data structures*. For instance, the position of the ship is maintained by a local data structure. For interacting with the RTI, the simulation layer contains structures (e.g., classes and data types) that are extended from the communication layer components. The integration with the communication layer is explained in Sect. 7.1.4. An example is presented in Chap. 6 depicting the structure of the simulation layer as a UML class diagram.

7.1.3 Communication Layer

The communication layer (also called the *access layer*) deals with the HLA RTI level communication to access federation-wide data, specifically, the objects and interactions exchanged in the federation execution. The communication layer also coordinates the use of all the functionality provided by management services such as federation management (e.g., joining a federation execution) and time management (e.g., advancing time). Therefore, its functionality and its structure are intricately related to the RTI. In this book, as a communication layer, we will use the RTI abstraction component for .NET (RACoN), which is introduced in Chap. 1.

7.1.4 Integration of Layers

To integrate the local simulation with the communication layer and the underlying RTI, you may use a manager class (e.g., CSimulationManager) to manage the (multiple) federation execution(s) and the (multiple instances of) federate(s). The federate class, Federate, is the representation of a joined federate (see Fig. 7.1). It is responsible for all the application-specific RTI interaction (the observable behavior of the federate). For example, when a new object is discovered, Federate takes the appropriate action for that object. It is derived from the abstract class CGenericFederate, which is the main extension point for application-specific federates provided by RACoN.

Eventually, for implementing the simulation layer, you must

- Extend the abstract federate class (Fig. 7.1—note 1),
- Override the abstract methods found in the abstract federate class to implement the application-specific behavior (Fig. 7.1—note 2), and
- Encapsulate the simulation local data structures of the simulation and/or the data structures found in the FFL with the provided class (by RACoN), namely CHlaObject (Fig. 7.1—note 3).

An example is presented in Chap. 8 to show how all pieces fit together.

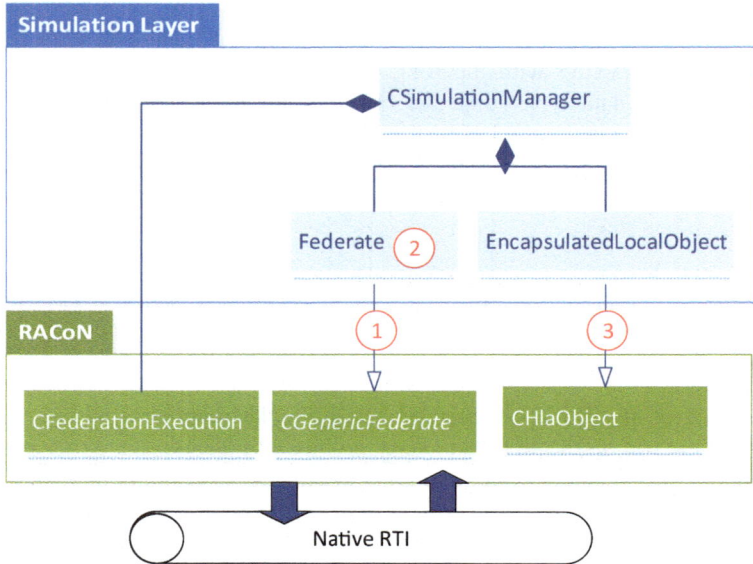

Fig. 7.1 Integration of the simulation layer and the communication layer. The simulation layer classes extend the RACoN generic classes and specialize the behavior

7.1.5 Encapsulation of Simulation Local Data Structures

Local data are encapsulated when they are to be exchanged in the federation execution. Encapsulation is not needed for all the local data structures. Only the relevant part of the data that will be shared in the federation by other federates must be considered. Remember that object instances are durable.[1] Therefore, we need to keep the state of an object (i.e., the current values of its attributes).

As seen in Fig. 7.2, by encapsulating a local data structure, we add some new properties and methods to the simulation local data structure such as a handle and type. When an object instance is registered (i.e., created) in the federation execution, the RTI assigns a unique *handle* to that instance. By keeping the handle, the application and the RTI are in agreement on which instance is under consideration. So, when some operations are done by some federate to an object instance, such as updating the value of an attribute of it, another interested federate knows the object with the help of the object handle and takes action accordingly.

See Fig. 7.3 for an example. Here, the Ship class is the local data structure that represents a ship in the environment. It is a domain entity, which has a

---

[1] "Durable" does not mean that object instances are kept in a database. In fact, they are more likely to be kept in main memory.

7.1 Federate Application Architecture

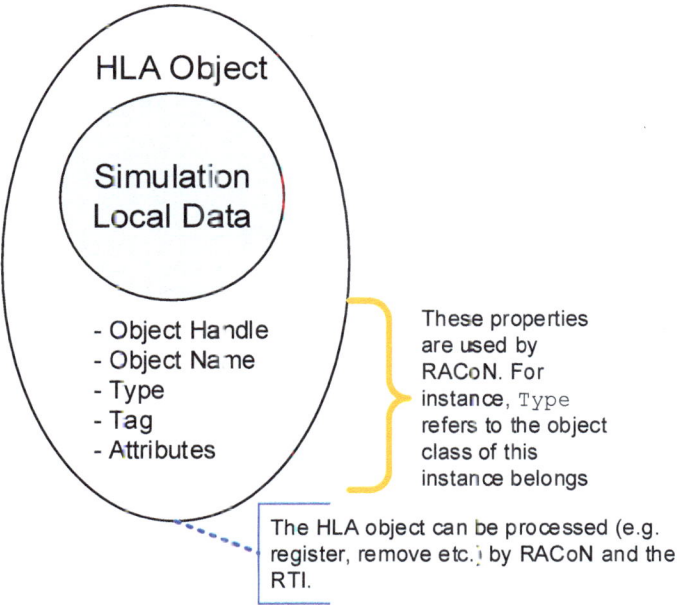

Fig. 7.2 Encapsulation of a local object as an HLA object. The HLA object brings new properties for the local object. These properties are crucial for the RTI interactions. Specifically, the object handle is used to keep the application and the RTI in agreement

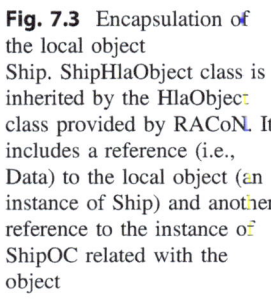

Fig. 7.3 Encapsulation of the local object Ship. ShipHlaObject class is inherited by the HlaObject class provided by RACoN. It includes a reference (i.e., Data) to the local object (an instance of Ship) and another reference to the instance of ShipOC related with the object

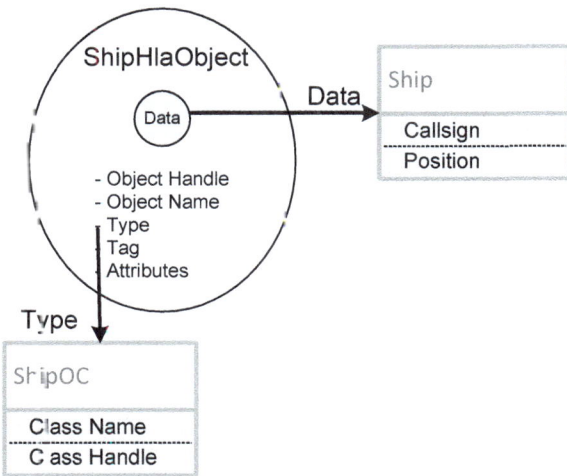

computational model that moves the ship in the virtual environment (see Chap. 3 for its computational model). You encapsulate it (or a part of it) as an HLA object by referencing the local data (`Ship`). So, the encapsulated object (`ShipHlaObject`) can be processed by the RTI.

Note that the skeleton of the wrapper class for encapsulation is generated with SimGe. You must manually create the link with the local data structure. More precisely, you must create an instance of the `Ship` class in the `ShipHlaObjectClass` by composition or aggregation. See Chap. 8 for the implementation and the code samples.

7.1.6 The Federation Foundation Library

Within the scope of an HLA federation, data are dispersed among federates and accessed through the RTI services (perhaps with the support of shared databases). The Federation Foundation Library (FFL) provides common data types, structures, and the supporter classes for the FOM to the federate applications. In addition, it helps address cross-cutting concerns across layers. The major cross-cutting concerns for many federations are the federation-wide data structures (object and interaction classes), support classes for FOM, exception management, logging, internationalization, standard look-and-feel GUI components (e.g., a federation clock for each federate), and security. The FFL is a federation-dependent auxiliary library accessed by the presentation and the simulation layers. This library encapsulates the federation-specific data structures (i.e., classes and data types) and each federate application uses this library to construct its local data structures. The FFL supports code reuse and facilitates code maintenance by keeping the common code in a central library. Consequently, a change in the FFL is reflected in all the federates using the FFL.

The use of an FLL is not mandatory from the architectural point of view, but when it is not used, each federate must implement some of the components (the functionality thereof) found in the FFL.

7.2 Development Environment Configuration

In the following subsections, we will present how to set up a development environment to begin implementing a federation using RACoN in a Windows operating system.

All the code samples are shown in C# language employing RACoN library. The integrated development environment (IDE) used in the implementation of the case studies is Microsoft Visual Studio (VS) (Microsoft 2017a, b). Please, note that all the tools and the libraries used in this book can be obtained freely; check references for the related links.

The following Chaps. 8 and 9 present the details showing how to implement a federate application using RACoN.

7.2 Development Environment Configuration

7.2.1 Prerequisites

Software requirements are presented in Table 7.1.

7.2.2 Operating Environment Configuration

As RACoN is only a wrapper library, we need to install a native RTI software. In this book, we will use OpenRTI (Portico 2017) as the baseline RTI implementation for the case studies, but the reader can select a different native RTI among supported RTIs by RACoN. The complete set of supported native RTIs within RACoN is listed in (RACoN 2016). In the following sections, we will present configuration information about OpenRTI, Portico, and DMSO RTI.

7.2.2.1 OpenRTI Configuration

To run and implement a federate application, we need to configure the operating system (OS) environment variables. First, select "System" by right-clicking "Windows" button and then click to "Advanced system settings." There, click "Environment Variables" button (see Fig. 7.4).

Add the following statements to the existing PATH variable found either in user variables or in system variables. Note that there can be one PATH variable for each set; hence, modifications must be done to the PATH variable.

- `C:\Program Files (x86)\OpenRTI\bin` for RTI dynamic link library (DLL) files.

7.2.2.2 DMSO RTI Environment Configuration

Instead of using OpenRTI as native RTI, you can use DMSO RTI NG 1.3 v6 for HLA 1.3 standard. Before adding the new environment variables to either system variables or user variables set, the DMSO RTI NG must be installed (Table 7.2).

Add the followings to the existing PATH variable. Modifications must be done to the PATH variable, where the RTI environment variable is defined.

Table 7.1 Software requirements

Category	Component
Native RTI	OpenRTI 0.8 (OpenRTI 2011), or DMSO RTI 1.3NGv6, or Portico 2.1 (Portico 2017)
Operating system	Windows 10
Runtime environment	Microsoft .NET Framework 4.6 (Microsoft 2016) Microsoft Visual C++ Redistributable package for Visual Studio 2015 (Microsoft 2017a, b)
Development environment	Microsoft Visual Studio 2015 Community Edition (Microsoft 2017a, b)

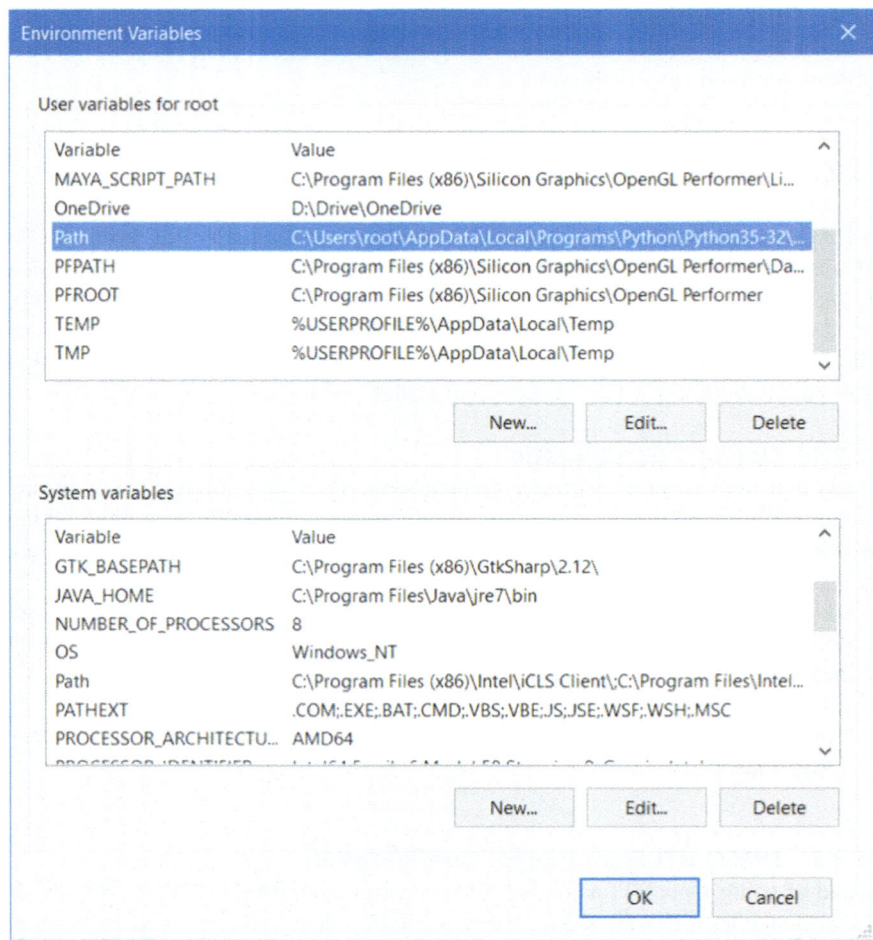

Fig. 7.4 Setting environment variables for Windows 10 OS

Table 7.2 RTI environment variables for DMSO RTI

RTI environment variables	
RTI_HOME	RTI home directory (typically C:\Program Files (x86)\DMSO)
RTI_BUILD_TYPE	RTI distribution type (i.e., RTI1.3NG-V6)

- RTI DLLs: %RTI_HOME%\%RTI_BUILD_TYPE%\Win2000-VC6\lib
- BIN DIR: %RTI_HOME%\%RTI_BUILD_TYPE%\Win2000-VC6\bin

7.2.2.3 Portico Configuration

Add the new environment variables to either system variables or user variables set (Table 7.3).

Add the following statements to the existing PATH variable. Note that there can be one PATH variable for each set, so modifications must be done to the PATH variable where the RTI environment variable is defined. If JAVA_HOME is defined in the user variables set, then modify the PATH variable in this set.

- `%RTI_HOME%\bin\vc10` for RTI dll files, where `vc10` stands for Visual C++ 10.
- `%JAVA_HOME%\bin\client` for `jvm.dll`.

7.2.2.4 Verifying Configuration

You may verify the configuration you made by opening a *console window* (i.e., Command Prompt) (using `cmd` command on "run") and then typing `path` command. Here, you will see the folders of the PATH variable. Note that if you change the content of the PATH variable, you must open a new command prompt to see the change.

You can check the configuration of the environment variables by executing the following commands.

For DMSO RTI, run `rtiexec.exe` process in the console window.

For OpenRTI, run `rtinode -i 127.0.0.1`.

Portico no longer uses a central RTI to run from the version v0.9 and upper. All federates operate in a peer-to-peer manner so there is no need to start an RTI process.

7.2.3 IDE Configuration

Before creating a VS project for federate implementation, you need to configure your VS project by installing the RACoN library. There are two methods to do that. The first method is installing the library using a *NuGet package*. The second is manually adding the DLL files to your project.

Table 7.3 RTI environment variables for Portico

RTI environment variables	
RTI_HOME	Portico home directory (typically C:\Program Files (x86)\Portico\portico-2.1.0)
JAVA_HOME	JRE home directory (e.g., C:\Program Files (x86)\Portico\portico-2.1.0\jre)

7.2.3.1 Configuration via Using a NuGet Package

RACoN library comes as a NuGet package. NuGet is "a package manager for the Microsoft (MS) developer platform including .NET" (.NET Foundation 2016). You can download and manually install RACoN NuGet package from (RACoN 2015). Or you can automatically install it by using the NuGet Package Manager found in MS Visual Studio. The package includes three DLL files (e.g., `Racon.dll`, `Racon.RtiLayer.dll`, and `Racon.RtiLayerNative.dll`).

7.2.3.2 Manual Configuration

As an alternative method, you can download the RACoN DLL files and then manually add them to your project using Visual Studio Reference Manager (Fig. 7.5). The steps are listed below.

- Create a Visual C# project.
- Right click to the "References" folder in solution explorer of the project just created. Select "Add reference."
- Select "Browse" tab.
- Download RACoN DLLs.
- Browse the folder that you copied the RACoN DLLs.
- Select one of the library files and then press OK (see Fig. 7.5).
- Repeat the steps for the other DLL files.

7.2.3.3 Namespace

To use the RACoN classes in your custom code, add "using RACoN;" statement to the top of your class code.

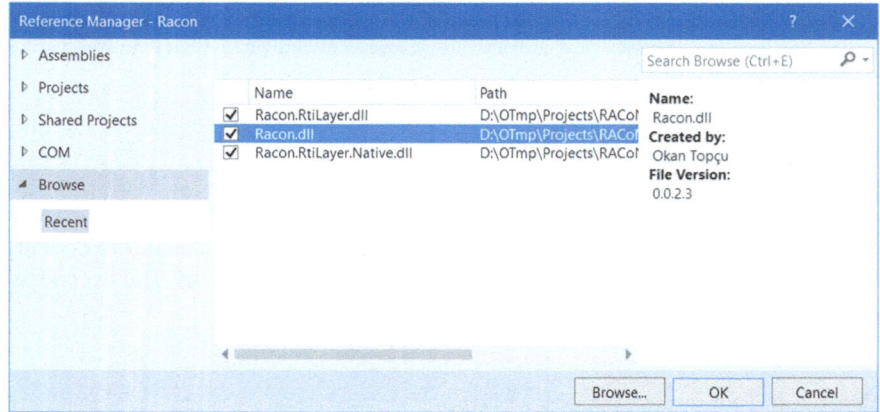

Fig. 7.5 Adding RACoN library files as reference to a project using the Visual Studio Reference Manager

7.3 Case Study: Running the STMS Federation

The subsequent chapters describe how to develop a federate application using the RACoN in detail, accompanied with a case study, the STMS federation. For a larger scale federation, see the maritime border surveillance simulation environment in Chap. 11. Furthermore, Naval Surface Tactical Maneuvering Simulation System (NSTMSS) (Topçu and Oğuztüzün 2005), a distributed interactive simulation, is implemented using the RACoN library.

The executables and the source code for the STMS federate applications can be downloaded from (STMS Web Site 2016).

First run the native RTI as specified in Sect. 7.2.2.4. Then, on a console (i.e., command prompt in Windows operating systems), use the following command line commands:

For ShipFdApp: `ShipFdApp.exe`
For StationFdApp: `StationFdApp.exe`

7.3.1 User Interface

ShipFdApp and StationFdApp applications are both console applications. In other words, they use console as standard input and output. The basic user interface for ShipFdApp is depicted in Fig. 7.6.

The gray text color is used for the status messages generated by the RACoN library while the yellow text is used to emphasize that a user input is required. The

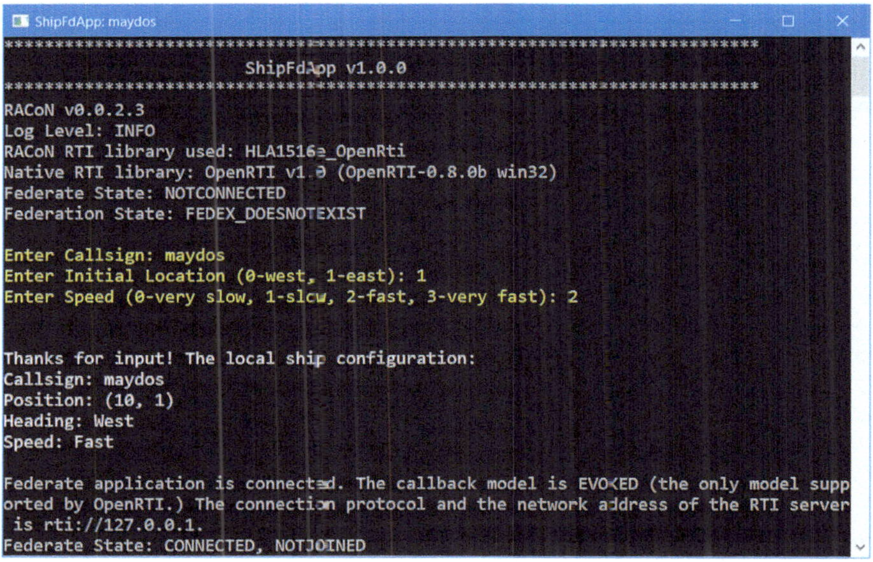

Fig. 7.6 ShipFdApp user interface showing the configuration interaction for the ship properties such as callsign and initial location

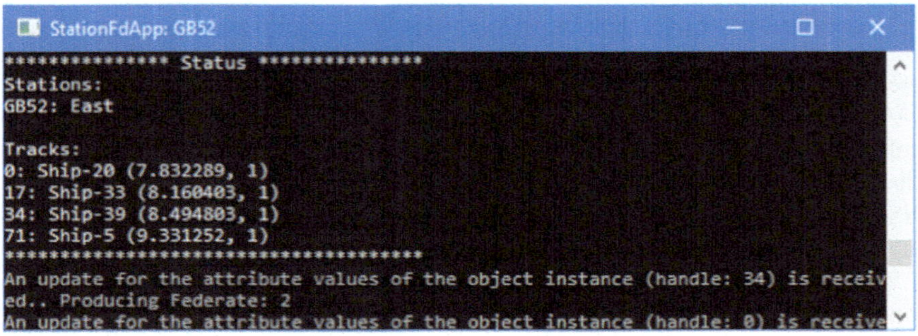

Fig. 7.7 StationFdApp user interface reporting the current tracks in its area of responsibility

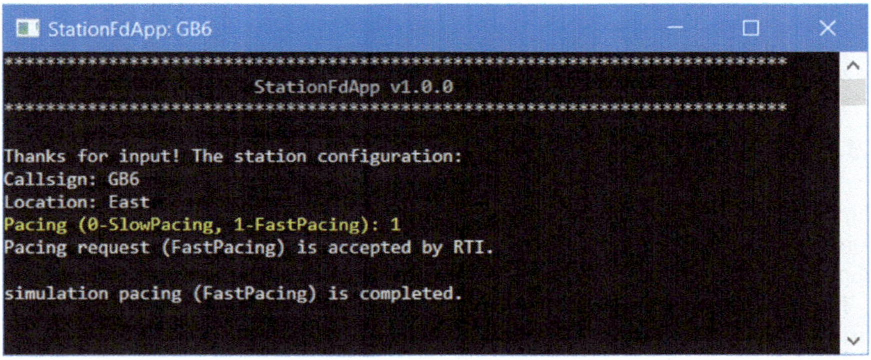

Fig. 7.8 StationFdApp user interface for controlling the simulation pace

ship reports in white text. The user can use keyboard keys to manage the applications. Below are some specific keys that work in both applications:

- In order to send a radio message, user may press "S" key anytime and begin typing the message. The message is sent as soon as the user presses the enter key.
- "P" key is used to print the status of the environment. Consequently, the application reports the entities in its environment. A screen shot is shown in Fig. 7.7.

Station federates are capable of setting the simulation pace in terms of slowing down or speeding up the ships; you can use "C" key to do that (see Fig. 7.8).

7.4 Summary

This chapter has presented a non-strict layered simulation architecture adopting the established layered architectural style for HLA federates. The layered architectural style provides a clear logical separation of the concerns of interface, simulation computation, and the HLA-specific communication, both at the conceptual and implementation levels. Layered architecture allows the separation of the layers so that each can be implemented and maintained individually. Moreover, layers become suitable for reuse in other applications, especially the lower levels, which are independent of the layers above.

RACoN is an application-independent component and can be reused in any HLA federation. To illustrate the implementation of a federate application that employs RACoN, the configuration of a typical development environment is presented.

The federation foundation library is a collection of classes and data structures that are commonly used in the implementation of federates in a typical federation. Its main goal is to handle the cross-cutting concerns (for example, the standardization of exception handling throughout the federation) implied by the federation architecture in a uniform way for each federate architecture. They are the shared components that address the cross-cutting concerns of the federation both in functionality and structure.

References

.NET Foundation. (2016). *NuGet*. https://www.nuget.org/. Accessed February 02, 2016.
Microsoft WPF. (2017). *Windows Presentation Foundation (WPF)*. https://blogs.msdn.microsoft.com/wpf/. Accessed April 18, 2017.
Microsoft. (2009). *Microsoft application architecture Guide: Patterns & practices*. 2nd edn. s.l.: Microsoft Press.
Microsoft. (2016). *Microsoft .NET framework 4.6*. https://support.microsoft.com/en-us/kb/3045557. Accessed October 03, 2016.
Microsoft. (2017a). *Microsoft visual C++ redistributable package for visual studio 2015*. https://www.microsoft.com/en-us/download/details.aspx?id=48145. Accessed April 18, 2017.
Microsoft. (2017b). *Microsoft visual studio*. https://www.visualstudio.com/. Accessed April 16, 2017.
OpenRTI. (2011). *OpenRTI project website*. https://sourceforge.net/projects/openrti/files/. Accessed April 18, 2017.
Oracle. (2017). *Java*. https://www.java.com/en/. Accessed April 18, 2017.
Portico. (2017). *The poRTIco project*. http://timpokorny.github.io/public/index.html. Accessed April 18, 2017.
RACoN. (2015). *RACoN distribution website*. https://www.nuget.org/packages/RACoN/. Accessed August 30, 2016.
RACoN. (2016). *RACoN project website*. https://sites.google.com/site/okantopcu/racon. Accessed August 30, 2016.
STMS Web Site. (2016). *STMS*. https://sites.google.com/view/distributed-simulation/stms. Accessed November 19, 2016.

Topçu, O., Durak, U., Oğuztüzün, H., & Yılmaz, L. (2016). *Distributed simulation: A model driven engineering approach* (1st ed.). Cham(Zug): Springer International Publishing.

Topçu, O., & Oğuztüzün, H. (2005). Developing an HLA based naval maneuvering simulation. *Naval Engineers Journal Winter, 117*(1), 23–40.

Topçu, O., & Oğuztüzün, H. (2013). Layered simulation architecture: A practical approach. *Simulation Modelling Practice and Theory, 32,* 1–14.

8. Federate Implementation: Basics

In this chapter, first we present how to implement the skeleton structure of a federate application. We, then, move on to how to implement a federate using the RTI basic services such as federation, data declaration, and object management services (IEEE 1516.1 2010).

8.1 Case Study: Federate Architecture

The federate applications, ShipFdApp and StationFdApp, are based on the same layered architectural style as explained in the previous chapter. In this chapter, we will only describe the ShipFdApp architecture as an example.

The static structure of an application can be represented as a *UML class diagram* showing the classes and the relationships among them. In this regard, Fig. 8.1 depicts how the classes of the ShipFdApp map to the layers. Physical separation can be achieved by packaging the classes found in each layer into an assembly. In our case study, we do not physically separate all layers; only the communication layer is separated as a runtime library. All classes in the presentation and simulation layers reside in a single process as long as our application is a console application, which simplifies the presentation layer (see Sect. 7.3 for user interface of ShipFdApp). But, you can easily separate them into different assemblies when you plan to port the user interface (of your application) to various platforms. For instance, you may prefer both a desktop and a web-based user interface for your application. In this case, it is a good practice to separate the simulation layer (e.g., as a separate assembly) from the user interface.

As seen from Fig. 8.1, most of the simulation layer classes are extended from the communication layer classes. Please remember that the federate SOM class (`FederateSom`) and related interaction and object classes (e.g., `CRadioMessageIC` and `CShipOC`) are generated using the SimGe tool. Moreover, the

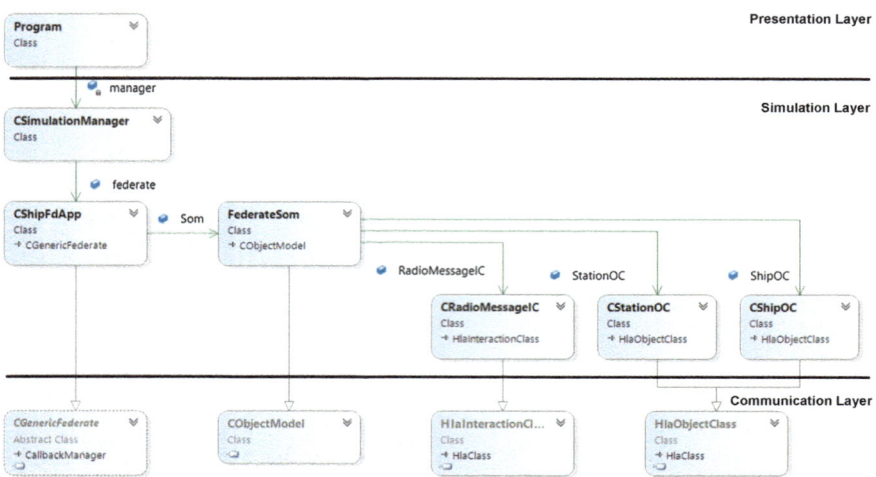

Fig. 8.1 UML class diagram of ShipFdApp. You can see how the layers are connected with each other

federate class (`CShipFdApp`) is generated as a partial class to enable the user to customize the generated code. The following sections describe how to customize and extend the application-specific federate class.

8.2 The Basics

We introduced the layered architectural style for a federate application in Chap. 7 and presented the static structure of the federate applications of our case study in the previous section. In this section, we expound on each class.

8.2.1 Namespace

The namespace for RACoN must be added before all class definitions related to RACoN. If required, the assemblies of the library may be added as follows:

```
1. using Racon;
2. using Racon.RtiLayer;
```

8.2.2 RACoN Methods

Before going further, it is time to discuss the RACoN methods. As RACoN encapsulates the entire native RTI *low-level methods* in order to simplify the

8.2 The Basics

repetitive, error-prone, and low-level implementation details of the HLA federate interface, it defines some *high-level methods*. The novice developers may employ high-level methods to easily accomplish a package of actions without thinking about the details. For instance, initializing federation execution involves some detailed actions such as creating the federation execution, joining into it, and declaring the object and interaction classes. Instead of dealing with each one by one, a single high-level method, InitializeFederation(), does all the job. But sometimes experienced developers may want to delve into the details of native RTI to adjust and control the behavior of the federate. Then, the low-level methods come to play. RACoN allows both approaches by providing the high-level methods as well as the low-level methods by wrapping each low-level method of the native RTI.

8.2.3 Creating the Simulation Manager

The simulation manager is the orchestrator among the HLA communication model (the inherited federate and its related data structures) (ln. 4 in the code segment below[1]), the local data structures (related to the simulation computational model) (ln. 7 and 8), and the simulation computational model, which is defined in the CShip class. The class definition and the declarations for the simulation manager are as follows:

```
1.  public class CSimulationManager
2.  {
3.      // Communication layer related structures
4.      public CShipFdApp federate; // Application-specific federate
5.
6.      // Local data structures and the computational models
7.      public BindingList < CShip > Ships; // Keeps the ships
8.      public BindingList < CStation > Stations; // Keeps the stations
9.  }
```

8.2.3.1 Initialization of the Federation Execution

In the constructor of the simulation manager, we need to instantiate the (application-specific) federate first (ln. 2), where this reference creates a back link between the manager and federate (see Fig. 8.2), and then we initialize the federation execution data: the name of the federation execution (ln. 4), type of federate (ln. 5), and the connection settings (ln. 6).

---

[1] ln. stands for "line number" in the following code snippet.

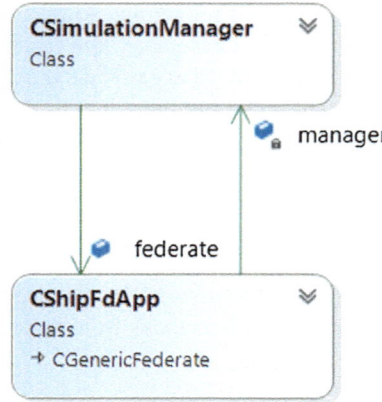

Fig. 8.2 References between the simulation manager and the federate classes.
A reference (a link) from the simulation manager to the federate class and a reference (a back link) from the federate to the simulation manager

```
1. // Initialize the application-specific federate
2. federate = new CShipFdApp(this);
3. // Initialize the federation execution
4. federate.FederationExecution.Name = "Dardanelles";
5. federate.FederationExecution.FederateType = "TestFederate";
6. federate.FederationExecution.ConnectionSettings = "rti://127.0.0.1";
7. // Handle RTI type variation
8. initialize();
```

To create a federation execution, we must also supply a FOM module. To specify a FOM, we must provide the name and the path of the related FED/FDD file. In this example, we provide the full name of the file with an absolute or relative path. Below is an example to specify the FDD file using a relative file. In this case, the federate application will try to reach the file in its execution directory.

```
1. FederationExecution.FDD = @".\MariSim.xml";
```

Note that HLA 1.3 and HLA 1516-2000 specifications only support one FOM module. On the other hand, HLA Evolved (IEEE1516 2010) specification supports multiple FOM modules. To load additional FOM modules, you may call the following method:

```
1. FederationExecution.FomModules.Add(@".\ACL.xml"); // add additional
   FOM modules
```

8.2.4 Creating the Federate Class

The first thing is to inherit your application-specific federate (i.e., CShipFdApp) from the RACoN generic federate.

8.2 The Basics

```
1. // CShipFdApp extends and specializes the generic federate
2. public partial class CShipFdApp : Racon.Federation.CGenericFederate
```

This class is generated as a partial class by SimGe spread into two files as `ShipFdApp.cs` and `ShipFdApp.simge.cs`. To customize and extend it, you are advised to work on the former. In this way, when you generate this file again, you will not lose the code you added.

As we want to reach to some local data structures declared in the simulation manager, we create a back link (see Fig. 8.2) to the simulation manager in the federates constructor.

```
1. public CShipFdApp(CSimulationManager parent): this() {
2.     manager = parent; // Set simulation manager
3. }
```

8.2.4.1 Native RTI Selection

In the constructor of the inherited federate class, you call the base constructor with your selection of the native RTI library type as a parameter, where RACoN supports various HLA 1.3 and HLA Evolved compliant RTIs. Using this parameter, RACoN selects the native RTI library to be used during federation execution. For OpenRTI HLA1516e, for example, the constructor code will be as follows:

```
1. public CShipFdApp(): base(RTILibraryType.HLA1516e_OpenRti)
```

8.2.4.2 Handling Multiple RTI Variation

HLA specifications differ not only from the perspective of providing new features and technologies, but also from the perspective of implementation. For instance, there are some naming variations on object models according to the HLA specifications. SimGe handles naming variations in agreement with the relevant HLA specification and generates code according to the code generator configuration parameters as explained in Chap. 6.

RACoN also supports multiple HLA specifications and handles RTI-specific variation. Before compiling the federation, you can change and select another native RTI (e.g., DMSO RTI 1.3NGv6, or HLA1516e OpenRTI) using the base constructor as described in the previous section. In this case, the generated code could not reflect the proper naming. To handle this situation, a special private method, named `initialize()` (ln. 2), is also auto-generated.

```
1.  // Handles naming variation according to HLA specification
2.  private void initialize() {
3.    switch (federate.RTILibrary) {
4.      case RTILibraryType.HLA13_DMSO:
5.      case RTILibraryType.HLA13_Portico:
6.      case RTILibraryType.HLA13_OpenRti:
7.        federate.Som.ShipOC.Name = "ObjectRoot.Ship";
8.        federate.Som.ShipOC.PrivilegeToDelete.Name = "privilegeToDelete";
9.        federate.FederationExecution.FDD = @".\StmsFom.fed";
10.       // …
11.       break;
12.     case RTILibraryType.HLA1516e_Portico:
13.     case RTILibraryType.HLA1516e_OpenRti:
14.       federate.Som.ShipOC.Name = "HLAobjectRoot.Ship";
15.       federate.Som.ShipOC.PrivilegeToDelete.Name = "HLAprivilegeToDeleteObject";
16.       // …
17.       federate.FederationExecution.FDD = @".\StmsFom.xml";
18.       break;
19.   }
20. }
```

8.3 Implementing the Simulation Object Model

FDD represents an agreement among federates on what to share within a federation during execution. The federates are responsible to implement the required data structures to represent this agreement. When a federate discovers an object, what it will do with it totally depends on the implementation of the federate. Furthermore, FOM is declarative. It limits what can be done at execution time, but does not dictate it. For example, who is the current owner of an object class at a particular time? P/S (publish/subscribe) is also a runtime behavior reflecting the changing capabilities and interests of a federate. To publish and subscribe, a federate needs the runtime ids (handles) of object classes for publish and subscribe or for register/delete. The handles may differ in each federation execution. Therefore, each federate needs to implement a representation (object model) for FOM/SOM data.

The simulation object model (SOM) includes the HLA object classes, interaction classes, and routing spaces.[2] The SOM class includes the instances of the HLA object model classes that can be used in the federate application.

The SOM class and the classes corresponding to each HLA class are defined in separate files in the application. It is recommended to let SimGe generate those classes completely, instead of manually coding each. The UML class diagram for the ship federate application, depicted in Fig. 8.3, shows the classes corresponding each HLA class in the SOM of the federate and their related attributes/parameters.

---

[2]For HLA 1.3 version.

8.3 Implementing the Simulation Object Model

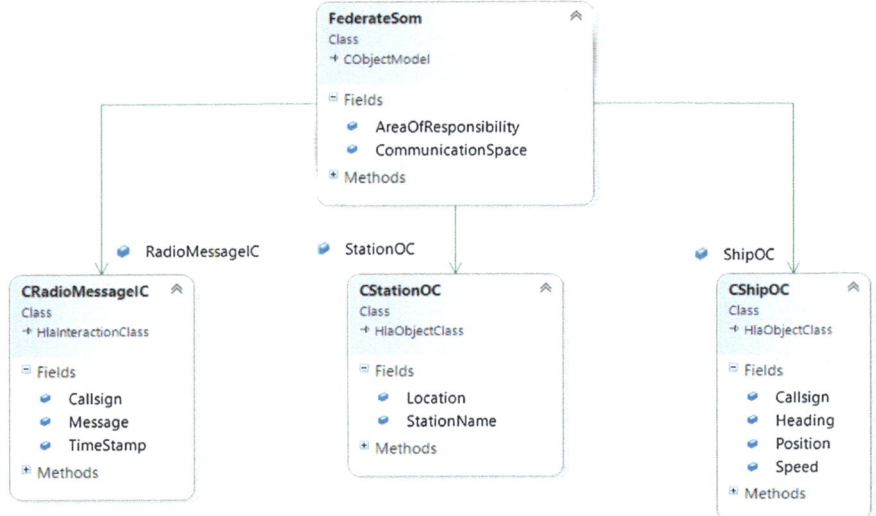

Fig. 8.3 UML class diagram for (a part of) SOM of the ship federate application

For small SOMs, however, the SOM can be defined directly in the federate class. But, we do not advise this for the sake of code modularity.

The SOM class, named `FederateSom` by default, must be inherited from the `CObjectModel`, and its constructor must call the base constructor as seen below.

```
1.  public class FederateSom: Racon.ObjectModel.CObjectModel
```

`FederateSom` class must declare all the classes representing the HLA object and interaction classes found in the federate SOM as well as the routing spaces for HLA1.3 specification.

```
1.  public stms.Som.CShipOC ShipOC;
2.  public stms.Som.CStationOC StationOC;
3.  public stms.Som.CRadioMessageIC RadioMessageIC;
4.  public stms.Som.CCommunicationSpace CommunicationSpace;
```

Then, in the constructor, you must instantiate (e.g., ship object class in ln. 3) and add each class to the object model of the federate (e.g., ln. 4). You repeat this process for all the classes that represent the HLA classes and the routing spaces (ln. 5–10). When extending a RACoN library by inheritance, always call the `base()` method in the constructor as seen in ln. 1. Because the base class does some initialization job at instantiation.

```
1.  public FederateSom(): base() {
2.      // Construct SOM
3.      ShipOC = new stms.Som.CShipOC();
4.      AddToObjectModel(ShipOC);
5.      StationOC = new stms.Som.CStationOC();
6.      AddToObjectModel(StationOC);
7.      RadioMessageIC = new stms.Som.CRadioMessageIC();
8.      AddToObjectModel(RadioMessageIC);
9.      CommunicationSpace = new stms.Som.CCommunicationSpace();
10.     AddToObjectModel(CommunicationSpace);
11. }
```

8.3.1 Defining an Object Class and Its Attributes

For each object class in the SOM, we define a class and then set its properties such as the class name, its P/S status, and its attributes.

The object class must be inherited from the `HlaObjectClass` of RACoN library. The following code snippets are for the ship object class.

```
1.  public class CShipOC : HlaObjectClass
```

Next, we need to declare all its attributes, where their type is `HlaAttribute`.

```
1.  public HlaAttribute Callsign;
2.  public HlaAttribute Position;
3.  public HlaAttribute Heading;
4.  public HlaAttribute Speed;
```

In its constructor, first we set the object class name (ln. 3) and its P/S status (ln. 4), and then we instantiate and initialize its attributes (e.g., ln. 6, 8, 10, and 12). After initialization, we add it to the related object class (e.g., ln. 7, 9, 11, and 13). Here, the attributes are stored in a list data structure (i.e., `BindingList` to support binding with graphical user interface).

The name of the object class and the name of each attribute must exactly be the same as those in the FED/FDD file. The object classes and interaction classes use fully qualified names, which show the hierarchy of the base classes (ln. 3).

8.3 Implementing the Simulation Object Model

```
1.  public CShipOC(): base() {
2.      // Initialize Class Properties
3.      Name = "HLAobjectRoot.Ship";
4.      ClassPS = PSKind.PublishSubscribe;
5.      // Create Attributes // Callsign
6.      Callsign = new HlaAttribute("Callsign", PSKind.PublishSubscribe);
7.      Attributes.Add(Callsign); // Position
8.      Position = new HlaAttribute("Position", PSKind.PublishSubscribe);
9.      Attributes.Add(Position); // Heading
10.     Heading = new HlaAttribute("Heading", PSKind.PublishSubscribe);
11.     Attributes.Add(Heading); // Speed
12.     Speed = new HlaAttribute("Speed", PSKind.PublishSubscribe);
13.     Attributes.Add(Speed);
14. }
```

An attribute's publish/subscribe status must match with the federate publish/subscribe behavioral pattern; see the Sect. 8.5 for declaration management.

8.3.2 Defining an Interaction Class and Its Parameters

The implementation approach followed for object classes is also used for interaction classes. The following code is for the radio message interaction.

```
1.  public class CRadioMessageIC: HlaInteractionClass {
2.      public HlaParameter TimeStamp;
3.      public HlaParameter Callsign;
4.      public HlaParameter Message;
5.      // Constructor
6.      public CRadioMessageIC(): base() {
7.          // Initialize Class Properties
8.          Name = "HLAinteractionRoot.RadioMessage';
9.          ClassPS = PSKind.PublishSubscribe;
10.         // Create Parameters
11.         TimeStamp = new HlaParameter("TimeStamp");
12.         Parameters.Add(TimeStamp);
13.         Callsign = new HlaParameter("Callsign");
14.         Parameters.Add(Callsign);
15.         Message = new HlaParameter("Message");
16.         Parameters.Add(Message);
17.     }
18. }
```

8.3.3 Connecting SOM and Federate

In the constructor of the federate class, we instantiate a SOM object and then tell the federate to use it as its object model (ln. 4).

```
1.  public CShipFdApp(): base(RTILibraryType.HLA1516e_OpenRti) {
2.      // Create and Attach Som to federate
3.      Som = new stms.Som.FederateSom();
4.      SetSom(Som);
5.  }
```

8.4 Calls and Callbacks

The federate interface services are provided in terms of methods. As explained in Chap. 2, methods are grouped as *federate-initiated* and *RTI-initiated*. When we ask the RTI to carry out something, we *call* a method. When the RTI has something to send us, we receive this as a *callback*.

8.4.1 Events

Callbacks are implemented as events in RACoN. *Event* is a message to signal the occurrence of an action such as an object discovery. In other words, RACoN provides notifications about HLA-related services to the federate by using the events; this is known as *event-based notification*. Eventually, an application-specific federate can handle events triggered from the communication layer by overriding the *event handlers*, which are subscribed by the base federate in order to customize their RTI-related behaviors; this is known as *delegated event handling*.

The .NET event handling structures are used for implementing events and event handling mechanism. Events are categorized according to their initiators:

- Federate Ambassador (FdAmb) events: The RTI-initiated events generated by the Federate Ambassador callbacks such as the object-discovered event. The callbacks from the RTI to the Federate Ambassador are queued as events to be processed at the end of each simulation cycle.
- RTI Ambassador (RtiAmb) Events: The federate-initiated events generated by the RTI Ambassador such as the federate-joined event.
- The RACoN events generated by the generic federate such as the federate-state-changed event.

Figure 8.4 depicts the federate, RTI, and RACoN events. The FdAmb events represent the RTI-initiated service callbacks such as object discovered, provided by the `CallbackManager` class. The event handlers are registered automatically by the generic federate (base federate class). The callbacks from the RTI to the Federate Ambassador are queued as events for processing at the end of each simulation cycle. The names of FdAmb event handlers begin with `FdAmb_` prefix. They are public methods; when required, they can be overridden by the federate class.

8.4 Calls and Callbacks

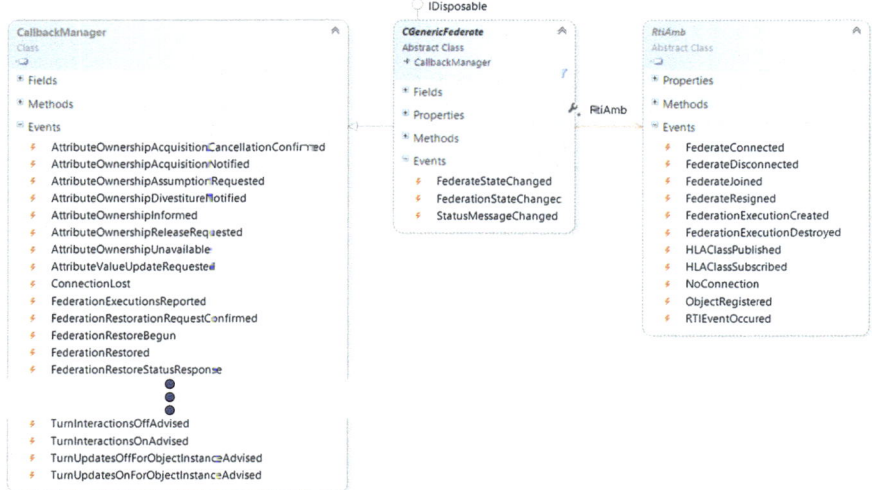

Fig. 8.4 Events. The class (CallbackManager) on the *left* provides the FdAmb events, the class (CGenericFederate) in the *middle* the RACoN events, and the class (RtiAmb) on the *right* the RtiAmb events

The RtiAmb events are the federate-initiated events like the `FederateJoined`. These events are normally used to keep track of the federate and federation state.

8.4.2 Event Handling

Event handlers (e.g., `FdAmb_InteractionReceivedHandler`) are implemented in the federate class by overriding the base virtual methods. The base class (the generic federate) has already subscribed to the RTI and the federate events. You can override and customize them as extending the federate class. SimGe generates the handler templates (the skeleton code) automatically in the generated federate class (e.g., in ShipFdApp.simge.cs, see Fig. 8.5) But when you want to customize and extend a handler, then it is advised that you move the handler code and definition to the federate file (i.e., ShipFdApp.cs for the case study) where the user code is implemented. Thus, when the federate file is regenerated by SimGe, you will not lose the manually added code.

8.4.3 Tracing the RTI

One specific RACoN event is the one that provides detailed information (in text) about what is going on "under the hood", that is, inside RACoN. This is specifically

```
ShipFdApp.simge.cs

    #region Event Handlers
    #region Federate Callback Event Handlers
    #region Federation Management Callbacks
    // FdAmb_InitiateFederateSaveHandler
    public override void FdAmb_InitiateFederateSaveHandler(object
sender, RACoN.RTILayer.CHlaFederationManagementEventArgs data)
    {
      // Call the base class handler
      base.FdAmb_InitiateFederateSaveHandler(sender, data);

      #region User Code
      throw new
NotImplementedException("FdAmb_InitiateFederateSaveHandler");
      #endregion //User Code
    }
```

Move to «ShipFdApp.cs» to override

Fig. 8.5 Overriding default event handlers. When overriding the event handler, you should not forget to call the base class handler (base.FdAmb_InitiateFederateSaveHandler) first

needed for debugging. By default, this capability is turned on for warning and error messages. To get the RTI execution traces regularly, you must follow these steps:

- First, the application-specific federate must hook to the `StatusMessageChanged` event.

  ```
  1. // Getting the information/debugging messages from RACoN
  2. manager.federate.StatusMessageChanged += Federate_StatusMessageChanged;
  ```

- Second, the information level must be set to a log mode within the values of TRACE, INFO, WARN, and ERROR. TRACE mode provides detailed information about the RTI events including the handles. INFO mode provides only important information like federate state changes. WARN mode reports the warnings in the RTI behavior, but the execution can continue. For example, when a federate tries to connect when it has already connected, a warning (i.e., AlreadyConnected), is generated. ERROR mode only reports the errors encountered during execution such as an RTI internal error exception.

  ```
  1. manager.federate.LogLevel = Racon.DebugLevel.TRACE;
  ```

- In the handler method, the `StatusMessage` of the federate carries the latest information message about the RACoN events (ln. 4). The type of `StatusMessage` is `String`, and it is a read-only property provided by the base federate.

8.4 Calls and Callbacks

```
1.  // Racon Information received
2.  private static void Federate_StatusMessageChanged(ob-
    ject sender, EventArgs e)
3.  {
4.      Console.WriteLine((sender as CShipFdApp).StatusMessage
5.          + Environment.NewLine);
6.  }
```

Moreover, RACoN keeps a trace log where all trace and information messages are kept. To dump this log to a file:

```
1.  // Dump trace log
2.  System.IO.StreamWriter file = new System.IO.StreamWriter(@".\TraceLog.txt");
3.  file.WriteLine(manager.federate.TraceLog);
4.  file.Close();
```

An example trace log is depicted in Fig. 8.6.

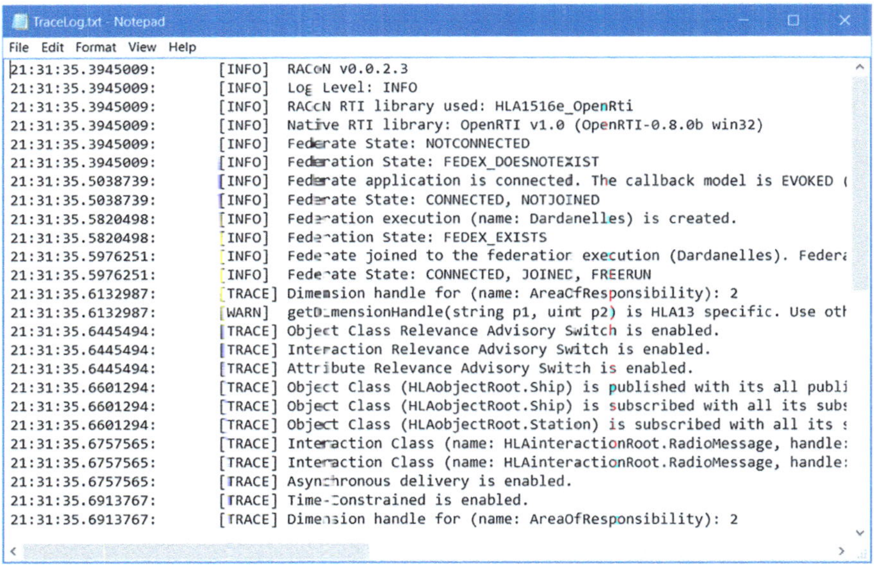

Fig. 8.6 An excerpt from the trace log of ShipFdApp. The log includes all the log entries generated during the federate lifecycle. A log entry is composed of a timestamp, a log level, and a message. Timestamp shows time when it is logged. As the trace messages are generated in high volumes, the precision of timestamp is high. The last seven digits show the milliseconds thereof. The log entries are ordered according to the timestamps

8.5 Federation Management

Before interacting with the RTI, the federate must connect to the RTI using the connect service to establish a connection. In calling the connect method, we supply the callback model (see Chap. 2) as a parameter as well as the local connection settings. The parameter for the local connection settings is optional. In OpenRTI, this parameter is used to specify the connection protocol and the network (IP) address of the RTI server (rtinode executable).

```
1. virtual public bool Connect(CallbackModel callbackModel = Callback-
   Model.EVOKED, string localSettingsDesignator = "rti://127.0.0.1")
```

After a successful connection establishment, the federate state changes to the CONNECTED and NOTJOINED state from the NOTCONNECTED state.

Please, note that the connect service is not available in HLA 1.3 specification.

8.5.1 Federation Execution Creation

To create a federation execution, we first initialize the federation execution properties (ln. 1–7) as described in Sect. 8.2.3.1. Then, we call the create federation execution service (ln. 10).

```
1.  // initalize federation execution properties
2.  FederationExecution.FederateName = "USV";
3.  FederationExecution.FederateType = "UsvAgentFederate";
4.
5.  // add additional FOM modules
6.  FederationExecution.FomModules.Add(@".\MariSim.xml");
7.  FederationExecution.FomModules.Add(@".\ACL.xml");
8.
9.  // Create federation execution
10. CreateFederationExecution(FederationExecution.Name, FederationExe-
    cution.FomModules);
```

There are two method overloads to call the `CreateFederationExecution()` method in HLA Evolved. In the first method overload, we provide the federation execution name and the FDD file name as parameters. The third parameter, logical time implementation name, is optional. If it is not provided, `HLAfloat64Time` representation of logical time is used as default. This call is the only way to create a federation execution in HLA 1.3. The third parameter has no effect in this case.

```
1. virtual public bool CreateFederationExecution(string fed-
   exName, string fomModule, string logicalTimeImplementation-
   Name = "")
```

8.5 Federation Management

The second overload of this method takes additional FOM modules instead of a single FDD file name. The additional FOM modules are provided as the (full) file names of each corresponding FDD file.

```
1. virtual public bool CreateFederationExecution(string fed-
   exName, List<string> fomModules, string logicalTimeImplementation-
   Name = "")
```

Alternatively, to create a federation execution with a customized (federation-specific) MIM module, you use the following method.

```
1. virtual public bool CreateFederationExecutionWithMIM(string fed-
   exName, List < string > fomModules, string mimMod-
   ule = "", string logicalTimeImplementationName = "")
```

The federation execution will be created as a result of these calls if it is not already created by another federate. The federation execution state will transit to the FEDEX_EXIST state from the FEDEX_DOESNOTEXIST state. If the federation execution is created previously, then a warning exception will be generated.

8.5.2 Joining the Federation Execution

After successful creation of a federation execution, the federate can join the federation execution. There are two method overloads for this service. In the first one, we provide the federate type, the federation execution name, which this federate is willing to join, and FOM module designators. The federate type is used to distinguish federate categories in a federation save-and-restore operation. The FOM module designators are optional and are used to provide additional FDD files. The contents of the additional FDD files cannot conflict with the current FDD specified at the creation of the federation execution.

```
1. virtual public bool JoinFederationExecution(string federate-
   Type, string federationExecutionName, List < string > fomMod-
   ules = null)
```

The second overload takes a federate name parameter additionally. The federate name supplied must be unique in the federation execution. The federate name must be kept by the federate application in case of a possible restore operation.

```
1. virtual public bool JoinFederationExecution(string federate-
   Name, string federateType, string federationExecution-
   Name, List < string > fomModules = null)
```

In the first method overload, the RTI is responsible to provide a unique name for the federate. To query the federate name, you may use a support service as specified below (ln. 1). You can also get the federate handle using the federate name (ln. 2).

```
1. federate.GetFederateName(manager.federate.FederateHandle);
2. federate.GetFederateHandle(manager.federate.FederationExecu-
   tion.FederateName);
```

For HLA 1.3, we call the method shown below with the federate and the federation execution name.

```
1. virtual public bool JoinFederationExecution(string federate-
   Name, string federationExecutionName)
```

After a successful join operation, the federate state changes to a combined state of CONNECTED, JOINED, and FREERUN. The FREERUN state is only used when the federation involves a scenario, and it indicates that a role is not assigned to the federate.

8.5.3 High-Level Method for Initialization

RACoN also provides a high-level method which simplifies federation initialization by combining several RTI services. This method returns true signaling a successful initialization.

```
6. bool result = manager.federate.InitializeFederation(federate.Feder-
   ationExecution);
```

Initialization method is a combination of method calls that connects, creates the federation execution (provided that federation execution does not exist), joins the federation execution, creates the regions, and declares the federate capabilities (including the interests), as seen in Fig. 8.7.

8.5.4 Finalization of Federation Execution

You can call the finalization method provided by the generic federate (ln. 2). At this stage, the resigning federate implicitly deletes any objects for which it holds the privilege-to-delete token and then releases ownership of any remaining owned attributes. This is the default resign action. Alternatively, you can also specify the resign action explicitly by providing a second parameter to the method (ln. 4).

8.5 Federation Management

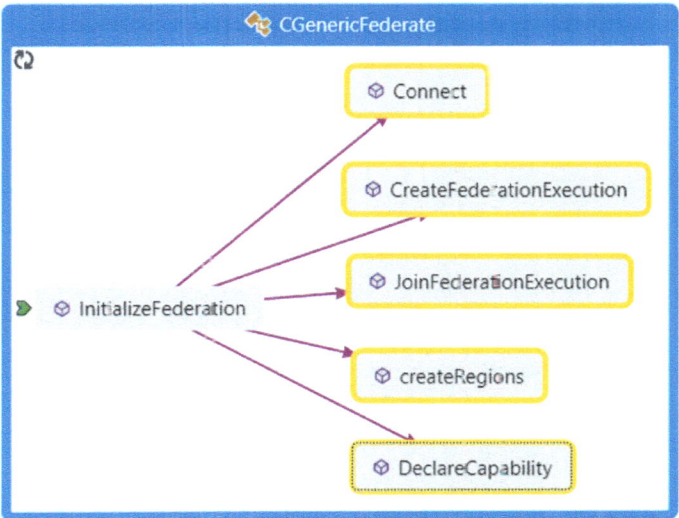

Fig. 8.7 Code map for InitializeFederation() method

```
1. // Leave federation with default resign action
2. bool result = manager.federate.FinalizeFederation(manager.feder-
   ate.FederationExecution);
3. // Leave federation with a resign action you choose
4. bool result = manager.federate.FinalizeFederation(manager.feder-
   ate.FederationExecution, Racon.ResignAction.DELETE_OBJECTS);
```

When the finalization method is called, first the federate resigns the federation execution and then tries to end (destroy) the federation execution. Destroying the federation execution succeeds only if there are no joined federates in the federation execution. Lastly, the federate disconnects as seen in Fig. 8.8.

8.5.5 Connection Lost

In some cases, such as in case of a crash of the RTI executive or a network breakdown, the federate will lose its connection to the RTI. In this situation, the federate is notified by a connection lost callback, and the federate enters into the NOTCONNECTED state (see Sect. 2.8 for federate states). You must implement a strategy to deal with this situation. For example, if the network failure is likely to be recovered shortly, you may try to reconnect to the RTI.

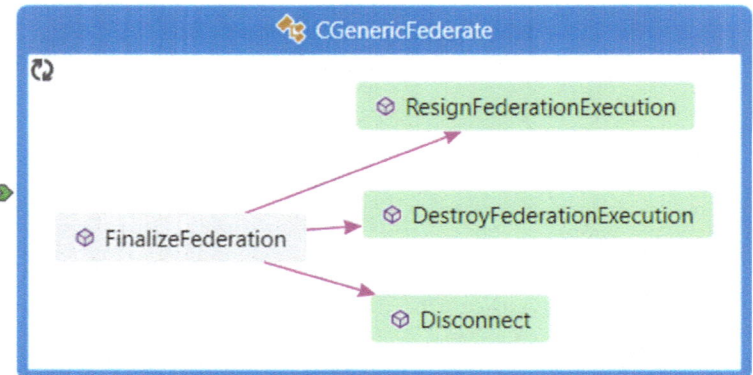

Fig. 8.8 Code map for FinalizeFederation() method. As you see, the finalize federation is an high-level method consisting of some low-level methods

8.6 Declaration Management

As stated in Sect. 8.2.3, the declaration of object and interaction classes is implicitly done when initializing the federation. Publishing/subscription is done in accordance with the federate SOM. Remember that each object class, attribute, and interaction class in SOM has a property to set its P/S status.

For instance, ShipFdApp subscribes to the Station object class and its attributes in consonance with its Station object class definition in its SOM. The P/S status is set as follows (ln. 3 for class, ln. 4 and 6 for attributes):

```
1.  public CStationOC(): base() {
2.      Name = "HLAobjectRoot.Station";
3.      ClassPS = PSKind.Subscribe;
4.      StationName = new HlaAttribute("StationName", PSKind.Sub-
    scribe);
5.      Attributes.Add(StationName);
6.      Location = new HlaAttribute("Location", PSKind.Subscribe);
7.      Attributes.Add(Location);
8.  }
```

Eventually, ShipFdApp not only subscribes to the Station object class, but also both publishes and subscribes to the Ship object class and the radio message interaction class as traced in Fig. 8.9.

At runtime, a federate may freely modify its P/S status depending on its changing interests and capabilities, depending on the stage of the simulation. For instance, federate may unpublish an interaction class, which it is currently publishing. To reverse P/S operations, a federate can use the declaration management services below:

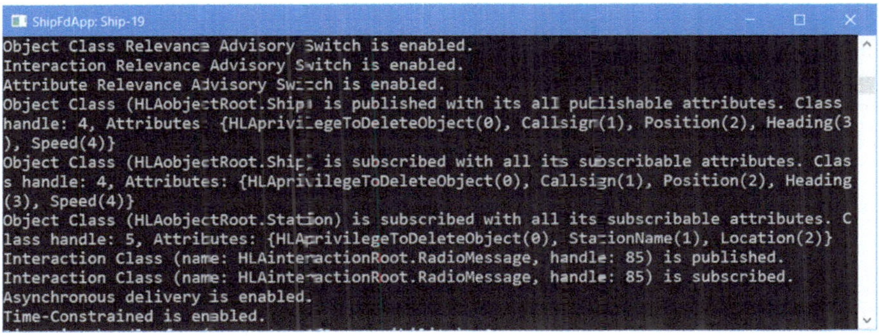

8.6 Declaration Management

```
ShipFdApp: Ship-19
Object Class Relevance Advisory Switch is enabled.
Interaction Relevance Advisory Switch is enabled.
Attribute Relevance Advisory Switch is enabled.
Object Class (HLAobjectRoot.Ship) is published with its all publishable attributes. Class
handle: 4, Attributes: {HLAprivilegeToDeleteObject(0), Callsign(1), Position(2), Heading(3
), Speed(4)}
Object Class (HLAobjectRoot.Ship) is subscribed with all its subscribable attributes. Clas
s handle: 4, Attributes: {HLAprivilegeToDeleteObject(0), Callsign(1), Position(2), Heading
(3), Speed(4)}
Object Class (HLAobjectRoot.Station) is subscribed with all its subscribable attributes. C
lass handle: 5, Attributes: {HLAprivilegeToDeleteObject(0), StationName(1), Location(2)}
Interaction Class (name: HLAinteractionRoot.RadioMessage, handle: 85) is published.
Interaction Class (name: HLAinteractionRoot.RadioMessage, handle: 85) is subscribed.
Asynchronous delivery is enabled.
Time-Constrained is enabled.
```

Fig. 8.9 A screen shot showing the P/S output of ShipFdApp after declaration is completed

- Unpublish object class attributes,
- Unpublish interaction class,
- Unsubscribe object class attributes,
- Unsubscribe interaction class.

8.7 Object Management

8.7.1 Implementing Simulation Objects

As introduced in Chap. 7, the simulation local data structures (i.e., the simulation classes) must be wrapped by the local representations of the HLA object classes. In STMS federation, ShipFdApp will track both ships and stations in the environment. Ships and stations are domain objects found in the conceptual model. Therefore, we create a class to represent them, called `CShip` and `CStation`. Then, we can define any local data (attributes, properties, or methods) in the class such as the call sign and position (ln. 3 and 4) for the ship class.

```
1.  // Local Domain Object
2.  public class CShip {
3.      public string callsign;
4.      public LocationEnum position, heading;
5.      public SpeedEnum speed;
6.      public Ship() {
7.          callsign = "";
8.          position = LocationEnum.East;
9.          heading = LocationEnum.West;
10.         speed = SpeedEnum.Fast;
11.     }
12. }
```

We need to encapsulate them in order to use them as HLA objects. Hence, to implement a simulation object, we must derive it from `HlaObject` class (ln. 1). The following code snippet shows how to encapsulate the domain object, `ship`. The constructor must call the base constructor to set the type (i.e., the object class) of the object (ln. 4).

```
1.  // Encapsulated Object for HLA
2.  public class CShipHlaObject: HlaObject {
3.      public CShip ship;
4.      public CShipHlaObject(HlaObjectClass _type): base(_type) {
5.          ship = new CShip();
6.      }
7.  }
```

Now, we can instantiate an object from the `CShipHlaObject` class to represent the local ship object and other ships found in the simulation environment. The most critical part is to set the type of the object. Here, the `ShipOC` is the class defined in SOM of the federate class (see Sect. 8.3.1).

```
1.  // Encapsulate our own ship and add it to the list
2.  CShipHlaObject encapsulatedShipObject = new CShipHlaObject(manager.federate.Som.ShipOC);
```

If the domain object is needed only to keep track of the environment, such as the station object for ShipFdApp, then we may directly define it in the encapsulation class. For `Station` object instance, we just define the encapsulated object class without an external domain object definition as seen in the code snippet below.

```
1.  // Encapsulated Object for HLA including the Local Domain Object
2.  public class CStationHlaObject: HlaObject {
3.
4.      public string stationName;
5.      public LocationEnum location;
6.
7.      public CStationHlaObject(HlaObjectClass _type): base(_type) {
8.          stationName = "";
9.          location = LocationEnum.East;
10.     }
11.     public CStationHlaObject(HlaObject _obj): base(_obj) {
12.         stationName = "";
13.         location = LocationEnum.East;
14.     }
15. }
```

Now, we are ready to keep all the object instances which we are interested, in the federation execution. In the simulation manager, we can create a list for each type of objects. For example, for ship objects:

8.7 Object Management

```
1.  ShipObjects = new BindingList<CShipHlaObject>();
```

Whenever we discover a ship object instance in the environment, we can instantiate a new ship HLA object and add it to the list.

8.7.2 Registering Objects

After a successful initialization of the federation execution, you may register each object (e.g., `ship`) instantiated in the previous section. Registering means creating an HLA object instance[3] from the perspective of the RTI so that other federates can discover them. As we manage our local ship, we register it, which is the first in our ship list.

```
1.  RegisterHlaObject(manager.ShipObjects[0]);
```

8.7.2.1 Object Class Relevance Advisory Switch

RTI smartly advises you when to start your object registration by sending *Start Registration For Object Class* callback (ln. 1). When a subscriber is found in the federation for your published object classes and its attributes, then this callback is generated. For object registration, it is better to put registration code inside this callback (ln. 7 and 8). We must ensure which object class is requested for registration by checking the handles of the object classes (ln. 7).

```
1.  public override void FdAmb_StartRegistrationForObjectClassAdvisedHandler
2.  (object sender, HlaDeclarationManagementEventArgs data)
3.  {
4.      // Call the base class handler
5.      base.FdAmb_StartRegistrationForObjectClassAdvisedHandler(sender, data);
6.      // Check that this is for the ShipOC
7.      if (data.ObjectClassHandle == Som.ShipOC.Handle)
8.          RegisterHlaObject(manager.ShipObjects[0]);
9.  }
```

When no subscribers exist in the federation execution, then *Stop Registration For Object ClassStart Registration For Object Class* callback is generated. Both advisory switches are controlled using the *Enable/Disable Object Class Relevance Advisory Switch* services. See Fig. 8.10

---

[3]Remember that an HLA object instance is the object exchanged in the federation execution. Not to be confused with instantiation of an object in the sense of OOP.

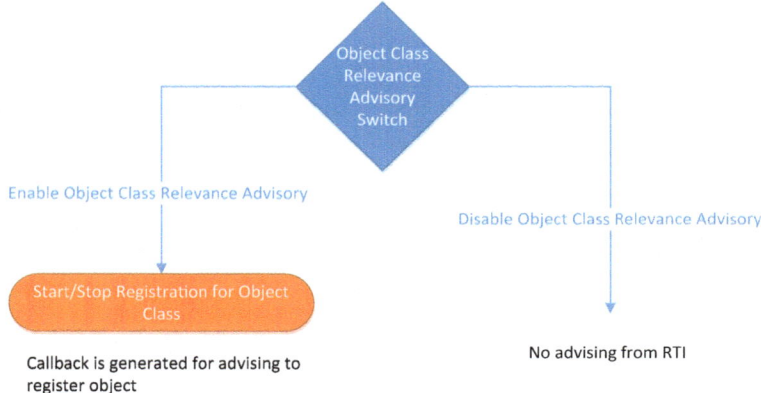

Fig. 8.10 Object class relevance advisory switch

8.7.3 Updating the HLA Object Attributes

After registering an object, we can update the values of its attributes. When a federate wants to update the values of the attributes it owned, then it calls the *Update Attribute Values* method. A federate can update only owned instance attributes. A federate may update the values of its owned attributes according to the update type and update condition of the attribute in the FOM.

- In our case study, the update type for the call sign, heading, and speed attributes is *static*. Thus, we only update those values upon registration and upon request (see Sect. 8.7.6). When a request is received for object update, it means some federate is waiting for our federate to do updates of the values of attributes for an object we owned. First, we find the object for which update is requested (ln. 2) and identify the attributes requested (ln. 4), and then we provide the updates (ln. 5–8).

```
1.  // !!! If this federate is created only one object instance, then it is suffi-
    cient to check the handle of that object, otherwise we need to check all the collec-
    tion
2.  if (data.ObjectInstance.Handle == manager.Ships[0].Handle) {
3.      // We can further try to figure out the attributes for which update is requested.
4.      foreach(var item in data.ObjectInstance.Attributes) {
5.          if (item.Handle == Som.ShipOC.Callsign.Handle) UpdateName(manager.Ships[0]);
6.          else if (item.Handle == Som.ShipOC.Heading.Handle) UpdateHeading(man-
    ager.Ships[0]);
7.          else if (item.Handle == Som.ShipOC.Position.Handle) UpdatePosition(man-
    ager.Ships[0]);
8.          else if (item.Handle == Som.ShipOC.Speed.Handle) UpdateSpeed(manager.Ships[0]);
9.      }
```

- The update type for the position attribute is *periodic* (see Fig. 8.11). Therefore, we periodically update the current value only according to the update condition (rate). Updating starts when Attribute Relevance Advisory switch tells our federate to do so by turning on attribute value updates (see the following subsection).

❌ Callsign	Ship	string	Static	NA
❌ Position	Ship	PositionType	Periodic	1/sec

Fig. 8.11 Update type and update condition of position attribute

Consequently, the current values of the instance attributes are sent to other federates when the value of an attribute is changed. To inform the change, one is required to create an update method that updates all attributes in one shot and/or specific methods that update only one or more attribute

In ShipFdApp, a new method for each ship instance attribute is defined for updating. Below, the code snippet for the update method for the call sign attribute of a ship instance is shown. The first thing is to add an attribute and its value as a pair to the attribute value pair set (ln. 3). We repeat this step as many as the number of attributes that we want to update. As you can see from the example, the first parameter is the attribute to be updated, and the second parameter is its current value, which comes from the local simulation. Then, we call the *Update Attribute Values* method to inform the RTI.

```
1.  private void UpdateName(CShip ship) {
2.      // Add Values
3.      ship.AddAttributeValue(Som.ShipOC.Callsign, ship.Local.Callsign);
4.      UpdateAttributeValues(ship);
5.  }
```

The `AddAttributeValue()` method serializes the attribute values, which is called *marshaling*. See Sect. 8.9 for data types that are supported for marshaling. For enums, there is a need for an explicit type conversion as figured below. The original type of Heading is an enum, and it is cast to uint (unsigned integer) first.

```
1.  ship.AddAttributeValue(Som.ShipOC.Heading, (uint) ship.Local.Heading);
```

8.7.3.1 Attribute Relevance Advisory Switch

RTI smartly advises our federate when to turn on attribute updates by sending *Turn Updates On for Object Instance* callback. When a subscriber is found in the federation for your object instances and the related attributes, then this callback is generated by the RTI (Fig. 8.12).

Employing the advisory switch, we can start or stop a timer (ln. 5) for updating the position attribute in time (i.e., 1/s) as specified in the FOM.

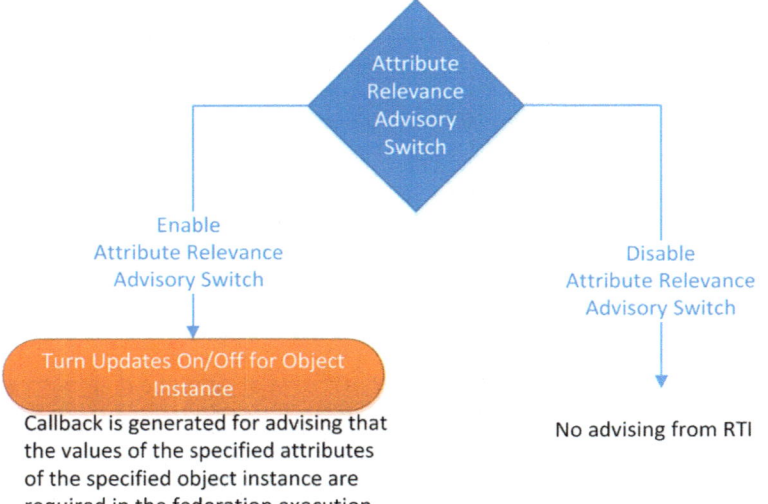

Fig. 8.12 Attribute Relevance Advisory Switch

```
1. public override void FdAmb_TurnUpdatesOnForObjectInstanceAd-
   visedHandler(object sender, HlaObjectEventArgs data) {
2.     // Call the base class handler
3.     base.FdAmb_TurnUpdatesOnForObjectInstanceAdvisedHandler(sender, data);
4.     // Start to update the position periodically
5.     manager.timer.Start();
6. }
```

When the timer is elapsed, it will update the position attribute (ln. 4).

```
1. // Update Ship Position
2. private void TimerElapsed(object sender, ElapsedEventArgs e) {
3.     // Display the position when this method got called.
4.     federate.UpdatePosition(Ships[0]);
5.     Console.WriteLine($"Position is up-
   dated: X={Ships[0].Local.Position}, Y={Ships[0].Local.Posi-
   tion} ");
6.     // Force a garbage collection to occur.
7.     GC.Collect();
8. }
```

8.7.4 Discovering Objects

When a federate registers an object belonging to an object class, which our federate is subscribed, a *Discover Object Instance* callback is generated, so that our federate

8.7 Object Management

can track the other object instances in the environment. Check the code segment below for an example. First, we check the class type of the discovered object (ln. 5), and we instantiate a local object to keep its state (ln. 7–10). Yet, we do not know the values of the attributes of the discovered object. Therefore, instead of waiting for a reflect callback, we can ask for an update from the owning federate to get the values of its attributes (ln. 12). See Sect. 8.7.6 how to request an update.

```
1.  public override void FdAmb_ObjectDiscoveredHandler(ob-
    ject sender, HlaObjectEventArgs data) {
2.      // Call the base class handler
3.      base.FdAmb_ObjectDiscoveredHandler(sender, data);
4.      // Check the class type of the discovered object
5.      if (data.ClassHandle == Som.ShipOC.Handle) // A ship
6.      {
7.          // Create and add a new ship to the list
8.          CShip newShip = new CShip(data.ObjectInstance);
9.          newShip.Type = Som.ShipOC;
10.         manager.Ships.Add(newShip);
11.         // Request Update Values of Attributes
12.         // !!! See section 8.7.6
13.     }
14. }
```

8.7.5 Reflecting the Attribute Values

When an attribute is updated by the owner federate, the federates that subscribed to its class will get a callback as *Reflect Attribute Values* service. When this callback is received, first thing to do is to find the object instance, which this update is intended for (ln. 6). Then get the parameter values and report the new values to the user if necessary (ln. 11).

```
1.  public override void FdAmb_ObjectAttributesReflectedHandler(ob-
    ject sender, HlaObjectEventArgs data) {
2.      // Call the base class handler
3.      base.FdAmb_ObjectAttributesReflectedHandler(sender, data);
4.      foreach(var item in manager.Ships) {
5.          // Find the Object
6.          if (data.ObjectInstance.Handle == item.Handle) {
7.
8.              // Get parameter values (Decoding)
9.              // See the next following code snippet
10.
11.             Console.WriteLine($"Callsign: {item.Local.Callsign}, Head-
            ing: {item.Local.Heading.ToString()}, Position: ({item.Local.Posi-
            tion.X}, {item.Local.Position.Y})" + Environment.NewLine);
12.         }
13.     }
14. }
```

To get the attribute values, you need to decode the attribute-value pairs. For this, you may employ two different methods. In the first method, you check whether the attribute is updated or not (e.g., ln. 2, 4, and 6). The result returned is false if the updated attribute set does not contain the attribute and its value. If the result is true, we decode the value by explicitly stating the data type of the value (e.g., ln. 3, 5, and 7). See Sect. 8.9 for data types supported for decoding the parameter values.

```
1.  // Get parameter values - 1st method
2.  if (data.IsValueUpdated(Som.ShipOC.Callsign))
3.     item.Local.Callsign = data.GetAttributeValue<string> (Som.ShipOC.Callsign);
4.  if (data.IsValueUpdated(Som.ShipOC.Heading))
5.     item.Local.Heading = (LocationEnum) data.GetAttributeValue<uint> (Som.ShipOC.Heading);
6.  if (data.IsValueUpdated(Som.ShipOC.Position))
7.     item.Local.Position = data.GetAttributeValue<PositionType> (Som.ShipOC.Position);
```

In the second method, we iterate through all the attribute-value pairs found in the updated set (ln. 2), and if the attribute is found in the set, then we decode its value (e.g., ln. 3 and 4).

```
1.  // Get parameter values - 2nd method
2.  foreach(var pair in data.ObjectInstance.Attributes) {
3.      if (pair.Handle == Som.ShipOC.Callsign.Handle)
4.         item.Local.Callsign = pair.GetValue<string>();
5.      else if (pair.Handle == Som.ShipOC.Position.Handle)
6.         item.Local.Position = pair.GetValue<PositionType>();
7.  }
```

8.7.6 Request an Update for Attribute Values

There are three ways to request an update for the attribute values from the owning federate. First, we may request an update for all attributes of a specific object instance (e.g., the object instance, we just discovered).

```
1.  // (1) Request update values of all attributes for a specific object instance
2.  RequestAttributeValueUpdate(newShip);
```

Second, we may request an update for the current values for all attributes of all object instances of a specific object class.

```
1.  // (2) Request an update for all attribute values of all object instances of a specific object class
2.  RequestAttributeValueUpdate(Som.ShipOC);
```

Last, we may request an update for the current values only for specific attributes, not for all. In this case, we prepare an attribute list that we want an update for.

8.7 Object Management

```
1.  // (3) Request Update Values for specific attributes only
2.  List < HlaAttribute > attributes = new List < HlaAttribute > ();
3.  attributes.Add(Som.ShipOC.Callsign);
4.  attributes.Add(Som.ShipOC.Heading);
5.  RequestAttributeValueUpdate(newShip, attributes);
```

Requesting attribute value update triggers the RTI to send a *Provide Attribute Value Update* callback to the owning federate of the attribute(s). The owning federate may respond by calling *Update Attribute Values* service as explained in the previous sections or may not respond at all.

8.7.7 Deleting and Removing an Object Instance

When a federate wants to delete an object from the federation execution, for which it owns the privilege-to-delete attribute, it must call the *Delete Object Instance* service.

```
1.  federate.DeleteObjectInstance(manager.Ships[0]);
```

Then, the RTI informs all the subscribed federates that an object instance has been deleted from the federation execution by sending the callback *Remove Object Instance*. Consequently, we find the local object corresponding to this HLA object instance in our list (e.g., list of ship objects) (ln. 11 and 12) and remove the local object from our list (ln. 14). Note that in order to make changes in the list while iterating it, we need a snapshot of the list first to avoid a loop enumeration exception (ln. 5–9).

```
1.  public override void FdAmb_ObjectRemovedHandler(object sender, HlaObjectEven-
    tArgs data) {
2.      // Call the base class handler
3.      base.FdAmb_ObjectRemovedHandler(sender, data);
4.
5.      // Lock while taking a snapshot - to avoid foreach loop enumeration excep-
    tion
6.      object[] snap;
7.      lock(thisLock) {
8.          snap = manager.Ships.ToArray();
9.      }
10.
11.     foreach(CShip ship in snap) {
12.         if (data.ObjectInstance.Handle == ship.Handle) // Find the Object
13.         {
14.             manager.Ships.Remove(ship);
15.             Console.WriteLine(%code%nbsp;"Ship: {ship.Local.Callsign} left. Num-
    ber of Ships Now {manager.Ships.Count}" + Environment.NewLine);
16.         }
17.     }
18. }
```

8.7.8 Sending an Interaction

As an interaction is a fire-and-forget type of data (i.e., non-durable), we do not consider encapsulating them. In order to send an interaction, first we instantiate an interaction and specify its type by referring to an interaction class (ln. 2). Then, we need to construct the parameter values. To do this, we simply call `AddParameterValue()` method for each parameter (ln. 4–6).

```
1.  public bool SendMessage(string txt) {
2.      HlaInteraction interaction = new Racon.RtiLayer.HlaInteraction(Som.RadioMessageIC, "RadioMessage");
3.      // Add Values
4.      interaction.AddParameterValue(Som.RadioMessageIC.Callsign, manager.ShipObjects[0].Ship.Callsign); // String
5.      interaction.AddParameterValue(Som.RadioMessageIC.Message, txt); // String
6.      interaction.AddParameterValue(Som.RadioMessageIC.TimeStamp, DateTime.Now); // DateTime
7.      // Send interaction
8.      return (SendInteraction(interaction));
9.  }
```

See Sect. 8.9 for data types supported for marshaling parameters.

8.7.8.1 Interaction Relevance Advisory Switch

Once more the RTI smartly advises our federate when to begin sending interactions by *Turn Interactions On* callback. When a subscriber is found in the federation for our published interaction class or its superclass, then this callback is generated. In this callback, you can just set a condition as true to indicate that now your federate may send interactions.

When no subscribers exist in the federation execution, then *Turn Interactions Off* callback is generated. Both advisory switches are controlled using the *Enable/Disable Interaction Relevance Advisory Switch* services. See Fig. 8.13.

8.7.9 Receiving an Interaction

In order to process interactions, we override the `InteractionReceivedHandler()` (ln. 1). Inside the handler, we need to identify to which class the interaction received belongs (ln. 5). The interaction-specific information and parameter values are provided by the `HlaInteractionEventArgs` argument. To get the parameter values, calling `GetParameterValues()` method is enough (ln. 13, 15, 17). Before that, we need to find out which parameter is updated. For this purpose, `IsValueUpdated()` method is used (ln. 12, 14, 16). If it returns true, we get the value of the parameter.

8.7 Object Management

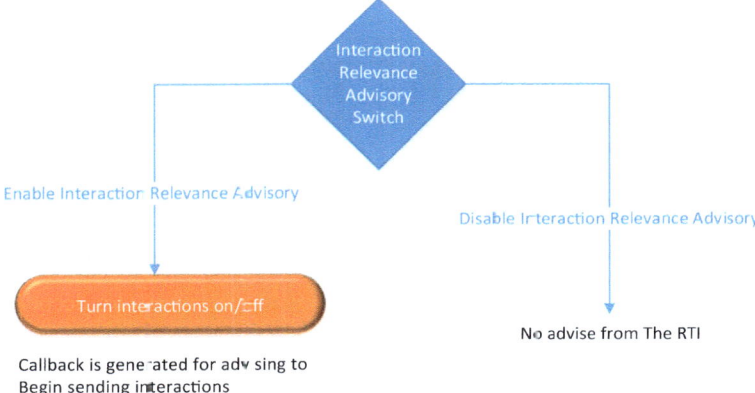

Fig. 8.13 Interaction relevance advisory switch

```
1.  public override void FdAmb_InteractionReceivedHandler(ob-
    ject sender, HlaInteractionEventArgs data) {
2.    // Call the base class handler
3.    base.FdAmb_InteractionReceivedHandler(sender, data);
4.    // Which interaction class?
5.    if (data.Interaction.ClassHandle == Som.RadioMessageIC.Handle)
6.    {
7.        string sentBy = "";
8.        string msg = "";
9.        var ts = new DateTime();
10.       // Get parameter values
11.       // 1st Method: check which parameter is updated
12.        if (data.IsValueUpdated(Som.RadioMessageIC.Callsign))
13.          sentBy = data.GetParameterValue<string>(Som.Radi-
    oMessageIC.Callsign);
14.        if (data.IsValueUpdated(Som.RadioMessageIC.Message))
15.          msg = data.GetParameterValue<string>(Som.Radi-
    oMessageIC.Message);
16.        if (data.IsValueUpdated(Som.RadioMessageIC.TimeStamp))
17.          ts = data.GetParameterValue<DateTime>(Som.Radi-
    oMessageIC.TimeStamp);
18.   }
19. }
```

Alternatively, you can iterate through parameter set (ln. 2), which holds all the parameters sent with the interaction. For this, you need to check which parameters are sent by comparing their parameter handles (ln. 3, 5, 7).

```
1.  // 2nd method: iterate through parameter set
2.  foreach(var item in data.Interaction.Parameters) {
3.    if (Som.RadioMessageIC.Callsign.Handle == item.Handle)
4.      sentBy = item.GetValue<string>();
5.    else if (Som.RadioMessageIC.Message.Handle == item.Handle)
6.      msg = item.GetValue<string>();
7.    else if (Som.RadioMessageIC.TimeStamp.Handle == item.Handle)
8.      ts = item.GeValue<DateTime>();
9.  }
```

As all incoming parameter values are encoded, we need to decode them according to the type of the expected value. Therefore, we need to unmarshal the sequence of bytes to their actual data types. See Sect. 8.9 for data types supported for encoding parameters.

8.8 Main Simulation Loop

In Chap. 2, we presented a typical federate program flow. The main simulation loop is at the heart of program flow. The *main simulation loop* involves the activities of a federate for the HLA services, generally the object management, the time management, and the ownership management services in a normal federate execution. Moreover, in the evoked callback model, we need to instruct the RTI to send federate callbacks regularly. In HLA Evolved, this is carried out by calling the EvokeCallback or EvokeMultipleCallbacks services regularly. In case of HLA 1.3, we call tick() method regardless of the callback model.

From the perspective of RACoN, the events pile up on the event queues. In order to dequeue and receive the events, we need to call Run() method in each iteration of the main simulation loop (ln. 6). Run method calls the tick() or EvokeCallback() method "behind the scene" and processes the event queues to pull a notification that an event has occurred.

Additionally, we process the state of our internal simulation models. In case of our running example of STMS, we update the position of the local ship (ln. 8).

```
1.  // **************************************************
2.  // Main Simulation Loop - loops until ESC is pressed
3.  // **************************************************
4.  do {
5.    // process rti events (callbacks) and tick
6.    if (manager.federate.FederateState.HasFlag(Racon.FederateStates.JOINED)) manager.federate.Run();
7.    // Move our local ship
8.    manager.ShipObjects[0].Ship.Move(GetTimeStep());
9.  } while (!Terminate && !ship.Exit);
```

8.8.1 Console Applications

Console applications include an explicit Main() method. So, we can create a main simulation loop inside this method simply by coding a loop construct such as a while loop.

8.8.2 Windows Forms Applications

In the main application class, override the Main() function. The code below shows how to create a simulation loop. DoSimulation() method (ln. 9), which includes the Run() method, is implemented in the main Form class.

```
1.  // The main entry point for the application
2.  static void Main() {
3.    Application.EnableVisualStyles();
4.    Application.SetCompatibleTextRenderingDefault(false);
5.    // Create the main UI and run it
6.      Form1 frm = new Form1();
7.      frm.Show();
8.      while (frm.Created) {
9.        frm.DoSimulation(); // The Main Simulation Loop
10.       Application.DoEvents();
11.     }
12. }
```

8.8.3 Windows Presentation Foundation (WPF) Applications

First, subscribe to the rendering event of the main window.

```
1.  public void RegisterMainSimulationLoop() {
2.    // Register Main Simulation Loop
3.    CompositionTarget.Rendering += new EventHandler(MainSimulation-
      Loop);
4.  }
```

And then, implement the main simulation loop.

```
1.  private void MainSimulationLoop(object sender, EventArgs e) {
2.    this.controller.DoSimulation();
3.  }
```

8.9 Parameter and Attribute Marshaling/Unmarshaling

During its execution, our federate mostly sends/receives information to/about other federates. This object exchange is done through RTI. RTI only knows the classes and properties of those objects with the help of the FOM (by feeding the FED/FDD file during the creation of a federation execution). The classes are the HLA object classes and the HLA interaction classes, where their properties are specified by the attributes and the parameters, respectively. At runtime, RTI does not know the type of the data sent and received; it only pushes byte sequences. This is an application-specific process. In other words, only the federate application knows the format of the received/sent data. Therefore, we need to specify the type of data especially at sending/receiving interactions and at updating/reflecting the attribute values. The RACoN presents the values in key–value pairs. The values are kept as a pointer to raw data.

The raw data are a bunch of bytes, and we need to specify its type to convert it back to a meaningful data. While sending an interaction or updating an attribute, marshaling is internally performed in RACoN library. The user simply uses the high-level abstracted methods. For example, to send an interaction, we only specify the parameter and its value by calling `AddParameterValue()` method (ln. 1–3), or we can explicitly state the data type (ln. 4). The RACoN converts the types of those values to the types (i.e., byte strings) that can be sent by the RTI.

```
1.  interaction.AddParameterValue(Som.RadioMessageIC.Callsign, man-
    ager.ShipObjects[0].Ship.Callsign); // String
2.  interaction.AddParameterValue(Som.RadioMessageIC.Mes-
    sage, txt); // String
3.  interaction.AddParameterValue(Som.Radi-
    oMessageIC.TimeStamp, DateTime.Now); // DateTime
4.  interaction.AddParameterValue<double>(Som.Radi-
    oMessageIC.TimeStamp, 5.5); // double
```

While receiving an interaction or reflecting an attribute update, the user must explicitly state the data type to unmarshal the received raw data pointer to a data type meaningful to (known by) the application federate. For example, while getting an attribute value, we use `GetAttributeValue()` method by stating the expected type (ln. 1–4).

```
1. item.Ship.Callsign = data.GetAttributeValue<string>(Som.ShipOC.Callsign);
2. item.Ship.Heading = (LocationEnum) data.GetAttributeValue<uint>(Som.ShipOC.Head-
   ing);
3. item.Ship.Position = data.GetAttributeValue<PositionType>(Som.ShipOC.Posi-
   tion);
4. item.Ship.Speed = (SpeedEnum) data.GetAttributeValue<uint>(Som.ShipOC.Speed);
```

8.9.1 Supported Data Types

Currently, the supported data types for marshaling/unmarshaling are `String` and `DateTime`, and the blittable value types[4]:

```
1. // Value Types (Only Blittables): (1) Structs (2) Enumerations
2. // Structs: (1) Numeric Types (2) bool (System.Boolean) (3) User-
   defined Structs
3. // Numeric Types: (1) Integral types (2) Floating-
   point Types (3) decimal (System.Decimal)
4. // Integral Types: sbyte, byte, char, short, ushort, int, uint, long, ulong
5. // Floating-point Types: float (System.Single), double (System.Dou-
   ble)
```

8.9.1.1 Date Time Type

Note that the MS.NET `DateTime` pattern supported in marshaling and unmarshaling in RACoN is the round-trip date/time pattern. With this format pattern, the formatting or parsing operation always uses the invariant culture (Microsoft MSDN, 2016). An example string representation is "2011-12-21T15:07:46.2061993+02:00". This pattern provides milliseconds, which may be required by some federates.

8.10 Summary

In this chapter, we learned how to implement a federate application by using one of the federate applications (ShipFdApp) of our running example, STMS. For implementing a federate application, we first reveal its modular architecture and then learn how to implement the simulation object of it. Then, we implement how to initialize a federation execution by using the basics of federation management services, how to declare federate's capability by using the declaration management

---

[4]A blittable data type is a value type that does not require conversion when they are passed between managed and unmanaged code in .NET framework. See Microsoft (2017).

services, how to send/receive an interaction, how to create object instances, and how to update/receive the values of attributes at runtime by using the object management services.

8.11 Questions for Review

1. What if a member federate resigns and joins again from the viewpoint of the RTI? For example, does it get back the same federate handle?
2. Indicate which of the following statements are true and which are false. Also, correct the false statements.

    (a) Discover an object instance is a federate-initiated service.
    (b) You can register an HLA object instance after publishing the related object class.
    (c) The layered architecture promoted in this book separates the Federate Ambassador and RTI Ambassador.
    (d) Event handling in RACoN is used to handle the callbacks.
    (e) Declaration management involves the sending and receiving interactions.

3. Assume that you will implement an interaction class for starting a scenario, named StartScenario. This interaction class has two parameters: ScenarioFile and Role. The scenario file is indicated with the name of the scenario as a string such as "EmergencyEvacuationScenario.xml". On the other hand, the role can take a value from an enumeration (Roles) specified as {ChiefWarden, EmergencyWarden, FirstAidOfficer, PersonWithDisability, InjuredPerson}. Implement the methods for sending and receiving interactions in type of StartScenarioIC class considering marshaling and unmarshaling of the parameter values.
4. Consider you have two domain classes: Student and Teacher. Write a wrapper class (only the skeleton) for each to use their instances as an HLA object.
5. Create and join a federation execution without using the high-level method for initialization (i.e., InitializeFederation). Hints: (i) You can freely choose the parameters such as the federation execution name and the connection settings, (ii) you need a connection to the RTI first.
6. Give an account of the steps a federate (say, simulating a drone) must take so that it may start sending attribute updates (say, its remaining battery charge). Your steps should refer to the RTI calls and callbacks, but you may use pseudocode notation.

References

IEEE 1516.1. (2010). *Standard for modeling and simulation (M&S) high level architecture (HLA) —Federate interface specification.* s.l.:IEEE.

Microsoft MSDN. (2016). *MS developer network.* [Online] Available at: https://msdn.microsoft.com/en-us/library. Accessed November 29, 2016.

Microsoft. (2017). *Blittable and non-blittable types.* [Online] Available at: https://msdn.microsoft.com/en-us/library/75dwhxf7(v=vs.110).aspx. Accessed April 24, 2017.

Part IV
Advanced Topics

Federate Implementation: Advanced 9

In this chapter, we will cover (somewhat) advanced topics for federation implementation, such as time management, where the theoretical background is given in Chap. 2. First, we will look at the time management (Fujimoto 2000). Then, we will see how to implement advanced federation management services such as save-and-restore and federation synchronization, data distribution management, and ownership management services in detail. The last section of this chapter will provide a look for computer-generated entities in the form of multiple (joined) federates generated in a single application and handling multiple federation executions at runtime.

9.1 Time Management

The federate has two predefined properties, time and lookahead, for keeping the logical federate time and the federate's lookahead value, respectively. You can initialize these properties according to the simulation time management requirements. Whenever the federate becomes a time-constrained (TC) or time-regulating (TR) federate, these values become essential for time management.

```
1.  // Time management
2.  federate.Lookahead = 1;
3.  federate.Time = 0;
```

For the basic notions of time management, see Chap. 2.

9.1.1 Time-Regulating Federates

To support time management, a federate has a role in relation to time. Initially, a federate is neither TC nor TR (NEITHER) by default. Not being TR, it does not influence the federation time flow; not being TC, it is not influenced by the other federates. Consequently, a NEITHER federate does not participate in the federation-wide time management. A federate is free to keep a local time by itself, unrelated to federation time.

When a non-TR federate wants to be TR federate to send TSO messages, then it can invoke *Enable Time Regulation* service any time by supplying a lookahead value as a parameter (ln. 1). *Lookahead* is a time interval, during which the federate guarantees that it will not send any TSO messages. To disable time regulation, a TR federate calls *Disable Time Regulation* service (ln. 2), and from then on, the federate switches into NEITHER or TC status as depending on its previous constrained status.

```
1.  manager.federate.EnableTimeRegulation(manager.feder-
    ate.Lookahead);
2.  manager.federate.DisableTimeRegulation();
```

When a TR request is done, RTI will reply using a *Time Regulation Enabled* callback supplied with the current logical time as a return argument (ln. 1). The federate's logical time must be set to this time (ln. 3), and its lookahead will be the one provided in the method call. Then, the federate will become a TR federate and may now send TSO messages and regulate the time advancement in the federation.

```
1.  public override void FdAmb_TimeRegulationEnabled(ob-
    ject sender, HlaTimeManagementEventArgs data) {
2.    base.FdAmb_TimeRegulationEnabled(sender, data);
3.    Time = data.Time; // Current logical time of the joined feder-
    ate set by RTI
4.  }
```

In HLA 1.3, this method takes two parameters instead of one: time to set federate's time and the lookahead value of federate. If the federate's status is NEITHER, when the federate calls `EnableTimeRegulation (time, lookahead)` method, the RTI confirms the federate's status as TR and sets the federate's initial federate time as the requested time (the first parameter of the method). If the federate's status is TC and this federate wants to be TR, other federates' statuses in the federation are significant in determining the federate's new federate time. This issue is decided by looking at LBTS (lower bound on timestamps). If LBTS is undefined (i.e., infinity), it means that there is no TR federate in the federation and all federates can advance to any time. Otherwise, there must be at least one TR federate in the federation and this federate limits how far the time may advance. In the former case, there is no constraint for the federate, and after calling `EnableTimeRegulation(time,lookahead)` method, the RTI confirms the federate's TR status and lets the federate to stay at its current federate time. In the latter case, the RTI confirms federate's TR status and sets federate's time as

9.1 Time Management

(LBTS—lookahead). In both cases, it must be considered that the time parameter must be equal to the current federate time, else the RTI raises an exception. Usage of these methods is shown below.

```
1.  {
2.      double initialTime = 5;
3.      double lookahead = 2;
4.      this.simulation.federate.EnableTimeRegulation(initial-
    Time, lookahead);
5.      this.simulation.federate.DisableTimeRegulation();
6.  }
```

All the alternatives explained above, for the HLA 1.3 specification, are shown in UML sequence diagram, depicted in Fig. 9.1.

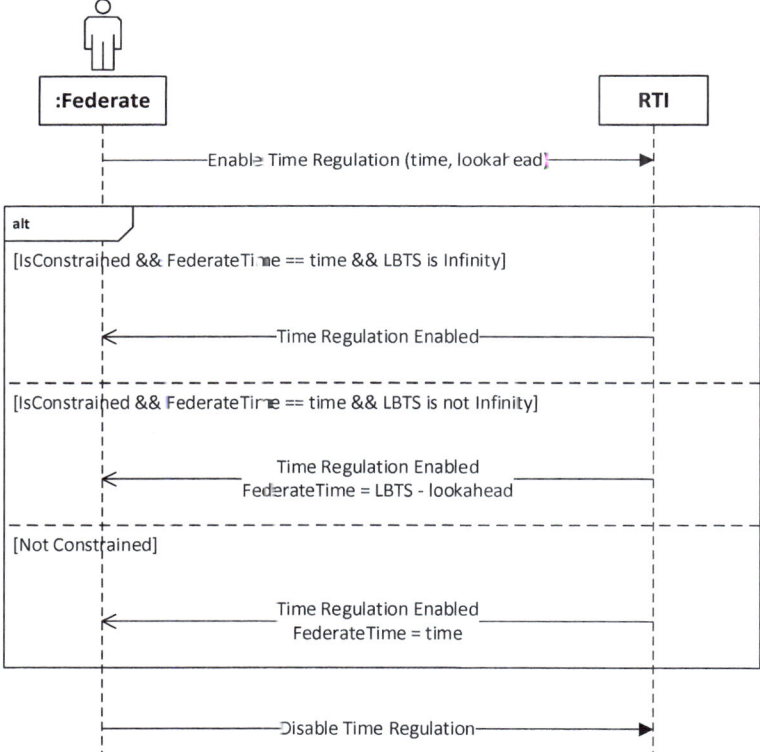

Fig. 9.1 UML sequence diagram for EnableTimeRegulation() and DisableTimeRegulation() methods in the HLA 1.3 specification

9.1.2 Time-Constrained Federates

A time-constrained (TC) federate can receive time stamp-ordered (TSO) messages. When a non-TC federate wants to be constrained, it can call *Enable Time Constrained* service at any time (ln. 1). This method does not take any parameters. When a federate does not want to be TC any more, it calls *Disable Time Constrained* method (ln. 2) and then the federate switches into NEITHER or TR depending on its previous regulating status.

```
1. manager.federate.EnableTimeConstrained();
2. manager.federate.DisableTimeConstrained();
```

When enabling time-constrained is requested, the RTI confirms the federate's status by invoking a *Time Constrained Enabled* callback supplied with a current logical time as a return argument (ln. 1). The federate's logical time, assigned by RTI, must be set as the current federate logical time (ln. 3). Then, the federate will be a TC federate and may now receive TSO messages.

```
1. public override void FdAmb_TimeConstrainedEnabled(ob-
   ject sender, HlaTimeManagementEventArgs data) {
2.    base.FdAmb_TimeConstrainedEnabled(sender, data);
3.    Time = data.Time; // Current logical time of the joined feder-
      ate set by RTI
4.    Report("Logical time set by RTI: " + Time);
5. }
```

In optimistic time management, timing errors are allowed, but they are immediately recovered from. In conservative time management, we restrict ourselves to where a constrained federate is guaranteed not to receive a TSO message from its past (i.e., whose timestamp is less than the federate time). In case when a TR federate decides to be constrained, then the federate's current logical time is checked. If it is equal to or less than LBTS, the RTI immediately confirms the federate as being constrained and the federate keeps its current time. But if the federate time is bigger than LBTS, the RTI holds confirmation until LBTS exceeds the federate time. It is not possible to set federate time as LBTS, because in HLA, time advances forward (provided that time management strategy is conservative). Then, the RTI confirms federate as being constrained and federate keeps its own federate time. To clarify, the alternatives explained above are shown in the UML sequence diagram, depicted in Fig. 9.2, for HLA 1.3.

9.1.3 Time Advancement

TC, TR, and both TC and TR (TC&TR) federates maintain their own federate logical time. They try to advance their current logical times (t_c) when they completed all local processing up to the current time. Time advancement can be in the

9.1 Time Management

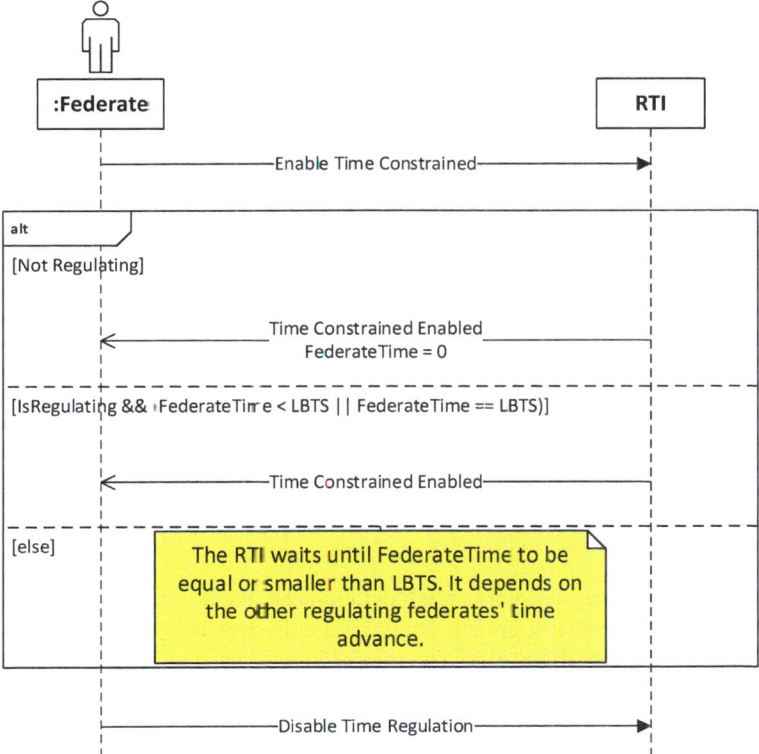

Fig. 9.2 UML sequence diagram for EnableTimeConstrained() and DisableTimeConstrained() methods in the HLA 1.3 specification

form of (i) time step advancement, (ii) event-based advancement, or (iii) optimistic advancement (Fujimoto 1998). For time advancement, the federate must take permission from the RTI by sending a time advancement request. The services for a time advancement request are listed as follows:

- For time step advancement
  - Time Advance Request,
  - Time Advance Request Available.

- For event-based advancement
  - Next Message Request,
  - Next Message Request Available.

- For optimistic advancement
  - Flush Queue Request.

Fig. 9.3 Time advancement for a TC federate

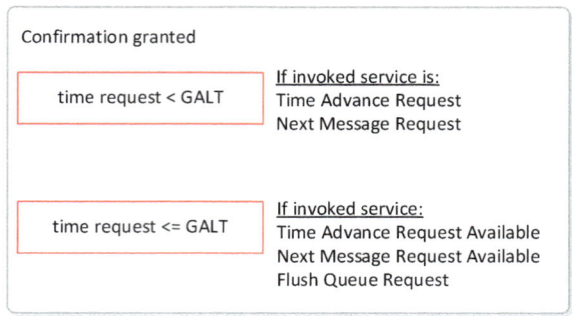

A federate can advance its time only if the RTI grants it by using the *Time Advance Grant* service.

For advancing logical time in time steps, *Time Advance Request* method is used with a time parameter indicating the requested logical time (t_r). By calling this method, a federate declares to the RTI its intention to advance its time to t_r. The t_r must be equal to or bigger than t_c; if not, the RTI raises a *Logical Time Already Passed* exception.

If the federate is only TR within the federation execution, the RTI grants the time advance and the federate's current logical time is updated. Be careful that the requested time cannot be less than the current logical time as stressed above.

If the federate is only TC federate, the RTI checks the conditions before confirmation of a time advancement according to the call made (Fig. 9.3). The RTI cannot grant a time request greater than the Greatest Available Logical Time (GALT).

UML sequence diagram in Fig. 9.4 shows Time Advance Request and grant sequence in detail.

The following code fragment shows how to call *Time Advance Request* with a parameter specifying the requested time (ln. 4). The RTI confirms advancement by invoking *Time Advance Grant* service (ln. 7–9).

```
1. {
2.    double currentFederateTime = this.simulation.federate.QueryFeder-
      ateTime();
3.    double timeStep = 2;
4.    this.simulation.federate.TimeAdvanceRequest(currentFeder-
      ateTime + timeStep);
5. }
6. // …
7. public override void FdAmb_TimeAdvanceGrant(object sender, CHlaTi-
   meManagementEventArgs data) {
8.    // …
9. }
```

9.1 Time Management

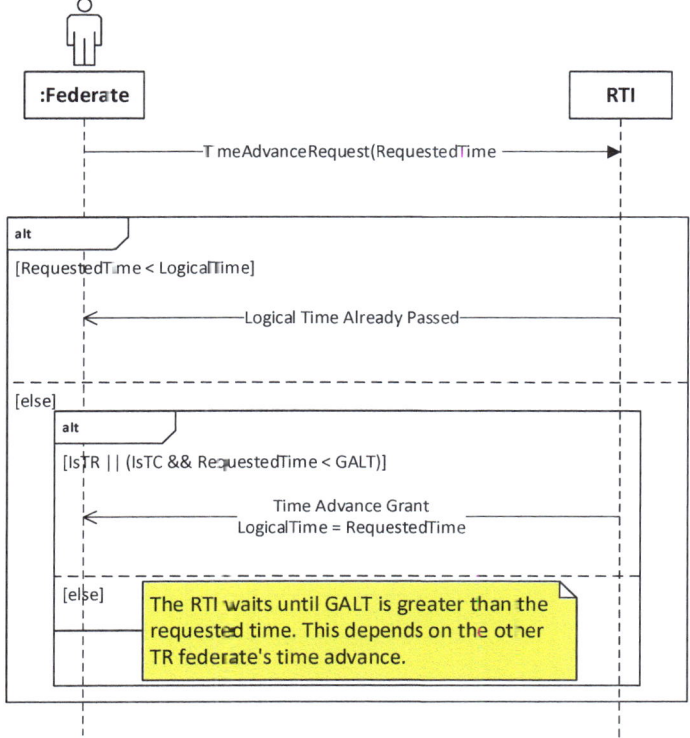

Fig. 9.4 UML sequence diagram for TimeAdvanceRequest() method

After the requested logical time is granted by the RTI, the federate will advance its logical time and it will no longer receive messages with a timestamp less than or equal to its new logical time. *Time Advancement Request Available* service is similar to the time advancement request. But in this case, a message with a timestamp equal to the logical time granted to the federate may arrive.

Next Message Request and *Next Message Request Available* services are used to request time advancement to the timestamp of the next TSO message in the federation for an event-based advancement.

9.1.4 Queries

During federation execution, federates can make queries about federation time issues. These queries return current logical time, GALT, federate's lookahead value, and LITS, which is the minimum timestamp of a message that federate can receive in future. UML sequence diagram is depicted in Fig. 9.5.

Fig. 9.5 UML sequence diagram for time management queries

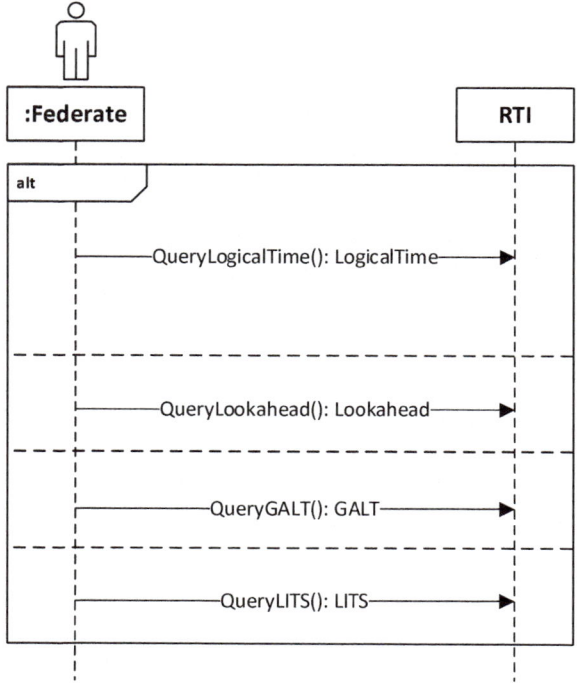

Querying logical time (ln. 1) and lookahead (ln. 2) is straightforward. The query returns the logical time and the current lookahead, respectively, as a result.

```
1. double time = manager.federate.QueryLogicalTime();
2. double lookahead = manager.federate.QueryLookahead();
```

If a non-TR federate queries for the lookahead value, then the query generates *Time Regulation is not Enabled* exception.

Querying GALT/LITS returns a Boolean value, which is true if GALT/LITS is defined and false otherwise. It takes an (optional) out parameter as the current value of invoking federate's GALT/LITS. You can call it without any parameter (ln. 3 and 6) or with an out parameter (ln. 2 and 5). The out parameter returns the value of GALT/LITS.

```
1. double galt;
2. bool res = manager.federate.queryGALT(out galt);
3. bool res2 = manager.federate.queryGALT();
4. double lits;
5. bool res4 = manager.federate.QueryLITS(out lits);
6. bool res3 = manager.federate.QueryLITS();
```

9.1 Time Management

As RACoN also supports the HLA 1.3 specification, you can use the HLA 1.3 specific calls for queries. These calls are as follows. *Query Federate Time*, *Query LBTS*, and *Min Next Event Time*.

9.1.5 Changing Preferred Order Types

The preferred order type for an interaction or an attribute is specified in the FOM. But a federate can dynamically change the order type of an attribute or a set of attributes of an object by calling the *Change Attribute Order* service. First, you must form the attribute list (ln. 1 and 2) and then make the call (ln. 3).

```
1.  List<Racon.RtiLayer.HlaAttribute> attributes = new List<Racon.Rti-
    Layer.HlaAttribute> ();
2.  attributes.Add(manager.federate.Som.StationOC.StationName);
3.  manager.federate.ChangeAttributeOrderType(station, attributes, Ra-
    con.OrderType.TimeStamp);
```

The following code snippet exemplifies changing the interaction order type. In this case, we need to pass the interaction class and preferred order type as parameters.

```
1.  manager.federate.ChangeInteractionOrderType(manager.feder-
    ate.Som.RadioMessageIC, Racon.OrderType.Receive);
```

9.1.6 Sending and Receiving TSO Messages

In order to send TSO messages, the federate must be TR. The federate cannot send a TSO message with a timestamp which is less than the granted logical time by the RTI (via Time Advance Grant) plus its current lookahead [see Eq. (9.1)]. Hence, it is guaranteed that a TR federate will not send any TSO message from its past or break its promise about its lookahead.

$$\text{Timestamp} \geq \text{Logical Time} + \text{Lookahead} \qquad (9.1)$$

If the lookahead is zero, then the restriction becomes tighter as stated in Eq. (9.2), assuming the federate has advanced its time by invoking one of the time advancement methods. Zero lookahead is useful for a federate that performs pure calculation, without generating a new state.

$$\text{Timestamp} > \text{Logical Time} \qquad (9.2)$$

You can query the lookahead value by calling the *Query Lookahead* method (ln. 1 and 3). The lookahead of a federate can be changed dynamically by invoking *Modify Lookahead* service (ln. 2).

```
1. Console.WriteLine("Lookahead: " + manager.federate.Que-
   ryLookahead()); // initial lookahead
2. manager.federate.ModifyLookahead(3); // modify lookahead
3. Console.WriteLine("Lookahead: " + manager.federate.Que-
   ryLookahead()); // modified lookahead
```

The TSO messages, which are the RTI services associated with a timestamp, are listed below. Sending a message means invoking a federate-initiated call such as send interaction, and receiving a message means receiving a callback from the RTI such as receive interaction.

- Update attribute values,
- Reflect attribute values (callback),
- Send interaction,
- Send interaction with regions,
- Receive interaction (callback),
- Delete object instance,
- Remove object instance (callback).

Receiving callbacks with a timestamp is exactly the same with using event handlers explained in Chap. 8. The event arguments in the handler provide time-related values such as a timestamp. In the succeeding subsections, we only provide sending and receiving an interaction as an example.

9.1.6.1 Sending Interactions with a Timestamp

You prepare an interaction as described at Chap. 8, and then simply add a timestamp as a parameter to send the interaction (ln. 1). The method call returns an event retraction handle to call off the message if required. See the Sect. 9.7 for event retraction.

```
1. EventRetractionHandle handle = SendInteraction(interac-
   tion, timestamp);
```

9.1.6.2 Receiving Interactions with a Timestamp

In order to receive a TSO interaction, a federate must be TC and the preferred delivery order of the message must be timestamp. The event arguments of the

9.1 Time Management

interaction received handler now provide additional properties such as the timestamp and the event retraction handle (ln. 3 and 5) as well as supplemental information (ln. 4).

```
1.  public override void FdAmb_InteractionReceivedHandler(object sender, HlaInteractionEventArgs data) {
2.    // TSO message - additional properties
3.    double timestamp = data.Time; // timestamp in case of a message sent with a timestamp
4.    var handle = data.SupplementalReceiveInfo.ProducingFederateHandle; // returns the federate handle of the federate, which produces this message
5.    var retractionHandle = data.RetractionHandle; // returns event retraction handle in acse of a TSO message
6.  }
```

Supplemental information is provided for the remove object instance, receive interaction, and reflect attribute values services in the form of *Supplemental Remove Info*, *Supplemental Receive Info*, and *Supplemental Reflect Info*, respectively.

9.1.7 Message Retraction

Some OM methods use message retraction designators to keep track of the messages sent to the other federates to retract them when required. For example, if a federate, using optimistic time management strategy, receives a message from its past, then the messages sent after that time may become invalid. So, the optimistic federate will retract the invalidated message using *Retract* service and all the federated that received the invalidated messages will get a *Request Retraction* callback. During runtime, the RTI automatically assigns a message retraction designator after *Update Attribute Values*, *Send Interaction*, *Send Interaction with Regions*, and *Delete Object Instance* calls. For example, as shown in Fig. 9.6, the `Retract` and `RequestRetraction` methods use the "Message Retraction Designator" reference resulting from some object management calls (e.g., send interaction and receive interaction).

9.2 Federation Synchronization

The synchronization mechanism is provided to synchronize activities of federates throughout federation execution. A *synchronization point* is used to specify a synchronization activity. The synchronization points are declared in the OMT

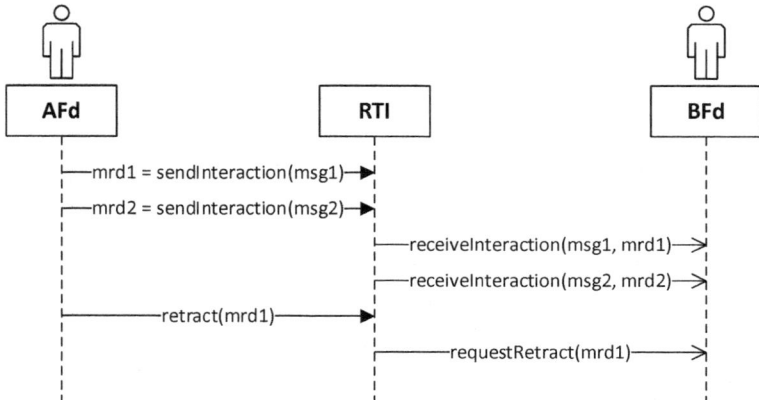

Fig. 9.6 Using message retraction designator to retract messages. The AFd retracts msg1 interaction after it is sent using the message retraction designator (mrd1) assigned. The RTI informs the federates (BFd) that received the related message

synchronization table for documentation purposes (see Chap. 5 how to declare a synchronization point in OMT).

For an example of the use of synchronization points, let us think about a common scenario where a group of entities will gather in a specific area at a certain time. Assume that a flotilla, composed of warships in the simulation, will gather in a rendezvous point. First, the commodore, who is in tactical command of the flotilla, will order the rendezvous. Then, each ship will move to the rendezvous point. When a ship arrives at the rendezvous point, it will report to the commodore. Once all ships gather at the rendezvous point, the commodore may begin an action (e.g., attack). Gathering all ships, in this case, imposes a synchronization among federates. Ordering means registering a synchronization point. When a federate gets to the synchronization point, it issues a report using a synchronization point achieved call. Once all the required federates reach the synchronization point, the synchronization is completed.

In our STMS case study, there are two synchronization points (i.e., `SlowPace`, `FastPace`), which are declared to control the pace of the simulation. The station federates can either adjust the acceleration or deceleration of the movement of ships by using these synchronization points. First, a station federate must register one of these synchronization points with the RTI. To do that, the user can select the pace for the simulation using the interface of StationFdApp (when the key C is pressed. See ln. 2), and then the selected pace is registered by the federate (ln. 13 and 18) using `RegisterFederationSynchronizationPoint()` call.

9.2 Federation Synchronization

```
1.    // Pacing control
2.    case ConsoleKey.C:
3.        Console.ForegroundColor = ConsoleColor.Yellow;
4.        int pacing = 0;
5.        bool cont = true;
6.        do {
7.            Console.Write("Pacing (0-SlowPacing, 1-FastPacing): ");
8.            bool res = int.TryParse(Console.ReadLine(), out pacing);
9.            if (res) {
10.               switch (pacing) {
11.                   case 0:
12.                       Pacing = (PacingEnum) pacing;
13.                       manager.federate.RegisterFederationSynchroniza-
    tionPoint(Pacing.ToString(), "Slow pacing is requested");
14.                       cont = false;
15.                       break;
16.                   case 1:
17.                       Pacing = (PacingEnum) pacing;
18.                       manager.federate.RegisterFederationSynchroniza-
    tionPoint(Pacing.ToString(), "Fast pacing is requested");
19.                       cont = false;
20.                       break;
21.                   default:
22.                       cont = true;
23.                       break;
24.               }
25.           }
26.       } while (cont);
27.       break;
```

When you want to synchronize only a subset of federates, specify the set of federate handles as a parameter in the call. In case you don't provide a federate list, then it implies that synchronization is intended for all the (joined) federates. To get the federate handles in the federation execution, you can use MOM classes (i.e., HLAobjectRoot.HLAmanager.HLAfederate.HLAfederateHandle) to report you the existing federate handles in the federation execution. Alternatively, if you know the names of federates, which are unique in the federation execution, you can ask the RTI to give you the federate handle by calling *Get Federate Handle* service, which takes a federate name and returns the federate handle.

After requesting a synchronization point registration, the RTI will respond with a *Synchronization Point Registration Succeeded* callback (lr. 1–5) indicating a successful registration or with a *Synchronization Point Registration Failed* callback indicating a failed registration with the reason.

```
1. public override void FdAmb_OnSynchronizationPointRegistrationCon-
   firmedHandler(object sender, HlaFederationManagementEven-
   tArgs data) {
2.   // Call the base class handler
3.   base.FdAmb_OnSynchronizationPointRegistrationCon-
   firmedHandler(sender, data);
4.   Report($ "Pacing request ({data.Label}) is ac-
   cepted by RTI." + Environment.NewLine);
5. }
```

If the synchronization point registration is successful, the RTI will announce the synchronization point to the other federates using the *Announce Synchronization Point* service (ln. 1). When a federate receives an announcement, it will try to achieve the synchronization point. In our example, the ships adjust their speed as requested (ln. 3–12) and report that the synchronization point is achieved (ln. 14).

```
1.  public override void FdAmb_SynchronizationPointAnnounced(ob-
    ject sender, HlaFederationManagementEventArgs data) {
2.    base.FdAmb_SynchronizationPointAnnounced(sender, data);
3.    PacingEnum Pacing;
4.    Enum.TryParse(data.Label, out Pacing);
5.    switch (Pacing) {
6.      case PacingEnum.SlowPacing:
7.        manager.ShipObjects[0].Ship.Speed = SpeedEnum.VerySlow;
8.        break;
9.      case PacingEnum.FastPacing:
10.       manager.ShipObjects[0].Ship.Speed = SpeedEnum.VeryFast;
11.       break;
12.   }
13.   // Report that the ship is adjusted her speed accord-
      ing to the requested pacing
14.   manager.federate.SynchronizationPointAchieved(data.La-
      bel, true);
15. }
```

Finally, when all federates successfully report the achievement of the synchronization point, the RTI will send a *Federation Synchronized* callback to each one (ln. 1–4).

```
1.  public override void FdAmb_FederationSynchronized(ob-
    ject sender, HlaFederationManagementEventArgs data) {
2.      base.FdAmb_FederationSynchronized(sender, data);
3.      Report($"simulation pacing ({data.Label}) is completed." + En-
    vironment.NewLine);
4.  }
```

9.3 Federation Save-and-Restore

The theoretical background for the federation save-and-restore operation is given in Chap. 2. Here, we will cover and exemplify the use of related services.

The *save-and-restore* operation is a mechanism to keep selected federation execution states during a federation execution. Thus, a federation execution may return to one of the previous states, which has been successfully saved (Fig. 9.7).

The responsibilities for the save-and-restore operation can be considered from the viewpoint of a federate application and that of the RTI. The RTI is responsible for coordinating the whole process and provides some federation-specific information to federates such as the federate handles at the time of save after the restoration. The federate application is responsible for deciding what data to save and in what format so that it can restore that state later. When save begins, all federates must save their application-specific data in a persistent data store (in a file or in a database).

A federate may request a federation save operation by invoking a *Request Federation Save* by supplying a unique save label. The save label identifies a particular federation save operation; hence, it must be unique. If required, a timestamp can also be provided. But in this case, there are some restrictions. First, the requesting federate must be either a time-regulating federate or a Greatest Available Logical Time (GALT) is defined for the federate to ensure that the supplied timestamp is larger than the logical time of all the time-constrained federates.

```
1.  federate.RequestFederationSave("SaveLabel_BeforeBigBang");
```

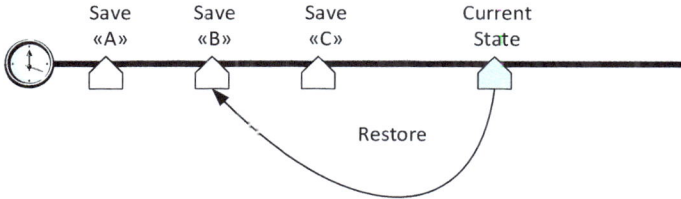

Fig. 9.7 Save-and-restore operation. Save A, B, and C are selected federation execution states kept during a federation execution. By a restore operation, you can revert the current federation execution state to a previously saved state

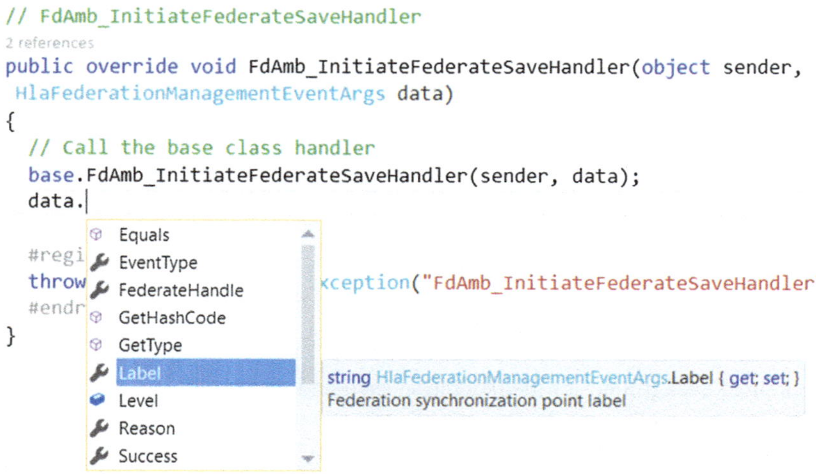

```csharp
// FdAmb_InitiateFederateSaveHandler
public override void FdAmb_InitiateFederateSaveHandler(object sender,
 HlaFederationManagementEventArgs data)
{
    // Call the base class handler
    base.FdAmb_InitiateFederateSaveHandler(sender, data);
    data.|
}
```

(IntelliSense dropdown showing: Equals, EventType, FederateHandle, GetHashCode, GetType, **Label**, Level, Reason, Success)

`string HlaFederationManagementEventArgs.Label { get; set; }`
Federation synchronization point label

Fig. 9.8 Initiate federate save service

After the Save Request service is called by the federate, the RTI invokes the *Initiate Federate Save* service to instruct all federates to save their states. The federate receives this callback by overriding the related callback method as shown in Fig. 9.8. For the restore operation, the user must provide the restore label, which must be the same as a prior save label.

The *Initiate Federate Save* callback has two parameters: the sender as `Object` and the event arguments for federation management, which provides some save-and-restore arguments: the label, the reason, and the success indicator. These arguments are valid according to the related callback. For example, the label argument gives us the federation save label.

After the RTI-initiated federation save, the joined federates call the *Federate Save Begun* service. With this method, the federate notifies the RTI that it is beginning to save its state. This method does not take any parameters (ln. 1). The federate saves its internal data to keep its state (ln. 3—commented because of application-specific handling). After the federate's saving process is completed, the federate invokes *Federate Save Complete* method with a success indicator to notify the RTI that the federate has completed its save attempt (ln. 5). This service takes one Boolean parameter, the save-success indicator. The save-success indicator informs the RTI that the federate save either succeeded (true) or failed (false).

9.3 Federation Save-and-Restore

```
1.  federate.FederateSaveBegun();
2.
3.  // Operations for Application Specific Saving of Federate State
4.
5.  federate.FederateSaveComplete(true);
```

After all the federates sent a federate save complete report, the RTI initiates the *Federation Saved* service, which informs all the federates that the federation save process is completed, and indicates whether it is completed successfully or not (ln. 4 and 7). If the federation save is failed, then the reason for the failure is also provided by the RTI (ln. 9). To receive the callback, we must override the method as shown below.

```
1.  public override void FdAmb_FederationSaved(object sender, HlaFeder-
    ationManagementEventArgs data) {
2.    // Call the base class handler
3.    base.FdAmb_FederationSaved(sender, data);
4.    if (data.Success) {
5.       // federation saved
6.    }
7.    else {
8.       // federation not saved. Report the save failure reason
9.       Report("The save failure reason: " + data.Reason);
10.   }
11. }
```

The restore operations are very similar to save operations. While initiating restoration of the federation, all federates must exist in the federation execution with the same type and the same numbers as in the save operation. If not, the RTI will throw an exception as shown in Fig. 9.9.

If the restoration label, which we supply in *Request Federation Restore* service, is different from the existed save labels, the RTI will throw an exception and the restoration process will not start. After RTI's checking result is feasible (true), *Confirm Federation Restoration Request* service is initiated by the RTI, and then the RTI initiates the *Federation Restore Begun* service. This service informs all the federates that a federation restoration is imminent. Then, the RTI sends *the Initiate Federate Restore* service for instructing all the federates to return to a previously saved state. After all the federates returned to a previously saved state (success or failure), they invoke the *Federate Restore Complete* method. This method takes one Boolean parameter (restore-success indicator). The restore-success indicator informs the RTI that the federate restoration either succeeded (true) or failed (false). Finally, the RTI sends a *Federation Restored* message, which informs all the federates that the federation restoration process is completed, and indicates whether it is completed successfully or not (with the failure reason).

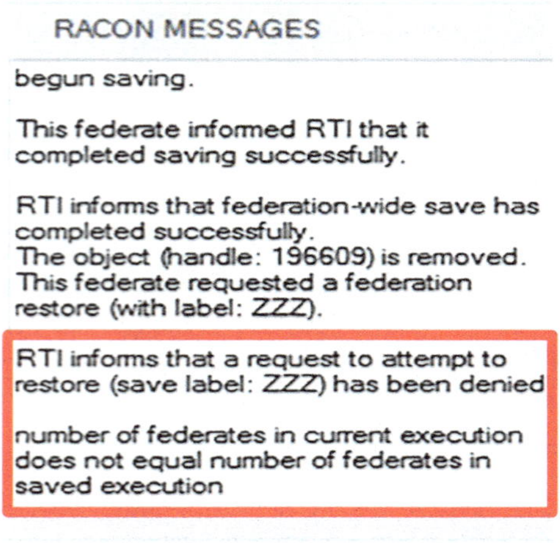

Fig. 9.9 Exception generated for restore operation in case a number of federates in the current execution are missing with regard to the number of federates in the saved execution

RACON MESSAGES

begun saving.

This federate informed RTI that it completed saving successfully.

RTI informs that federation-wide save has completed successfully.
The object (handle: 196609) is removed.
This federate requested a federation restore (with label: ZZZ).

RTI informs that a request to attempt to restore (save label: ZZZ) has been denied

number of federates in current execution does not equal number of federates in saved execution

9.4 Data Distribution Management

In order to demonstrate how to implement the data distribution management (DDM) services, we present two case studies. The first case study is our running example Strait Traffic Monitoring Simulation (STMS). The second one is the Extended Chat Application, where we extend the basic Chat federate application introduced in Chap. 4. The first case study demonstrates the use of class attributes with regions, while the second one the use of interactions with regions. Furthermore, the second case study demonstrates the HLA 1.3 specific implementation of DDM services, which differs from the later specifications.

9.4.1 Case Study 1: STMS

In our running example, we define a geographical region to specify the area of responsibility of a traffic monitoring station. Thus, each ship updates its position, velocity, and heading attributes in the zone they are located so that only the responsible traffic station receives the attribute updates.

There is a single dimension defined in the FOM for specifying the area of responsibility. All the attributes of the ship object class defined in FOM are associated with this dimension. Dimension specification is presented in Fig. 9.10.

Here, we use a linear enumerated normalization function listed in (IEEE Std 1516.2-2010 2010). The form is depicted below.

$$\text{linearEnumerated (domain, mappedSet)} \qquad (9.3)$$

9.4 Data Distribution Management

OMT View

Name	Data Type (1)	Dimension Upper Bound (2)	Normalization Function	Value When Unspecified (3)
❌ AreaOfResponsibility	AreaEnum	2	LinearEnumerated(Location, [West, East])	[0 .. 2]

FDD View

```
- <dimensions>
  - <dimension>
    <name>AreaOfResponsibility</name>
    <dataType>AreaEnum</dataType>
    <upperBound>2</upperBound>
    <normalization>LinearEnumerated(Location, [West, East])</normalization>
    <value>[0 .. 2]</value>
  </dimension>
</dimensions>
```

Fig. 9.10 Area of responsibility dimension specification

The ship location is used as the domain parameter, which is an enumerated value known to the ship federate. The `mappedSet` argument is the set of enumerated values that the domain parameter can take. In our case, we have two values: East and West. Mapping is carried out according to Eq. (9.4).

$$[\text{positionInMappedSet}(\text{domain})/(\text{mappedSetLength} - 1] \times (\text{DUB} - 1) \quad (9.4)$$

The `positionInMappedSet` is a function giving the position of the domain parameter in the mapped set starting at zero. Mapped set length is the number of elements in the mapped set. DUB stands for the dimension upper bound.

According to this mapping, for instance, if the location of the ship is East, then:

```
domain = "East"
positionInMappedSet(domain) = 1 (starting from 0)
mappedSetLength = 2
DUB = 2
Mapping value = [1/(2-1)] * (2-1) = 1
```

Using this one-dimensional space, we create two regions corresponding to the areas of responsibility (AORs) in terms of the West and East sectors. As we are using an enumeration function, mapping is done to a point. The schematic representation of the coordinate system with regions is depicted in Fig. 9.11.

In the case study, the federates use different DDM services as depicted in Fig. 9.12.

The interactions are presented in Fig. 9.13. Both federates need to create the related regions dynamically. As the StationFd is stationary, it only creates one region corresponding to its location. But, as ShipFd changes zones during Strait passage, it creates and deletes the related region according to its zone. Moreover, the ShipFd registers its `Ship` object instance with the related region. The StationFd must subscribe the `Ship` object class and attributes with the associated region, and then it may request attribute value updates.

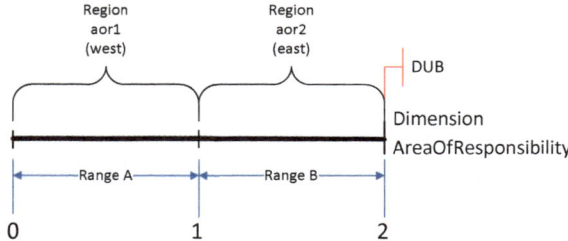

Fig. 9.11 One-dimensional coordinate system and regions for STMS

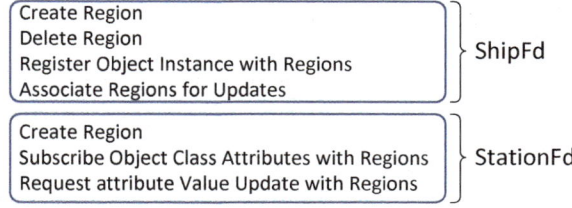

Fig. 9.12 DDM services used by STMS federates

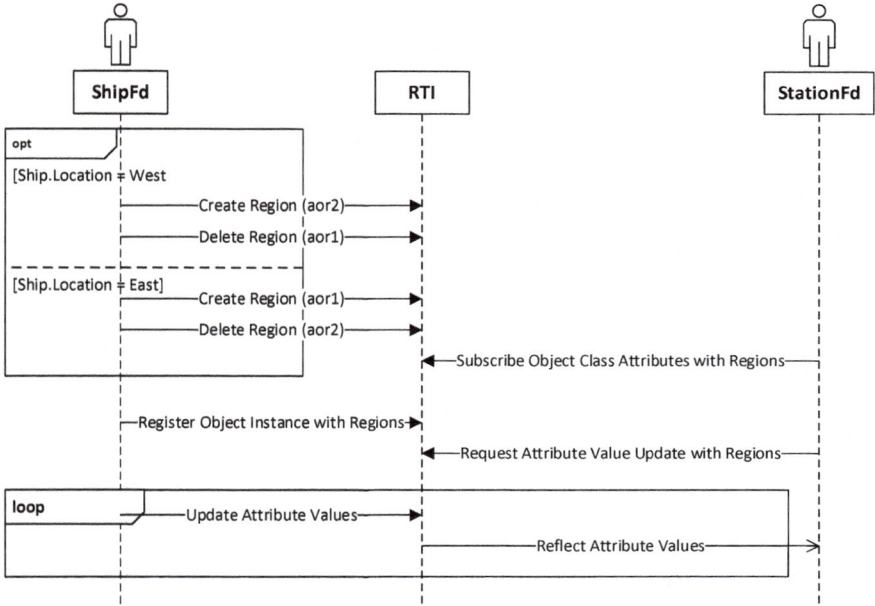

Fig. 9.13 UML sequence diagram for DDM service interactions

9.4.2 Creating Regions

Before using any data services related to DDM, we need to create regions, set range bounds, and commit region modifications, in this order. To create a region, we need to specify the associated dimensions. First, we get the dimension handles (ln. 3) and then prepare a dimension set (ln. 8–10) as an argument for the *Create Region* method (ln. 13). The RTI provides the region handle for further use. Specifically, the region handle ensures the association of the declaration and object management services, such as subscribe interaction class with region. The second step is to adjust the range of lower and upper bounds for each dimension of the region. Finally, we call the *Commit Region Modification* method to inform the RTI about the ranges of the regions (ln. 23).

```
1.  public void CreateWestRegion() {
2.    // Get all dimension handles associated with the region
3.    GetAllDimensionHandles();
4.
5.    // Instantiate a region object
6.    aor1 = new HlaRegion("aor1");
7.
8.    // Create a set of dimensions related with this region
9.    List < HlaDimension > dimensions = new List < HlaDimension > ();
10.   dimensions.Add(Som.AreaOfResponsibility);
11.
12.   // Create region
13.   CreateRegion(aor1, dimensions);
14.
15.   // Set range lower and upper bounds for each dimension
16.   SetRangeBounds(aor1.Handle, Som.AreaOfResponsibility.Han-
      dle, 0, 1);
17.
18.   // create a set of regions
19.   List < HlaRegion > regions = new List < HlaRegion > ();
20.     regions.Add(aor1);
21.
22.   // Commit region modifications
23.   CommitRegionModifications(regions);
24. }
```

At runtime, we can delete a region. For instance, when a ship in the strait moves to another zone (say from aor1 to aor2), it must re-adjust its data filters. First, it deletes the region (aor1) corresponding to its previous zone (ln. 4 and 9) and creates the new region (aor2) corresponding to its current zone (ln. 5 and 10). Second, it must register the ship object instance and its attributes with the new zone (see the following sections).

```
1.  // Zone transfer
2.  if (ship.Location == LocationEnum.West) // New zone
3.  {
4.    manager.federate.DeleteRegion(manager.federate.aor2);
5.    manager.federate.CreateWestRegion();
6.  }
7.  else
8.  {
9.    manager.federate.DeleteRegion(manager.federate.aor1);
10.   manager.federate.CreateEastRegion();
11. }
```

Now, we are ready to use the data services with regions.

9.4.3 Subscribing an Object Class with Regions

The attributes of an object instance can be associated with the regions created to form a data distribution filter. In order to do that we need to specify which attributes are associated with which regions. Thus, we create a set of attributes and a set of regions, associated as a pair (ln. 4–11). We can create as many pairs as necessary. In our running example, the StationFd subscribes to the Ship object class to receive the updates of the attribute values of a Ship object in its AOR.

```
1.  // DDM - subscribe object class with regions
2.
3.  // Create a list of attribute set and region set pairs
4.  AttributeHandleSetRegionHandleSetPairVector pairs = new At-
    tributeHandleSetRegionHandleSetPairVector();
5.
6.  // Construct the region set
7.  List < HlaRegion > regions = new List < HlaRegion > ();
8.  regions.Add(aor1);
9.
10. // Populate the pairs. Here we use all the attributes of the object
    class
11. pairs.Pairs.Add(new KeyValuePair < List < HlaAttrib-
    ute > , List < HlaRegion >> (ShipOC.Attributes, regions));
12.
13. // register object attributes with related regions
14. SubscribeObjectClasswithRegions(ShipOC, pairs);
```

To explain how to associate the attributes with regions, let us look at a hypothetical example. We have an object class *OC1* with attributes $\{x, y, w, z\}$ and assume that we have four regions $\{r1, r2, r3, r4\}$ created dynamically by the federate. Also, the association of the attributes with regions is asked as depicted in Fig. 9.14. To publish an instance of *OC1*, we need to pack each attribute and region as shown in Fig. 9.14.

9.4 Data Distribution Management

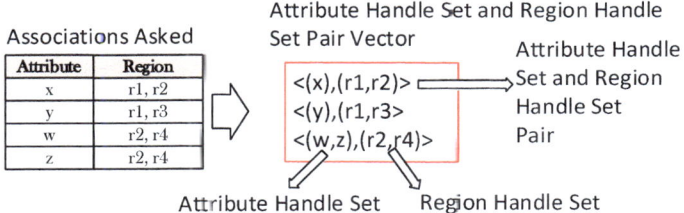

Fig. 9.14 Preparing a collection of attribute designator set and region designator set pairs

It is also possible to unsubscribe an object class associated with a region at runtime.

```
1. federate.UnsubscribeObjectClassWithRegions(feder-
   ate.Som.ShipOC, pairs);
```

We can request attribute value update associated with regions by calling *Request Value Update with Regions*.

```
1. federate.RequestClassAttributeValueUpdateWithRegions(feder-
   ate.Som.ShipOC, pairs, "user-supplied tag");
```

9.4.4 Registering an Object Instance with Regions

In our running example, the ShipFd registers the Ship object and its attributes associated with the region corresponding to its location. So, the updates of the attributes are distributed only to this region. Thus, the responsible traffic station gets the updates while the other stations do not. Before registering the object instance, we again need to construct a collection of the attribute set and region set pairs as explained in the previous section.

```
1. // DDM - register object with regions
2. // Create attribute set and region set pairs
3. // register object attributes with related regions
4. RegisterHlaObject(obj, pairs);
```

9.4.5 Associating Regions for Updates

We need to associate the attributes of a registered object with the distribution regions for providing the attribute value updates through the associated regions. To do so, we call the *Associate Regions for Update* service before beginning to update the values of the attributes. We can also remove the association using *Unassociate Regions for Updates* service. Note that it is important to register an object instance before associating it with the regions for update. Otherwise, the RTI will not be able to match the object instance with any region and raise an *object not known* error.

9.4.6 Case Study 2: Extended Chat Application

In the chat application, the users can select a nickname, enter the chat room, and send/receive messages from other users (federates). With the use of DDM services, the users will be able to enter exclusive chat rooms and communicate each other in private. To this end, we extend the Chat object model by introducing a routing space (i.e., ChatWorld) and a dimension (i.e., Rooms). A *routing space* is an HLA 1.3 specific concept to hold a set of dimensions. As depicted in Fig. 9.15, the routing space has only one dimension divided into two distinct regions.

The routing spaces and the dimensions must be defined in the FED file. A sample definition for the Chat is depicted below.

```
1.  (FED
2.    (Federation SimGe_Chat_DDM)
3.    (FEDversion v1_3)
4.    (spaces
5.      (space ChatWorld
6.        (dimension Rooms
7.        )
8.      )
9.  )
```

In HLA 1.3 specification, the attributes and interaction classes are associated with the routing spaces, not with the dimensions. The association of interaction class with spaces also must be done at the FOM construction time. The definition of the Chat interaction class, as a part of the FED, is depicted below (ln. 1–8). Notice that the class is related to the routing space ChatWorld (ln. 1).

```
1.  (class Chat reliable timestamp ChatWorld
2.    (parameter Sender
3.    )
4.    (parameter Message
5.    )
6.    (parameter TimeStamp
7.    )
8.  )
```

Now the federate is ready to create regions at runtime and to send chat messages according to the room. As an interaction class is treated as all or nothing, all the parameters are routed in the associated space. Remember that SimGe generates the FED file automatically from a given FOM.

9.4 Data Distribution Management

Fig. 9.15 Routing space design for Chat federate application. The routing space (ChatWorld) includes one dimension (Rooms) that is used to create two regions: Room1 and Room2

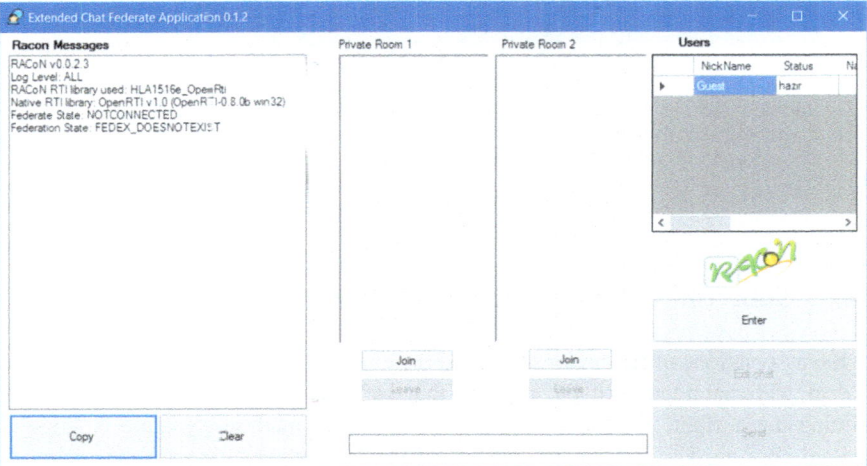

Fig. 9.16 Screen shot of the user interface of the Chat federate application

A screen shot of the user interface of the Chat application is shown in Fig. 9.16. Here, there are two (static) rooms that the user can join. Using the DDM services, the user receives the messages only sent from the room he/she joined.

SimGe generates a routing space template class (i.e., CChatWorldSpace) for each routing space. Using this class, in the federate SOM class (i.e., FederateSom), a routing space is created automatically as follows:

```
1. // Create Routing Space
2. ChatWorldSpace = new Chat_DDM.Som.CChatWorldSpace();
3. this.AddToObjectModel(ChatWorldSpace);
```

You must manually create the regions. Note that the dimensions related to the routing space are generated automatically by SimGe (ln. 2–3). To create a region, we need to create extents. The *extent* terminology is also HLA 1.3 specific. It corresponds to a range in the HLA Evolved specification.

```
1.  // Create Dimensions
2.  Rooms = new RACoN.ObjectModel.CDimension("Rooms", this);
3.  this.Dimensions.Add(Rooms);
4.
5.  // Create Extends
6.  exOd1 = new RACoN.ObjectModel.CExtent(Rooms, 2, 3);
7.  exOd2 = new RACoN.ObjectModel.CExtent(Rooms, 4, 5);
8.
9.  // Room1 Region (2-3)
10. Room1Region = new RACoN.ObjectModel.CRegion("Room1Region");
11. Room1Region.Extents.Add(exOd1); // Add extent to the region
12. this.Regions.Add(Room1Region); // Add region to the Space
13.
14. // Room2 Region (4-5)
15. Room2Region = new RACoN.ObjectModel.CRegion("Room2Region");
16. Room2Region.Extents.Add(exOd2); // Add extent to the region
17. this.Regions.Add(Room2Region); // Add region to the Space
```

9.4.7 Subscribing Interactions with Regions

As the associations of the regions with interactions are at class level, we do not need to deal with parameters in the manner that we deal with object classes such as defining the attribute set and region set pairs. So, the method signature is straightforward. We need to supply the handles of the interaction class and the region as arguments (ln. 2). The unsubscribe service call also uses the same parameter set.

```
1. // Subscribe
2. federate.SubscribeInteractionClass(ChatIC, Room1Region);
3. federate.UnSubscribeInteractionClass(ChatIC, Room1Region);
```

For HLA Evolved, we use a list of regions instead of a single region as a parameter.

9.4.8 Sending and Receiving Interactions Using Regions

To send an interaction, our federate calls the *Send Interaction with Regions* method by providing an interaction with parameter values as described in Chap. 8. Additionally, we add a region list, which is associated with the interaction, as a method argument. In HLA 1.3 specification, instead of a region list, we use only one region. If we want to send this interaction to multiple regions, then we must call this service with each region.

1. SendInteraction(interaction, region)

To receive an interaction with a region is not different from the normal use of receive interaction. The RTI ensures the interaction is delivered to the subscribed federates.

9.5 Ownership Management

Ownership management (OwM) is used by federates and the RTI to transfer ownership of instance attributes among federates. The key ideas of ownership management are highlighted below.

- Every instance attribute is owned by some federate, or is un-owned.
- An instance attribute effectively comes into existence when its instance is registered.
- Instance attributes remain in existence, and are owned or un-owned, until they are deleted.
- The federate that owns an instance attribute is responsible for updating its value as necessary. Only the federate that owns an instance attribute can update its value.
- A federate must be publishing the corresponding class attribute if it is to own an instance attribute.
- An instance attribute is never owned by more than one federate at a time.
- Ownership of an attribute can be transferred unambiguously from one federate to another.
- Ownership of an instance attribute cannot be gained or lost by a federate without its consent.
- Different attributes of an object instance can be owned by different federates.

9.5.1 Ownership Management Services

HLA 1.3 has 14 services for OwM including supporting functions such as cancellation and queries. These services are listed below (IEEE Std 1516.1-2010 2010).

- Unconditional Attribute Ownership Divestiture,
- Negotiated Attribute Ownership Divestiture,
- Request Attribute Ownership Assumption,
- Attribute Ownership Acquisition Notification,
- Attribute Ownership Acquisition,

- Attribute Ownership Acquisition If Available,
- Attribute Ownership Unavailable,
- Request Attribute Ownership Release,
- Cancel Negotiated Attribute Ownership Divestiture,
- Cancel Attribute Ownership Acquisition,
- Confirm Attribute Ownership Acquisition Cancellation,
- Query Attribute Ownership,
- Inform Attribute Ownership,
- Is Attribute Owned By Federate.

HLA Evolved specification adds four more additional services to overcome some deficiencies in OwM services found in HLA 1.3. These are discussed at the end of this section. The additional services introduced in HLA Evolved are as follows:

- Request Divestiture Confirmation (callback),
- Confirm Divestiture,
- Attribute Ownership Release Denied,
- Attribute Ownership Divestiture If Wanted.

9.5.2 Pull Strategy

As explained in Chap. 2, a *pull strategy* is followed when a federate is willing to take the ownership of some attributes of a specific object instance. When the attributes are un-owned or divested by its owner, then a federate can ask the permission of RTI to acquire the ownership of these attributes by calling *Attribute Ownership Acquisition If Available* service as shown in Fig. 9.17. The RTI responds with *Attribute Ownership Acquisition Notification*. Whenever this callback is received, the federate owns the specified attributes and the responsibility thereof. On the other hand, if the attributes are already owned, then the RTI does not look for a negotiation with the requesting federate and the owner federate; it simply replies with *Attribute Ownership Unavailable*.

For the *intrusive pull*, where the RTI negotiates between the requesting federate and the owner federate, the negotiation begins with *Attribute Ownership Acquisition* service called by the acquiring federate. Then, the RTI informs the owner federate by sending *Request Attribute Ownership Release* message if the owner federate is not in the waiting-for-a-new-owner state. In that case, the RTI must invoke the *Request Divestiture Confirmation* service. In the HLA Evolved standard, you can respond to the request either with *Attribute Ownership Divestiture If Wanted*, *Unconditional Attribute Divestiture*, or *Negotiated Attribute Ownership Divestiture* calls for a positive response. For a negative response, you can use *Attribute Ownership Release Denied* service. In HLA 1.3 specification, you can give a positive response by calling *Attribute Ownership Release Response*.

9.5 Ownership Management

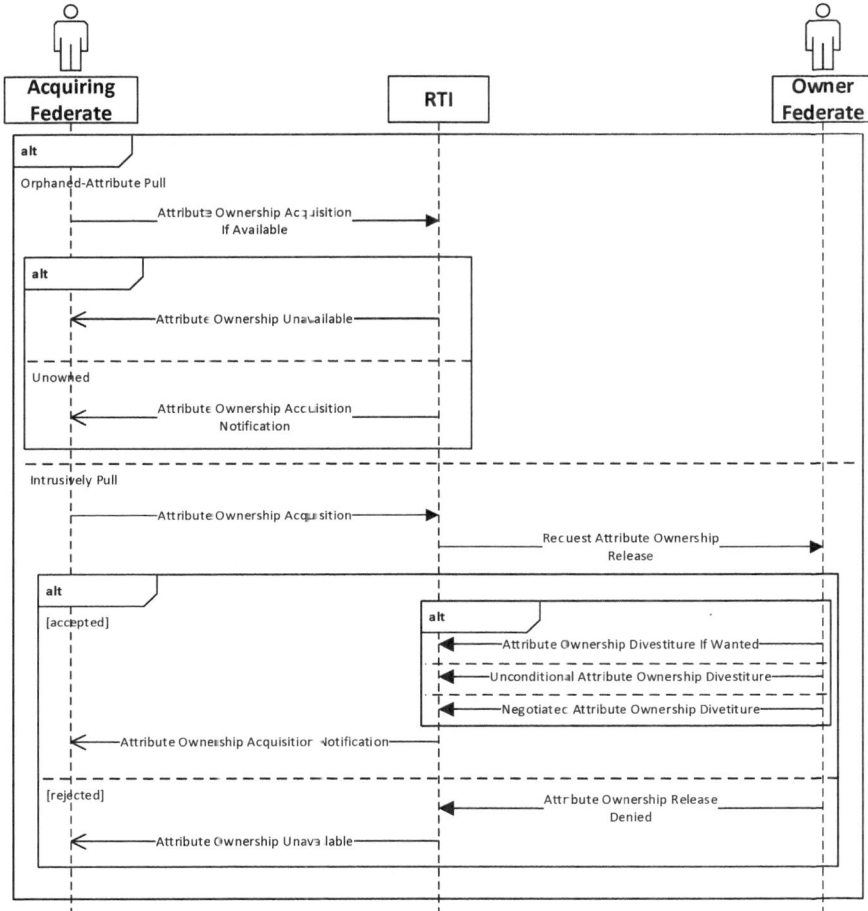

Fig. 9.17 Ownership pull strategy

9.5.3 Push Strategy

In *unconditional push*, the federate with the ownership of attributes (this may also include the privilege-to-delete attribute) unconditionally and willingly drops ownership immediately after calling the *Unconditional Attribute Ownership Divestiture*. The attributes become un-owned and then the RTI tries to find federates that are willing to take the ownership of these attributes by sending *Request Attribute Ownership Assumption* message. In case of a *negotiated push* strategy, the divesting federate (who currently has the ownership and is willing to give the responsibility to another federate) starts the process by issuing *Negotiated Attribute Ownership Divestiture* service. Again, the RTI transmits this request by sending *Request Attribute Ownership Assumption* message.

In both cases, a willing federate may call *Attribute Ownership Acquisition* or *Attribute Ownership Acquisition If Available* as stated in pull strategy. If attributes are un-owned as in the case of an unconditional push, then there is nothing to do further; the RTI gives the responsibility to the willing federate. In case negotiation is required, due to the presence of a divesting federate, the RTI informs the divesting federate that a new owner federate is found by invoking the *Request Divestiture Confirmation* service. Now, the divesting federate may cancel or confirm the divest operation by calling *Cancel Negotiated Attribute Ownership Divestiture* and *Confirm Divestiture*, respectively. By this call, the ownership transfer is completed (Fig. 9.18).

For HLA 1.3, there is no action for confirmation of a divestiture operation. When an attribute acquisition is made, then the RTI sends only an *Attribute Ownership Divestiture Notification* to the divesting federate.

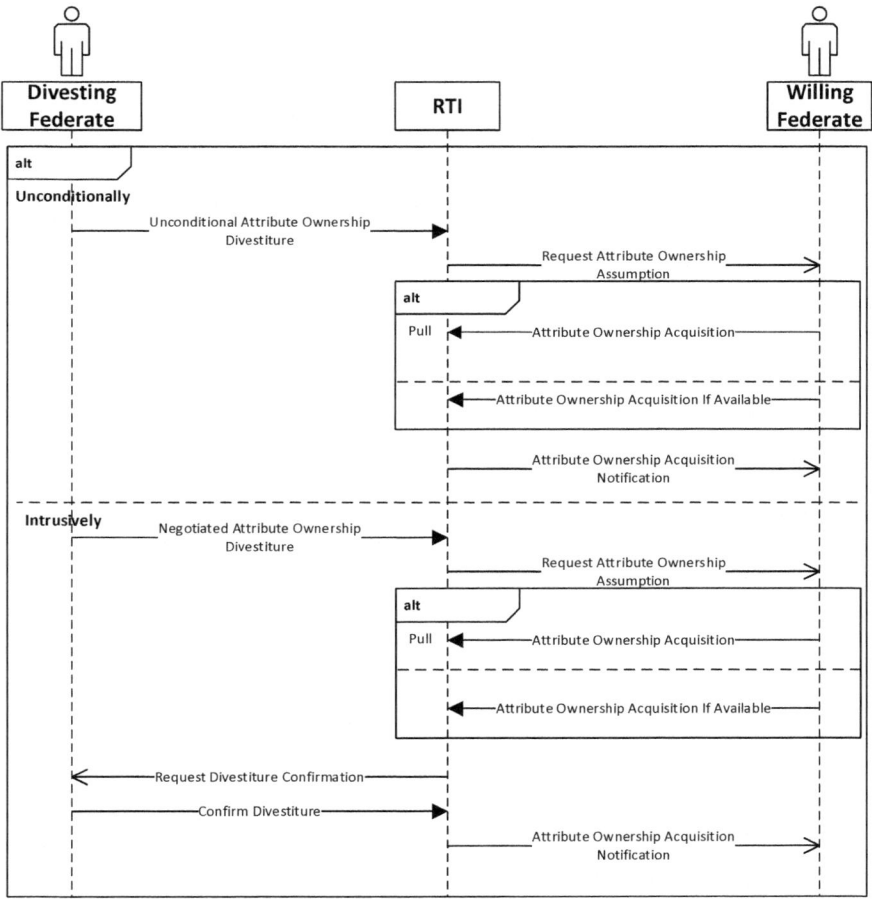

Fig. 9.18 Interactions for the ownership push strategy

9.5.4 Case Study: Transferring Tracks Among Traffic Stations

In our running example, remember that the traffic monitoring stations are responsible to track the ships in their area of responsibility. When a ship is detected entering the strait, then the responsible StationFd creates a track that represents the ship. The tracks are also shared by the stations. When a ship enters a new responsibility area of a station while moving along the strait, then the responsible StationFd, which is created the track for that ship, transfers the ownership of the track to the new responsible station. Thus, the area of responsibility for traffic monitoring stations indicates the ownership of tracks.

In STMS, a push strategy is implemented. Whenever a track of a StationFd is out of its area of responsibility, then the federate first creates an attribute list of the related track (ln. 2–7) and sends an *Unconditional Attribute Ownership Divestiture* message (ln. 12) and immediately becomes free of its responsibility.

```
1.  private void HandleTrackOutOfZone(object sender, COu-
    tofZoneArgs data) {
2.    // Construct attribute list
3.    List < HlaAttribute > attributes = new List < HlaAttrib-
    ute > ();
4.    attributes.Add(Som.TrackOC.TrackNumber);
5.    attributes.Add(Som.TrackOC.TrackPosition);
6.    attributes.Add(Som.TrackOC.TrackHeading);
7.    attributes.Add(Som.TrackOC.TrackSpeed);
8.    if (data.Zone == OutOfZoneEnum.OutOfStrait) {
9.       DeleteObjectInstance(data.Track);
10.   }
11.   else
12.      UnconditionalAttributeOwnershipDivestiture(data.Track, attrib-
    utes);
13.
14.   // remove this track
15.   Program.MyTracks.Remove(data.Track);
16. }
```

The RTI issues a *Request Attribute Ownership Assumption* message (ln. 1), and the new responsible StationFd informs the RTI about its willingness to take the ownership by calling *Attribute Ownership Acquisition* (ln. 4).

```
1.  public override void FdAmb_AttributeOwnershipAssumptionRe-
    quested(object sender, HlaOwnershipManagementEventArgs data) {
2.    CTrackHlaObject track = new CTrackHlaObject(Som.TrackOC);
3.    track.Handle = data.ObjectHandle;
4.    AttributeOwnershipAcquisition(track, "DivestitureRequestTag");
5.  }
```

After this step, the RTI sends an *Attribute Ownership Divestiture Notification* message to the divesting federate (the giver) and an *Attribute Ownership Acquisition Notification* message to the new owner (the taker).

9.5.5 Querying the Ownership

It is possible to query the ownership of an attribute of a specific object instance by using the *Query Attribute Ownership* service.

```
1. federate.QueryAttributeOwnership(station, federate.Som.Sta-
   tionOC.PrivilegeToDelete);
```

The RTI answers this query by sending an *Inform Attribute Ownership* message. This callback encapsulates a federate handle of the owner, if the attribute is owned. If the attribute instance is not owned by a joined federate, then the *attributeIsnotOwned* callback is sent to indicate that the attribute is un-owned, or the *attributeIsOwnedByRTI* message is sent to indicate the attribute is owned by RTI and available for acquisition (Fig. 9.19). Typically, the RTI is the owner of the attributes of MOM object instances.

Alternatively, one can ask the RTI whether an attribute is owned by the local federate (the invoking federate) or not using *Is Attribute Owned By Federate* method, which returns a Boolean value, true or false.

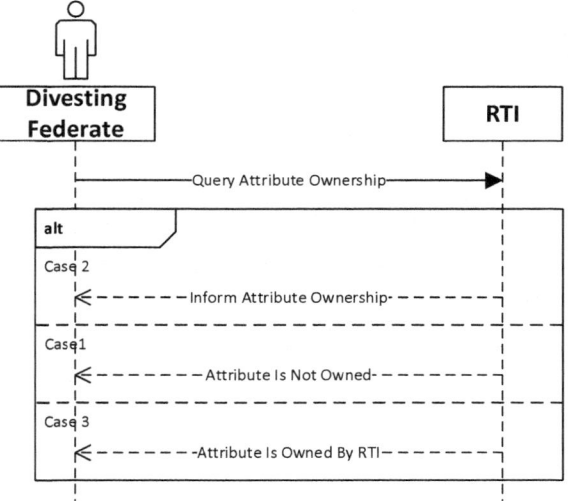

Fig. 9.19 Querying the ownership

9.5.6 Problems in OwM of HLA 1.3

As you noticed, the HLA Evolved specification introduced some additional services for ownership management over the HLA 1.3 specification. The HLA 1.3 specification was found inadequate regarding the divesting/acquiring of ownership operations. First, there is no mechanism implemented in the RTI 1.3 that allows a federate to reject an attribute release and divest ownership if wanted. Second, the Attribute Ownership Release Response service, which is HLA 1.3 specific only, is problematic when an acquiring federate cancels its acquisition request before the RTI receives an *Attribute Ownership Release Response* from the owner federate (DMSO 2002).

9.6 Handling Multiple Federation Executions

A federate application can interact with more than one federation execution at the same time. Sometimes, this ability is used to bridge different federation executions as logically depicted in Fig. 9.20.

As discussed in Chap. 2, a federate can query the existing federation executions executed by the RTI using *List Federation Executions* service. The RTI informs the federate by sending a list of pairs, where each pair consists of the name of a federation execution and its time representation, using *Report Federation Executions* callback service.

To exemplify the situation using our running example STMS, let us assume that we want to run two different federation executions at the same time to simulate the strait traffic under different parameters. The first federation execution is to simulate Dardanelles Strait and the second federation execution Bosporus Strait. Actually, both federation executions are instances of the STMS federation; thus, they share the same FOM. Instead of running different StationFdApp for each execution, we

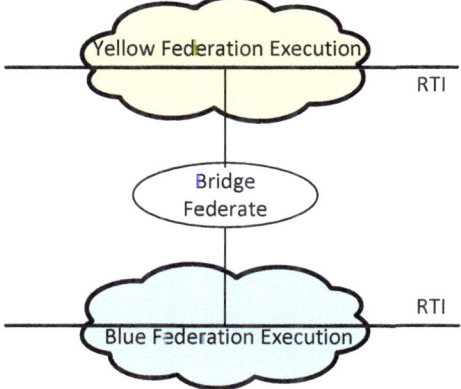

Fig. 9.20 Bridging multiple federation executions

simply run one StationFdApp that will handle both executions. In other words, the StationFdApp will interact with two federation executions at the same time.

As the layered architecture of the federate application provides a good separation of concerns, the implementation is straightforward. To handle multiple federation executions, the federate application creates an instance of federate class of RACoN (ln. 2), where each one is handling a different federation execution. The federate application then initializes (ln. 3–8), connects (ln. 11), tries to create a new federation execution (ln. 14), and joins it (ln. 17) as described previously. The following code samples are related to the Bosporus federation execution. Implementing the federate for Dardanelles federation execution is similar.

```
1.  // Initialize the second federation execution
2.  CStationFdApp federateForBosporus = new CStationFdApp();
3.  federateForBosporus.StatusMessageChanged += Federate_StatusMes-
    sageChanged;
4.  federateForBosporus.LogLevel = LogLevel.ALL;
5.  federateForBosporus.FederationExecution.Name = "Bosporus";
6.  federateForBosporus.FederationExecution.FederateType = "StationFed-
    erate";
7.  federateForBosporus.FederationExecution.ConnectionSet-
    tings = "rti://127.0.0.1";
8.  federateForBosporus.FederationExecution.FDD = @".\StmsFom.xml";
9.
10. // Connect
11. federateForBosporus.Connect(Callback-
    Model.EVOKED, federateForBosporus.FederationExecution.ConnectionSet
    tings);
12.
13. // Create federation execution
14. federateForBosporus.CreateFederationExecution(federateForBospo-
    rus.FederationExecution.Name, federateForBosporus.FederationExecu-
    tion.FomModules);
15.
16. // Join federation execution
17. federateForBosporus.JoinFederationExecution(federateForBospo-
    rus.FederationExecution.FederateName, federateForBosporus.Federa-
    tionExecution.FederateType, federateForBosporus.FederationExecu-
    tion.Name, federateForBosporus.FederationExecution.FomModules);
18.
19. // Declare Capability
20. federateForBosporus.DeclareCapability();
```

A conceptual view of the situation is depicted in Fig. 9.21.

Fig. 9.21 Participating into two federation executions at the same time

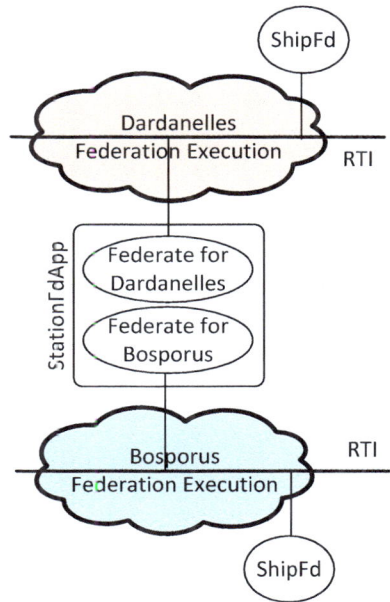

9.7 One Federate Application, Multiple Federates

In most cases, a federate is a single application. But in some cases, a federate application may host multiple joined federates in a single federation execution. One such case is the computer-generated (virtual) entities such as agents, which act by themselves. A single application creates and manages many agents, which are also federates, not objects, in a single federation execution. An application is presented in Chap. 11, where the agent manager handles multiple boat agents as joined federates.

To illustrate the situation, here we will use a simpler example, where a federate application creates a new federate, and that federate joins and resigns to/from the federation execution whenever the user presses the create and remove buttons. The objective of the exercise is to simulate the free fall of balls from a predefined height. Each ball is represented as a joined federate. The logical federate architecture is depicted in Fig. 9.22.

The user interface of the federate application enables the user to add and remove balls before starting the simulation. Adding and removing a ball represents adding a new federate (i.e., ball) to the federation execution. The graphical user interface (GUI) of the simulation is depicted in Fig. 9.23.

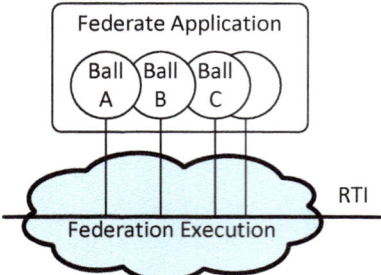

Fig. 9.22 Managing multiple joined federates in a federation execution by a single federate application

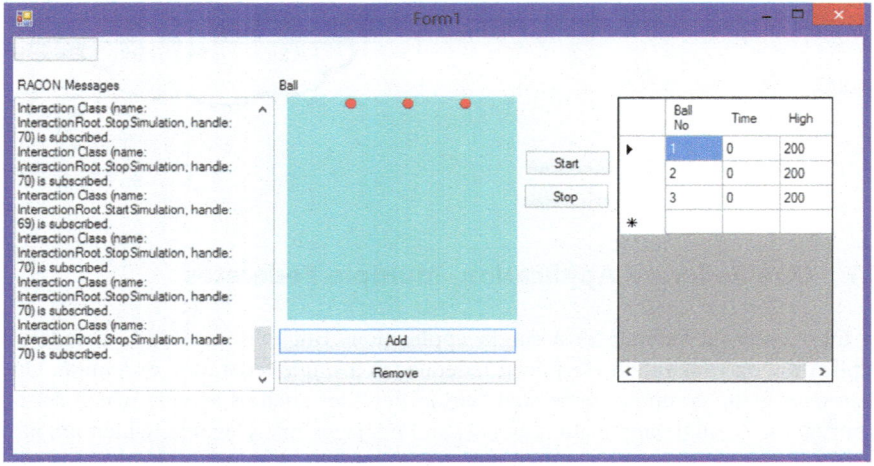

Fig. 9.23 A screen snapshot of free fall of balls

When the manager federate sends start and stop interactions to ball federates, then each ball federate registers a ball object and then updates the value of the height attribute of the ball object. So, there are two interaction classes published by the manager federate and a ball object class published by a ball federate and subscribed by the manager federate.

Using the same implementation approach, it is straightforward to create and delete joined federates. In the button clicked event of Add button, we instantiate and initialize a new federate and then we call the join federation execution service.

9.7 One Federate Application, Multiple Federates

```
1.  private void AddButton_Click(object sender, RoutedEventArgs e) {
2.    // initalize federation execution properties
3.    FederationExecution.FederateName = "Ball";
4.    FederationExecution.FederateType = "BallFederate";
5.    FederationExecution.FomModules.Add(@".\FreeFall.xml");
6.    // Try to create federation execution
7.    CreateFederationExecution(FederationExecution.Name, FederationExe-
      cution.FomModules);
8.    // Join feceration execution
9.    JoinFederationExecution(FederationExecution.FederateType, Federa-
      tionExecution.Name, FederationExecution.FomModules);
10. }
```

In the event of Remove button clicked, we finalize the last added federate from the federation execution.

```
1.  private void RemoveButton_Click(object serder, RoutedEven-
    tArgs e) {
2.    // Resign federation execution
3.    ResignFederationExecution(ResignAction.NC_ACTION);
4.    // Try to destroy the federation execution
5.    DestroyFederationExecution(FederationExecution.Name);
6.  }
```

9.8 Summary

In this chapter, we learned how to implement a federate application by working through one of the federate applications, ShipFdApp, of our running example, STMS. For implementing a federate application, we first bring about its static architecture and then implement the simulation object of it. Then, we learned to implement how to initialize a federation execution by using the basics of federation management services, how to declare the federate's capabilities and interest by using the declaration management services, and how to send/receive interaction, how to create objects, and how to update/receive the values of attributes at runtime by using the object management services. Lastly, handling multiple federation executions was discussed.

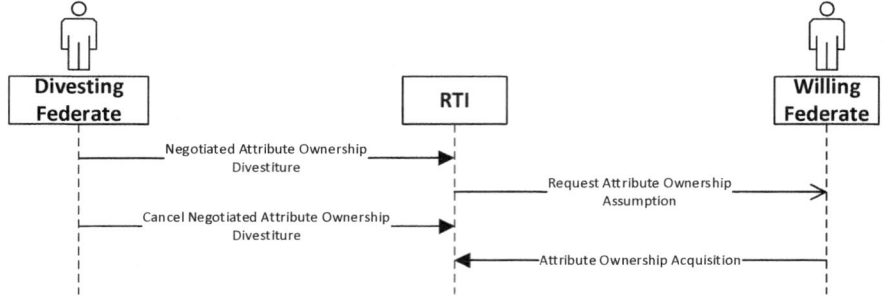

Fig. 9.24 Cancel negotiated attribute ownership divestiture

9.9 Questions for Review

1. Assume you use the linear enumerated normalization function introduced in Sect. 9.4.1 for representing the values of two dices, how is the value of 7 mapped to a dimension with an upper bound 13?
2. a. Discuss the differences of HLA ownership management services specified in HLA 1.3 and HLA Evolved standard.
   b. What are the problems and inefficiencies in ownership management services in HLA 1.3 specification?
3. Describe what happens when *Cancel Negotiated Attribute Ownership Divestiture* service is called following the *Negotiated Attribute Ownership Divestiture* service and the RTI sent a *Request Attribute Ownership Assumption* to other federates as depicted in Fig. 9.24.
4. Suppose that you're porting a legacy simulation from the code base of HLA 1.3 specification to the HLA Evolved standard. In the ownership management calls, you come across an *Attribute Ownership Release Response* method call. You notice that this service is not available in the HLA Evolved specification. How do you port this code to the HLA Evolved?
5. Same question as 4 considering the *Attribute Ownership Divestiture Notification* callback.
6. Regarding the HLA 1.3, describe what happens when a federate cancels its acquisition request when the *Attribute Ownership Release Response* call of the owner federate reaches the RTI after this cancellation is confirmed as depicted in Fig. 9.25.
7. Is it possible to allow a federate to reject an attribute release and divest ownership in the HLA 1.3 specification?
8. The developer of a real-time federate thinks she does not need to use time management services. Then, how can she keep the federate time?

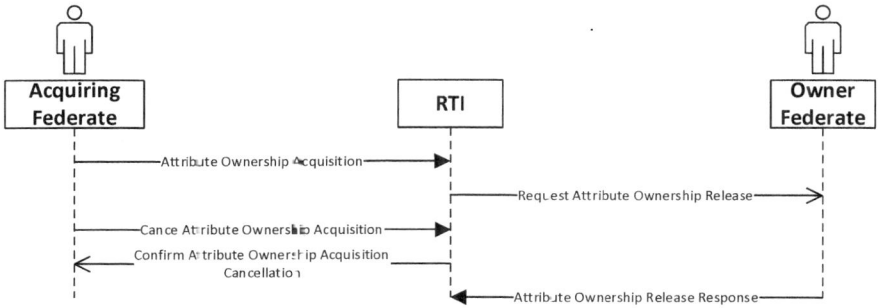

Fig. 9.25 Cancel attribute ownership acquisition request

9. Describe a hypothetical, yet sensible, federation where one of the federates is time regulating (only), another one is time constrained (only), and yet another one is both.
10. Assume that the underlying network protocol supports multicasting. How does it help with RTI in terms of data management and data distribution management?

References

DMSO. (2002). *High level architecture run-time infrastructure RTI 1.3-Next generation programmer's guide version 6*. s.l.: Department of Defense Defense Modeling and Simulation Office.

Fujimoto, R. M. (1998). Time management in the high level architecture. *Simulation, 71*(6), 388–400.

Fujimoto, R. M. (2000). *Parallel and distributed simulation systems* (1st ed.). s.l.: Wiley.

IEEE Std 1516.1-2010. (2010). *Standard for modeling and simulation (M&S) high level architecture (HLA)—Federate interface specification*. s.l.: IEEE.

IEEE Std 1516.2-2010. (2010). *Standard for modeling and simulation (M&S) high level architecture (HLA)—Object model template specification*. s.l.: IEEE.

Integration of Agents into HLA 10

We can identify two main approaches for achieving synergies between multi-agent systems and distributed simulation. The first one is to incorporate agents into a simulation environment, specifically into an HLA federation, using interoperability techniques. The second is to build an agent environment based on HLA so that the RTI is employed to serve as the baseline for agent communication and management. In this chapter, first we will briefly introduce agent-based simulation and describe a cognitive agent architecture as an example of an agent architecture. Then, we will discuss how to integrate an agent-based simulation into an HLA-based distributed simulation and how to utilize HLA as agent communication medium.

10.1 Agent-Based Simulation

Agent-Based Modeling and Simulation (ABMS), specifically multi-agent simulation, is maturing as a scientific approach to analyze the emergent behavior and to help solve the related problems of complex systems. Emergent behavior is the result of interactions of autonomous agents with each other in an environment. In this approach, the parts of a complex system are modeled as interacting autonomous agents, where each agent's observed behavior is individually specified and modeled by simple rules and interactions with its environment. By modeling the system from the bottom up as agents and then letting them interact with each other in a specified environment will often lead to self-organization and create an emerged behavior that reflects the dynamic behavior of the complex system under consideration, which is not preprogrammed (Macal and North 2010). Due to its expressive power and flexibility, multi-agent simulation is used as a technique in a broad range of areas from social sciences to finance.

A (software) agent is a computer program that has the ability to perceive its environment via sensors and to perform actions via its actuators (Russell and Norvig 2010). Specifically, an autonomous agent possesses the characteristics of autonomy, proactivity, adaptation, and social abilities. *Social ability* imposes on agents that they are commonly situated in an environment composed of other (software or human) agents. To accomplish their tasks, agents can engage in dialogs with other agents and interact in cooperative or competitive ways (Braubach and Pokahr 2009). Some tasks cannot be accomplished by only one agent therefore they require collaboration. On the other hand, sometimes agents compete for tasks. Both requirements dictate that agents must be *interactive*, where they communicate in order to cooperate or compete when they execute a common task. *Autonomy* imposes on agents the need to decide on its own in order to accomplish given tasks and goals as well (Shiffman 2012). In this regard, the goal-oriented agents need a *goal deliberation* mechanism. Moreover, context-awareness has impact on goal deliberation, where goal validity is related to specific contexts. Here, goal validity refers to the acceptance of a goal and context is the information about the agent itself and its environment that can be used to characterize the situation of an agent. For instance, a goal might not be acceptable in a specific context. The *proactivity* property of an agent is also a result of the goal deliberation reasoning. Agents pursue their own goals, not only react to events. The adaptation, as well as the autonomy, of an agent requires the provision of a *learning* ability. Learning can employ activity-awareness ability and event reaction mechanisms as in reactive agents.

In an agent-based simulation, the behavior of an autonomous agent is influenced by its decision-making ability. *Decision making* can be defined as a high-level cognitive process resulting in the selection of a course of action among several alternatives to achieve some goal. Decision-making process relies on *situational awareness*. One reason is that, in the presence of changing and uncertain environmental conditions and situations, a plausible decision in a specific context cannot remain to be valid. Moreover, an emergent situation may dictate the derivation of a new execution plan based on the goals that lead the agent to adapt to the new situation. Therefore, the behavior of an autonomous agent depends on its decision-making mechanism and the result of the decision-making process is mostly related to the agent's situational awareness and its adaptation to the new context and situation.

10.1.1 A Cognitive Agent Architecture

From the viewpoint of agent-based simulation discipline, we may narrow down autonomy to decision making and decision making to *goal deliberation* for an agent. Making the right decision can be interpreted as choosing the more coherent alternative. Thus, goal deliberation can be formulated as a constraint satisfaction problem (Thagard and Verbeurgt 1998), where the goals and the tasks found in an execution plan of an autonomous agent have relations among them setting constraints such as facilitation and inhibition. For example, a constraint can be specified such as "a task facilitates a goal" or "a task inhibits the accomplishment of a goal," where in the former case, the task and goal cohere with each other, and, in the latter, they incohere. The coherence considerations in goal reasoning bring the

10.1 Agent-Based Simulation

deliberative coherence—*Theory of Deliberative Coherence* (TDC) (Millgram and Thagard 1996), which is based on the Explanatory Coherence Theory (Thagard 1989). Thagard and Millgram (1995) present a scheme for goal inference based on deliberative coherence. In their approach, constraint satisfaction is computed by using a parallel distributed processing algorithm (McClelland 2014); the inference is concluded by selecting the most satisfied constraints among the goals and tasks, called elements, where satisfaction increases among elements that fit together (the case of coherence) and decreases otherwise (the case of incoherence). Then, the elements are divided into two sets as accepted or rejected, where the former set forms the most satisfied constraints and thus it is selected as the inferred plan to execute (or the decision made). The elements in the plan and their constraints constitute a model called a *connectionist network* (model), which can be seen as a kind of recurrent neural network (Haykin 2009). In this network, the elements correspond to units and the constraints to links. This connectionist network forms the structure of decision making, where the goals and tasks are not formally distinguished.

To this end, for illustrative purposes, we introduce a reference architecture for a cognitive agent, called *deliberative coherence-driven agent (DeCoAgent)*, specifically targeting an adaptive decision-making capability. The reference architecture is represented as a SysML internal block diagram (OMG 2012) and depicted in Fig. 10.1 (Topçu 2014). The classical agent block represents a known agent structure such as model-based reflex agent (Russell and Norvig 2010) or a known agent architecture such as BDI (Belief-Desire-Intention) agent (Bratman 1987).

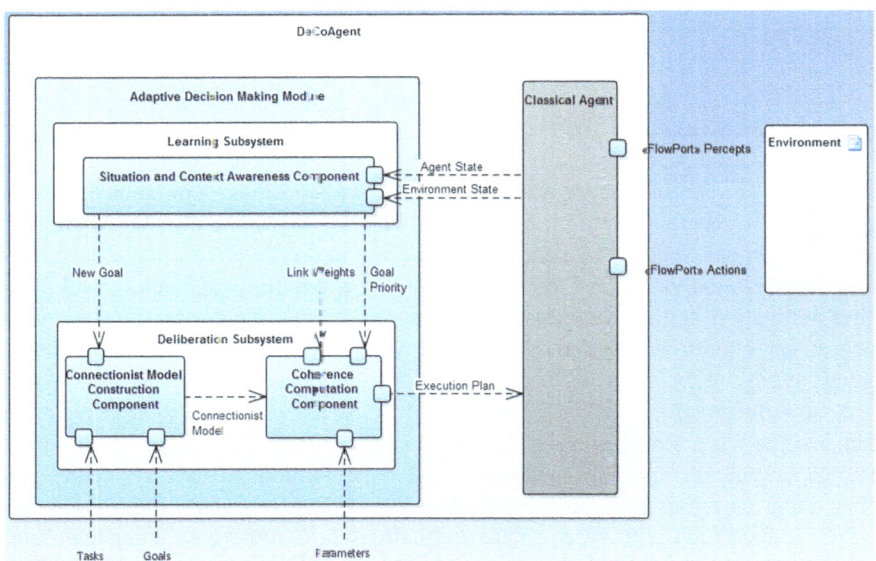

Fig. 10.1 Architecture for adaptive decision making (Topçu 2014)

The coherence computation component is responsible for the goal deliberation process, where it maintains a connectionist network of tasks, goals, and the relations among them and calculates the activations and the total coherence of the connectionist network. The coherence computation continues until the activation of nodes in the connectionist network becomes stable. The monitoring component is called the situation and context-awareness component, and it is responsible for dynamically adjusting the goal priority and relation strengths (i.e., weights) among the goals and tasks. The situation and context-awareness component and the connectionist model construction component together support the agent in adapting to the mission objectives in the presence of shifting and competing goals.

The tasks that an agent performs depend on the context. According to the context, the priority of the goals that the agent pursues may change. When a goal priority changes, the relevant actions (i.e., tasks) need to change accordingly.

Developing autonomous agents with cognitive abilities such as decision making is a complicated task. In Chap. 11, we provide a full-blown HLA-integrated agent-based simulation example that employs the reference architecture discussed in this section.

10.2 Integration of Agents into HLA-Based Simulations

To integrate agents into an HLA-based simulation for both using interoperability techniques and using HLA as an agent environment, different architectural approaches are proposed (Zhuang et al. 2006). The following sections introduce some of fundamental abstract architectural approaches and then an example architecture.

10.2.1 Architectural Approaches

Distributed simulation brings the capability to link various simulations. In this sense, the interoperability of an agent-based simulation with a distributed simulation environment, such as a federation, can be required. The obvious challenge is to provide the shared data in two directions: to other simulation applications and from other simulation applications, by the means of the RTI. The conceptual view of such an integration is depicted in Fig. 10.2, where the RTI serves as a communication layer.

A straightforward solution is to develop an *HLA gateway*, to mediate data exchange between simulations as depicted in Fig. 10.3. In this scheme, within the agent-based simulation, the agents continue to communicate directly with each other using an *agent communication language* (ACL), but when they require or provide shared data with other simulation entities (i.e., non-agent federates), then the HLA gateway performs the necessary data mediation in the form of HLA objects and interactions conforming to the federation object model. The major

10.2 Integration of Agents into HLA-Based Simulations

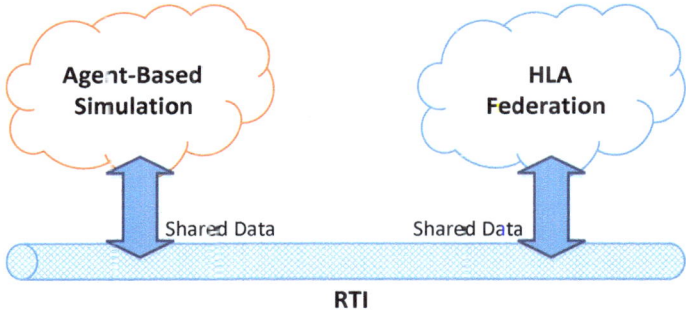

Fig. 10.2 Integration of an agent-based simulation with an HLA federation. Our goal is to integrate agents with an HLA-based simulation; to this end, we employ interoperability techniques

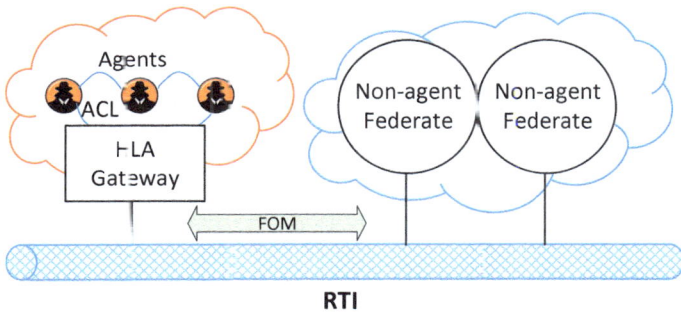

Fig. 10.3 Integration with using an HLA gateway

advantage of this integration architecture is that it clearly keeps the separation of concerns. The agent-based simulation remains as is. In general, the life cycle of an agent in an agent-based simulation is managed by using a central *agent manager* (e.g., to create an agent). In this case, the agent manager can be extended as an HLA gateway. The HLA gateway behaves (possibly) as an agent in the agent-based simulation and (definitely) as a federate in the federation.

Although this solution approach is straightforward, the development of the HLA gateway is not trivial. First, the agent manager must keep track of each agent and must handle the distribution of incoming data among agents. Second, it must perform the encapsulation of data, coming from different types of agents, according to the federation object model. Third, it must manage the various RTI services related to simulation management such as time management on account of all the agents. Therefore, the HLA gateway may become a bottleneck in terms of availability and performance.

An alternative approach for the integration is to extend each agent with an RTI component (RTILib) or to wrap the agent as a federate application, so that each agent behaves as a separate federate as depicted in Fig. 10.4. In this case, the agents

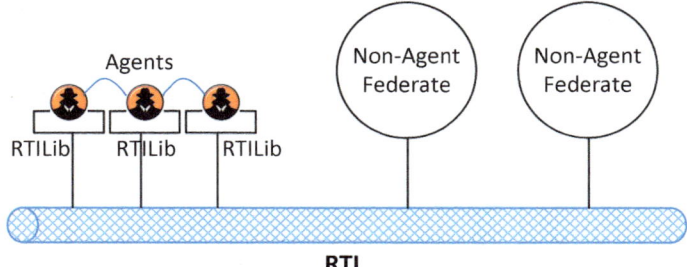

Fig. 10.4 Integration by extending/wrapping each agent as a federate

continue to communicate with each other using an agent communication language within the agent-based simulation as well as they behave like a federate for interfederate communication with other simulation entities. This approach enables the distribution of simulation to the full extent and from the viewpoint of an HLA practitioner, the implementation becomes comparable to federate application implementation.

The limitation of this approach is that it can be employed only if we have access to the source code of the agent or if we develop it from scratch. In addition, we need compatible libraries with the RTI software for agent and RTI component implementation. In the following section, we provide a concrete example of this type of integration.

10.2.2 A Concrete Architecture

Taking the advantage of the federate-layered architecture (see Fig. 10.5) introduced in Chap. 7, we can quickly integrate the simulation and communication layers (i.e., RACoN) into an agent development framework (i.e., the agent layer). To simplify the architecture, we omit the presentation layer (assuming the agent has its own user interface), and we call the *HLA Layer* the combination of communication and simulation layers. The HLA layer incorporates the RTI library, which includes the Federate and the RTI Ambassadors to handle the RTI services.

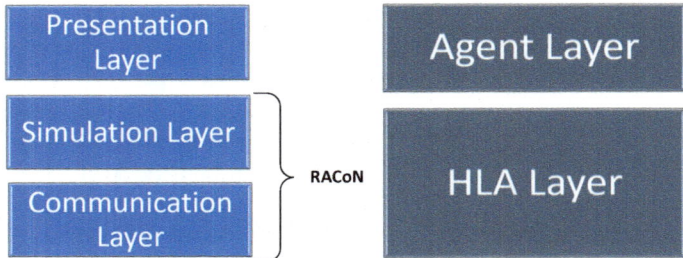

Fig. 10.5 Integration layers for an HLA-enabled agent

10.2 Integration of Agents into HLA-Based Simulations

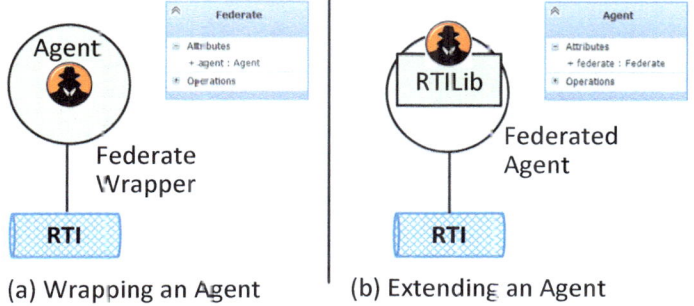

Fig. 10.6 Extending and wrapping an agent so that it can act as a federate

The integration can be implemented by either wrapping an agent with federate code (Fig. 10.6a) or extending the agent with the RTI library (Fig. 10.6b). The former can be described as *federate hosting an agent*. The federate application involves an agent so that it can mediate data between the agent and the federation execution. In the latter technique, an agent has an RTILib so that it can interact with a federation execution.

To concretize the integration, we will use the *Coherence-Based Agent Framework* (CogAgentLib) (CogAgentLib 2017) as the agent platform in the agent layer and the RACoN library in the HLA layer. The agent library incorporates the library for HLA capability (IHlaAgent) as well as some cognitive capability libraries such as decision making (IDeCoAgent) as depicted in Fig. 10.7. So, it is not an arbitrary agent framework; it anticipates HLA integration. A cognitive agent becomes HLA-capable, denoted as *Federated Agent* (HlaAgent), by implementing the HLA agent interface (IHlaAgent) provided by the CogAgentLib. The HLA interface serves as a bridge to the RACoN library.

In Chap. 11, we give a full-blown example on how to implement a federated agent based on this architecture.

10.2.3 Using HLA as Agent Communication Medium

Although HLA is not intended to be a multi-agent platform, it is noted that the collection of services provided by the RTI meets many common requirements expected from an agent platform, such as data (control and information) distribution, providing environment information, event management, and time management (Andersson and Löf 1999). However, the RTI is found short of a fine-tuned communication standard among agents as an agent hardly acts in isolation in an environment and it requires proper communication means, explicitly tuned for agent communication. Therefore, there are some studies (Andersson and Löf 1999; Göktürk and Polat 2003) that propose to extend the RTI with an agent communication language (ACL).

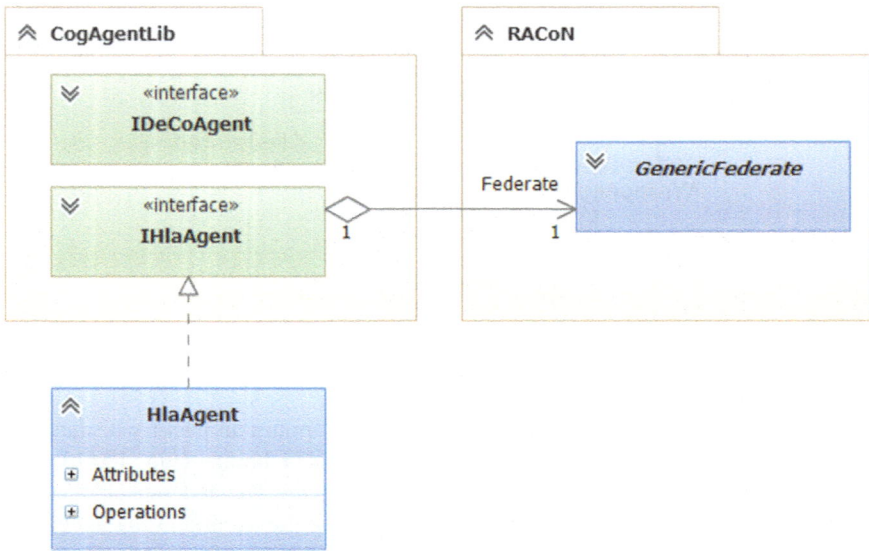

Fig. 10.7 Class diagram for HLA-capable agent. This diagram shows how two different assemblies (CogAgentLib and RACoN) are integrated to define an HLA-capable agent (HlaAgent)

In a multi-agent system, the agents interact with each other for collaboration using an *ACL*. *FIPA* (Foundation for Intelligent Physical Agents), a standards committee of the IEEE Computer Society, provides an ACL with a message structure (FIPA-SC00061G 2012), an ontology-based standard language, Semantic Language (SL) (FIPA-SC00008I 2002), and various transport protocols for agent communication (Poslad 2007). Another specification for ACL is *Knowledge Query and Manipulation Language* (KQML) (Finin et al. 1994). Both approaches provide an architectural basis for the agent communication involving the discovery of other agents and their abilities, directory services, communication protocols, and messages.

To narrow the discussion down, we focus on ACL messages. From the viewpoint of the RTI, an ACL message is only transient data that originates from an agent and is exchanged between federates and then delivered to another agent. As we discussed at length, the data communication in HLA occurs in the form of object classes or interaction classes. Therefore, an ACL message can be exchanged by sending and receiving an interaction or by using the object attribute update and reflect mechanism. The former approach, representing an ACL message as an HLA interaction to employ the RTI as a communication medium among agents, is more straightforward. As shown in Fig. 10.8, a regular agent (appears in the right side of the figure) has a communication component of its own, apart from the federate's communication layer for handling the ACL messages (e.g., decoding and parsing) for instance in the form of a KQML message. The federated agent has another component for handling the representation of an ACL message to an HLA

10.2 Integration of Agents into HLA-Based Simulations

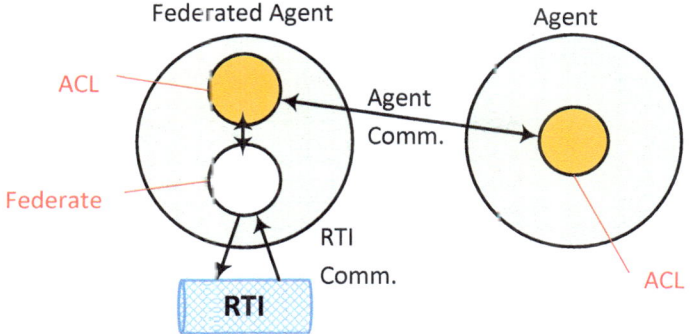

Fig. 10.8 Using RTI as a communication medium

interaction and vice versa. At the sender side, the federated agent represents the ACL message in the form of an interaction and then sends it via RTI. The other federated agent receives and decodes the interaction and delivers the ACL message to the agent's communication component for further decoding and processing.

The federation object model must consist of suitable interaction classes for encapsulating an ACL message. There are some studies to offer interaction classes for both KQML (Andersson and Löf 1999; Göktürk and Polat 2003) and FIPA-ACL. The `CcgAgentLib` provides some interaction classes for relaying such ACL messages. A typical FIPA-ACL message includes a header to indicate the type of communicative act or performative information as well as other header fields to specify identification information such as the sender, receiver, protocol, language, and ontology used. The content is the actual message (Poslad 2007). A sample template of an interaction class for FIPA-ACL communicative act message is depicted in Fig. 10.9.

Taking the advantage of FOM modularity, introduced in the HLA Evolved specification, the ACL extensions made to FOM can be designed as a FOM module. So, the federated agents may load this module separately from its application-specific FOM. In Chap. 11, we demonstrate how to use an ACL-extended FOM module side by side with the federation FOM.

As far as the agent communication is carried out by point-to-point links and the RTI communication uses publish/subscribe mechanism, the major drawback of encapsulating the actual ACL message within an interaction is forcing all federated agents to subscribe the interaction classes used for encapsulation. As the actual message has its own sender and receiver, the RTI must limit the message distribution in the federation. A particular solution is to use the RTI data distribution management services, where each federate creates its own region to send and receive such interactions. Another problem arises when the transportation of an ACL message requires send-order reception. As discussed in Chap. 2, HLA only supports receive-order and timestamp-order messages. For some solutions to this problem, see (Göktürk and Polat 2003).

Fig. 10.9 Snapshot taken from SimGe depicting the parameters of the interaction class for FIPA-ACL

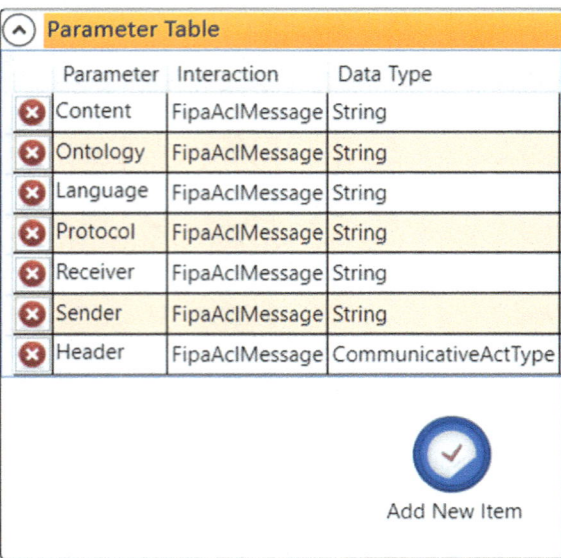

10.3 Summary

In this chapter, the synergy between the agent-based simulation and the distributed simulation was highlighted and an approach for realizing it was discussed. If our aim is to integrate the agents (in an agent-based simulation or in a multi-agent system) with an HLA-based simulation, we can employ interoperability methods. An HLA gateway is implemented to enable the interoperability between two, where it behaves as an agent in the agent-based simulation and as a federate in the federation. Another approach is to extend or wrap an agent so that it acts as a federate in its own in addition to acting as an agent in the agent-based simulation. Lastly, HLA can be used as an agent communication medium. The straightforward method here is to represent an ACL message as an HLA interaction. But for all cases, we need agent platforms (or libraries) that anticipate HLA integration. In this regard, we introduced an agent development library called as CogAgentLib. In Chap. 11, we provide a case study that employs (a subset of) this library. You can freely obtain this library from its Web site (CogAgentLib 2017; DeCoAgent 2015).

References

Andersson, J., & Löf, S. (1999). *HLA as conceptual basis for a multi-agent environment*. Orlando: s.n.
Bratman, M. (1987). *Intention, plans, and practical reason*. s.l.: Harvard University Press.
Braubach, L., & Pokahr, A. (2009). Using rule-based concepts as foundation for higher-level agent architectures. In: *Handbook of research on emerging rule-based languages and technologies: Open solutions and approaches* (pp. 493–524). s.l.: s.n.
CogAgentLib. (2017). *CogAgentLib*. https://sites.google.com/site/okantopcu/coagent. Accessed April 22, 2017.
DeCoAgent. (2015). *DeCoAgent framework web site*. https://sites.google.com/site/okantopcu/decoagent. Accessed 22 Apr 2017.
Finin, T., Fritzson, R., McKay, D., & McEntire, R. (1994). *KQML as an agent communication language* (pp. 456–463). Gaithersburg: ACM.
FIPA-SC00008I. (2002). *FIPA SL content language specification*. Geneva, Switzerland: Foundation for intelligent physical agents.
FIPA-SC00061G (2012). *FIPA ACL message structure specification*, Geneva, Switzerland: FIPA.
Göktürk, E., & Polat, F. (2003). *Implementing agent communication for a multi-agent simulation infrastructure on HLA* (pp. 619–626). Paris: Springer.
Haykin, S. (2009). *Neural networks and learning machines*. New Jersey: Pearson.
Macal, C., & North, M. (2010). Tutorial on agent-based modeling and simulation. *Journal of Simulation, 4*, 151–162.
McClelland, J. L. (2014). *Explorations in parallel distributed processing: A handbook of models, programs, and exercises* (2nd ed.) Stanford.
Millgram, E., & Thagard, P. (1996). Deliberative coherence. *Synthese, 108*(1), 63–88.
OMG. (2012). *OMG systems modeling language (SysML) Version 1.3*. s.l.: OMG.
Poslad, S. (2007). Specifying protocols for multi-agent systems interaction. *ACM Transactions on Autonomous and Adaptive Systems (TAAS), 2*(4), 15:1–15:24.
Russell, S., & Norvig, P. (2010). *Artificial intelligence a modern approach* (3rd ed.). Upper Saddle River (New Jersey): Prentice Hall.
Shiffman, D. (2012). *The nature of code*. s.l.: s.n.
Thagard, P. (1989). Explanatory coherence. *Behavioral and Brain Sciences, 12*(3), 435–502.
Thagard, P., & Millgram, E. (1995). Inference to the best plan: A coherence theory of decision. In A. Ram & D. B. Leake (Eds.), *Goal-driven learning* (pp. 439–454). Cambridge: MIT Press.
Thagard, P., & Verbeurgt, K. (1998). Coherence as constraint satisfaction. *Cognitive Science, 22*(1), 1–24.
Topçu, O. (2014). Adaptive decision making in agent-based simulation. *Journal of Simulation: Transactions of the Society for Modeling and Simulation International, 90*(7), 815–832.
Zhuang, Y., Zhang, Z., Cheng, J., & Du, H. (2006). *Research on multi-agent simulation environment based on HLA* (pp. 154–159). Dalian: IEEE.

11 A Complete Case Study

In this chapter, we will present a complete case study, named "Maritime Border Surveillance Using Unmanned Surface Vehicles," abbreviated MariSim, which involves interoperability of an agent-based simulation and an HLA-based simulation. Moreover, we discuss the properties of an intensive 3D graphics federate application, paying attention to the planning of its main simulation loop.

11.1 Prelude

Maritime surveillance, especially on unpopulated and scarcely populated coastal areas, is an important factor of border security. A continuous surveillance is necessary to increase the situational awareness in complex maritime environments, specifically to control and stop illegal immigration through the sea. In the near future, unmanned vehicles will gain importance both in civilian operations (e.g., border security) and military operations (e.g., fighting sea piracy). In this respect, all the unmanned systems will be capable to carry out the tasks found in those workflows. To perform a continuous maritime surveillance, which is a strenuous and weary mission for humans, we take the advantage of autonomous unmanned surface vehicles (USVs) to detect and identify refugee boats on sea border and to support current border control systems and the manned law enforcement vessels (e.g., coast guard).

A USV patrols and monitors its assigned area of responsibility (AOR). It is capable of detecting and identifying refugee boats. When it identifies a refugee boat, it informs the coast guard command center and it escorts the refugee boat until a manned boat arrives, and then resumes its surveillance. USVs are not equipped with weapons. Whenever necessary, they request an armed intervention from the coast guard, which is capable of boarding and conducting maritime interdiction operations. A coast guard boat (CGB) is a manned surface vessel; when it receives an identification report from the USV, it navigates to the area and seizes the refugee boat. On the other hand, a refugee boat (RB) is simply a boat (a big dinghy), carrying a full load of people.

The USV is fully autonomous, capable of making its own decisions (i.e., selecting which goal/task to pursue). It is a *cyber-physical system* that has the ability to drive plans from goals, to determine goals, to cooperate and collaborate with others to accomplish a task, and to deliberate about plans (choosing what to do). They conduct patrol for the tasks of detecting, locating, identifying, and monitoring all the surface contacts in their AOR. A USV is constructed as an intelligent agent and as an HLA federate. On the other hand, the refugee boats are simple reactive agents that randomly appear in the area and follow a routine path. Unlike the others, a CGB is modeled as a federate with a three-dimensional (3D) graphical user interface for a human operator. This type of a simulation application is usually called a *human-in-the-loop simulation*.

11.1.1 Simulation Environment

Our case study is in the maritime domain (i.e., MariSim) including some naval entities (i.e., NavySim). The ensemble of our simulation environment is depicted in Fig. 11.1.

There are two groups of simulation entities: the *computer-generated entities* (a.k.a. constructive entities) and the *human-operated simulation entities* (a.k.a virtual entities). The computer-generated entities consist of the USVs and RBs and modeled as software agents. The human-involved entities consist of the environment federate as well as an interactive coast guard boat simulator, also called a *virtual boat*. The federation monitor federate is a passive data-collector federate that collects RTI-collected data. On account of this, the overall architecture of the simulation of the case study is composed of two types of simulations, an agent-based simulation and an HLA-based distributed simulation, which are composed of some federates of an existing Naval Simulation (NavySim), called as Naval Surface Tactical

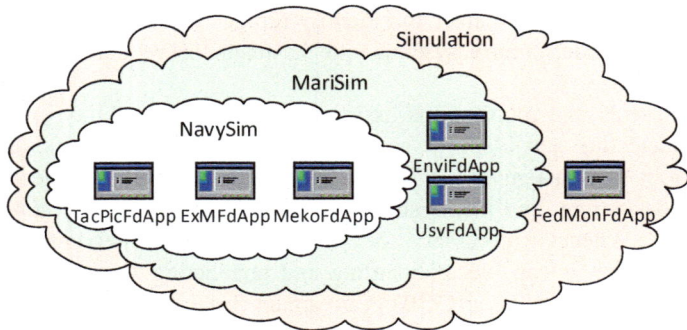

Fig. 11.1 Ensemble of our simulation environment

11.1 Prelude

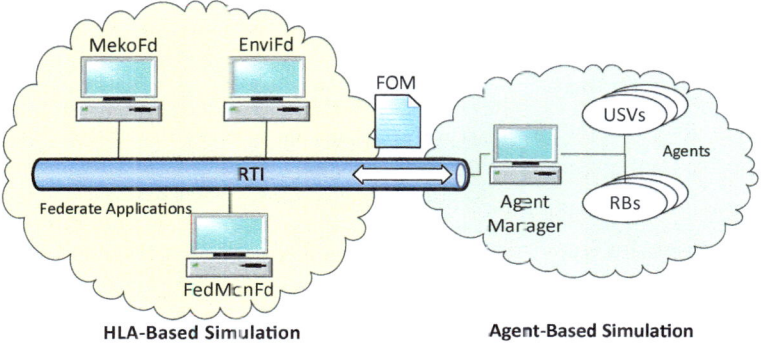

Fig. 11.2 Maritime simulation architecture

Maneuvering Simulation System (NSTMSS, pronounced "Nistmiss") (see Fig. 11.2). This is a testimony to HLA facilitating reusability.

We refer to the overall simulation environment created by integrating both simulations as Maritime Border Surveillance Using Unmanned Surface Vehicles, *Maritime Simulation* (MariSim) in short.

11.2 Naval Simulation

NSTMSS (Topçu and Oğuztüzün 2005; NSTMSS 2016) is an HLA-based distributed simulation that is composed of 3-dimensional (3D) ship handling simulators (virtual ships), a tactical-level simulation of operational area, a virtual environment manager (Environment Federate Application—EnviFdApp), and a simulation monitoring federate (i.e., data collection tool). There are three federate applications, which will be reused with slight modification to fit the scenario execution of the case study (Table 11.1).

11.2.1 Virtual Environment

All federate applications share a common *virtual environment*. The EnviFdApp enables a user (i.e., simulation trainer) to control the environment dynamically. A simulation trainer can adjust the time of day for the virtual environment and the cloud density; can select among four different types of waves; can configure waves by setting their direction, speed, length, amplitude, and exponential properties; can choose the fog type (e.g., linear and exponential fog), and minimum and maximum fog ranges; can set the wind direction and speed; and can determine the sea state, which represents a predefined configuration for the wind and waves. For a detailed description of the EnviFd, refer to Topçu and Oğuztüzün (2013). The EnviFdApp,

Table 11.1 MariSim federate applications

Federate application	Description
Environment controller federate application (EnviFdApp)	EnviFdApp is used both to model the environment and to control the environmental (i.e., sea) effects (e.g., sea state and waves) and the atmospheric (i.e., weather) effects (e.g., fog, wind, and time of day) in the virtual environment
	Its code base is completely reused for this case study
Federation monitor federate application (FedMonFdApp)	The FedMonFdApp enables us to monitor the RTI-related data. For instance, it keeps the interactions sent and object attribute updates. It uses the MOM
	Its code base is completely reused for this case study
Coast guard boat simulator	An existing Meko-type frigate federate application (MekoFdApp) is reused to represent a coast guard boat, which is a human-in-the-loop interactive 3D simulator
	It is implemented reusing the existing MekoFd with modifications

periodically or at will, sends a weather report to the participating federates, including information such as sea state and wind speed.

Some selected environmental parameters are presented in Table 11.2. Those parameters are effective on task execution. For instance, USVs cannot undertake a traversing task in sea state 4. A thick fog considerably limits the photograph and video taking activities for the identification task.

These environmental parameters are also considered in the visualization of the virtual environment for the 3D virtual ships (i.e., MekoFdApp) besides task execution. For example, in a sky dome visualization, the sky is changed according to the virtual environment weather conditions (e.g., cloudy sky). Furthermore, its functionality can be extended to cover sky effects such as sun, moon with its phase, stars, movement of the clouds (according to the wind), rain, and snow to enhance the sense of reality.

Table 11.2 MariSim virtual environment parameters

Virtual environment parameters	
Sea control	
Sea state	A predefined configuration for the wind and waves. For example, a sea state 1 expresses a calm sea (glassy) with no wave, where a sea state 4 describes a moderate sea with 1.5 m wave height
Atmosphere control	
Fog	The fog type (e.g., linear and exponential fog), minimum and maximum fog ranges
Wind direction	The direction of the wind
Wind speed	The speed of the wind
Time of day	Virtual environment wall-clock time. That is "physical" time (time in the physical system, i.e., simuland), e.g., scenario takes place in the morning

11.2 Naval Simulation

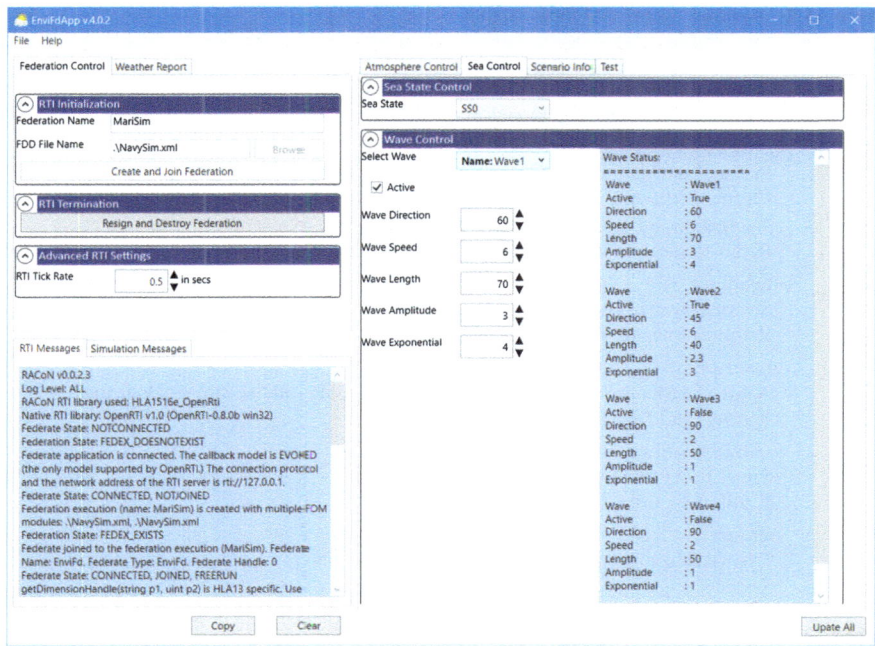

Fig. 11.3 EnviFdApp screen shot depicting sea configuration tab. You can select a preconfigured sea state or modify the wave parameters

A screen shot of the EnviFdApp is shown in Fig. 11.3. The federate architecture of EnviFdApp is presented in Chap. 7 of Topçu et al. (2016).

11.3 Agent-Based Simulation

An *agent manager* is responsible to create the agents in the simulation. There are two types of agents, which are the main actors of the simulation, summarized in Table 11.3. The primary agent is the USV agent, which is context-aware, adaptive, and interactive. This agent is represented as a federate in the simulation. This is the *federated agent* described in Chap. 10. The other is a simple reflexive agent and it exists only in the scope of the agent-based simulation. For simplicity, we assume that the MariSim components, such as the coast guard boat, do not interact with the RB agents via the RTI or any other means.

The characteristics of the *task environment*, where the agents interact with each other, are presented in Table 11.4. For the detailed explanation of characteristics, refer to the well-known artificial intelligence book of Russell and Norvig (2010).

Table 11.3 MariSim agents and their characteristics

Agents		
USV	*Cognitive ability*	
	Ability to make goal deliberation	
	Sensors	
	Surface (navigation) radar (to detect surface contacts)	
	Electro-optic sensor (i.e., camera) to identify a contact	
	Navigation aid system for positioning (e.g., GPS, gyroscope, speedometer)	
	Radio to receive the radio messages and the weather reports	
	Actuators	
	Steering system (propellers and rudder)	
	Radio to transmit the identification reports	
	Agent state	
	A list of tasks and goals, current position, heading, and speed, residual fuel capacity, and fuel consumption rate	
RB	*Characteristics*	
	Small boats filled with people	
	It follows a predefined route	
	Sensors	
	Eye visualization (assumed range 20 nautical miles)	

Table 11.4 MariSim task environment characteristics

Task Environment	
1	Dynamic by nature (see the virtual environment parameters specified in the previous section)
2	Partially observable due to limited sensor ranges and weather conditions
3	Stochastic (random appearing of RB agents)
4	Adversarial (due to RB agents) (competitive multi-agent environment)
5	Continuous (movements of agents are continuous)
6	Uncertainty (sensor limits, adversaries, stochastic movement)

11.3.1 Goal Reasoning

As the agents are autonomous, they have the ability to make their own decisions about which goal to follow and which task to execute, which is known as *goal reasoning* or *goal deliberation*. To gain this ability, we modeled and implemented the agents in this case study as a *Deliberative Coherence Driven Agent* (*DeCoAgent*) Topçu (2014) using the DeCoAgent Framework (DeCoAgent 2015).

A *DeCoAgent* is a cognitive agent that possesses an adaptive decision-making ability, based on the deliberative coherence theory (Millgram and Thagard 1996). The DeCoAgent has a deliberation subsystem, which is responsible for the goal deliberation process. This subsystem maintains a connectionist network of tasks, goals, and the relations among them and calculates the activations and the total coherence of the connectionist network.

Table 11.5 Goals and tasks for USV agents in MariSim

Goals and tasks for USV agent	
Patrol	Patrol the AOR by executing a traverse plan
Ingress	Move to AOR and do not leave the area during the execution of the tasks
Escort	Escort the RB to guard until a CG boat arrives or RB exits the AOR of the USV[a]
Safety	Maneuver according to the International Regulations for Preventing Collisions at Sea (IMO 2003)
Identify	Whenever a contact is detected, approach it until identification range arrived, then identify the contact via digital camera
Move	Move according to the heading and current speed
Communicate	Communicate with radio to send identification reports to a coast guard boat

[a]USV does not leave its AOR, even when escorting

Coherence-Based Agent Framework (*CogAgentLib*), which is introduced in Chap. 10, provides the tools, the process, and the formalism to prototype an agent-based simulation, where the cognitive model of the agent is factored out and can be generated from an authoritative source such as a command and control (C2) system. The framework includes the programming libraries for agent implementation; various generators to automatize and accelerate the development; the metamodels to formalize the domain models and rules; and a graphical modeling environment for the domain user. From the technical perspective, the framework adopts the model-driven engineering (MDE) (Bezivin 2005) approach to facilitate tool support for agent-based simulation development. Thus, the framework supports rapid prototyping of agent-based simulation.

The goals and tasks assigned for USV agents are assumed as presented in Table 11.5. On the other hand, the goal of an RB agent is simply to follow a predefined route.

Let us clarify the USV communication ability. When the Communicate task is active, the USV sends an identification report to the coast guard by using its radio. This is a behavior derived from the user requirements of the conceptual model. On the other hand, the USVs are free to communicate with each other to cooperate to complete the tasks voluntarily. To do this, the USV is capable to send agent communication language (ACL) messages via the RTI. This is an agent-characterized behavior.

11.3.2 Agent Manager

The agent manager is a central application to create and monitor the agents of USV and RB. Each agent is shown as a *contact* on a map. A screen shot is depicted in Fig. 11.4. As seen from the screen shot, you can create a USV or a refugee boat by using the contact manager by initializing the position, course, speed, and call sign of the agent. The agent manager is integrated with a geographical information system (GIS) such as Google Maps to open real-life maps. The manager also

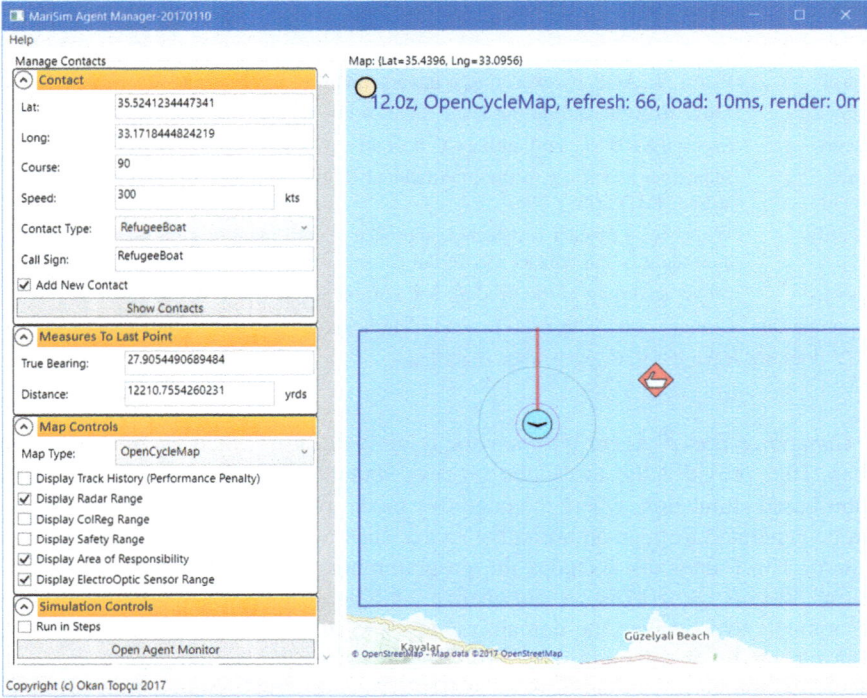

Fig. 11.4 The screen shot of the MariSim agent manager. The agent manager provides controllers for contacts, map, and simulation (each is grouped as seen on the *left* panel). Using the contact manager, you can configure a USV or an RB and then create it. Using the map controller, you can configure the map, for example, changing the map type. Using the simulation controller, you can start, pause, or run the simulation in steps

enables you to control and use some map properties, for instance, a switch to control the Radar range visibility on the map and a measure displayer to show the distance. Lastly, the agent manager is used to control the simulation run, with such commands as start, pause, and reset. Furthermore, if you want, you can run simulation step-by-step. So, you can check the agent monitor to look at the current state of an agent such as the current task selection. See the next section for more on the agent monitor.

The agent manager also maintains the tactical map of the operational area and displays it. The symbols for contacts (USV, refugee boats, and coast guard boats) are adapted from the joint military symbology of DoD (2014).

11.3.3 USV Agent

In order to adapt the USV agent to the HLA federation, we extend the USV agent with an RTI library to form a federated agent as described in Chap. 10. We will refer to the extended USV agent as *UsvFd*. The USV agent is extended using the

11.3 Agent-Based Simulation

Fig. 11.5 A part of the UML class diagram of UsvAgent. You can see which classes are used to extend the UsvAgent class

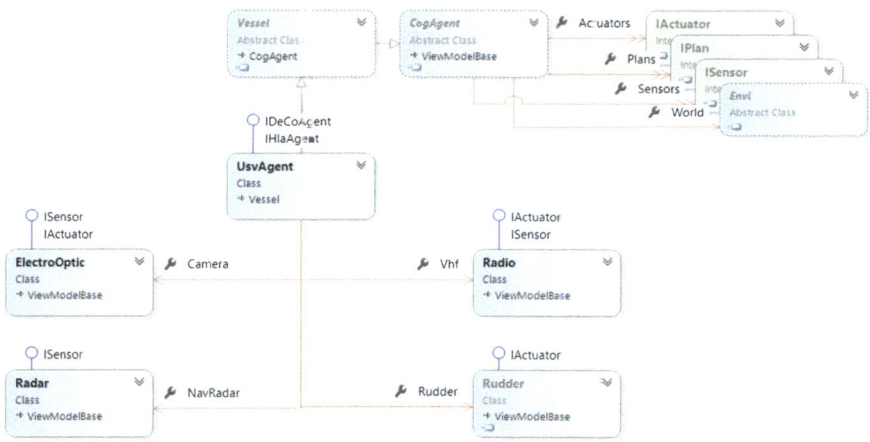

Fig. 11.6 USV agent architecture

CogAgent abstract class and the interfaces of IDeCoAgent and IHlaAgent from the CogAgentLib as depicted in Fig. 11.5.

Then, the sensor and actuator classes such as Radar and Radio classes are extended by implementing the IActuator and ISensor interfaces. A part of class diagram is depicted in Fig. 11.6.

At runtime, the state of the USV agent can be monitored by using the agent monitor. The user interface of the agent monitor is depicted in Fig. 11.7. We will not go into the agent monitor details here, but in a nutshell, you can monitor the RTI behavior (the log on the right side of Fig. 11.7), the simulation run (the log in the middle of Fig. 11.7), and the dynamic task selection (the log on the left side of Fig. 11.7). Moreover, it has user interfaces to monitor the sensors and the actuators of the agent. It maintains situational awareness and keeps track of the cognitive abilities of the agent using the tabs (at the bottom of Fig. 11.7).

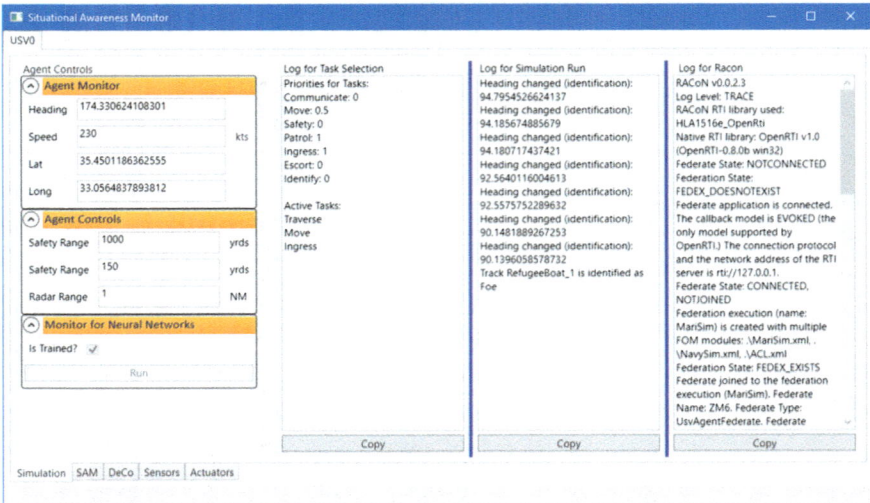

Fig. 11.7 USV agent monitor user interface

11.4 Object Model

In MariSim, we use three standalone FOM modules side by side (see Chap. 2 for FOM modularity). The first FOM module is the MariSim application-specific FOM, which includes the definitions of concepts found in the domain of application. The second FOM module is used by the NSTMSS federates. And, the third FOM module is used for agent communication language and it includes the interface class definitions for ACL message encapsulation. The third FOM module and the related classes are provided with the `CogAgentLib`. In order to simplify the composition of the FOM modules, we carry out a linear composition of the standalone FOM modules assuming no conflict occurs among modules. The schematic composition of the FOM modules is depicted in Fig. 11.8.

First, let us describe the application-specific object model. For the illustration purposes, we provide a part of the FOM module in Fig. 11.9. The boat object class specifies a boat in the virtual environment while the radio message interaction is used to transmit and receive a radio message between a USV and a coast guard boat.

The USVs are capable to communicate with each other to collaborate. For instance, when two USVs identify a refugee boat at the same time, then they can come to an agreement who will escort the boat and who will continue its patrol task for a more effective task execution. The communication between agents takes place in ACL. As we discussed in Chap. 10, to use the RTI as an ACL communication medium, the USV agents need the representation of the ACL message as an HLA interaction to send it via the RTI using an ACL-extended FOM. This is provided as

11.4 Object Model

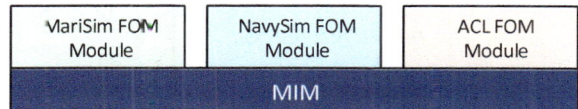

Fig. 11.8 Composition of the FOM modules

Fig. 11.9 A part of the MariSim FOM module (MariSim.xml)

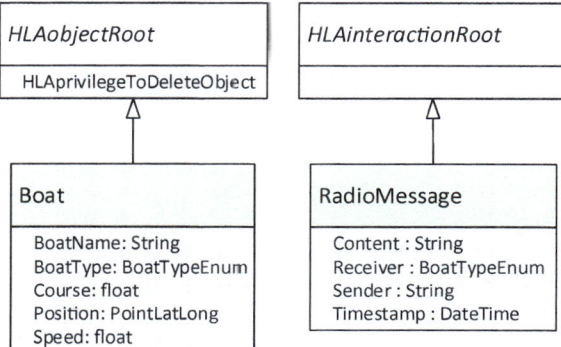

a FOM module by `CogAgentLib`. A basic interaction template for FIPA-ACL messages is depicted in Fig. 11.10.

Each FOM module is loaded when both creating and joining the federation execution. The following code snippet shows how to initialize a federation execution with multiple FOM modules. Here, we specify each module (ln. 6–8), then create the federation execution (ln. 11), and join it (ln. 14).

```
1.  // initalize federation execution properties
2.  FederationExecution.FederateName = "USV";
3.  FederationExecution.FederateType = "UsvAgentFederate";
4.
5.  // add FOM modules
6.  FederationExecution.FomModules.Add(@".\MariSim.xml");
7.  FederationExecution.FomModules.Add(@".\NavySim.xml");
8.  FederationExecution.FomModules.Add(@".\ACL.xml");
9.
10. // Create feceration execution
11. CreateFederationExecution(FederationExecution.Name, FederationExecution.FomModules);
12.
13. // Join federation execution
14. JoinFederationExecution(FederationExecution.FederateName, FederationExecution.FederateType, FederationExecution.Name, FederationExecution.FomModules);
```

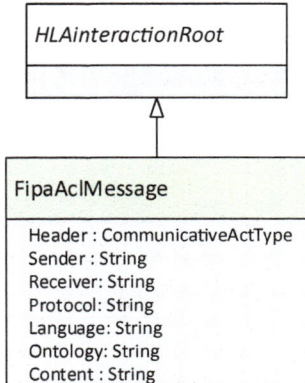

Fig. 11.10 ACL FOM module (ACL.xml) for wrapping an FIPA-ACL message

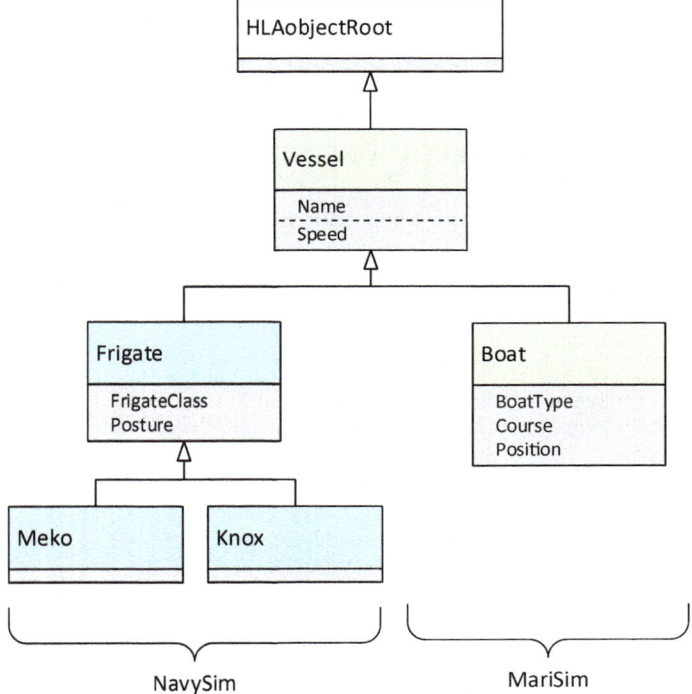

Fig. 11.11 Combined FOM (monolithic view) for MariSim—object classes

As a result, the RTI combines all the FOM modules. Figures 11.11 and 11.12 illustrate a part of the monolithic view of the combined FOM for the object classes and the interaction classes, respectively.

11.4 Object Model

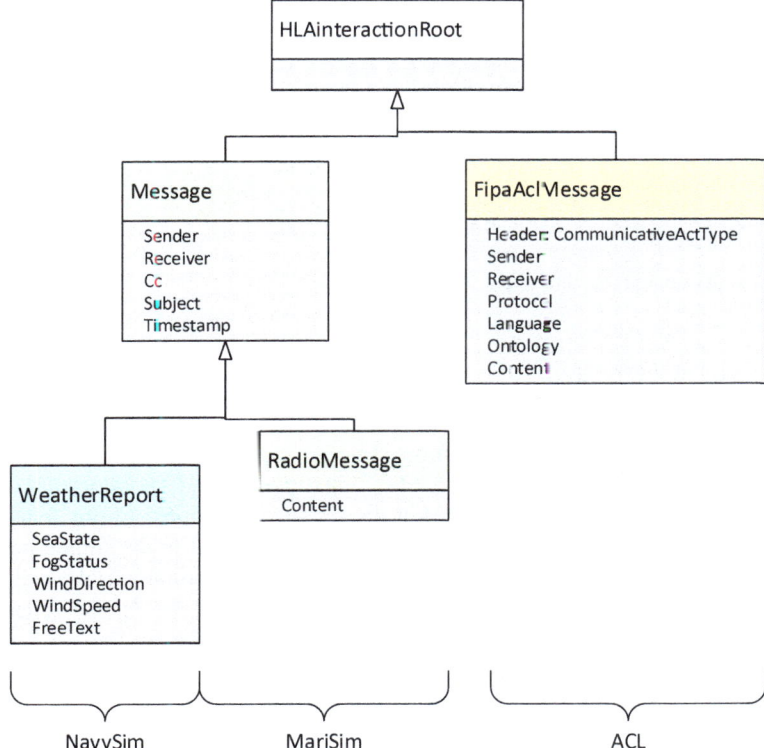

Fig. 11.12 Combined FOM (monolithic view) for MariSim—interaction classes

In the composition of the object classes, the Vessel object class acts as a melting pot, a placeholder for the union of the Frigate and Boat elements. Both NavySim and MariSim FOM modules include the same definition for the vessel.[1] The Message interaction class also acts the same for the interaction class hierarchy. Another approach for using placeholder is to use a dummy (empty) placeholder. As one FOM module holds the full definition, the other one defines only the name of the placeholder.

As a result of the modular FOM structure of the HLA Evolved, it is possible to publish and subscribe the HLA classes found in the separate FOM modules. For example, EnviFd publishes a weather report as the UsvFd subscribes it as depicted in Fig. 11.13. This is especially helpful for the USV agent to perceive the virtual environment weather state.

---

[1] If the definitions do not exactly match, then InconsistentFDD exception is generated by the RTI. For example, if one module defines the order type of an interaction class as TimeStamp and the other one defines it as Receive, then the FOM modules will not be composed and an exception will be generated thus.

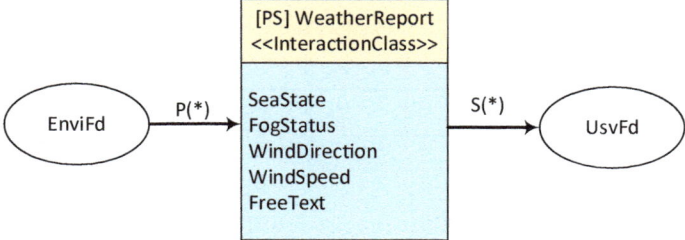

Fig. 11.13 Weather report interaction class P/S diagram

11.5 Federation Structure

The lollipop diagram for the federation structure is depicted in Fig. 11.14. The EnviFd and FedMonFd are the federates that manage and monitor the virtual environment and the RTI as described in the previous sections. In our federation execution, one instance of these federates is sufficient to control the simulation run. The MekoFd represents a coast guard boat and is a 3D ship simulator. According to the case study, one or two coast guard boats must be present in the federation execution for manned intervention when called for by the USVs. The USV agents are packaged as USV federates in the federation execution. They are centrally created and monitored by the agent manager application, which is not a member of the federation. Please note that the refugee boat agents are purely agents and not related to the RTI, so they are shown in the diagram, but not connected to the RTI.

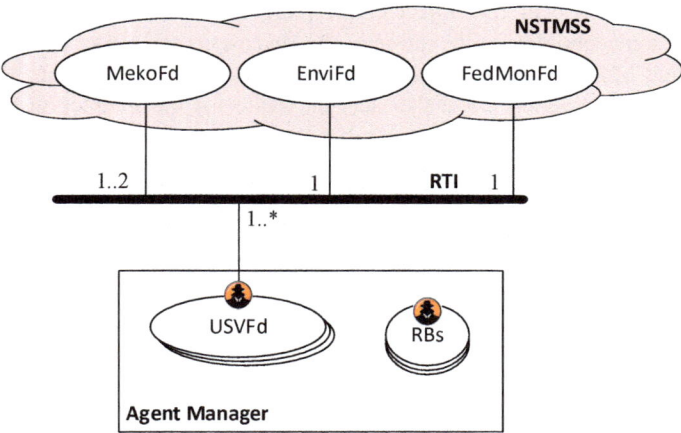

Fig. 11.14 Lollipop diagram for MariSim federation structure

11.6 Deployment and Execution

The agent-based simulation runs on a single machine by design.[2] Therefore, all the USV and RB agents reside on a single machine (Node 3 in Fig. 11.15). On the other hand, as the CGB is a 3D graphics-intensive federate application, each one (represented by a MekoFd) should execute on a standalone graphics-powerful machine (Node 1 and 2 in Fig. 11.15). As the FedMonFdApp and EnviFdApp are generally used by an exercise manager (or trainer), they can run on another single machine as well as the RTI software (e.g., `rtinode` for OpenRTI software) (Node 4 in Fig. 11.15). Putting all this together, the typical deployment and execution environment for the case study is depicted in Fig. 11.15.

11.7 Federate Application with Intensive Graphics

In this case study, the coast guard boats are brought into the federation by the Meko-class frigate federate, which is a platform-level simulation allowing a person to steer the ship in (nearly) real time. The frigate federate implements a three-dimensional ship handling interactive simulator of a frigate with a single user interface. They provide the means and the abilities for the user (aka officer of the watch—OOW):

- To adjust the ship's course either through the use of rudder by ordering a specific rudder angle or by directly ordering the course,
- To adjust the ship's velocity by controlling the ship's engines,
- To keep track of the position of the ship in terms of latitude and longitude by looking at the indicators,
- To view the other ship echoes in the radar display,
- To view the environment through the bridge windows, and
- To receive/send messages from/to other ships.

Many coast guard boats can join into virtual environment. We reuse an existing ship federate, which simulates a Meko-class frigate as the coast guard boat. A screen shot is depicted in Fig. 11.16.

There are numerous indicators and tools on the bridge, some of which serve for the safety of navigation, and some for military purposes. The simulated bridge equipment is chosen in a manner that the bridge officers often use these widgets in navigation. The user interface of the ship federate includes:

- A ship control center: The ship control center interface includes the bridge equipment necessary for ship handling such as a helm. The OOW can use this

---

[2]In other words, the design requires all agents run on a single machine.

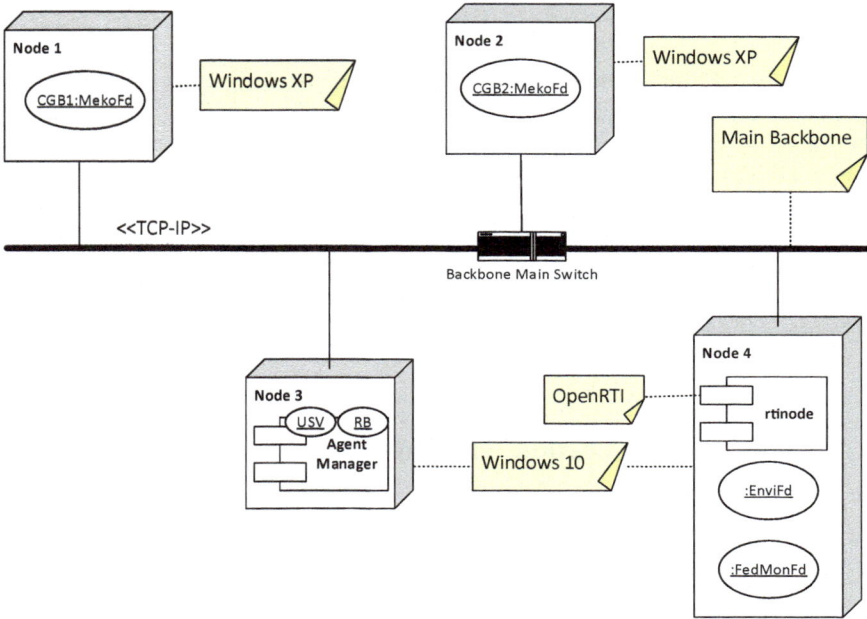

Fig. 11.15 Typical deployment and execution environment for a basic MariSim federation execution

Fig. 11.16 A screen shot of the coast guard boat

11.7 Federate Application with Intensive Graphics

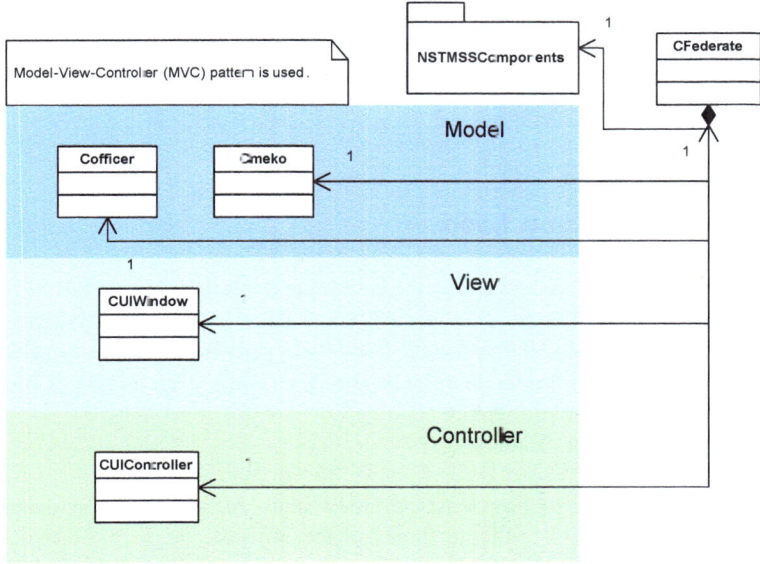

Fig. 11.17 Main class diagram for MekoFd

equipment to maneuver the ship or can order a specific course, and then, the ship control center will control the helm automatically to turn to the ordered course.
- A message control center, which provides the necessary tools to send and to receive radio messages in addition to providing controls for reviewing the old received and transmitted messages.
- A navigation control center, which includes a simple traditional radar display and an advanced tactical display for the use in navigation.
- A GPS, with the ability to display the ship's position in terms of latitude and longitude. It shows the values in a readable format: "degrees minutes seconds" (e.g., 123° 45′ 13″W).

The Model-View-Controller (MVC) (Burbeck 1992) is used as the design pattern. In this pattern, View and Controller packages manage the graphical user interface while the Model package models the ship. The main class diagram is presented in Fig. 11.17.

For the original hydrodynamics and maneuvering model, refer to Topçu and Oğuztüzün (2005).

Ship federate also includes a track manager, a tracking subsystem (TSS), to keep track of each ship detected in the virtual environment. The TSS module accurately represents the common virtual environment as perceived by this federate and tracks other entities in the virtual environment by using a *dead-reckoning* algorithm

(Grosswiler et al. 1994). In the dead-reckoning algorithm, each entity in the virtual environment is kept as a ghost and the positions of ghosts are continuously calculated using the ship's old position and speed until an update is received from the entity.

11.8 Main Simulation Loop

In a graphics-intensive federate application, the main simulation loop has to handle activities associated with scene drawing. A typical HLA-based interactive graphical simulation repeatedly calls the preframe, frame, and post-frame stages as presented in Fig. 11.18. A *frame* is the scene to be drawn. The average frame rate of MekoFd is over 30 frames per second (fps).

Let us examine the preframe stage:

- First thing we do is to broadcast our own state to the federation execution. In HLA terms, we update the attributes of the objects.
- We read the callbacks and the incoming messages sent by the RTI. So that, we can discover new objects or reflect the attribute updates done by other federates.
- Lastly, we update the scene graph (e.g., the transformation and rotation nodes). The scene graph is the geometry tree drawn to the screen. See the following section.

After all the necessary calculations are done in preframe, we draw (i.e., render) the scene graph on the screen (e.g., a view of the virtual environment in 3D). The frame phase, although dependent to the graphics system used, typically consists of two stages: *Cull* determines which geometries in the scene are visible in the viewing frustum. *Draw* renders all visible geometries.

At the post-frame stage, the snapshot of user input queues, both from keyboard and mouse, are captured and handled. The GUI is updated in response to user inputs. We also send interactions, triggered by the user inputs (e.g., sending a message when the user clicks the send button).

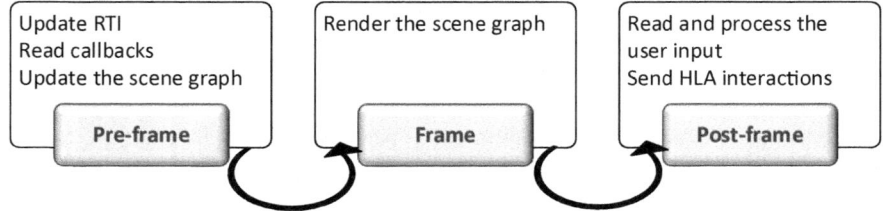

Fig. 11.18 Main simulation loop for a typical graphics-intensive simulation

11.9 Graphics API Integration

Graphics-intensive federate applications, such as flight or ship simulators, can be two-dimensional (2D) or three-dimensional (3D) according to the application requirements, and they are implemented using a graphics library. A *graphics library* provides the necessary API to render graphics to the screen. From the programming perspective, the graphics libraries can be categorized as *low-level graphics libraries* such as OpenGL (OpenGL 2017), Vulkan (Khronos 2017), and DirectX (Microsoft DirectX 2017), and *high-level graphics libraries*, which are in the form of a scene graph library such as OpenSceneGraph (OpenSceneGraph 2007) and OpenSG (OpenSG 2013). A *scene graph* is a graph-based data structure that includes all the geometrical and functional nodes of a scene, which can be potentially drawn on the screen (not necessarily all because of cull).

Furthermore, a *game engine*, such as Unity (Unity 2017) and CryEngine (Crytek 2017), is usually provided as a software framework on top of the graphics libraries so that they add more functionality to facilitate the game and virtual environment development such as access to a physics engine, collision detection, and the user interface gadgets. The game engines also support portability of applications to various platforms, including the mobile platforms.

In simulation applications, instead of programming at low level, the general tendency is to use a high-level graphics library, which provides additional functionality on top of low-level libraries. In this case, you simply add the graphics library to your federate application project and implement the graphics. But, in case you want to use a game engine in a federate application, then you need an integration package that links the game engine and the RTI such as VR-Link for Unity (VT MAK 2017). In Unity, the integration package is provided in the form of an asset package to bring a Unity-based game into a federation execution (see Fig. 11.19) so that you take advantage of both worlds.

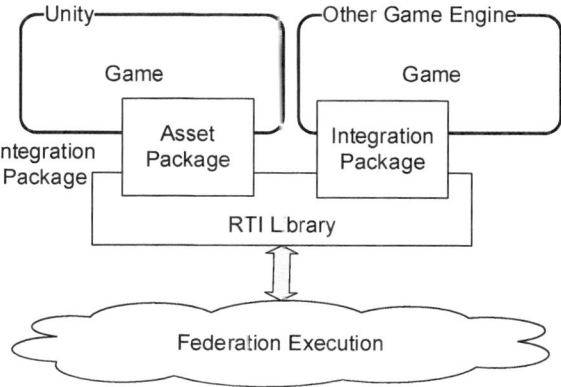

Fig. 11.19 Game engine and the RTI integration

11.10 Summary

In this chapter, we presented a full-blown case study, where an agent-based simulation and an HLA-based simulation interoperate via the RTI. The case study involves various types of federate applications. One is the federated agents—USVs, where they have both cognitive capability in the sense of decision-making and HLA capability. They sense the environment, act accordingly, and communicate both with other agents in the environment via agent communication means and with other federates via the RTI. Another federate type is a 3D interactive (human-in-the-loop) simulator—virtual ship, which involves an intensive graphics environment. We also have a stealth federate application—FedMonFd that monitors the federate and the RTI interactions.

From another standpoint, our case study is a testimony to HLA facilitating reusability. Some federate applications (MekoFdApp, EnviFdApp, and FedMonFdApp) found in an existing federation are reused as is or slightly modified for our purpose.

All the applications that are presented in this chapter are obtainable from MariSim (2017).

11.11 Questions for Review

1. Suppose that two federates in a federation keep their environmental data in their own formats. Devise a scheme for data format conversion so that they can exchange environmental data. Consider the layered federate architecture.
2. In a federation where the federates employ dead reckoning, the member federates keep the "ghosts" of their own entities (in addition to keeping the ghosts of other federates' entities). Describe the logic for maintaining your own ghost object.

References

Bezivin, J. (2005). On the unification power of models. *Software and Systems Modeling, 4*(2), 171–188.
Burbeck, S. (1992). *Applications programming in smalltalk-80(TM): How to use model-view-controller (MVC)*. Retrieved December 19, 2015 from http://www.dgp.toronto.edu/~dwigdor/teaching/csc2524/2012_F/papers/mvc.pdf
Crytek.(2017). *CryEngine*. Retrieved March 11, 2017 from https://www.cryengine.com/
DeCoAgent. (2015). *DeCoAgent framework web site*. Retrieved January 8, 2017 from https://sites.google.com/site/okantopcu/decoagent
DoD. (2014). *MIL-STD-2525D joint military symbology*. Philadelphia: DoD Interface Standard.
Grosswiler, R., Laferriere, R., Keller, M., & Pausch, R. (1994). An introductory tutorial for developing multi-user virtual environments. *Presence, 3*(4), 255–264.

References

IMO. (2003). *COLREG: convention on the international regulations for preventing collisions at sea, 1972. Consolidated edition 2003* (4th ed.). London: IMO (International Maritime Organisation).

Khronos. (2017). *Vulkan*. Retrieved March 11, 2017 from https //www.khronos.org/vulkan/

MariSim. (2017). *Maritime simulation (MariSim)*. Retrieved January 8, 2017 from https://sites.google.com/site/okantopcu/marisim

Microsoft DirectX. (2017). *DirectX*. Retrieved March 11, 2017 from https://msdn.microsoft.com/en-us/library/windows/desktop/hh309467(v=vs.85).aspx

Millgram, E., & Thagard, P. (1996). Deliberative coherence *Synthese, 108*(1), 63–88.

NSTMSS. (2016). *Naval surface tactical maneuvering simulation system (NSTMSS) web site*. Retrieved January 8, 2017 from http://www.ceng.metu.edu.tr/~otopcu/nstmss/

OpenGL. (2017). *OpenGL website*. Retrieved March 11, 2017 from https://www.opengl.org/

OpenSceneGraph. (2007). *OpenSceneGraph*. Retrieved March 11, 2017 from http://trac.openscenegraph.org/projects/osg/

OpenSG. (2013). *OpenSG*. Retrieved March 11, 2017 from http://www.opensg.org/

Russell, S., & Norvig, P. (2010). *Artificial intelligence A modern approach* (3rd ed.). Upper Saddle River: Prentice Hall.

Topçu, O. (2014). Adaptive decision making in agent-based simulation. *Journal of Simulation, 90*(7), 815–832.

Topçu, O., Durak, U., Oğuztüzün, H., & Yılmaz, L. (2016). *Distributed simulation: A model driven engineering approach* (1st ed.). Cham: Springer.

Topçu, O., & Oğuztüzün, H. (2005). Developing an HLA based naval maneuvering simulation. *Naval Engineers Journal, 117*(1), 23–40.

Topçu, O., & Oğuztüzün, H. (2013). Layered simulation architecture: A practical approach. *Simulation Modelling Practice and Theory, 32*, 1–14.

Unity. (2017). *Unity*. Retrieved January 1, 2017 from https://unity3d.com/

VT MAK. (2017). *VR-link for unity*. Retrieved March 11, 2017 from http://www.mak.com/products/link/vr-link-for-unity

Appendix A: SimGe Installation and Remarks

In this appendix, we will give step-by-step instructions for installing SimGe on a Windows operating system. Then, we present some remarks about usage of SimGe.

Hardware and Software General Prerequisites

Before going into installation, let's first check the hardware and software prerequisites. SimGe does not require specialized or high-end hardware. Table A.1 presents a typical configuration. On the software side, the requirements are presented in Table A.2.

Installation

SimGe is freely downloadable from (SimGe 2015) and comes in a zipped file. Extract the zipped file to a folder. Right click to SimGe.msi and select install. Program installer will check whether SimGe is already installed. If a current version of SimGe installation is detected, the installer will ask whether to remove it or to repair it. If a previous version of SimGe installation is detected, then the installer will uninstall it first.

The installation program is prepared with Windows Installer XML (WiX) toolset (WiX 2017). The installation begins with the License Agreement screen as depicted in Fig. A.1.

Once you accept the terms in the license agreement, you can proceed with install or select the advanced setup options by clicking the related button. Click the Install button, and then installation will take place and an installation completed dialog will appear as depicted in Fig. A.4. Click the Advanced button, and then you can select a different installation folder than the default one (see Fig. A.2).

After clicking Next button, Product features dialog will appear as in Fig. A.3. Currently, SimGe is offered as one package. Just click Next in this screen.

The installation will end with a success message as seen in Fig. A.4. The user may now launch SimGe.

Table 1 Hardware requirements

Component	Absolute minimum configuration (MB)	Recommended minimum configuration
RAM	512	1 GB
Hard disk space	20	32 MB
Video graphics card	–	–

Table 2 Software requirements

Component	Absolute minimum configuration
Operating system	Windows 10
Runtime environment	Microsoft .NET framework 4.0 client profile package
Installation needs local administration rights	

Fig. A.1 License agreement dialog

Please note that the installation wizard associates the .fap (SimGe Project file extension) files with SimGe. Therefore, it needs administrator privileges.

Appendix A: SimGe Installation and Remarks

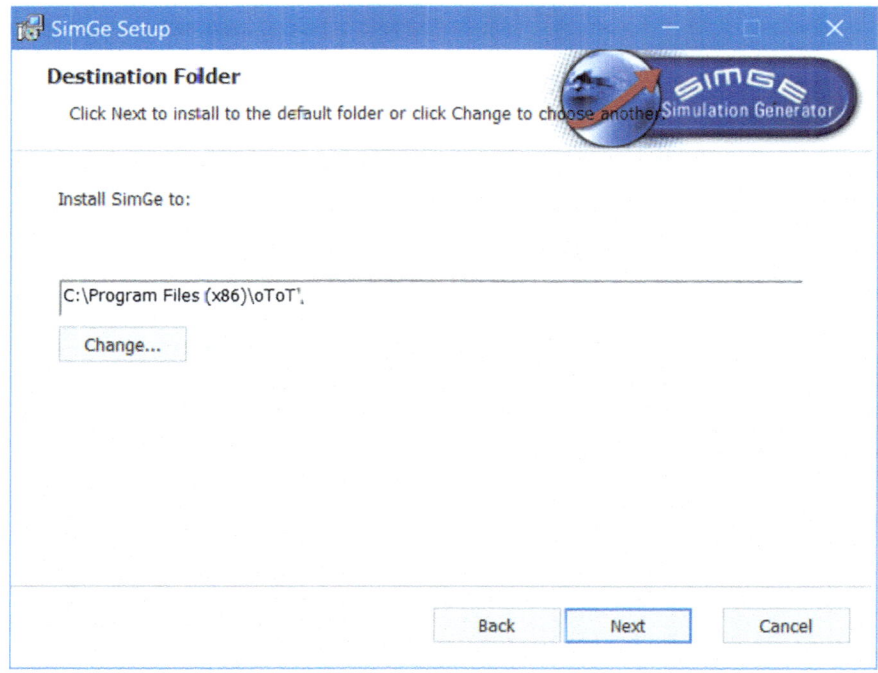

Fig. A.2 Selection dialog for installation folder

Uninstallation

The user can uninstall SimGe by using *Windows Programs and Features* or the shortcut to uninstall SimGe at SimGe folder in Programs Menu.

File Extensions for SimGe and HLA Related Files

The file extensions related to SimGe and HLA are presented in Table A.3.

Remarks

Here are some points you need to be aware of when using SimGe.

- Please note that SimGe versions do not adhere to backward compatibility policy. New versions sometimes do not load an older object model.

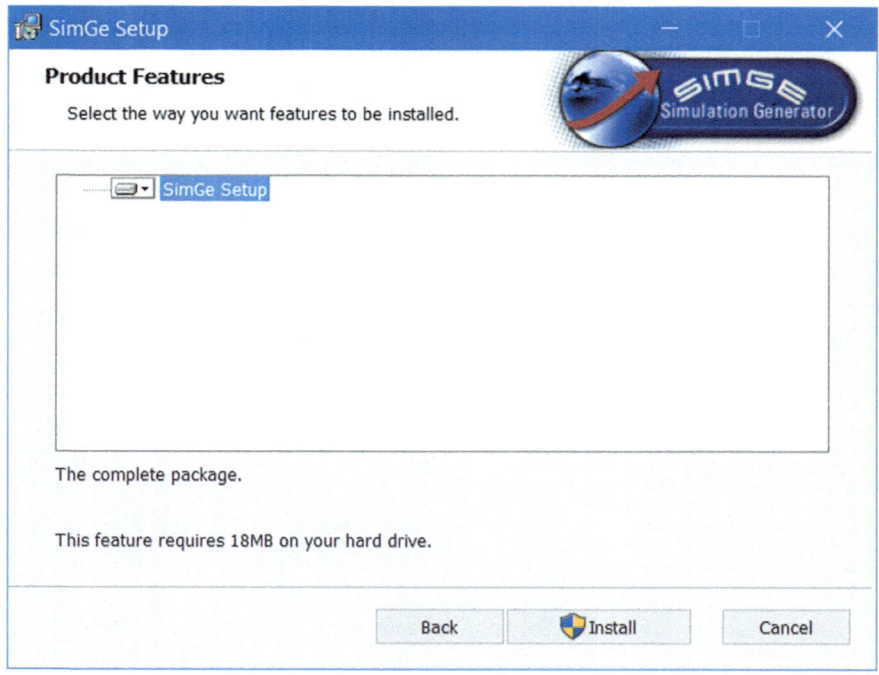

Fig. A.3 Product features dialog

- The user interface of OME always uses the local culture format of the operating system, where SimGe is installed at. That said, if the operating system culture information is set to a continental European country, the floating-point values are separated by a comma (for most of them) as opposed to the USA where the floating-point format uses a dot as a separator. The culture format of the artifacts (e.g., FDD file) generated by SimGe conforms to their related specifications. For instance, a dot is used as a separator for the values for the update rates.
- The default page layout for the report generator is as follows: Its orientation is portrait, and its size is A4 (29.7 cm × 21 cm). But, the US users may always print the report in the Letter size. Please note that the generation of the first report may take a while.

Appendix A: SimGe Installation and Remarks

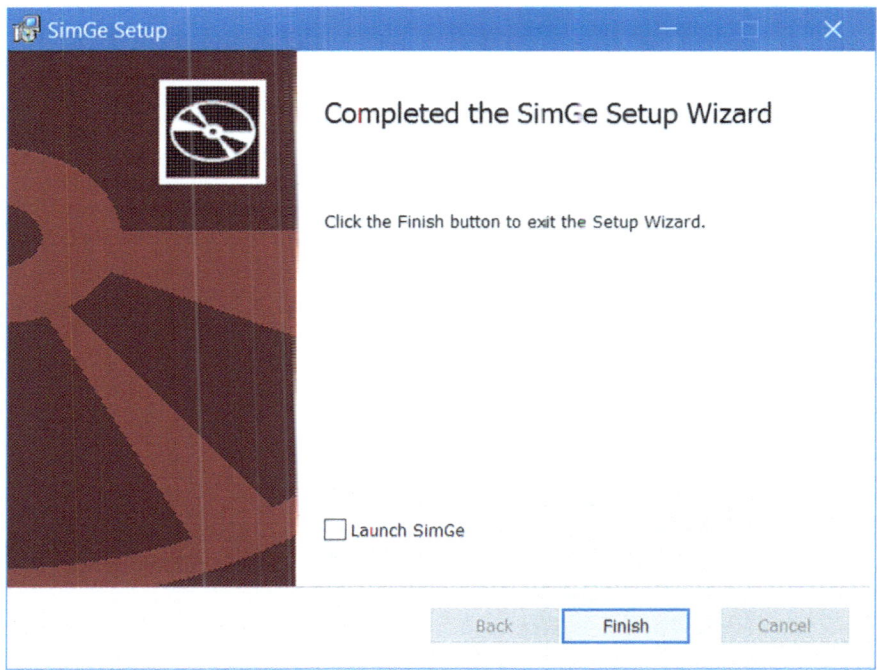

Fig. A.4 Installation completed dialog

Table 3 File extensions

Extension	File
.fap	SimGe federation architecture project
.fom	SimGe object model of a project
.fed	FED file
.xml	FDD file
.xsd	XML Schema file for DIF XML Schema (IEEE1516.2-2010 DIF XML Schema 2010), FDD Schema (IEEE1516.1-2010 FDD Schema 2010), and OMT Schema (IEEE1516.2-2010 OMT Schema 2010)

References

IEEE1516.1-2010 FDD Schema. (2010). *EEE1516-FDD-2010.xsd*. [Online] Available at: http://standards.ieee.org/downloads/1516/1516.1-2010/IEEE1516-FDD-2010.xsd. Accessed April 15, 2017.
IEEE1516.2-2010 DIF XML Schema. (2010). *OMT DIF XML Schema*. [Online] Available at: http://standards.ieee.org/downloads/1516/1516.2-2010/IEEE1516-DIF-2010.xsd. Accessed April 15, 2017.
IEEE1516.2-2010 OMT Schema. (2010). *IEEE1516-DIF-2010.xsd*. [Online] Available at: http://standards.ieee.org/downloads/1516/1516.2-2010/IEEE1515-OMT-2010.xsd. Accessed April 15, 2017.
SimGe. (2015). *SimGe web site*. [Online] Available at: https://sites.google.com/site/okantopcu/simge. Accessed November 2016.
WiX. (2017). *WIX toolset*. [Online] Available at: http://wixtoolset.org/. Accessed February 27, 2017.

Index

A
Abstraction, 5
Access layer, 171
ACL, FIPA, 268
Acquire, 124
Acquiring, 61
Agent-based modeling and simulation, 261
Agent communication language, 264
Agent manager, 265, 277, 279
Aggregate Level Simulation Protocol (ALSP), 13
Announce synchronization point, 234
Application Programming Interface (API), 48
Area of responsibility, 84, 88
Array data type, 135
Array datatype table, 125
Arrays, 135
Associate regions for update, 243
Attribute, 5, 39
Attribute ownership acquisition notification, 248
Attribute ownership release response, 252
Attribute ownership unavailable, 248
Attribute relevance advisory switch, 60
Attribute table, 44
Automatic resign action, 132
Autonomy, 262

B
Basic data representations table, 133
Behavior of a system, 5, 24
Best effort delivery, 130

C
Call, 48, 192
Callback, 48, 192
Callback methods, 48
Centralized federation management, 70
Change attribute order type, 67

Change interaction order type, 67
Chat client, 101
Chat room, 101
C# language, 174
Class-based P/S diagrams, 56
Code explorer, 159
CodeGen, 157
Code generation configuration dialog, 164
Code generator, 98
Coherence-based agent framework, 267
Commit region modification, 240
Communication layer, 159, 170, 171
Component, 5
Composite state, 73
Computer-generated entities, 274
Conceptual model, 81
Conceptual validation, 81
Confirm federation restoration request, 237
Connectionist network, 263
Conservative time management, 65
Console window, 177
Contact, 279
Continuous time models, 9
Coupling, 30
Create region, 239
Cross-cutting concerns, 170
CRUD, 116
Cull, 290
Cyber-physical system, 274

D
Data distribution management, 47, 62
Data Interchange Format (DIF), 42
Dead-reckoning, 289
Decision making, 262
Declaration management, 47, 54
DeCoAgent, 263, 278
DeCoAgent framework, 279
Default region, 63

Default routing space, 56
Delegated event handling, 192
Delete object instance, 209
Deliberative coherence-driven agent, 263, 278
Dependent module, 46
Deployment, 72
Detailed (application) design, 87
Dimension, 63, 126
Dimensions table, 122
Discover object instance, 206
Discrete event models, 9
Discrete events, 9
Discrete-time models, 10
Dispersion, 11
DIS protocol, 12, 38
Distributed interactive simulation, 12
Distributed simulation, 11
Distributed Simulation Engineering and Execution Process (DSEEP), 15, 79
Divest, 124
Divest/acquire, 124, 143
Divesting, 61
Domain entities, 8
Draw, 290
Dynamic link library, 175

E
Enable/disable interaction relevance advisory switch, 210
Encapsulation, 172
Endianness, 133
Entity, 5
Enumerated datatype table, 135
Enumeration, 135
Enumerator, 135
Environment, 5
Event, 5, 170, 192
Event-based advancement, 65
Event-based notification, 170, 192
Event handler, 192
Evoked callback model, 50
Evoking, 49
Exceptions, 47
Executable form, 7
Experiment with, 4
Extent, 245

F
FAM folder, 101
FEDEP, 79
Federate, 32
Federate Ambassador, 49, 159
Federate application, 81
Federate architecture, 87

Federate-based P/S diagrams, 56
Federated agent, 267, 277
Federate hosting an agent, 267
Federate-initiated, 192
Federate-initiated methods, 48
Federate interface, 48
Federate restore complete, 54, 237
Federate rules, 34
Federate save complete, 52, 236
Federate states, 73
Federation, 33
Federation agreement, 42
Federation architecture, 81, 104
Federation architecture model, 104
Federation architecture modeling environment, 98
Federation architecture project, 101
Federation design, 81
Federation execution, 33
Federation Execution Details (FED), 16, 38
Federation execution lifecycle, 68
Federation execution properties, 106
Federation execution states, 73
Federation Foundation Library (FFL), 170, 174, 181
Federation management, 47
Federation management services, 50
Federation name, 71
Federation Object Model (FOM), 44, 45
Federation Object Model (FOM) Document Data (FDD), 16
Federation restore begun, 54, 237
Federation restored, 237
Federation rules, 34
Federation saved, 236
Federation structure, 82
Federation synchronized, 234
FedExec, 48
Fidelity, 6, 7
FOM Document Data (FDD), 38
FOM folder, 101
FOM modules, 45
Frame, 290
Functional behavior, 5

G
Game engine, 89, 291
General purpose programming language, 7
Geodetic coordinate system, 89
Get federate handle, 233
Get update rate value, 59
Get update rate value for attribute, 59
Goal deliberation, 262, 278
Goal reasoning, 278

Index

Graphical user interface, 170
Graphics library, 89, 291
Graphics termination, 71
Greatest available logical time, 65

H

Handle, 40, 172
Heterogeneity, 11
High Level Architecture, 13
High-level graphics libraries, 291
High-level method, 185
HLA, 30
HLAbestEffort, 129
HLA class, 38
HLA evolved, 14, 29
HLA federate interface specification, 14
HLA framework and rules, 14, 31
HLA gateway, 264
HLA layer, 266
HLA object model, 38, 159
HLA object model template, 14
HLAreliable, 129
Human-operated simulation entities, 274
Hybrid automata, 10

I

Immediate callback model, 50
Initialization, 70, 71
Initiate federate save, 235
Input data analysis, 6
Integrated development environment, 89, 157, 174
Interaction, 40
Interaction class structure table, 44, 122
Interactive, 262
Interface specification (IF), 32
Interface specification services usage table, 141
Interoperability, 30
Intrusive pull, 61, 248

J

Joined federate, 32

K

Knowledge query and manipulation language, 268

L

Layered architectural style, 169
Layered architecture, 158
Layered simulation architecture, 159
Layering, 169
Learning, 262
Least incoming time stamp, 66

Level of accuracy, 6
Level of detail, 6, 7
List federation executions, 253
Local data structures, 160, 171
Local model termination, 71
Logical time, 65
Lollipop diagram, 82
Lookahead, 65, 222
Low-level graphics libraries, 291
Low-level methods, 184

M

Main simulation loop, 71, 212
Management Object Model (MOM), 36, 45, 145
Man-in-the-loop simulation, 274
Maritime simulation, 275
Marshalling, 205
Master-slave table, 6, 135
Mathematical programming language, 7
MATLAB, 6
Member application, 15
Message exchange, 37
Messages, 65
Method calls, 170
Middleware, 34
MIM, 45, 112
Model, 4
Modeling, 4
Modeling and simulation, 3
MOM and initialization module, 145
MOM data by an Initialization Module (MIM), 45
Monolithic simulation, 10, 24

N

Negotiated push, 62, 248
Network information, 72
Next message request, 67
Node, 72
Non-centralized federation management, 70
Note, 141
Notes table, 141
NSTMSS, 179
NuGet package, 177

O

Object, 39
Object class structure table, 43
Object exchange, 37
Object instance name, 60
Object management, 47, 59
Object model editor, 97
Object Model Identification Table, 42

Object Model Template (OMT), 32, 42
Object not known error, 243
OM explorer, 146
Operation, 71
Operational systems, 8
Optimistic advancement, 65
Optimistic time management, 65
Options, 103
Orphaned attribute, 61
Orphaned-attribute pull, 61
Ownership management, 47, 60, 246

P
Parallel simulation, 11, 24
Parameters, 40
Parameter table, 44
Partial class, 163
Physics-based models, 9
Post-conditions, 47
Pre-conditions, 47
Preferred order type, 67
Presentation layer, 159, 170
Proactivity, 262
Process, 5
Processing layer, 170
Project explorer, 99
Project home folder, 100
Project settings, 102
Project Start Page, 102
Project workspace, 99
Protocol Data Units (PDUs), 13
Provide attribute value update, 209
Publish/subscribe pattern, 36, 38
Publishable, 55
Publish and Subscribe (P/S), 38
Publish and subscribe diagram, 55
Publishing, 38
Publish interaction class, 55
Publish object class attributes, 55
Pull strategy, 61, 248
Push strategy, 62

R
RACoN, 15, 16, 98, 171
Range, 63
Reality, 4, 9, 81
Receive interaction, 60
Receive order, 122
Receive order message, 49
Record data type, 137
Record fields, 137
Referent, 7
Reflect attribute values, 207
Region, 63

Region realization, 63
Region specification, 63
Region template, 63
Reliable delivery, 130
Remove object instance, 209
Report federation executions, 253
Report generator, 98, 149
Request federation restore, 53, 237
Request federation save, 52, 235
Request retraction, 231
Request value update with regions, 242
Reserve object instance name, 60
Resolution, 7
Results validation, 6, 81
Retract, 231
Reusability, 11
Routing space, 56, 142, 243
Routing spaces Table, 142
RTI Ambassador, 49, 159
RtiExec, 48
RTI executive, 48
RTI-initiated, 192
RTI-initiated methods, 48
RTI library type, 166
RTI method, 48
RTI service, 46, 48
RTI termination, 71
Runtime Infrastructure (RTI), 14, 16, 30, 33

S
Save-and-restore, 235
Scenario, 6
Scene graph, 291
Send interaction, 60
Send interaction with regions, 246
Ship application, 83
Shutdown, 71
SimGe, 15, 16, 97
SimGe object model editor, 111
SIMNET, 12
Simple data type, 134
Simuland, 5, 10, 24
Simulation conceptual model, 8
Simulation conceptual model and fidelity, 8
Simulation data exchange model, 33
Simulation engineering, 8
Simulation environment, 15
Simulation execution, 6
Simulation Interoperability Standards
    Organization (SISO), 14
Simulation layer, 159, 170
Simulation manager, 185
Simulation Object Model (SOM), 44
Simulation-oriented programming language, 7

Simulation project, 98
Simulation run, 6
Simulation user, 6
Situational awareness, 262
Skeleton code, 158
Smart update reduction, 58, 131
Social ability, 262
Software design, 81
SOM, 45
Source code folder, 101
Stand-alone desktop application, 170
Standalone module, 46
Start registration for object class 203
Start/stop registration for object instance, 60
States, 5
Station application, 84
Stop registration for object class, 203
Subscribe interaction class, 55
Subscribe/unsubscribe, 55
Subscribing, 38
Support services, 47
Switch, 131
Switches table, 131
Synchronization point, 51, 128, 231
Synchronization point achieved, 51
Synchronization point registration failed, 233
Synchronization point registration succeeded, 233
Synchronization table, 51, 129
SysML, 9
System, 5
System initialization and termination, 70

T
Task environment, 277
Termination, 70, 71
The enable/disable object class relevance advisory switch, 203
Theory of deliberative coherence, 263
Ticking, 49
Time, 9
Time advance grant, 67
Time advancement strategies, 65
Time advance request, 67
Time axis, 9, 65

Time constrained enabled, 224
Time dimension, 9
Time management, 47, 64
Time management mechanisms, 65
Time-stamp, 52
Time-stamp order, 122
Time-stamp-order message, 49
Time step advancement, 65
Transferable/acceptable, 143
Transportation table, 122
Try-catch, 48
Turn interactions off, 210
Turn interactions on, 210
Turn updates on for object instance, 59, 205

U
UML, 9
UML class diagram, 183
Unassociate regions for updates, 243
Unconditional attribute ownership divestiture, 250
Unconditional push, 62, 248
Unpublish interaction class, 55
Unpublish object class attributes, 55
Updateable/reflectable, 143
Update attribute values, 205, 209
Update rate, 53, 131
Update rate designator, 58
Update rate table, 131
Update reduction, 58, 131
User interface controller, 170
User interface layer, 170
UsvFd, 280

V
Variant record, 139
Verb-noun analysis, 85
Verification, 6, 81
Virtual boat, 274
Virtual environment, 275

W
Web client, 170

Printed by Printforce, the Netherlands